Iran

WORLD BIBLIOGRAPHICAL SERIES

Robert L. Collison (Editor-in-chief)

John J. Horton   Ian Wallace

Hans H. Wellisch   Ralph Lee Woodward, Jr.

Robert L. Collison (Editor-in-chief) is Professor emeritus, Library and Information Studies, University of California, Los Angeles, and was a President of the Society of Indexers. Following the war, he served as Reference Librarian for the City of Westminster and later became Librarian to the BBC. During his fifty years as a professional librarian in England and the USA, he has written more than twenty works on bibliography, librarianship, indexing and related subjects.

John H. Horton is Deputy Librarian of the University of Bradford and currently Chairman of its Academic Board of Studies in Social Sciences. He has maintained a longstanding interest in the discipline of area studies and its associated bibliographical problems, with special reference to European Studies. In particular he has published in the field of Icelandic and of Yugoslav studies, including the two relevant volumes in the World Bibliographical Series.

Ian Wallace is Professor of Modern Languages at Loughborough University of Technology. A graduate of Oxford in French and German, he also studied in Tübingen, Heidelberg and Lausanne before taking teaching posts at universities in the USA, Scotland and England. He specializes in East German affairs, especially literature and culture, on which he has published numerous articles and books. In 1979 he founded the journal *GDR Monitor*, which he continues to edit.

Hans H. Wellisch is Professor emeritus at the College of Library and Information Services, University of Maryland. He was President of the American Society of Indexers and was a member of the International Federation for Documentation. He is the author of numerous articles and several books on indexing and abstracting, and has published *The conversion of scripts* and *Indexing and abstracting: an international bibliography*. He also contributes frequently to *Journal of the American Society for Information Science, The Indexer* and other professional journals.

Ralph Lee Woodward, Jr. is Chairman of the Department of History at Tulane University, New Orleans, where he has been Professor of History since 1970. He is the author of *Central America, a nation divided*, 2nd ed. (1985), as well as several monographs and more than sixty scholarly articles on modern Latin America. He has also compiled volumes in the World Bibliographical Series on *Belize* (1980), *Nicaragua* (1983), and *El Salvador* (forthcoming). Dr. Woodward edited the Central American section of the *Research guide to Central America and the Caribbean* (1985) and is currently editor of the Central American history section of the *Handbook of Latin American Studies*.

VOLUME 81

Iran

Reza Navabpour
Compiler

CLIO PRESS
OXFORD, ENGLAND · SANTA BARBARA, CALIFORNIA
DENVER, COLORADO

British Library Cataloguing in Publication Data

Navabpour, Reza
Iran. — (World bibliographical series; 81).
1. Iran — Bibliography
I. Title   II. Series
016.955   Z3366

ISBN 1–85109–036–3

Clio Press Ltd.,
55 St. Thomas' Street,
Oxford OX1 1JG, England.

ABC-Clio Information Services,
Riviera Campus, 2040 Alameda Padre Serra,
Santa Barbara, CA 93103, USA.

Designed by Bernard Crossland.
Typeset by Columns Design and Production Services, Reading, England.
Printed and bound in Great Britain by
Billing and Sons Ltd., Worcester.

Valid
2/20/05
[signature]

THE WORLD BIBLIOGRAPHICAL SERIES

This series, which is principally designed for the English speaker, will eventually cover every country in the world, each in a separate volume comprising annotated entries on works dealing with its history, geography, economy and politics; and with its people, their culture, customs, religion and social organization. Attention will also be paid to current living conditions – housing, education, newspapers, clothing, etc. – that are all too often ignored in standard bibliographies; and to those particular aspects relevant to individual countries. Each volume seeks to achieve, by use of careful selectivity and critical assessment of the literature, an expression of the country and an appreciation of its nature and national aspirations, to guide the reader towards an understanding of its importance. The keynote of the series is to provide, in a uniform format, an interpretation of each country that will express its culture, its place in the world, and the qualities and background that make it unique.

VOLUMES IN THE SERIES

1 *Yugoslavia*, John J. Horton
2 *Lebanon*, Shereen Khairallah
3 *Lesotho*, Shelagh M. Willet and David Ambrose
4 *Rhodesia/Zimbabwe*, Oliver B. Pollack and Karen Pollack
5 *Saudi Arabia*, Frank A. Clements
6 *USSR*, Anthony Thompson
7 *South Africa*, Reuben Musiker
8 *Malawi*, Robert B. Boeder
9 *Guatemala*, Woodman B. Franklin
11 *Uganda*, Robert L. Collison
12 *Malaysia*, Ian Brown and Rajeswary Ampalavanar
13 *France*, Frances Chambers
14 *Panama*, Eleanor DeSelms Langstaff
15 *Hungary*, Thomas Kabdebo
16 *USA*, Sheila R. Herstein and Naomi Robbins
17 *Greece*, Richard Clogg and Mary Jo Clogg
18 *New Zealand*, R. F. Grover
19 *Algeria*, Richard I. Lawless
20 *Sri Lanka*, Vijaya Samaraweera
21 *Belize*, Ralph Lee Woodward, Jr.
23 *Luxembourg*, Carlo Hury and Jul Christophory

24 *Swaziland*, Balam Nyeko
25 *Kenya*, Robert L. Collison
26 *India*, Brijen K. Gupta and Datta S. Kharbas
27 *Turkey*, Merel Güçlü
28 *Cyprus*, P. M. Kitromilides and M. L. Evriviades
29 *Oman*, Frank A. Clements
31 *Finland*, J. E. O. Screen
32 *Poland*, Richard C. Lewański
33 *Tunisia*, Allan M. Findlay, Anne M. Findlay and Richard I. Lawless
34 *Scotland*, Eric G. Grant
35 *China*, Peter Cheng
36 *Qatar*, P. T. H. Unwin
37 *Iceland*, John J. Horton
39 *Haiti*, Frances Chambers
40 *Sudan*, M. W. Daly
41 *Vatican City State*, Michael J. Walsh
42 *Iraq*, A. J. Abdulrahman
43 *United Arab Emirates*, Frank A. Clements
44 *Nicaragua*, Ralph Lee Woodward, Jr.
45 *Jamaica*, K. E. Ingram
46 *Australia*, I. Kepars

47 *Morocco*, Anne M. Findlay, Allan M. Findlay and Richard I. Lawless
48 *Mexico*, Naomi Robbins
49 *Bahrain*, P. T. H. Unwin
50 *The Yemens*, G. Rex Smith
51 *Zambia*, Anne M. Bliss and J. A. Rigg
52 *Puerto Rico*, Elena E. Cevallos
53 *Namibia*, Stanley Schoeman and Elna Schoeman
54 *Tanzania*, Colin Darch
55 *Jordan*, Ian J. Seccombe
56 *Kuwait*, Frank A. Clements
57 *Brazil*, Solena V. Bryant
58 *Israel*, Esther M. Snyder (preliminary compilation E. Kreiner)
59 *Romania*, Andrea Deletant and Dennis Deletant
60 *Spain*, Graham J. Shields
61 *Atlantic Ocean*, H. G. R. King
63 *Cameroon*, Mark W. Delancey and Peter J. Schraeder
64 *Malta*, John Richard Thackrah
65 *Thailand*, Michael Watts
66 *Austria*, Denys Salt with the assistance of Arthur Farrand Radley
67 *Norway*, Leland B. Sather
68 *Czechoslovakia*, David Short

69 *Irish Republic*, Michael Owen Shannon
70 *Pacific Basin and Oceania*, Gerald W. Fry and Rufino Mauricio
71 *Portugal*, P. T. H. Unwin
72 *West Germany*, Donald S. Detwiler and Ilse E. Detwiler
73 *Syria*, Ian J. Seccombe
74 *Trinidad and Tobago*, Frances Chambers
76 *Barbados*, Robert B. Potter and Graham M. S. Dann
77 *East Germany*, Ian Wallace
78 *Mozambique*, Colin Darch with the assistance of Calisto Pacheleke
79 *Libya*, Richard I. Lawless
80 *Sweden*, Leland B. Sather and Alan Swanson
81 *Iran*, Reza Navabpour
82 *Dominica*, Robert A. Myers
83 *Denmark*, Kenneth E. Miller
84 *Paraguay*, R. Andrew Nickson
85 *Indian Ocean*, Julia J. Gotthold with the assistance of D. W. Gotthold
86 *Egypt*, Ragai N. Makar
87 *Gibraltar*, Graham J. Shields
88 *The Netherlands*, Peter King and Michael Wintle
89 *Bolivia*, Gertrude M. Yeager

To: *Farideh,*
Pupak, and
Saghar

Contents

INTRODUCTION xiii

THE COUNTRY AND ITS PEOPLE 1

GEOGRAPHY AND GEOLOGY 6

TRAVELLERS' ACCOUNTS 14

TOURISM AND TRAVEL GUIDES 18

FLORA AND FAUNA 20

PREHISTORY AND ARCHAEOLOGY 23

HISTORY 27
    General   27
    Ancient pre-Islamic era   31
    Mediaeval Islamic period (7th–15th centuries)   36
    Modern Islamic period (16th–19th centuries)   42
    The age of constitutionalism, secularism and modernism (late 19th and 20th centuries)   50

BIOGRAPHIES, DIARIES AND MEMOIRS 56

POPULATION 63

EMIGRATION AND MIGRATION 67

NATIONALITIES AND MINORITIES 70
    General   70
    Nomads and pastoral settlers   72

LANGUAGE 75
    Grammars and linguistic studies   75

Contents

Readers   78
Dictionaries   79

RELIGION 81
Islam   81
Christianity and Judaism   88
Zoroastrianism   89

SOCIAL STRUCTURE AND SOCIAL CHANGE 92
General   92
Women   101

SOCIAL SERVICES, HEALTH AND WELFARE 105

POLITICS 108

AYATOLLAH KHOMEINI AND THE IRANIAN
REVOLUTION, 1979–   120
General   120
Religious ideology   128
Human rights   131
The hostage crisis   132

FOREIGN RELATIONS 134
General   134
With the Gulf States   139
With the Superpowers   141

THE GULF WAR, 1980–   147

CONSTITUTION AND THE LEGAL SYSTEM 151

THE MILITARY AND DEFENCE 156

ECONOMY 158

TRADE 168

OIL, INDUSTRY AND INDUSTRIALIZATION 171
Oil   171
Industry and industrialization   174

AGRICULTURE AND IRRIGATION 177
Agriculture   177
Irrigation   181

TRANSPORT 183

Contents

EMPLOYMENT AND MANPOWER 185

LABOUR MOVEMENT AND TRADE UNIONS 188

STATISTICS 191

URBANIZATION AND PLANNING 193

EDUCATION 196

SCIENCE AND TECHNOLOGY 199

LITERATURE 201
    Literary history and criticism   201
    Classical literary works   214
    Modern literary works   219

THE ARTS 223
    Visual arts   223
    Architecture   226
    Music   230
    Theatre and film   231
    Folk art, customs and handicrafts   232

IRANIAN COLLECTIONS IN FOREIGN LIBRARIES,
    MUSEUMS AND ART GALLERIES 237

BOOK PRODUCTION, DECORATION AND CALLIGRAPHY 241

MASS MEDIA 244

PROFESSIONAL PERIODICALS 246

BIBLIOGRAPHIES 249

INDEX OF AUTHORS, TITLES AND SUBJECTS   255

MAP OF IRAN 309

Introduction

Iran is notable for its geographical and strategic position, for its historical, cultural and social characteristics, and for the role it has played in Islamic civilization, regional politics, and international affairs. The country covers an area of 638,000 square miles and its population was recently estimated at just under fifty million. It occupies the area north of the Persian Gulf, the Strait of Hormuz and the Gulf of Oman, and, consequently, has the potential for strategic dominance over a vast area — an area which contains many of the Middle East's oil-fields, and also a sea route which is crucial to Western interests. Furthermore, Iran shares a 1,500-mile border with the USSR and, as a result, has been a buffer zone for 200 years: first for British colonial interests, and then, since the early 1950s, for the economic and political interests of the Western bloc in general, and the USA in particular. Other neighbours of Iran include Afghanistan and Pakistan to the east, and Turkey and Iraq to the west.

Modern Iran is descended from an ancient civilization dating back to around the 10th century BC, when the Elam societies emerged in what is now the southwestern province of Khuzestan. The Persian empire, established by Cyrus the Great and his dynasty and known as Achaemenian, lasted from 550 to 320 BC. The Achaemenian empire was followed by the Parthians (247 BC–AD 224), who were in turn followed by the Sassanians (AD 226–651). During the rule of the Sassanian dynasty, Zoroastrianism was the main religion. It was recognized as the state religion, at the expense of a number of other religions which were suppressed. In the 7th century AD the Arabs invaded and conquered the country and brought with them a new religion known as Islam.

From the fall of the Persian empire until the establishment of the Safavid dynasty at the beginning of the 16th century, Iran was ruled by non-Iranian Arab caliphs, Mongol Khans and Turkish/

Turkoman sultans, and, occasionally, by short-lived, self-appointed local Iranian houses. Throughout this period of Iranian history, during which Zoroastrianism was wiped out, the most zealous Zoroastrians migrated to India to escape Islamic persecution. Although Islam became the dominant religion of Iran, the Iranians, unlike many other nations defeated by the Muslim Arabs, preserved their Iranian identity and resisted full Arabization. In fact the Persian system of administration actually helped in the establishment of the Islamic empire, and since that time, Persian culture and the Iranian people have played a significant and influential role in the evolution of Islamic civilization. Indeed, Islam was refined and moulded in Iran so that it achieved a uniquely Persian identity.

A major quarrel among early Islamic leaders resulted in the formation of a separate sect and the growth of Shi'ism; this was later declared the country's state religion by the Safavids in the 16th century. Although Shi'ism has followers in other parts of the Islamic world, Iran is the only country to recognize it as the state religion. This has had mixed effects on Iran. On the one hand, it once helped the Iranians to resist the political influence of the Ottoman empire and, consequently, to preserve their Persian identity; on the other hand, with the growth of Western interests in the Middle East in the last two centuries, it has conflicted with the potential benefits of the pan-Islamic philosophy. Pan-Islamism, which aims to unify all Muslim peoples, surfaced in the 19th century among Muslim intellectuals who sought to protect their countries from foreign encroachment.

Iranian formal literature and folk-literature both reflect hostility towards the Arabs throughout the Islamic period. More recently, the Gulf War is a conflict between two Muslim nations, Shi'ite Iran and Sunni Iraq. The continuation of the war after the Iraqis' retreat was mainly justified as a campaign for the protection of Islam, threatened by the rulership of an infidel, i.e. Saddam Hussein. The historical rift is strongly highlighted by the fact that, even today, Shi'ite 'olamā (Islamic clerics) often compare Saddam Hussein with Yazid, a Sunni caliph of the early Islamic period (680–683 AD), who led a bloody campaign against Hosein, the revered third Shi'ite Imam and grandson of the Prophet.

For various reasons it can be said that Iran is a divided land occupied by a divided people. The country is fragmented by high mountain ranges: the Alborz to the north, and the Zagros stretching across the western and southern parts of the country.

The lowlands too are divided by vast, arid deserts. This variety of geographical conditions gives rise to climatic extremes: whilst the temperature falls to minus 30°C in some parts of the northwest, it rises to over 50°C in desert regions and in areas of the Persian Gulf. The amount of rainfall also varies considerably, with an average of forty inches around the shores of the Caspian Sea, and as little as two inches in desert regions. The rain falls mainly in the highland areas where cultivatable land is limited, while the lowlands in most parts of the country suffer from water scarcity. The population of the lowlands is thinly spread in small remote villages, except for a few large towns which have historically been centres of tax-collection, or market-places on the old caravan routes. In the western heights of the country, in contrast, the people live in tribal and pastoral communities, while the northern heights and lowlands of the country are more densely populated, the people being mainly involved in cultivation.

Besides these varied physical conditions which have contributed to social division and disintegration over the centuries, Iran is the home of many different ethnic groups, including Kurds, Turks, Baluchis, Turkomans and Arabs. Together they total nearly twenty million, and are often more closely allied to their neighbours over the borders than to other Iranian groups. There are also numerous linguistic and religious minority groups. The physical isolation of Iranian minority groups has, however, undergone some changes with the introduction of modernization, particularly in the 1960s and 1970s. The last three decades have witnessed a continuous flow of migrants from the rural areas and small towns to the provincial capitals and to Tehran. The population of Tehran rose from 2.7 million to well over 10 million between 1966 and 1986. The oil industry too has engendered much migration from different parts of the country to Khuzestan, although this has been reversed to some extent since the beginning of the Gulf War. Whilst efforts at modernization have helped the country to progress, and have encouraged the populace to integrate more, the speed of change and the high rate of migration have contributed to a sudden disintegration in the traditional communal structure and social balance. The environmental dislocation of a great proportion of the population has caused the migrants to forfeit their identity. For many Iranians, the 1979 Islamic Revolution represented a return to the traditional paternalistic social structure; it offered comfort to many who were naturally confused and had failed to keep up with the pace of modernization.

Introduction

It is not surprising to find that the policies introduced by the modernist, constitutionalist governments when they emerged at the beginning of the 20th century have now been reversed. The Constitutional Revolution of 1905–09, influenced by Western ideas, curtailed the influence of the Islamic clerics who had achieved power since the establishment of the Islamic state in the 16th century, and had enjoyed considerable authority during the 19th-century Qajar period. With the 1979 Islamic Revolution, the *'olamā* (Islamic clerics) resumed their charismatic position of authority which they had been denied for several decades. Their control now extends into all areas of national life, both secular and religious, representing a degree of power that they had never previously possessed.

Since the 1978–79 Islamic Revolution Iran has played an important role in international politics in general, and in regional politics in particular. The US Embassy hostage crisis brought the country to the headlines of most newspapers and journals throughout the world for more than a year. The Iran–Iraq war, which began in September 1980, is another topic which has received continuing wide coverage. The war has had regional as well as international repercussions, both in economic and political terms. It has so far claimed about one million casualties and cost both countries enormous sums of money.

The Islamic Revolution has brought about a revival of traditional Islamic institutions at the expense of modernist attitudes and a Western life-style. Together with the Iran–Iraq war it has forced a great number of mostly educated middle-class Iranians into self-exile throughout the world. On the other hand, it has opened a new political horizon for many Muslims in other countries who look to the Islamic government of Iran as a leading example of independence from Western decadence.

The bibliography

This volume follows the general guidelines of the *World Bibliographical Series* in providing a selective annotated bibliography of Iran, aimed at an audience ranging from the informed general reader to the scholar who wishes to obtain background information in a field other than his own.

Both works of extreme scholasticism and those of an ephemeral nature (such as articles from newspapers and popular journals) have mostly been omitted, but a number of works from the former category are included as they were considered to be of good and lasting reference value. Priority has always been given to works which can reasonably be expected to be found in the Middle East sections of university or large public libraries, and will therefore be available to most readers either directly or through the inter-library loan system. More recent works which are still in print and widely available have been preferred throughout, and it is owing to these factors that some collections, such as *The Cambridge history of Iran*, have been extensively referred to. As reference has been limited to those works available for consultation, a number of works which otherwise would have been included have been omitted, and in some cases an older edition of a book has been cited even though later publications are available.

The selection of which works should be included and which omitted was no easy task. No work was, however, omitted simply because of its subjectivity or for the type of opinions expressed. In fact, it has been the compiler's intention to include a variety of works representing different viewpoints and opinions, whether pro-Shah, pro-Khomeini, left or right wing. Material on issues such as the Gulf War, prepared by both hostile camps, has also been included, though not without some accompanying critical comments. These comments, however, are not intended to pass political judgement on the works concerned, but to guide users of the bibliography towards finding the works which are most appropriate for their purposes.

Finally, the volume neither claims nor is intended to be an exhaustive bibliography. While remaining in line with the general aims of the *World Bibliographical Series*, it corresponds to the special features and topical issues of contemporary Iran. This explains the limited coverage of areas of less immediate interest, such as 19th-century travel accounts, and the more extensive attention given to topical aspects such as Khomeini, the Islamic Revolution, and the Gulf War.

Acknowledgements

Thanks are due to a number of friends and colleagues for the encouragement, support and assistance they have given me throughout the compilation of this bibliography. The following is only an incomplete list: Dr. Richard Davis, Mr. Malcolm Ferguson, Mr. Ali Gheissari, Mrs Norma Gough, Mrs Susan Haberis, Miss Louise Jones, Dr. Richard Lawless, Dr. Paul Luft, Mrs Susan McBreen, Dr. Robert Neville, Dr. Paul Starkey and Mrs Sue Watts.

I should also like to express my gratitude to Farideh for her fathomless patience.

The Country and Its People

1 **The Iranians: how they live and work.**
John Abbott.   London: David & Charles, 1977. 161p. map. bibliog.
A general handbook on the country and its people. It covers the land, the people
and their history, and various social institutions. It also considers the way the
people live, work, learn, and amuse themselves.

2 **The legacy of Persia.**
Edited by A. J. Arberry.   Oxford: Oxford University Press, 1968.
3rd ed. 387p.
Illustrates the many facets of Persian culture and its influence on the country's
neighbours and on other nations. The volume contains thirteen articles on, for
example, history, religion, arts, language and literature, and carpets. It also
includes a table of the dates of the accession to the throne of Iranian rulers from
708 BC to 1941 AD (p. 389–97).

3 **Iran and Islam: in memory of the late Vladimir Minorsky.**
Edited by C. E. Bosworth.   Edinburgh: Edinburgh University Press;
Chicago: Aldine Publishing Company, 1971. 574p. 4 maps.
This is the second volume of essays to appear after the Russian Orientalist
Vladimir Minorsky's death in 1966, celebrating his contribution to Iranian studies.
Minorsky emigrated to France in 1919 where he taught Persian, Turkish and
Islamic history. Thirteen years later he moved to England and continued his
teaching at the School of Oriental and African Studies. He has left over 200
academic articles and books printed in different languages. This volume contains
thirty-six essays on various topics mostly on the history, culture and literature of
Iran.

1

The Country and Its People

4   **Persia: history and heritage.**
Edited by John A. Boyle.   London: Henry Melland, 1978. 120p.
map.
Aimed at the general reader, the volume focuses on various aspects of Persian
civilization, history, language and poetry, miniatures, architecture, pottery and
carpets. It also contains some interesting colour illustrations.

5   **Iran: continuity and variety.**
Edited by Peter J. Chelkowski.   New York: New York University
Press, 1971. 75p. (The Centre for Near Eastern Studies and the
Centre for International Studies).
A collection of four articles which were contributed to New York University's
fourth Annual Round Table Series, held in 1970–71 and organized in celebration
of the 2,500th anniversary of the establishment of the Iranian state. The articles
are as follows: 1, 'Continuity and change in rural Iran: the eastern deserts', by
Brian Spooner (p. 1–19); 2, 'Development of Persian drama in the context of
cultural confrontation', by Ehsan Yar-Shater (p. 21–38); 3, 'Shi'ism in the
medieval Safavid, and Qajar periods: a study in ithna "ashari continuity"', by
Michael Mazzaoui (p. 39–57); and 4, 'Variety and continuity in popular literature
in Iran', by William Hanaway (p. 59–75).

6   **Studies in art and literature of the Near East.**
Edited by Peter J. Chelkowski.   Utah: Middle East Centre,
University of Utah; New York: New York University Press, 1974.
289p.
This volume is in honour of, and was presented to, Richard Ettinghausen, the
universally recognized authority on the history of Islamic art. It includes a set of
studies on various aspects of Near Eastern culture and civilization. Most essays
are, however, on the Iranian arts, culture and literature and are by both Iranian
and non-Iranian scholars. A list of the writings of Richard Ettinghausen running
to 221 entries is included.

7   **The Persian Gulf states, a general survey.**
Edited by Alvin J. Cottrell, C. Edmund Bosworth, R. Michael
Burrell, Keith McLachlan, Roger M. Savory.   Baltimore, Maryland;
London: Johns Hopkins University Press, 1980. 536p. 4 maps.
bibliog.
A gazetteer-type handbook on the Persian Gulf region. Following an introductory
paper on 'The nomenclature of the Persian Gulf' (p. xvii–xxxiv) the volume
contains eighteen essays on four topics investigating various issues relating to the
Persian Gulf and the surrounding nations. The titles of these four parts are as
follows: 1, 'The history of the Persian Gulf'; 2 'Economics and urban development in the Persian Gulf'; 3, 'Culture, religion, language and literature'; 4, 'Arts
and society in the Persian Gulf'. The book is supported by twelve appendixes on
topics which include climate and oceanography, mineral resources, flora and
fauna, and demography. It also includes sixty-six informative tables.

2

8 Iran who's who.
  Echo of Iran.   Tehran: Echo of Iran, 1974. 2nd ed. 623p. map.
A revision of the first edition of *Iran who's who* in 1972. It contains about five thousand biographical entries of the contemporary Iranian élite.

9 Iran almanac and book of facts.
  Echo of Iran.   Tehran: Echo of Iran, 1977. 16th ed. 497p. 37 maps.
Contains basic information on various aspects of Persian life and culture divided into seven chapters. These are entitled: 1, 'History and geography'; 2, 'National affairs'; 3, 'Mass media'; 4, 'Foreign relations'; 5, 'Economic aspects'; 6, 'Demographic and social characteristics'; 7, 'Cultural life'.

10 Fall of the peacock throne: the story of Iran.
  William H. Forbis.   New York: Harper & Row, 1980. 290p. map.
  bibliog.
A collection of unconnected tales about Persian life and culture, with which the author intends 'to get behind the headlines and explore more profoundly the country and its people'. This readable volume is recommended for the reader wishing to gain a basic general knowledge of Iranian society, its history and its culture.

11 Iran: past, present and future.
  Edited by Jane W. Jacqz.   New York: Aspen Institute for
  Humanistic Studies, 1976. 465p.
The Aspen Institute for Humanistic Studies, sponsored by the Pahlavi Foundation of Iran and encouraged by the Shah's wife, Farah Pahlavi, organized a symposium in September 1975 in Persepolis. Scholars favourably inclined to the Pahlavi régime from North America, Europe, Asia and Africa, as well as from Iran, were invited to contribute. This volume includes papers presented to the symposium, followed by comments and discussions. The main theme of the volume is the general modernization policy of the government. A list of all participants is also included.

12 Iran: religion, politics and society.
  Nikki R. Keddie.   London: Cass, 1980. 239p.
A collection of eight essays, brought together under two topics: 1, 'Religion and politics'; 2, 'Socio-economic change'. Except for two chapters (three and four) all the other chapters have been published elsewhere. A detailed list of the author's printed works is included.

13 Iranica: twenty articles.
  Vladimir Minorsky.   Tehran: Publications of the University of
  Tehran (vol. 775), 1964. 332p. 4 maps.
Contains twenty articles by the author on various aspects of the Persian arts, literature, history and culture. Most of the papers are in English but some are in French. The arrangement of the articles is chronological according to when they

were written. Also included is a chronological list of Professor Minorsky's publications.

14 **Persia.**
    Admiralty War Staff, Naval Intelligence Division, Great
    Britain. London: HM Stationery Office, 1945. 583p. 38 maps.
    (Geographical Handbook Series, BR 525).
This volume still remains a reliable handbook on Iran (which was named Persia until 1935), providing a useful overview of the country's geographical features, as well as its climate, history and people. The work also covers aspects of the life and social system in Iran in the 1930s and early 1940s, which may be useful for research.

15 **Persian cooking: a table of exotic delights.**
    Nesta Ramazani. Charlottesville, Virginia: University Press of
    Virginia, 1982. 279p. map.
Provides recipes for a variety of Persian dishes and includes a shopper's guide.

16 **Area handbook for Iran.**
    Harvey H. Smith, William W. Cover, John B. Folan,
    Michael L. Meissenburg, Julius Szentadorjany, Suzanne
    Teleki. Washington, DC: US Government Printing Office, 1971.
    603p. 6 maps. bibliog.
Provides general information on the social, political and economic bases of Iranian society, and the developments in the main features of the government's reform programme conducted in the mid-1970s.

17 **Islam and its cultural divergence.**
    Edited by Girdhari L. Tikku. Urbana, Illinois; Chicago; London:
    University of Illinois Press, 1971. 248p.
A collection of studies in honour of, and some written by, Gustave Edmund von Grunebaum, Professor of History and Director of the New Eastern Centre at UCLA (University of California at Los Angeles). The works of Grunebaum are listed at the end of the book in the order in which they first appeared, followed by reviews of his works by other scholars also in order of publication. 'Secrets for Muslims in Parsi scriptures' by Sven S. Hartman (p. 63–75); 'Arabic orthography and some non-semitic languages' by C. Mohammad Naim (p. 113–44); 'Dāniyal-Nāme: an exposition of Judeo-Persian' by Amnon Netzer (p. 145–63); and 'Some socio-religious themes in modern Persian fiction' by the editor (p. 165–79) are amongst the topics most relevant to Iran.

18 **Contemporary Iran.**
    Donald Wilber. London: Thames & Hudson, 1963. 212p. bibliog.
This handbook attempts to provide a picture of social tensions in modern Iran, with reference to the country's institutions, attitudes of its society, and the

4

interwoven relationships between the forces of authority and social traditions. The volume's first two chapters – out of a total of five – provide a primary background, describing the land and its people. Chapter three gives a brief analytical study of the patterns of change and continuity, while contemporary and future times are discussed in the last two chapters.

19   **Iran: past and present.**
Donald Wilber.   Princeton, New Jersey: Princeton University Press, 1975. 331p. map. bibliog.
Provides pro-Pahlavi information about Iran as a whole, with special emphasis on modern developments up to the early 1970s. This is the 7th edition, and the eighth printing of the book, which first appeared in 1948. It contains eight chapters, of which the first three are concerned with the past, and are collectively entitled 'Iran's heritage'. Chapters 4–8 deal with the Pahlavi period and the government's attempts at modernization.

20   **Iran faces the seventies.**
Edited by Ehsan Yar-Shater.   New York; Washington; London: Praeger, 1971. 380p.
A collection of fifteen essays on various aspects of Iranian life and culture, concerning land reform, economy, politics, social and religious issues, education, mass media, literature and the arts.

21   **Cultural development in Iran.**
Ehsan Yar-Shater.   In: *Iran: past, present and future.* Edited by Jane W. Jacqz. New York: Aspen Institute for Humanistic Studies, 1976. p. 407–19.
A brief overview of Persian culture and the arts, aimed at the general public. Some of the topics covered include the historical awareness that the Persians have of their Iranian identity; the development of their culture and religious thought; and the emergence, progress and decline of the Persian arts and literature.

22   **Encyclopaedia Iranica.**
Edited by Ehsan Yar-Shater.   London; New York: Routledge & Kegan Paul, 1982–   .
This is the first systematic encyclopaedia of Iran in English providing up-to-date articles on topics of archaeological, geographical, ethnographic, historical, artistic, literary, religious, linguistic, philosophical, scientific and folklore interest. Articles are arranged alphabetically. The encyclopaedia is designed to appear in successive fascicles of 112 pages each. The fascicles forming volume one were first published in one volume in 1985. Half a dozen fascicles of volume two are in print.

A year amongst the Persians . . .
See item no. 53.

5

Geography and Geology

23 **Historical gazetteer of Iran: Tehran and northwestern Iran.**
Ludwig W. Adamec. Graz, Austria: Akademische Druck- u.
Verlagsanstalt, 1976. 714p. map.

An alphabetically-arranged list of the geographical features, villages and towns
found in north-western Iran. It provides a primary geographical source, enriched
with ethnographic and statistical data, as well as information on the history and
culture of the area. A map of the region is also included in fragments at the end
of the volume. A second volume by the same author, entitled *Historical gazetteer
of Iran: Mashad and northeastern Iran*, was published in 1981 and contains 690
pages. Covering the north-eastern region, its format is similar to volume one.

24 **The Shatt al-Arab river dispute in terms of law.**
Khalid al-Aziz. Baghdad: Iraqi Ministry of Information, 1972.
159p. map. bibliog.

Presents an historical and legal study of the Shatt al-Arab border dispute between
Iran and Iraq. The book is divided into two parts. Part one deals with the history
of the conflict; while the legal aspects of the dispute, substantiated by facts and
documentary evidence, are studied in part two. It is based on the author's
doctoral dissertation, which was approved by the State University of Groningen,
Groningen, The Netherlands. The dispute is studied objectively and is based on
both Iraqi and Iranian sources.

25 **A history of Persian earthquakes.**
N. N. Ambraseys, C. P. Melville. Cambridge, England:
Cambridge University Press, 1982. 198p. 76 maps. bibliog.

An investigation of geological processes and earthquakes based on historical
sources and modern field-studies. This survey, although concerned with Iran, is
not confined to the country's modern boundaries and for this reason the authors
have deliberately referred in their title to Persia rather than Iran.

26 **Baluchestan: its political economy and history.**
Āyandegān. In: *RIPEH: Review of Iranian Political Economy and History*, vol. 4, no. 1 (Spring 1980), p. 68–93.

A translation of an article entitled 'Baluchestan: political, geographic, historical appraisal', which was published in the Tehran daily *Āyandegān* from 22–24 July 1979. The article examines the appalling economic conditions in the south-eastern province of Sistan-Baluchestan, with reference to the political history of the area. Some interviews are also included.

27 **An historical geography of Iran.**
W. Barthold, translated from the Russian by Svat Soucek.
Princeton, New Jersey: Princeton University Press, 1984. 242p.
2 maps. bibliog.

An analytical and descriptive exploration of Iran's historical geography based on a critical study of basic classical Iranian and Greek sources, Arabic geographical texts, travelogues, diaries and European studies. The translation has been edited by C. E. Bosworth who also wrote the introduction.

28 **Bartholomew world travel map: the Middle East.**
Edinburgh: Bartholomew. scale 1:4,000,000. irregularly updated.
(World Travel Series).

A useful map for the traveller, showing the main political and geographical features with a note as to the major cities and towns. The most recent edition is 1982.

29 **The Middle East: a geographical study.**
Peter Beaumont, Gerald H. Blake, J. Malcolm Wagstaff. London; New York; Sydney; Toronto: John Wiley, 1977. 508p. maps. bibliog.

An extensive introduction to the political, cultural and economic geography of the Middle Eastern countries, with a detailed study of the region's landscape features, natural resources, environmental conditions and ecological evolution. Frequent references to Iran are made throughout the text.

30 **Yazd and its hinterland: a central place system of dominance in the central Iranian plateau.**
Michael Edward Bonine. Marburg, Lahn, FRG: Selbstverlag des Geographischen Institutes der Universität Marburg, 1980. 190p.
72 maps. bibliog. (Marburger Geographische Schriften, Heft 83).

Examines the city of Yazd and its relationship with the hinterland. The study, which was originally prepared in 1975 as a dissertation in geography at the University of Texas at Austin, Texas, is based on the author's field-work, carried out in Iran from autumn 1969 through to the summer of 1971, i.e., before the occurrence of expansion and change in the relationships between the city and its hinterland. Its primary data are, however, valuable, and this work provides a worthwhile contribution to central place and settlement studies.

Geography and Geology

31   **The Iranian city of Shiraz.**
     John I. Clarke.   Durham, England: University of Durham, 1963.
     55p. 5 maps. (Department of Geography, Research Papers Series,
     No. 7).

A study of Shiraz in the south-west, based on a field-study which was carried out
in the city throughout August and September 1962. It deals with the
contemporary social and physical structure of the city, and reference to the past is
made only to provide background information, or in relation to contemporary
findings.

32   **Kermanshah: an Iranian provincial city.**
     J. I. Clarke, B. D. Clark.   Durham, England: University of
     Durham, 1969. 137p. 14 maps. (Centre for Middle Eastern and
     Islamic Studies, No. 1; Department of Geography, Research Papers
     Series, No. 10).

An urban study of Kermanshah, a provincial centre in western Iran, based on
field-work which was carried out by a team of three researchers in September and
October 1966. It attempts to examine the city's morphology, its function and its
relationship with the rest of the region.

33   **Semnan: Persian city and region.**
     Edited by John Connel.   London: University College, London,
     1969. 105p. 3 maps.

A study of Semnan city in the north and its region, based on field-work carried
out by a small team from the Department of Geography, University College,
London. It surveys the physical environment, climate, and vegetation; the
region's historical background and social structure; the patterns and functions of
the traditional and modern economies; and water use and urban agriculture.

34   **Soils.**
     M. L. Dewan, J. Famouri.   In: *The Cambridge history of Iran,*
     vol. I: the land of Iran. Edited by W. B. Fisher. Cambridge,
     England: Cambridge University Press, 1968. p. 250–63. 2 maps.

Briefly examines the soils of the plains and valleys of Iran. The country is divided
into four areas, each having its own distinctive physiographic characterstics. Some
notes on clays are also included.

35   **The Cambridge history of Iran, vol. I: the land of Iran.**
     Edited by W. B. Fisher.   Cambridge, England: Cambridge
     University Press, 1968. 740p. maps. bibliog.

A compendium of information about the physical and economic geography of
Iran, as well as its anthropology, demography, flora and fauna. It includes twenty-
two articles arranged into sections covering the land, the people, and the
economic life. It concludes with a general survey by the editor, pointing out the
country's distinctive characteristics. The volume includes numerous maps, figures,
plates and tables.

36 **Physical geography.**
W. B. Fisher. In: *The Cambridge history of Iran, vol. I: the land of Iran*. Edited by W. B. Fisher. Cambridge, England: Cambridge University Press, 1968. p. 3–110. 22 maps. bibliog.
Provides a geographical observation of the different regions in Iran, placing special emphasis on their physical characteristics.

37 **Climate.**
M. H. Ganji. In: *The Cambridge history of Iran, vol. I: the land of Iran*. Edited by W. B. Fisher. Cambridge, England: Cambridge University Press, 1968. p. 212–49. 16 maps.
Examines pressure and wind, temperature conditions and rainfall. It also includes monthly climatic data for forty-one stations throughout the country.

38 **Iranian cities.**
Heinz Gaube. New York: New York University Press, 1979. 132p. 25 maps.
Herat, Isfahan and Bam, three cities of different sizes, situated in different parts of historical Iran and each representing different facets of life, are studied in this book. An introductory chapter entitled 'Origins', briefly discusses two modern Iranian cities, Tehran and Malayer, and provides a guide and a link for the rest of the book, which is concerned with the origins, the contours, the growth, and the functions of the cities under consideration.

39 **Geology.**
J. V. Harrison. In: *The Cambridge history of Iran, vol. I: the land of Iran*. Edited by W. B. Fisher. Cambridge, England: Cambridge University Press, 1968. p. 111–85. 15 maps. bibliog.
Provides a general observation of the geological characteristics of Iran. Harrison studies the stratigraphical details of the Iranian plateau, the landform, and its structure. He discusses the main structure lines, and examines the Alburz system, the Tabas wedge, the East Iranian quadrangle, the volcanic and complex belts, the zone of normal folding, and the Makran area.

40 **Minerals.**
J. V. Harrison. In: *The Cambridge history of Iran, vol. I: the land of Iran*. Edited by W. B. Fisher. Cambridge, England: Cambridge University Press, 1968. p. 489–516. 3 maps. bibliog.
A general overview of Iran's mineral resources, dealing with coal, iron, manganese, copper, lead, zinc, chromite, gold and marble, although oil has been omitted.

41   **Comment on the Iranian claims concerning the Iraqi-Iranian**
     Frontier Treaty of 1937 and the legal status of the frontier between
     the two countries in Shatt al-Arab.
     Iraqi Government.   Baghdad: Iraqi Ministry of Foreign Affairs,
     1969. 33p. map.
An official Iraqi view of the Frontier Treaty of 1937 between Iran and Iraq. It
includes the text of the Frontier Treaty of 1937.

42   **Alamut and Lamasar: two medieval Ismaili strongholds in Iran.**
     W. Ivanow.   Tehran: Ismaili Society Series 'C', No. 2, 1960. 81p.
     3 maps.
A survey of Alamut, an Ismaili stronghold during the 12th and 13th centuries,
dealing with the area's geographical position and geological conditions. Some
historical notes and other contemporary issues are examined, and there are three
appendixes, the first of which is concerned with the folklore of Alamut. Also
included are eighty-two pictures, mainly of the area's mountain rocks.

43   **Iran: highway map.**
     Ministry of Roads.   Tehran: Planning and Programming Division,
     1970.
Although relatively outdated, this is still a useful selection of the roadmaps of
Iran in both Persian and English. A name index is included.

44   **Historical atlas of Iran.**
     Edited by Seyyed Hossein Nasr, Ahmad Mostofi, Abbas
     Zaryab.   Tehran: Tehran University, 1971. 29 maps.
Contains historical maps of Iran, showing the territories of Iranian dynasties
from before the middle of the 5th millennium BC to the time of the Pahlavis. The
work also includes a brief general history of Iran in Farsi, English and French.
Each map, too, is accompanied by a relevant short historical note in these three
languages.

45   **The origin of the Zagros defiles.**
     M. Oberlander.   In: *The Cambridge history of Iran, vol. I: the land*
     of Iran. Edited by W. B. Fisher. Cambridge, England: Cambridge
     University Press, 1968. p. 195–211. 4 maps.
Examines the geological characteristics of the Zagros mountain range which, in
the author's view, represents an extremely unusual situation, that is, disharmony
between the drainage and the deformational patterns manifested in the parallel
ranges of gorges. The work studies the setting, drainage anomalies and streams.

46   **Map of Iran: river basins.**
     'Abbās Sahāb.   Tehran: Sahab (Geographic and Drafting
     Institute), 1963. scale 1:300,000.
A relatively outdated map of Iran focusing on the river basins and dams which
had been constructed at that time. The names are given in both Persian and
English.

47 **Atlas of geographical maps and historical documents on the Persian Gulf.**

Edited by 'Abbās Sahāb. Tehran: Sahab (Geographic and Drafting Institute), 1971. 282p. 373 maps. bibliog.

Brings together a collection of historical charts and maps with the main intention of proving that the Gulf, which lies to the south of Iran, has, from ancient times, been known as the Persian Gulf.

48 **Atlas of Iran: White Revolution proceeds and progresses.**

Edited by 'Abbās Sahāb. Tehran: Sahab (Geographic and Drafting Institute), 1971. 190p. 111 maps.

This volume attempts, largely, to give a glorious picture of Iran: this is seen as the result of the introduction of the White Revolution and its developments, presented in the form of diagrams incorporated into the maps of Iran. Titles, keys and other explanatory notes are in Persian and English, while a list of contents is given in Persian, English and French.

49 **Geomorphology.**

K. Scharlan. In: *The Cambridge history of Iran, vol. I: the land of Iran*. Edited by W. B. Fisher. Cambridge, England: Cambridge University Press, 1968. p. 186–94. bibliog.

A brief examination of the extent of rainfall in various areas of Iran and the pattern of its distribution determined by the country's geomorphological characteristics.

50 **Notes on the toponymy of the Persian Makran.**

Brian Spooner. In: *Iran and Islam*. Edited by C. E. Bosworth. Edinburgh: Edinburgh University Press, 1971. p. 517–33. map.

A descriptive account of the geographical features of the Makran area, which lies in the south-east of Iran and west of Pakistan. The study focuses on the part of the area which is under Iranian territory and deals with the human influences on the area, the different ethnic elements, and the social and anthropological characteristics. Included are two alphabetical lists, the first containing constituent toponymical elements and geographical terms, and the second selected toponyms.

51 **Iran: official standard names approved by the US Board on Geographic Names.**

US Board on Geographic Names. Washington, DC: Office of Geography, Department of the Interior, 1956. 578p. (Gazetteer).

Contains about 46,000 entries of the approved standard names of places and features in Iran. The unapproved variant names are cross-referenced with the standard names.

Geography and Geology

The Iranians: how they live and work.
See item no. 1.

The Persian Gulf states, a general survey.
See item no. 7.

Iran almanac and book of facts.
See item no. 9.

Contemporary Iran.
See item no. 18.

Persian diary 1939–1941.
See item no. 58.

Ten thousand miles in Persia . . .
See item no. 65.

Vegetation.
See item no. 74.

The vegetation of Hormoz . . .
See item no. 77.

A history of Persia.
See item no. 97.

Elam.
See item no. 103.

Persia and the Persian question.
See item no. 152.

Geography of settlement.
See item no. 241.

Who are the Baluch? . . .
See item no. 244.

A dictionary of scientific terms.
See item no. 267.

International and legal problems of the Gulf.
See item no. 459.

Industrial activities.
See item no. 525.

Agriculture.
See item no. 532.

Irrigation in the Zagros mountains.
See item no. 542.

The water-supply in the margin of Dasht-e-Kawir (central Iran).
See item no. 543.

Tehran: an urban analysis.
See item no. 569.

Tehran: a demographic and economic analysis.
See item no. 571.

Iran: a bibliographic research survey.
See item no. 776.

Travellers' Accounts

52 **Through Persia by caravan.**
   Arthur Arnold.   London: Tinsley Brothers, 1877. 2 vols.
The travel diary of Arthur Arnold, the author of *From the Levant* (London:
Chapman & Hall, 1868), who, accompanied by his wife, set out from London on
his travels in the summer of 1875. The diary notes, however, commence at
Warsaw. He and his wife journeyed through Iran from the period between
October 1875 and February 1876.

53 **A year amongst the Persians: impressions as to the life, character,
   and thought of the people of Persia received during twelve months'
   residence in that country in the years 1887–1888.**
   Edward Granville Browne.   Cambridge, England: Cambridge
   University Press, 1926. 2nd ed. 635p. map.
This is a most fascinating travel book, a classic, providing lively and entertaining
descriptions of the country and its people, as well as casting some light on
contemporary developments and new dimensions in the fields of literature and
thought. The volume includes some introductory notes by Denison Ross on the
author and the significance of his book.

54 **The road to Oxiana.**
   Robert Byron.   Bungay, Suffolk, England: Picador, 1981. new ed.
   5 maps. 277p.
A record of the English scholar Robert Byron's journey in 1933–34 to Persia and
Afghanistan in search of the origins of Islamic architecture. It is divided into five
parts, each containing a map displaying the author's route, leading from Venice to
Persia and on to Afghanistan, then back to Persia, journeying to Afghanistan for
a second time before travelling to India and back to England. The author's vivid
observations of the people he encountered and the places he visited are expressed

quite poetically. The 1981 edition includes an introduction by Bruce Chatwin which is more concerned with modern politics and the Russian presence in Afghanistan than with the book itself, which was originally published in 1937 by Macmillan.

55   Checkmate: fighting tradition in central Asia.
F. A. C. Forbes-Leith.   New York: Middle East Collection, 1973. 242p.

In late 1917, when Iran was in the grip of famine and occupying forces, and the Russians were engaged in civil war, the British War Office entrusted Major General Dunsterville with the mission of crossing Iran and supporting the establishment of a non-Soviet Armenian state in the Caucasus regions. The author was sent to join the 'Dunsterforce' in the summer of 1918. After the failure of the mission he stayed in Iran, serving a wealthy Iranian. The book is a telling story of his experience amongst the Persians from the summer of 1918 to the crowning of Reza Shah in 1925, and deals with various aspects of social structure, agriculture, economy and modernization attempts. The present volume is a reprint of the original which was published in 1927.

56   Behind the veil in Persia and Turkish Arabia: an account of an Englishwoman's eight years' residence amongst the women of the East.
M. E. Hume-Griffith.   London: Seeley & Company, 1909. 328p. map.

Presents an account of the author's experience of living conditions in Kerman at the beginning of the 20th century when her husband served as a medical officer for the Church Missionary Society. The book provides rare and interesting insights into the everyday lives of the Persian people. It consists of two parts: the first gives a general account of the author's experiences in Iran (p. 17–169); while the second is concerned more specifically with the physical and social life in Kerman, Yazd and the desert. Some of the important topics she highlights include women and health.

57   The ship of Sulaiman.
Ibn Mohammad Ibrahim, translated from the Persian by John O'Kane.   London: Routledge & Kegan Paul, 1972. 248p.

A translation of *Safineh-ye Suleimani*, which is an account of a Persian deputation sent to Siam during the latter part of the 17th century. The author was secretary to the envoy and made a record of his observations while at sea, and while in Siam and other countries in the Far East, notably China, Japan and the Philippines. Amongst the subjects covered by the author is a description of the Iranian community in Siam.

15

Travellers' Accounts

58 **Persian diary 1939–1941.**
Walter N. Koelz. Ann Arbor, Michigan: Museum of
Anthropology, University of Michigan, 1983. 227p. map.
(Anthropological Papers, no. 71).
Selections from a diary written during the author's travels in the Iranian
countryside between 1939–41 on a project sponsored by the US Department of
Agriculture to study the country's plant formations. This book concentrates on
the life of the Iranian nomads and peasantry with whom he came into contact
whilst carrying out his research.

59 **The glory of the Shia world: the tale of a pilgrimage.**
Nurollah Khan, translated and edited by P. M. Sykes. London:
Macmillan, 1910. 279p.
Translates the diary kept by Nurollah Khan whilst on a pilgrimage to the tomb of
the Shi'ite holy man Imam Reza in Mashhad. Khan was the son of Haji Abol
Hasan Khan, the original and famous title character in James Morier's satirical
Adventures of Hajji Baba of Ispahan (1824) and *The Adventures of Hajji Baba of
Ispahan in England* (1828). The diary was finished shortly before its translation. It
contains numerous fascinating colour and black-and-white illustrations, and also
includes a plan of the beautiful Mashhad shrine.

60 **Vakil Abad, Iran: a survivor's story.**
Richard Savin. Edinburgh: Canongate & Q Press, 1979. 240p.
The author's diary of his journey to Iran in 1976 and his experience in Vakil Abad
prison in Mashhad where he served a sentence after being convicted on drugs
charges.

61 **Travels into Persia.**
Sir Antony Sherley. Westmead, Hampshire, England: Gregg
International, 1972. 139p. 2nd ed.
Sir Antony Sherley's celebrated account of his travels into Persia early in the 17th
century. The present volume is an offset print of the original, which was printed
in London in 1613.

62 **World War in Iran.**
Clarmont Skrine. London: Constable & Company, 1962. 253p.
3 maps.
An illustrated narrative of observations made by the author, who lived and
worked in Iran during both World Wars and also, from time to time, between
them. The author's personal experience is incorporated with summaries of the
events which occurred during his periods of absence from Iran, based on pro-
British materials. Some of the photographs are of historical significance.

16

63   **Blind white fish in Persia.**
Anthony Smith.   London: Allen & Unwin, 1966. 207p. 2nd ed.
Describes the adventurous expedition of four Oxford students who set off for the
city of Kerman in September 1950 with the purpose of studying the *qanats*, the
underground water channels, of the area. The book was first published in 1953
and has been published in several editions under different imprints ever since.

64   **Old routes of western Iran.**
Sir Aurel Stein.   London: Macmillan, 1940. 422p. 7 maps.
A narrative record of the author's archaeological journey, undertaken between
1932 and 1936, in the southern and western areas of Iran. It contains a descriptive
and illustrated examination of some antiquities, and includes an additional map,
in the pocket at the end of the volume, of those parts of the western provinces of
Iran which were covered and surveyed by the author.

65   **Ten thousand miles in Persia or eight years in Iran.**
Percy M. Sykes.   London: John Murray, 1902. 458p. 8 maps.
A major late-19th-century travelogue dealing exhaustively with the geography of
various provinces, towns and villages in Iran, with frequent reference to their
geological and mineral importance, the inhabitants' social characteristics, and
some historical events. The volume includes an abundant selection of magnificent
illustrations.

66   **Shah Mozaffar Al-Din's European tour, AD 1900.**
G. M. Wickens.   In: *Qajar Iran: political, social and cultural
change, 1800–1925*. Edited by E. Bosworth, C. Hillenbrand.
Edinburgh: Edinburgh University Press, 1983. p. 34–47.
A study of the European journal kept by Mozaffaroddin Shah (the fifth Qajar
monarch (1896–1907)) on his first visit to Europe in the year 1900. His diary is a
major historical document.

To Persia for flowers.
See item no. 75.

Persian art through the eyes of nineteenth-century British travellers.
See item no. 690.

Tourism and Travel Guides

67 **Persian landscape: a photographic essay.**
Warwick Ball, Antony Hutt.   London: Scorpion Publications,
1978. [no pagination]. map.

A photographic introduction to Iran giving an impressionistic view of the awe-inspiring beauty of Iran's landscape. It contains fifty-nine colour and black-and-white pictures on alternate pages with a brief annotation on the opposite page.

68 **Isfahan, pearl of Persia.**
Wilfred Blunt, Wim Swaan.   London: Elek Books, 1974. 200p.
bibliog.

A general introduction to the history of Isfahan and its architecture, enriched by numerous black-and-white and colour illustrations, and providing a fascinating guide for travellers to Iran. The text, by Blunt, concentrates on the Safavid period (16th–18th centuries), but also deals with pre-Safavid architecture and the 19th-century Qajars, as well as the 20th-century innovations. The illustrations, by Swaan, include drawings, miniatures, art objects and buildings of architectural significance.

69 **Persia.**
A. Costa.   London: Thames & Hudson, 1957. 105p. map.
Reprinted, 1961.

Contains 105 pictures in black-and-white, and five colour plates with annotations, with a brief introduction to Iran's history, territory and people by L. Lockhart. A chronological table of important events from 4500 BC to 1954 AD is also included.

70 **Know the Middle East.**
John Laffin.   Gloucester, England: Alan Sutton, 1985. 186p. map.
bibliog.
A pocket-sized general handbook prepared for businessmen, travellers, tourists,
politicians and journalists, covering the Arab world as well as Iran, Sudan,
Turkey, Israel and Cyprus.

71 **Persia: an archaeological guide.**
Sylvia A. Matheson.   London: Faber, 1972. 283p. 9 maps. bibliog.
2nd rev. ed. 1976.
Attempts to provide the latest possible information on most of the excavations in
progress up to 1972. There is also a guide on travelling to Iran, and some useful
addresses for tourists. It includes an appendix providing a chronological and
historical table showing principal periods of main sites.

72 **Touring Iran.**
Philip Ward.   London: Faber, 1971. 163p. 6 maps.
This book has been prepared with the intention of offering a practical handbook
to those travellers wanting to travel around the country, see interesting places and
spend moderately. It contains forty-six plates and a chapter providing useful
information, as well as a chronology of Iranian rulers and great events from
4000 BC to 1971.

A list of the historical sites and ancient monuments of Iran.
See item no. 84.

Flora and Fauna

73 **Zoogeographic analysis of the lizard fauna of Iran.**
S. C. Anderson. In: *The Cambridge history of Iran, vol. 1: the land of Iran.* Edited by W. B. Fisher. Cambridge, England: Cambridge University Press, 1968. p. 305–71. map. bibliog.
A brief study of the amphibians and reptiles of Iran; their major distribution patterns and the historical origins of these patterns; and the determining factors of the present distribution in Iran and in relation to the whole of south-west Asia.

74 **Vegetation.**
H. Bobek. In: *The Cambridge history of Iran, vol. I: the land of Iran.* Edited by W. B. Fisher. Cambridge, England: Cambridge University Press, 1968. p. 280–93. map. bibliog.
Surveys the vegetation of Iran with references to the factors of diversification, such as, climatic situation, geographical characteristics, varied topography and the effect of human activity upon the vegetation.

75 **To Persia for flowers.**
Alice Fullerton. Oxford: Oxford University Press, 1938. 195p.
A diary of the author's journey to Iran in 1935 with the object of exploring the flowers of Iran. There is an appendix of Persian flowers and twenty-four illustrations.

76   **A guide to the mammals of Iran.**
Compiled and edited by Fred A. Harrington, Jr. in collaboration
with personnel of the Iran Department of the Environment with an
introduction by Eskander Firouz.   Tehran: Department of the
Environment, 1977. 88p. 3 maps.
The Iranian environment and the classification of its mammals are outlined in a
brief introduction, together with maps and a table (p. 1–19). The book presents
thirty-four plates of the mammals of Iran on alternate pages (p. 20–87) with
relevant notes on the facing page.

77   **The vegetation of Hormoz, Qeshm and neighbouring islands
(southern Persian Gulf area).**
Günther Kunkel.   Vaduz, Liechtenstein: J. Cramer, 1977. 177p.
map. bibliog.
Examines the vegetation of Hormoz, Qeshm and the neighbouring islands in
general, with the objective of providing a base for the purpose of conservation.
The field-work took place during March and April 1974. The volume includes
enumeration of species.

78   **Mammals.**
X. De Misonne.   In: *The Cambridge history of Iran, vol. I: the land
of Iran.* Edited by W. B. Fisher. Cambridge, England: Cambridge
University Press, 1968. p. 294–304. 3 maps. bibliog.
Surveys the mammals of Iran and their classification. It also studies the country's
ecology and domestic animals.

79   **Ornithology.**
S. Jervis Read.   In: *The Cambridge history of Iran, vol. I: the land
of Iran.* Edited by W. B. Fisher. Cambridge, England: Cambridge
University Press, 1968. p. 372–92. bibliog.
The author broadly divides the approximately 450 species of bird which can be
found in Iran into four main categories of residents, summer visitors, winter
visitors and passage migrants.

The Persian Gulf states, a general survey.
See item no. 7.

Semnan: Persian city and region.
See item no. 33.

Persian diary 1939–1941.
See item no. 58.

Flora and Fauna

A history of Persia.
See item no. 97.

A dictionary of scientific terms.
See item no. 267.

Prehistory and Archaeology

80 **Persian metal technology 700–1300 AD.**
James W. Allan. London: Ithaca Press, 1979. 152p. 9 maps.
bibliog. (Faculty of Oriental Studies and the Ashmolean Museum,
University of Oxford).

Traces in detail the movement of various metals; the way in which they were
purified and made into objects, alloys and so on in mediaeval Persian society.
The chapter headings are: 'Mercury, gold and silver'; 'Copper and its alloying
metals'; and 'Iron and steel'. An appendix on the elemental composition of
mediaeval Persian metal objects by A. Kaczmarczyk and R. E. M. Hedges is
included, as well as a number of plates, mostly displaying metal objects, with brief
captions.

81 **The small finds.**
John Curtis, with an introduction by David Stronach. London:
British Institute of Persian Studies, 1984. 57p. bibliog. (Nush-i Jan
III).

This is an illustrated fascicule of the final report on the excavations at Tape Nush-i
Jan, in Western Iran during the period 1967–77. It contains a description of the
objects found in the Median and Parthian periods and includes four chapters:
'The silver hoard'; 'Other finds of the Median period'; 'Finds of the Parthian
period'; and 'Unstratified and surface finds'. The book is substantiated by two
appendixes on the purity of the objects from the silver hoard and the methods
used to produce the silver wire contained in the jewellery from the hoard.

82   **The Islamic city of Gurgan.**
     M. Y. Kiani.   Berlin, FRG: Dietrich Reimer Verlag, 1984. 90p.
     3 maps. bibliog. (Archäologische Mitteilungen aus Iran,
     Ergänzungsband 11).

An historical and architectural study, with its findings, of the old city of Gorgan in
the north. There are seven chapters covering the historical background, town
planning, architectural decoration and the various objects which were excavated.
It also includes numerous figures, plates and plans.

83   **Village ethnoarchaeology: rural Iran in archaeological perspective.**
     Carol Kramer.   London; New York: Academic Press, 1982. 272p.
     map. bibliog.

Attempts to present the ethnographic characteristics of Aliabad, a village near
Kangavar, as an undifferentiated community with a view from the perspective of
an archaeologist. It is based on the author's observations during her archaeological
research and her later visits to the area during 1967–75.

84   **A list of the historical sites and ancient monuments of Iran.**
     Compiled by Nosratollah Meshkati, translated by
     H. A. S. Pessyan.   Tehran: Ministry of Culture and Arts Press,
     1974. 283p. (National Organization for the Protection of Historical
     Monuments of Iran, Publication No. 5).

Offers a brief introduction to the mounds, historical monuments and archaeological sites of Iran. It provides a useful guide, but is in need of a list of contents
and some introductory notes for those unfamiliar with Iran, its history and its
culture.

85   **The memorial volume of the Vth International Congress of Iranian
     Art and Archaeology.**
     Ministry of Culture and Arts.   Tehran: Ministry of Culture and
     Arts, 1972. 2 vols. map.

This collection of papers was presented to the fifth International Congress of Art
and Archaeology held in Tehran, Isfahan and Shiraz from 11–18 April 1968.
Vol. I contains essays on the background and archaeology of the prehistoric and
pre-Islamic periods. Vol. II is confined to papers on the Islamic era and East-
West relations. Numerous illustrations and drawings are included. Most of the
papers are in English, but a few are in other European languages or in Farsi.

86   **Preliminary report on Marlik excavation.**
     Ezat O. Negahban.   Tehran: University of Tehran, 1964. 130p.
     2 maps.

A report, in English and Farsi, of the 1961 archaeological excavation and
discoveries at Marlik (Cherāgh-Ali Tape) near Rudbar. It includes numerous
colour plates and black-and-white figures.

87 **Pasargade.**
David Stronach.   Oxford: Oxford University Press, 1978. 295p.
3 maps.
A report on the excavations conducted by the British Institute of Persian Studies
(London) at Pasargade from 1961 to 1963. The volume consists of a descriptive
study of Pasargade's archaeological sites and the discoveries made there, with
some historical notes supported by numerous figures, fold-outs and plates.

88 **Early man in Iran.**
E. Sunderland.   In: *The Cambridge history of Iran, vol. I: the land
of Iran*. Edited by W. B. Fisher. Cambridge, England: Cambridge
University Press, 1968. p. 395–408. bibliog.
An overview of prehistoric man in Iran with reference to the archaeological
discoveries made in 1933 in the south-east of Shiraz, and in 1949 in a cave near
Kirmanshah. It examines the geographical and biological origins of the early
migrants to the area which is now within the present boundaries of Iran.

89 **Archaeological ethnography in western Iran.**
Patty Jo Watson.   Tucson, Arizona: University of Arizona Press,
1979. 301p. 6 maps. bibliog. (Viking Fund Publications in
Anthropology, no. 57).
This is a study of three Kurdish villages: Hasanabad, Shirdasht and Ain Ali, with
an interdisciplinary purpose. In the first part descriptive data on details of social
and physical life are provided offering a source of material for archaeologists
working in the same area. This part forms the bulk of the book (p. 11–288). The
second section (p. 291–301) is a brief theoretical discussion on the archaeological
benefits which may be derived from the ethnographic data provided in the first
part.

90 **The first cities.**
Ruth Whitehouse.   Oxford: Phaidon Press; New York: Dutton,
1977. 207p. map. bibliog.
Studies the whereabouts, structure and development of the first cities which, it is
claimed, were built in the late 4th and 3rd millennia BC in Iran, Iraq and
Pakistan. Babylon, Nineveh, Ur and Mohenjo-Daro are discussed at length,
considering the land, people, buildings, language, culture and general way of life
in the light of archaeological and documentary evidence. The book is
substantiated by 105 illustrations, sixteen of them in colour.

91 **Persepolis: the archaeology of Parsa, seat of the Persian kings.**
Donald N. Wilber.   New York: Thomas Y. Crowell Company,
1969. 109p. 2 maps. bibliog.
An illustrative popular study of the site of Persepolis and its archaeological
findings, set against its background.

Prehistory and Archaeology

Old routes of western Iran.
See item no. 64.

Persia: an archaeological guide.
See item no. 71.

The Cambridge history of Iran, vol. 2 . . .
See item no. 108.

The king and kingship in Achaemenid art . . .
See item no. 113.

The Kūfic inscription in Persian verses in the court of the royal palace of Mas'ūd III at Ghazni.
See item no. 588.

Sasanian stamp seals in the Metropolitan Museum of Art.
See item no. 731.

Ancient bronzes from Luristan.
See item no. 736.

Ancient Iran.
See item no. 738.

Iran: Journal of the British Institute of Persian Studies.
See item no. 764.

History

General

92 Études mithriaques.
Actes du 2e Congrès International, Tehran, du ler au 8 septembre
1975.   Tehran; Liège, Belgium: Bibliothēque Pahlavi; Leiden, The
Netherlands: E. J. Brill, 1978. 563p. (Acta Iranica, 17).
Contains a number of essays, in English and other European languages, presented
to the second International Congress on Mithraism which was held in Tehran
from the 1st to the 8th September 1975. They discuss many different aspects of
Persian culture, including Mithraism, which, with Mithra, the Persian god of light
and wisdom, as its principal deity, and its many similarities to Christianity,
became a worldwide cult in the 2nd and 3rd centuries AD. Forty-eight relevant
plates are included at the end of the volume.

**93   A medical history of Persian and the eastern Caliphate: from the
earliest times until the year AD 1932.**
Cyril Elgood.   Cambridge, England: Cambridge University Press,
1951. 595p.
The author suggests that the part played by the Persians in the history of medicine
throughout the world is as important as Persian poetry and Persian miniatures,
and yet it has been more or less neglected. He thus attempts to provide a
perspective of the art and practice of medicine in Iran and the bordering countries
from the earliest times. He also discusses the introduction of Western medicine
into Iran.

94   **The tradition of sacred kingship in Iran.**
     Pio Filippani-Ronconi.   In: *Iran under the Pahlavis*. Edited by
     George Lenczowski. Stanford, California: Stanford University
     Press, 1978. p. 51–83. bibliog.
Surveys kingship as a sacred legacy of Iran, dealing with its spiritual features, its
influence on the Roman Empire, its continuity after the introduction of Islam and
its revival under the Pahlavis.

95   **Research in Iranian history.**
     B. G. Fragner.   In: *Orientalia Romana, 6: The first European
     colloquium of Iranology (Rome, June 18th–20th, 1983)*.   Edited by
     Gherardo Gnoli. Rome: IsMEO, 1985. p. 93–107.
Surveys the tradition of studying Iranian history, concentrating on the portrayal of
the history of Islamic Iran. It shows how various types of source were made
accessible, discusses the problems encountered, and studies such relevant
disciplines as research, analysis and historiography.

96   **The golden age of Persia: the Arabs in the East.**
     R. N. Frye.   London: Weidenfeld & Nicolson, 1977. 2nd ed. 236p.
     2 maps. bibliog.
A broad study of the cultural history of Iran from the Sasanian period (3rd
century) to the end of the 10th century. It shows how the major Iranian tradition
was amalgamated with Arab-Islamic customs and beliefs, and its features made
more representative by regional cultures. The author also describes the
emergence of a new Persian Islamic culture in the eastern realm of the caliphate
and its dissemination through the expanding rule of Turkish dynasties into Asia
Minor and the Fertile Crescent.

97   **A history of Persia.**
     Sir Percy Sykes.   London: Macmillan, 1915. 2 vols. 7 maps.
     bibliog.
A general history of Iran from the earliest record of the Persian Empire in the 3rd
millennium BC to the granting of the Iranian Constitution in 1906. The book is
arranged into two volumes. Volume one, covering the history of Iran until the rise
of Islam in the 7th century, includes chapters on configuration and climate, the
physical geography of Iran, flora, fauna and minerals. Volume two contains
background chapters on Islam, the prophet Mohammad and his early career,
battles, the first four caliphs (Abubakr, Omar, Osman and Ali, in whom the unity
of the Islamic world was preserved after the death of the Prophet), and the
tragedy of Kerbela. The book has been issued in further editions, the latest of
which was published by Routledge and Kegan Paul (London, 1969.), and includes
an additional chapter covering the post-constitutional period, the First World
War, the rise of Reza Shah and the Pahlavi dynasty from its foundation until
1930.

The Iranians: how they live and work.
See item no. 1.

The legacy of Persia.
See item no. 2.

Iran and Islam: in memory of the late Vladimir Minorsky.
See item no. 3.

Persia: history and heritage.
See item no. 4.

The Persian Gulf states, a general survey.
See item no. 7.

Iran almanac and book of facts.
See item no. 9.

Iranica: twenty articles.
See item no. 13.

Persia.
See item no. 14.

Contemporary Iran.
See item no. 18.

Historical gazetteer of Iran.
See item no. 23.

A history of Persian earthquakes.
See item no. 25.

Baluchestan: its political economy and history.
See item no. 26.

An historical geography of Iran.
See item no. 27.

Alamut and Lamasar . . .
See item no. 42.

Historical atlas of Iran.
See item no. 44.

Atlas of geographical maps and historical documents on the Persian Gulf.
See item no. 47.

Atlas of Iran: White Revolution proceeds and progresses.
See item no. 48.

Checkmate: fighting tradition in central Asia.
See item no. 55.

The glory of the Shia world . . .
See item no. 59.

World War in Iran.
See item no. 62.

Ten thousand miles in Persia . . .
See item no. 65.

Shah Mozaffar Al-Din's European tour, AD 1900.
See item no. 66.

Isfahan, pearl of Persia.
See item no. 68.

Touring Iran.
See item no. 72.

Iran's men of destiny.
See item no. 199.

Imam 'Ali: source of light, wisdom and might.
See item no. 200.

Mary Bird in Persia.
See item no. 208.

The English amongst the Persians during the Qajar period, 1787–1921.
See item no. 238.

The Qashqa'i nomads of Fars.
See item no. 240.

Who are the Baluch? . . .
See item no. 244.

The legacy of Islam.
See item no. 280.

The teachings of the Magi: a compendium of Zoroastrian beliefs.
See item no. 296.

The dawn and twilight of Zoroastrianism.
See item no. 297.

Women of Iran: the conflict with fundamentalist Islam.
See item no. 318.

Women and the family in Iran.
See item no. 321.

Women in Shi'i *fiqh*: images through the *hadith*.
See item no. 322.

In the shadow of Islam . . .
See item no. 333.

The Islamic Revolution in Iran.
See item no. 391.

The foreign policy of Iran . . .
See item no. 424.

Judicial authority in Imami Shi'i jurisprudence.
See item no. 475.

Shahanshah: a study of the monarchy of Iran.
See item no. 480.

British Society for Middle Eastern Studies Bulletin (BRISMES).
See item no. 761.

International Journal of Middle East Studies (IJMES).
See item no. 763.

Iranian Studies . . .
See item no. 765.

Iran: a bibliographic research survey.
See item no. 776.

An index of articles in Western journals.
See item no. 784.

Ancient pre-Islamic era

98 **Alexander in Iran.**
E. Badian.   In: *The Cambridge history of Iran, vol. 2: the Median and Achaemenian periods.* Edited by Ilya Gershevitch.   Cambridge, England: Cambridge University Press, 1985. p. 420–501. map. bibliog.
An account of the campaigns of Alexander the Great (336–23 BC) focusing on his conquest of Iran (334–31 BC). The article includes a chronological table of the most important events of Alexander's march to Asia.

99 **The Greeks and the Persians from the sixth to the fourth centuries.**
Hermann Bengtson with Edda Bresciani, Werner Caskel, Maurice Meuleau, Morton Smith.   London: Weidenfeld & Nicolson, 1968. 437p. 8 maps. bibliog.
Twenty readable articles, the majority of which are on the history of the Greeks and the Persians, from Darius I to Alexander the Great. The volume refrains, however, from drawing historical parallels.

100 **A history of Zoroastrianism.**
Mary Boyce. Leiden, The Netherlands; Cologne, FRG:
E. J. Brill, 2 vols. Vol. I: 1975, 330p. bibliog. Vol. II: 1982, 292p.
bibliog.

An objective contribution to the history of Zoroastrianism. Volume I provides a background history to the various pagan cults and their gods, the prehistoric period of the faith and Zoroaster (628?–?551 BC) and his teachings. Volume II discusses the period during which Zoroaster was known to be in Iran and the spread of Zoroastrianism, with reference to the historic achievements and religious beliefs of Cyrus the Great (550–30 BC) and the following rulers of Persia to Darius III (336–31 BC). The second volume is a more systematic and uniform study.

101 **Persia and the Greeks.**
A. R. Burn. In: *The Cambridge history of Iran, vol. 2: the Median and Achaemenian periods*. Edited by Ilya
Gershevitch. Cambridge, England: Cambridge University Press,
1985. p. 292–391. 4 maps. bibliog.

Examines the Greeks and their imperial expansion up to 500 BC, the great wars from 499–49 BC, and the following years of turmoil which lasted until 334 BC.

102 **The rise of the Achaemenids and establishment of their empire.**
J. M. Cook. In: *The Cambridge history of Iran, vol. 2: the Median and Achaemenian periods*. Edited by Ilya
Gershevitch. Cambridge, England: Cambridge University Press,
1985. p. 200–91. 3 maps. bibliog.

Following a study of the principal sources for early Achaemenid history, the author describes and discusses the rise of the Achaemenid empire since its foundation by Cyrus the Great in ca. 559 BC. The article outlines the country's social and economic characteristics, and its system of administration.

103 **Elam.**
I. M. Diakonoff. In: *The Cambridge history of Iran, vol. 2: the Median and Achaemenian periods*. Edited by Ilya
Gershevitch. Cambridge, England: Cambridge University Press,
1985. p. 1–24. bibliog.

'Elam' is the biblical name for the region which was later called Khuzestan, and in which the level of urban civilization emerged before any other region of present-day Iran. The author covers the history of Elam from the earliest times to the 6th century BC, as well as its cultural, geographical and archaeological significances.

104 **Media.**
I. M. Diakonoff. In: *The Cambridge history of Iran, vol. 2: the Median and Achaemenian periods*. Edited by Ilya Gershevitch. Cambridge, England: Cambridge University Press, 1985. p. 36–148. 4 maps. bibliog.
The area of the Iranian highlands called Media is the subject of the author's study, dealing with that region's population structure, and dating as far back as the end of the 23rd century BC. Iranian-speaking tribes; the emergence of urbanization at the end of the 9th century BC; the neighbouring countries and their advances into Median territory; the rise of the Median kingdom in ca. 673–72 BC, and its campaigns; the society, culture and religion of Media; and, finally, the fall of the Median empire to the Persians in the 6th century BC are the main topics covered.

105 **The Western response to Zoroaster.**
J. Duchesne-Guillemin. Oxford: Oxford University Press, 1958. 104p. bibliog.
A collection of a series of six historical lectures devoted to various aspects of Zoroastrianism, with particular emphasis on the religion's impact on Greece and Israel.

106 **The heritage of Persia.**
Richard N. Frye. London: Weidenfeld & Nicolson, 1962. 292p. 4 maps. bibliog.
The history of Iran and its culture from the earliest times to the Islamic conquest of the 7th century, designed to provide basic information for students of Iranian studies, as well as an interesting narrative for general readership.

107 **The political history of Iran under the Sasanians.**
R. N. Frye. In: *The Cambridge history of Iran, vol. 3: the Seleucid, Parthian and Sasanian periods*. Edited by Ehsan Yar-Shater. Cambridge, England: Cambridge University Press, 1983. p. 116–80. map. bibliog.
Provides a general history of Iran under the Sasanians, who created the last pre-Islamic Iranian empire (224–651). It studies the rise of the dynasty; the major historical epochs and the reigns of the most formidable monarchs; some important reforms regarding taxation; internal administration and foreign relations; and, finally, the decline of the empire.

108 **The Cambridge history of Iran, vol. 2: the Median and Achaemenian periods.**
Edited by Ilya Gershevitch. Cambridge, England: Cambridge University Press, 1985. 869p. 17 maps. bibliog.
This volume of *The Cambridge history of Iran* contains articles on the country's history from the earliest recorded periods in the late 3rd millennium BC to the end of the Achaemenian era in 331 BC. Also included are articles on the Greeks,

Alexander in Iran, and on archaeological finds, old Iranian culture, religion and the arts.

109 **Iran: from the earliest times to the Islamic conquest.**
R. Ghirshman, translated and edited by M. E. L. Mallowan.
Harmondsworth, England: Penguin Books, 1961. 377p. 6 maps.
bibliog.
A readable narrative history of Iran from the earliest times, when the first settlers arrived, until the Islamic conquest, when the Persian empire collapsed in the 7th century, and Iranian civilization entered a new historical era.

110 **Zoroaster's time and homeland: a study on the origins of Mazdeism and related problems.**
Gherardo Gnoli. Naples, Italy: Istituto Universitario Orientale, 1980. 247p. map. (Seminario di Studi Asiatici, Series Minor VII).
Attempts to establish the time of Zoroaster and his homeland with emphatic reference to the historical geography of the Zoroastrian book, *Avesta*. Zoroaster and his work are also studied, although only briefly, to provide support for the book's main theme. An historical perspective of Zoroastrianism from its origins to the Sasanian period is also presented.

111 **Cyrus the Great (558–529 BC).**
Max Mallowan. In: *The Cambridge history of Iran, vol. 2: the Median and Achaemenian periods*. Edited by Ilya Gershevitch.
Cambridge, England: Cambridge University Press, 1985.
p. 392–419. map. bibliog.
Also printed in *Iran*, X (1972), p. 1–17, the article provides a chronology of Cyrus' campaigns in the 6th century BC, examining the vast distances covered by his army. It also explains the symbol and style of his authority, his foreign policy, introduction of coinage, and religion.

112 **Ionians in Pasargadae: studies in old Persian architecture.**
Carl Nylander. Uppsala, Sweden: Almqvist & Wiksells Boktrykkeri Aktiebolag, 1970. 149p. bibliog. (Acta Universitatis Upsaliensis – Boreas, Uppsala Studies in Ancient Mediterranean and Near Eastern Civilisations, 1).
Investigates the sources of Achaemenian art and its transformation under foreign influences and inspiration. Particular emphasis is placed on masonry and stonework, and the work includes numerous illustrations and drawings.

113   **The king and kingship in Achaemenid art: essays on the creation of an iconography of empire.**
Margaret Cool Root.   Leiden, The Netherlands: E. J. Brill, 1979.
311p. bibliog. (Acta Iranica, Vol. IX).
An expanded and revised version of the author's doctoral dissertation, which was presented to the Department of Classical and Near Eastern Archaeology of Bryn Mawr College, Pennsylvania in 1976. It attempts to demonstrate the nature of the process of the creation of Achaemenid imperial iconography as a complex cultural system of influences, and as the central figure of their own cultural history. Also included is a catalogue of the known official imperial monuments, coin types and seals, followed by a series of iconographical essays.

114   **The Persian expedition.**
Xenophon, translated by Rex Warner.   Harmondsworth, England: Penguin Books, 1967. 301p. map.
An outstanding record of one of the most famous marches in history, during the early 4th century BC, in which the author took part by joining Cyrus' army of Greek mercenaries. While narrating the long march into Persia, and the tedious return to Greece, the author also presents a genuine picture of the social life in general.

115   **The Cambridge history of Iran, vol. 3: the Seleucid, Parthian and Sasanian periods.**
Edited by Ehsan Yar-Shater.   Cambridge, England: Cambridge University Press, 1983. 2 vols. 16 maps. bibliog.
A detailed history of Iran from the emergence of the Seleucid empire in 312 BC to the collapse of the Sasanian empire in AD 651. The book is arranged into two volumes and nine parts. Volume one contains four parts (seventeen articles) covering the period's political history, numismatics, traditions, and Iran's neighbours. The index and bibliography to this volume are given at the end of the second volume, which contains five parts (twenty articles), concentrating on institutions, religion, arts, languages and literature, historical sources and bibliography.

The memorial volume of the Vth International Congress of Iranian Art and Archaeology.
See item no. 85.

The letter of Tansar.
See item no. 289.

Iran's cultural identity and the present day world.
See item no. 306.

Mediaeval Islamic period (7th–15th centuries)

116 **Religion in the Saljuq period.**
A. Bausani. In: *The Cambridge history of Iran, vol. 5: the Saljuq and Mongol periods.* Edited by J. A. Boyle. Cambridge, England: Cambridge University Press, 1968. p. 283–302. bibliog.
A general survey of the main aspects of Iran's religious history during the 11th and 12th centuries, outlining the developments of Sunnism, the evolution of Shi'ite ideas, and Sufism. Isma'ilis, their movement and their religious ideas, dominating the best part of the Saljuq period, are, however, not included as they are covered elsewhere in the same volume of *The Cambridge history of Iran* (q.v.).

117 **Religion under the Mongols.**
A. Bausani. In: *The Cambridge history of Iran, vol. 5: the Saljuq and Mongol periods.* Edited by J. A. Boyle. Cambridge, England: Cambridge University Press, 1968. p. 538–49.
A brief study of the state of religion in Iran in the 13th and 14th centuries – focusing on the development of Shi'ite tendencies.

118 **The political and dynastic history of the Iranian world (AD 1000–1217).**
C. E. Bosworth. In: *The Cambridge history of Iran, vol. 5: the Saljuq and Mongol periods.* Edited by J. A. Boyle. Cambridge, England: Cambridge University Press, 1968. p. 1–202. 4 maps. bibliog.
The author says that for nearly a thousand years – until the present century – Iran was ruled by non-Persians of whom the Saljuq Turks, coming to power in the first half of the 11th century, were the first. They, however, were compelled by circumstances to adopt Iranian culture and employ Iranian officials. The development of the political events during their domination in different parts of the Iranian world in the 11th and 12th centuries is the subject of this study.

119 **Sīstān under the Arabs, from the Islamic conquest to the rise of the Saffārids (30–250/651–864).**
Clifford Edmund Bosworth. Rome: Istituto Italiano per il Medio ed Estremo Oriente (IsMEO), 1968. 123p. bibliog.
Attempts to study the history of Iran during a tumultuous period through the history of Sistan in eastern Iran which is geographically of significance, even though it is relatively small. The work contains five chapters covering the history of Sistan during the period before the coming of Islam, after the Islamic conquest, the

Umayyads, Abbasids, and finally the rise of Ya'qūb b. Laith. The work is indebted to the unparalleled and brilliant *Tarikh-e Sistan* (History of Sistan), which was written in the 11th century although the author remains anonymous.

120 **The medieval history of Iran, Afghanistan and Central Asia.**
C. E. Bosworth. London: Variorum Reprints, 1977. 374p.

A collection of twenty-three off-prints dealing with the mediaeval history of the old eastern Islamic world. Even though Iran forms only one part of the book, the influence of Persian culture and civilization is in evidence throughout the other two sections as well. The section dealing with Iran contains eight articles, entitled: 1, 'The rise of the Karāmiyyah in Khurasan'; 2, 'On the chronology of the Ziyārids in Gurgān and Ṭabaristān'; 3, 'Military organisation under the Buyids of Persia and Iraq'; 4, 'The Taharids and Persian literature'; 5, 'Dailamīs in Central Asia'; 6, 'The Banu Ilyās of Kirman (320–57/932–68); 7, 'The heritage of rulership in early Islamic Iran and the search for dynastic connections with the past'; 8, The Kūfichis or Qufs in Persian history'.

121 **The Cambridge history of Iran, vol. 5: the Saljuq and Mongol periods.**
Edited by J. A. Boyle. Cambridge, England: Cambridge University Press, 1968. 679p. 6 maps. bibliog.

The history of Saljuq and Mongol Iran from the 11th to the 14th centuries is covered in this volume of *The Cambridge history of Iran*. It includes ten articles dealing with the political, religious, cultural, administrative and socio-economic history of Iran in this period.

122 **Dynastic and political history of the Il-Khans.**
J. A. Boyle. In: *The Cambridge history of Iran, vol. 5: the Saljuq and Mongol periods*. Edited by J. A. Boyle. Cambridge, England: Cambridge University Press, 1968. p. 303–421. bibliog.

The years between 1219–31 witnessed one of the bloodiest periods of Iranian history, during which the Mongols conquered Iran. After that, although they ruled in Iran until the mid-14th century, they were, ironically, absorbed into the Iranian culture and system of administration. This article offers an account of the Mongols' campaign, their rule in Iran, and the political developments of the period.

123 **The political and social history of Khurasan under Abbasid rule, 747–820.**
Elton L. Daniel. Chicago: Bibliotheca Islamica, 1979. 200p. 2 maps. bibliog.

An analytical study of revolts and manifestations of discontent in Khurasan during the second century after the Arab conquest of Iran. Deals with the Abbasid revolt supported by Iranians, Abu Moslem's attempts and failure, rural discontents and the relationship between Khurasan and the central government.

124 **The Cambridge history of Iran, vol. 4: the period from the Arab invasion to the Saljuqs.**
Edited by R. N. Frye. Cambridge, England: Cambridge University Press, 1975. 664p. 6 maps. bibliog.
This volume of *The Cambridge history of Iran* covers the period from the Arab conquests to the emergence of the Saljuq dynasty (7th–10th centuries). This period of Iranian history is closely linked with the history of Islamic expansion. The volume contains twenty-two articles dealing with the general history of Iran, as well as the social, political, religious and cultural developments of the period.

125 **Islamic Iran and Central Asia (7th–12th centuries).**
Richard N. Frye. London: Variorum Reprints, 1979. 380p.
A collection of studies on the history of Iran and Central Asia from the Arab conquest of Iran till the Mongol conquests. All the articles were previously printed in various journals and they appear, in this book, in their original form. The volume has, therefore, no independent pagination, nor is it consistent with regard to publication format, transliteration, style of footnotes and references, etc. The articles are, however, concerned with a central theme of the change in the period under consideration. Altogether, it includes thirty-six items composed of general historical studies, articles focusing on Central Asia and Khorasan, notes on the rise of the new Persian language, and a number of texts and translations.

126 **The Ismaili state.**
M. G. S. Hodgson. In: *The Cambridge history of Iran, vol. 5: the Saljuq and Mongol periods.* Edited by J. A. Boyle. Cambridge, England: Cambridge University Press, 1968. p. 422–82. 2 maps.
From 1090 to 1256, until they were defeated by the Mongols, the Isma'ilis formed a political force backed by religious ideology to challenge the Saljuq state. The movement of the Isma'ilis, their doctrine and methods of their early struggle, their later periods of stalemate and resurrection, and finally their decline and collapse, are traced in this article.

127 **The occultation of the Twelfth Imam: a historical background.**
Jassim M. Hussain. London: Muhammadi Trust, 1982. 204p. bibliog.
A study of the Imami-Shi'ite movement from the time of Ja'far al-Sadeq, the sixth Imam in the 8th century, to the end of the lesser occultation of the Twelfth Imam in the mid-10th century.

128 **The history of the world-conqueror.**
'Ala-ad-Din 'Ata-Malek Juvaini, translated by John Andrew Boyle. Manchester, England: Manchester University Press, 1958. 2 vols. bibliog.
A translation of the brilliant historical accounts of the Mongols by an author who played an important role in the history of that period, and who knew a number of

key Mongol figures, including the conqueror of the Caliph seat of Baghdad, Il-Khan Hulagu, who respected him as a confidant.

129   **The exact sciences in Timurid Iran.**
E. S. Kennedy.   In: *The Cambridge history of Iran, vol. 6: the Timurid and Safavid periods.*   Edited by Peter Jackson.
Cambridge, England: Cambridge University Press, 1986.
p. 568–80. bibliog.

Presents an account of the development and study of the exact sciences in Iran during the period between 1350–1500. It covers various aspects of mathematics and observational astronomy.

130   **The prophet and the age of Caliphates: the Islamic Near East from the sixth to the eleventh century.**
Hugh Kennedy.   London; New York: Longman, 1986. 349p.
5 maps. bibliog.

An interpretative introduction to the history of the Middle East in the early Islamic period, from the time of the prophet Mohammad in the 6th century, to the 11th century. It discusses the birth of Islam, the Rashidun, Umayyad and Abbasid caliphs, and other political forces including the origins, expansion and decline of the Iranian dynasty, the Buyid, in the northern provinces of Iran during the 10th and 11th centuries (p. 212–49). The work also studies the role played in this period by the Kurds. A comprehensive bibliography and six genealogical tables are included.

131   **The internal structure of the Saljuq empire.**
A. K. S. Lambton.   In: *The Cambridge history of Iran, vol. 5: the Saljuq and Mongol periods.*   Edited by J. A. Boyle. Cambridge, England: Cambridge University Press, 1968. p. 203–82. bibliog.

The author argues that although the Iranian administrative system survived the Arab conquest of Iran and continued to be practised throughout the early Islamic period, the old institutions were crystallized in the 11th and 12th centuries under the Saljuqs and gained new dimensions. The article offers a study of these developments.

132   **European contacts with Persia, 1350–1736.**
Laurence Lockhart.   In: *The Cambridge history of Iran, vol. 6: the Timurid and Safavid periods.*   Edited by Peter Jackson.
Cambridge, England: Cambridge University Press, 1986.
p. 373–411. map. bibliog.

Studies the development of contact between the Persians and the West. The author argues that the traffic was not only West-eastward, but that there were also Iranian travellers, fewer in number, visiting Europe, although their accounts failed to become known. The article outlines the main incentives for the development of relations from the mid-14th century until the collapse of the Safavid dynasty in 1736.

133 The Shu'ubiyah controversy and the social history of early Islamic Iran.
Roy P. Mottahedeh. Princeton, New Jersey: Princeton University Press, 1980. 22p. (Program in Near Eastern Studies, Princeton Near East Paper, no. 28).

An off-print previously printed in the *International Journal of Middle East Studies*, vol. 7 (1976), p. 161–82. It studies the controversy over the position of Arabs and non-Arabs in Persia, with special reference to the Iranians, and focusing in particular on the movement of Shu'ubis, who claimed not only equality but superiority to the Arabs during the early Islamic era.

134 The socio-economic condition of Iran under the Il-Khans.
I. P. Petrushevsky. In: *The Cambridge history of Iran, vol. 5: the Saljuq and Mongol periods*. Edited by J. A. Boyle. Cambridge, England: Cambridge University Press, 1968. p. 483–537. bibliog.

Examines the socio-economic conditions in Iran during the period between the 1220s and the 1380s, divided into three consecutive areas of decline: from the 1220s–90s – caused by the Mongol invasion and the taxation policy; the economic upsurge between the 1290s and 1335 brought forward by Ghazan reforms, especially in agriculture; and the feudal partitioning and political disintegration of 1335–80s.

135 The successors of Genghis Khan.
Rashid al-Din Fazl Allāh, translated by John Andrew Boyle. London; New York: Columbia University Press, 1971. 330p. map. bibliog.

A translation of the first section of the world history by Rashid al-Din, dealing with 'The Turkish and Mongol tribes'; 'Genghis Khan and his ancestors'; 'The successors of Genghis Khan'; and 'The Il-Khans of Persia'.

136 The Jalayirids, Muzaffarids and Sarbadārs.
H. R. Roemer. In: *The Cambridge history of Iran, vol. 6: the Timurid and Safavid periods*. Edited by Peter Jackson. Cambridge, England: Cambridge University Press, 1986. p. 1–41. map. bibliog.

The power vacuum created by the end of the Il-Khanid empire in the 14th century resulted in a power struggle between the princes of different dynasties and local houses, which lasted for approximately 50 years before the advent of Timur (Tamerlane). The political scene of this period, the major social and religious issues, and the struggle of the dynasties and their rivals, are discussed in this article.

137 **The successors of Timur.**
H. R. Roemer. In: *The Cambridge history of Iran, vol. 6: the
Timurid and Safavid periods.* Edited by Peter Jackson.
Cambridge, England: Cambridge University Press, 1986.
p. 98–146. map. bibliog.
Complements the author's study on Timur (Tamerlane) in Iran, printed in the
same volume of *The Cambridge history of Iran* (q.v.). It deals with the successors
of Timur and their rivals in the 15th century. The article also includes notes on
the social and political conditions, economic affairs, religious and cultural
activities, architecture, arts and literature of the period.

138 **Timur in Iran.**
H. R. Roemer. In: *The Cambridge history of Iran, vol. 6: the
Timurid and Safavid periods.* Edited by Peter Jackson. Cambridge,
England: Cambridge University Press, 1986. p. 42–97. bibliog.
In the second half of the 14th century Iran was the scene of a power struggle
caused by the end of the Il-Khanid empire. Timur (Tamerlane) rose to power by
first conquering eastern Iran, gradually defeating his rivals and achieving the
reunification of the country. His advent and the political conditions of the period
are studied in this article.

139 **The Turkmen dynasties.**
H. R. Roemer. In: *The Cambridge history of Iran, vol. 6: the
Timurid and Safavid periods.* Edited by Peter Jackson. Cambridge,
England: Cambridge University Press, 1986. p. 147–88. 2 maps.
bibliog.
A general study of the Turkmen dynasties and their rivals in the second half of
the 14th century and the 15th century. It examines in closer detail the origins and
history of two Turkmen groups, Aq Quyunlu and Qara Quyunlu, their formidable
rulers, their dominions and the political situation during that period.

140 **Caliphate and kingship in medieval Persia.**
Amir Hasan Siddiqi. Philadelphia: Porcupine Press, 1977. 114p.
(Studies in Islamic History, no. 14).
A reprint of a collection of articles first published in *Islamic Culture* (Hyderabad,
vols. 9–11, 1935–37), dealing with the institution of the caliphate at Baghdad and
its relation with the Iranian minor dynasties, against a background of
contemporary political and historical events. Unfortunately, however, the work is
seriously marred by the lack of an introduction, a list of contents, author and
subject indexes, and even page numbers.

141   **Ya'qūb the coppersmith and Persian national sentiment.**
      S. M. Stern.   In: *Iran and Islam*. Edited by C. E. Bosworth.
      Edinburgh: Edinburgh University Press, 1971. p. 535–55.
A study of the identity of the Persian nation in the Islamic land, with reference to
Persian literature and its revival under the Safavids in the south-eastern province
of Sistan during the 11th century.

142   **Toward a theory of historical narrative: a case study in Perso-
      Islamicate historiography.**
      Marilyn Robinson Waldman.   Columbus, Ohio: Ohio State
      University Press, 1980. 142p. 3 maps. bibliog.
An analytical study of the 11th-century historian Abu al-Fazl Beihaqi's *Tarikh-e
Beihaqi* (Beihaqi's history). Its historical method, thematic patterns, structural
features and language style are examined as a case-study for the application of a
methodological approach to the study of historical narrative.

143   **Eternal cosmos and the womb of history; time in early Ismaili
      thought.**
      Paul E. Walker.   In: *International Journal of Middle East Studies*,
      vol. 9, no. 3 (1978), p. 355–66.
Investigates the issue of 'time and history' in Isma'ili thought. This allows
astronomical calculation, as a result of which their theory stands in contrast to
those of all other Islamic sects, in whose view time is reduced to a series of
recurrent instants.

**The memorial volume of the Vth International Congress of Iranian Art
and Archaeology.**
See item no. 85.

Modern Islamic period
(16th–19th centuries)

144   **British interests in the Persian Gulf, 1747–1780.**
      Abdul Amir Amin.   Leiden, The Netherlands: E. J. Brill, 1967.
      141p. map. bibliog.
Investigates the position of the British in the Persian Gulf during the
18th century, and examines their increasing interests in the area, particularly in
connection with the growth and decline of trade between the East India Company
and the Persian Gulf nations. The book is supported by a number of documents in
the appendix, but has no indexes.

145 **The shadow of God and the Hidden Imam: religion, political order, and societal change in Shi'ite Iran from the beginning to 1890.**
Said Amir Arjomand.   Chicago; London: University of Chicago
Press, 1984. 340p. bibliog. (Publications of the Centre for Middle
Eastern Studies, no. 17).

Analyses the role of religion in political action and societal change in Iran,
drawing on the sociology of Max Weber. The work also studies the establishment
and consolidation of Shi'ite Islam as the state religion of Iran covering its
historical background, and focusing on the Safavid and Qajar periods (16th–19th
centuries). The contents of the work are as follows: Part I: 'the historical and
cultural background of the emergence of a Shi'ite polity in Iran': 1, 'sectarian
Shi'ism within the Islamic body politic 8–13th century'; 2, 'millenarian religion and
political movements in the 14th and 15th centuries'; 3, 'the shadow of God on
Earth'. Part II: 'Shi'ism as the state religion under the Safavids, 1501–1722';
4, 'Safavid religious policies and the establishment of twelver Shi'ism'; 5, 'the
"clerical notables" and the final emergence of a Shi'ite hierocracy in Iran';
6, 'from sectarian Shi'ism to Shi'ism as a national religion'; 7, 'two variants of
Safavid Shi'ism and their respective political implications'; 8, 'Shi'ism, the
patrimonial ethos, and sociopolitical action'; 9, 'world-rejecting tendencies in the
Shi'ite religion'. Part III: 'the Shi'ite hierocracy and the state 1785–1890'; 10, 'the
impact of Shi'ism on the Qajar polity and its limits'; 11, 'religion and
sociopolitical action in the Qajar polity'; 12, 'conclusion'.

146 **Russia and Iran, 1780–1828.**
Muriel Atkin.   Minneapolis, Minnesota: University of Minnesota
Press, 1980. 187p. 2 maps. bibliog.

A critical study of Russian expansionist policies and methods in the eastern
Caucasus, and the responses of the Iranian government and the inhabitants of the
disputed territories. It examines the last two turbulent decades of the 18th
century, when Agha Mohammad Khan struggled to establish the Qajar dynasty,
and the following period of war, culminating in the humiliating Turkmanchai
treaty in 1828 between Iran and the Russian empire.

147 **An enquiry into the outbreak of the second Russo-Persian war, 1826–28.**
P. W. Avery.   In: *Iran and Islam*. Edited by C. E. Bosworth.
Edinburgh: Edinburgh University Press, 1971. p. 17–45. map.

Investigates the social and political causes of the outbreak of the second Russo-
Persian war only thirteen years after the first, concluded by the Treaty of
Golestan, had ended.

148 **Iran: monarchy, bureaucracy and reform under the Qajars: 1848–1896.**
Shaul Bakhash.   London: Ithaca Press (for the Middle East
Centre, St. Antony's College, Oxford), 1978. 373p. bibliog.

A major study of the reforms introduced during the reign of Naser al-Din Shah
Qajar (1848–96) into the government and administration of Iran. The volume is

arranged in six chapters, covering: the factors necessitating the reforms; the proposals and ideas expressed for reform; the measures introduced in the effort to reform; and reasons for the failure of the reforms during the period under consideration. Some biographical notes are also included.

149 **The failure of reform: the Prime Ministership of Amin al-Dawla, 1897–8.**
Shaul Bakhash. In: *Qajar Iran: political, social and cultural change, 1800–1925.* Edited by Edmund Bosworth and Carole Hillenbrand. Edinburgh: Edinburgh University Press, 1983, p. 14–33.

Amin al-Dawla's unsuccessful attempt to reform the Iranian government and administration was the last such attempt prior to the 1905 Constitutional movement, and marks the struggle between the reformists and those who were committed to the *status quo.* These efforts to reform, and the struggle between the two factions within the government, are the subjects of the article.

150 **Qajar Iran, political, social and cultural change, 1800–1925.**
Edited by Edmund Bosworth, Carole Hillenbrand. Edinburgh: Edinburgh University Press, 1983. 392p. bibliog.

A collection of twenty-one articles arranged into two parts concentrating on the political history, and the social and cultural history of Iran under the Qajars in the 19th century and the first quarter of the 20th century. The volume, which was dedicated to the late Professor Elwell-Sutton, a prominent Orientalist, on the occasion of his retirement, includes a bibliography of his 134 works in chronological order.

151 **A chronicle of the Carmelites in Persia and the papal mission of the XVIIth and XVIIIth centuries.**
The Carmelite Order. Edited and translated by H. Chick.
London: Eyre & Spottiswoode, 1939. 2 vols. map.

A detailed account of the Catholic position in Persia and Mesopotamia focusing on the Carmelite Order in Isfahan in the 16th, 17th and 18th centuries, although the thread of the narrative is maintained by reference to the other Orders which from time to time replaced the Carmelites in Julfa. The descriptions of the religious life of the missionaries are often interrelated with Iranian social conditions, and related in chronological order, dealing in particular with the Safavid Shahs, as well as their followers, through to the 18th century. Also included are descriptions of Christian residences in other towns in the South of Iran, supplemented by a corresponding map.

152 **Persia and the Persian question.**
George N. Curzon. London: Longmans, 1892. 2 vols.

This is a major source of reference for the study of 19th-century Persian history and politics, closely linked at that time to the interests and policies of the British government in the region in general and in Iran in particular. The work covers many aspects of Persian life and culture in the different provinces, the government, public institutions, and trade, as well as the British and Russian policy in Persia.

153 **Safavid medical practice: or the practice of medicine, surgery and gynaecology in Persia between 1500 AD and 1750 AD.**
Cyril Elgood. London: Luzac, 1970. 288p.
Deals with the history of medicine, surgery and gynaecology in Iran during the Safavid period of the 16th–18th centuries.

154 **History of Shah 'Abbas the Great.**
Eskandar Beg Monshi, translated by Roger M. Savory. Boulder, Colorado: Westview Press, 1978. 2 vols. (Persian Heritage Series, 28).
Shah 'Abbas I the Great, who ruled Persia from 1585–1629, was not only the most prominent ruler of the Safavid dynasty, but probably the most celebrated king in the entire Islamic era of Iranian history. His reign was recorded by Eskandar Beg Monshi, a secretary, in a compendious history entitled *Alamara-ye 'Abbasi*, which also includes valuable information about the earlier Safavid Shahs and the neighbouring countries, most significantly the Ottoman Empire. The state of arts and science in Iran, and biographies of numerous artists of the period, are also covered, thus making *Alamara* the most comprehensive source of Safavid history.

155 **History of Persia under Qajar rule.**
Hasan Fasa'i, translated from the Persian by Heribert Busse.
New York; London: Columbia University Press, 1972. 420p. bibliog.
A critical translation of the first volume of the celebrated chronicle *Farsnameh-ye Naseri* (Naserian history of Fars), which covers nearly a century of Qajar rule. It contains a treatise on the history of Persia, especially the southern province, Fars, from the beginning of Islam to the late 19th century.

156 **Social and internal economic affairs.**
Bert Fragner. In: *The Cambridge history of Iran, vol. 6: the Timurid and Safavid periods*. Edited by Peter Jackson. Cambridge, England: Cambridge University Press, 1986. p. 491–567. bibliog.
The author makes a distinction between the rural and the urban economic situations of Iran in the 14th–18th centuries. Whereas the former is based on farming, the latter is generated by commerce and industry. He outlines the rural economic activities (agriculture, cattle-breeding, hunting, fishing and mining) and the landholding institutions, as well as the urban sector of economy focusing on home-trade and industrial production, and also describing the financial and taxation systems.

History. Modern Islamic period (16th–19th centuries)

157 **The history of Nadir Shah, formerly called Thamas Kuli Khan, the present emperor of Persia.**
James Fraser. Westmead, Hampshire, England: Gregg
International Publishers, 1971 (2nd ed.). 234p. map.
This is an offset print of the original, which was first published in London in 1742.
The history of Nadir Shah (1736–47) is preceded by a brief history of the Moghul
emperors. A catalogue of about two hundred manuscripts, mainly in Farsi, is also
included.

158 **The economic history of Iran, 1800–1914.**
Edited by Charles Issawi. Chicago; London: University of
Chicago Press, 1971. 386p. bibliog. (A publication of the Centre
for Middle Eastern Studies).
A companion volume to the author's *The economic history of the Middle East,
1800–1914* (Chicago, 1966), this volume covers the Iranian economy in the 19th
and early 20th centuries. The main topics studied are the integration of Iran into
the international commercial and financial network; foreign trade and transport;
market-oriented agriculture; handicrafts and the introduction of modern industry;
the rise of the petroleum industry; and banking and finance.

159 **The Cambridge history of Iran, vol. 6: the Timurid and Safavid
periods.**
Edited by Peter Jackson, Laurence Lockhart. Cambridge,
England: Cambridge University Press, 1986. 994p. 7 maps. bibliog.
A basic source of reference for the history of Iran from the early 14th century,
when a vacuum was created with the collapse of the Il-Khanid empire, to the mid-
18th century when a similar condition was caused by the fall of the Safavids. The
volume contains eighteen articles examining the history of the period in general,
dealing with various political and economic issues, religion, arts and literature,
science and crafts.

160 **Artisans and guild life in the later Safavid period: contributions to
the social-economic history of Persia.**
Mehdi Keyvani. Berlin: Klaus Schwarz Verlag, 1982. 258p.
bibliog.
Attempts to cast light on the social and economic characteristics of the bazaar
craftsmens' and tradesmens' guilds and their institutions during the later Safavid
period (17th–18th centuries). A description and classification of the guilds; their
governmental administration and its method of control; the internal organization
of the guilds; and their social and political activities are some of the major topics
covered. It also includes a selection of *Shahr-ashub* verses, in translation, which
include reference to various trades and crafts of the time.

161   **The case of Hajjī 'Abd al-Karim: a study on the role of the**
      merchant in mid-nineteenth-century Persia.
      A. K. S. Lambton.   In: *Iran and Islam*. Edited by
      C. E. Bosworth. Edinburgh: Edinburgh University Press, 1971.
      p. 331–60.
Studies the role of the Iranian merchants in Iran in the mid-19th century as an
internal source of influence in contrast to the political role of the European
powers in Iranian affairs.

162   **Nadir Shah: a critical study based mainly upon contemporary**
      sources.
      Laurence Lockhart.   London: Luzac, 1938. 281p. 9 maps. bibliog.
The defeat of Isfahan in 1722 by Afghans, brought the Safavid empire
(1501–1722) to its end, and, in spite of the attempts of Prince Tahmasb Mirza to
revive the Safavid dynasty, the history of Iran in the following twenty-five years
was woven by Nadir Ooli Afshar who, after defeating Afghans and Turks and
subduing other rebels, made himself Shah *de jure* as well as *de facto* in 1736. He
was assassinated some eleven years later for his brutality. The volume presents an
account of Nadir's origin and his early career, his campaigns, including the
invasion of India and Turkistan, and his fate at the hands of his own trusted men.

163   **The fall of the Safavi dynasty and the Afghan occupation of Persia.**
      Laurence Lockhart.   Cambridge, England: Cambridge University
      Press, 1958. 472p. 2 maps. bibliog.
An analytical account of events in the late 17th and early 18th centuries, which
led to the fall of the Safavid empire. The book is arranged into thirty-seven
chapters dealing with chronological events as well as social, political and
economic developments, and foreign relations. It also contains six appendixes
including a genealogical table of the Safavid dynasty, and a brief study of art and
literature in the late Safavid period.

164   **Karim Khan Zand: a history of Iran, 1747–1779.**
      John R. Perry.   Chicago; London: University of Chicago Press,
      1979. 301p. bibliog. (A publication of the Centre for Middle
      Eastern Studies, no. 12).
A comprehensive and detailed study of Iranian history during the rule of Karim
Khan Zand, 1747–79. It is arranged in three parts, of which the first two deal with
Karim Khan's struggle for power, 1747–63, and the consolidation and expansion
of his state, 1763–79. The third part concentrates on the state's administration as
well as on social and economic issues.

165   **Indo-Persian relations: a study of the political and diplomatic**
      relations between the Mughul empire and Iran.
      Riazul Islam.   Tehran: Iranian Culture Foundation, 1970. 186p.
      map. bibliog.
This is the first volume in a study of the relations between the Moghul Emperors
and the Shahs of Iran from the early 16th to the mid-18th century. It provides the

background information to the period while the second volume, entitled *A calendar of documents on Indo-Persian relations (1500–1750)* by the same author (1982. 393p. bibliog.) presents the specific details of numerous correspondences, summaries and comments.

166 **The Safavid period.**
H. R. Roemer. In: *The Cambridge history of Iran, vol. 6: the Timurid and Safavid periods*. Edited by Peter Jackson. Cambridge, England: Cambridge University Press, 1986. p. 189–350. map. bibliog.

After centuries of foreign rule, the Safavid dynasty, founded by Isma'il in 1501, established a strong political structure in Iran which lasted until the early 18th century. The dynasty's typical features included the recognition of Shi'ite Islam as the state religion. The article examines the background of the Safavids, the foundation of the dynasty, and Isma'il and his successors. It also deals with the Safavid dynasty in the context of political and social background. A map of Iran under the Safavids and a table of the Shahs are also included.

167 **History of the Shah Isma'il Safawi.**
Ghulam Sarwar. New York: AMS Press, 1975 (Reprint). 109p. bibliog.

Shah Isma'il Safavi was the founder of the celebrated Safavid dynasty that restored the Persian empire and recreated the Persian nationality in 1501 after an eclipse of more than eight centuries following the Arab conquest of Iran. The book is arranged in three parts, describing the ancestors of Isma'il and his childhood; his campaigns and life as a new ruler; and his character and system of administration. The volume is a reprint of the original edition printed in Aligarh in 1939.

168 **Iran under the Safavids.**
Roger Savory. Cambridge, England: Cambridge University Press, 1980. 267p. map.

A history of Iran during the Safavid period (1501–1736) aimed at the general reader, although it may also be useful for a more particular study of Iran. The main structure of the book is primarily concerned with the rise, growth, decline and fall of the Safavids, but other issues, such as the social and economic structure of the country, intellectual life and the arts are also covered. The work includes a wide selection of black-and-white illustrations.

169 **The Safavid administration system.**
R. M. Savory. In: *The Cambridge history of Iran, vol. 6: the Timurid and Safavid periods*. Edited by Peter Jackson. Cambridge, England: Cambridge University Press, 1986. p. 351–72. bibliog.

Presents a study of three principal phases in the development of the Safavid administrative system in the 16th-18th centuries, with some reference to the social structure of the period and the Safavid authority. It also deals with the provincial administration.

170 **Persian science in Safavid times.**
H. J. H. Winter. In: *The Cambridge history of Iran, vol. 6: the Timurid and Safavid periods.* Edited by Peter Jackson. Cambridge, England: Cambridge University Press, 1986. p. 581–609. bibliog.

An historical survey of the condition of science in Iran during the Safavid period, based mainly on information extracted from the accounts of European travellers. It deals with astronomy and related sciences, mechanics and technology, and medicine.

Travels into Persia.
See item no. 61.

The memorial volume of the Vth International Congress of Iranian Art and Archaeology.
See item no. 85.

Observations on Nasir al-Din Shah.
See item no. 215.

Religion in the Timurid and Safavid periods.
See item no. 270.

Spiritual movements, philosophy and theology in the Safavid period.
See item no. 277.

The trade from the mid-14th century to the end of the Safavid period.
See item no. 515.

Agricultural and rural development in Iran . . .
See item no. 528.

Land reform and modernization of the farming structure in Iran.
See item no. 529.

The agricultural development of Iran.
See item no. 530.

Modernization of rural economy in Iran.
See item no. 534.

Bibliography on Qajar Persia.
See item no. 785.

The age of constitutionalism, secularism and modernism (late 19th and 20th centuries)

171 **The causes of the constitutional revolution in Iran.**
Ervand Abrahamian. In: *International Journal of Middle East Studies*, vol. 10, no. 3 (1979), p. 381–414.
An analytical investigation of the roots of the modernist and secularist movements in Iran at the beginning of the 20th century, culminating in the establishment of a parliamentary constitutional government in 1907. Amongst the topics examined are the impact of the West and the emergence of the intelligentsia in contrast to traditional institutions and conservative forces.

172 **Iran between two revolutions.**
Ervand Abrahamian. Princeton, New Jersey; Guildford, Surrey, England: Princeton University Press, 1983. 2nd printing with corrections. 537p. map. bibliog. (Princeton Studies on the Near East).
Analyses the social bases of Iranian politics, focusing on the fractionalization of Iranian forces and on the gradual transformation of Iranian politics from the late 19th century, when the growing concern for rationalism and secular constitutionalism culminated in the constitutional revolution in the first decade of the 20th century, to the triumph of the Islamic Revolution in February 1979. The volume is divided into three parts: part I provides an historical background covering the period from the late 19th century to the fall of Reza Shah in 1941; part II, based on the author's PhD dissertation ('Social bases of Iranian politics', Columbia University, Ohio, 1969), is the strongest chapter and forms a greater proportion of the work, although it covers the shortest of the three periods, from 1941 to 1953. The remaining period (1954–79) is discussed in part III. The book is well documented and soundly argued.

173 **Religion and politics in contemporary Iran: clergy-state relations in the Pahlavi period.**
Shahrough Akhavi. Albany, New York: State University of New York Press, 1980. 185p.
Studies the religious community of the Shi'ite *'olamā* (learned theologians) and their power politics during different stages of the Pahlavi secularization. Hence the division of the book into chapters (seven altogether, including introduction and conclusion) based on political epochs. The work is well documented, and contains additional appendixes of comparative data and informative tables.

History. The age of constitutionalism, secularism and modernism (late 19th and 20th centuries)

174 New light on the Iranian constitutional movement.
F. R. C. Bagley. In: *Qajar Iran: political, social and cultural change, 1800–1925*. Edited by E. Bosworth and C. Hillenbrand. Edinburgh: Edinburgh University Press, 1983. p. 48–64.

A critical study of some of the themes expressed by the Persian historian, Fereidun Adamiyat, in his *Ideoloji-ye nehzat-e mashrutiyat-e Iran* (Ideology of the Iranian constitutional movement) (Tehran: Payam, 1976.) and his other historical studies.

175 The modernization of Iran: 1921–1941.
Amin Banani. Stanford, California: Stanford University Press, 1961. 173p. map. bibliog.

This short description provides a basic study of the major attempts and measures taken by the Pahlavi régime to modernize Iran. The book is divided into seven chapters, four of which are confined to the creation of the modern bureaucratic system.

176 The cultural implications of the constitutional revolution.
Mangol Bayat. In: *Qajar Iran: political, social and cultural change, 1800–1925*. Edited by E. Bosworth and C. Hillenbrand. Edinburgh: Edinburgh University Press, 1983. p. 65–75.

Assesses the attempts to achieve secularization and cultural modernism in the constitutional revolution of 1905–11 against a background of resistance put up by the traditionalist clergy and the conservative forces.

177 The Persian revolution of 1905–1909.
Edward G. Browne. London: Cass, 1966. rev. ed. 400p.

Gives a liberal view of the origins, development and history of the Iranian constitutionalist and nationalist tendencies which culminated in the 1905–09 constitutional movement in opposition to the absolute government and religious fundamentalists. It includes a translation of the Constitutional Fundamental Laws and the Supplementary Fundamental Laws of 1906 and 1907 as well as the Electoral Laws of 1906 and 1909. A number of documentary notes and photographs are also included.

178 Nationalism in Iran.
Richard W. Cottam. Pittsburgh, Pennsylvania: University of Pittsburgh Press, 1979 (2nd ed.). 363p. map.

An assessment of modernist nationalism in Iran, with the purpose of providing a key to the understanding of Iranian attitudes and political behaviour. It analyses the phenomenon of nationalism in its historical perspective, and in connection with religious and ethnic minorities. The 1979 edition of the book is an updated volume and includes an additional chapter dealing with the fifteen-year period following the first publication of the book in 1964.

History. The age of constitutionalism, secularism and modernism
(late 19th and 20th centuries)

179 **Iran in the service of world peace.**
Zaven N. Davidian. Tehran: University of Isfahan, 1971. 315p.
The author paints a glorious picture of Iran under the Pahlavis, focusing mainly
on the post-war period, although he also presents a brief narrative history of Iran
from ancient times to the Shah's coronation in 1967. The economy and
development plans, the 1963 White Revolution and its twelve points, Iran's
foreign policy, oil and gas, industry, fiscal policy and social services are all
outlined.

180 **The forces of modernization in nineteenth century Iran: an
historical survey.**
Hafez Farman Farmayan. In: *Beginnings of modernization in the
Middle East; the nineteenth century*. Edited by William R. Polk,
Richard L. Chambers. Chicago; London: University of Chicago
Press, 1968. p. 119–51.
Examines the emergence and growth of the idea of modernization, and deals
with: the first group of Persian students abroad (19th century); the inauguration
of the first Iranian technical college in 1851; the modernizing attempts of the 19th-
century Qajar monarch Naser al-Din Shah (1848–96) and his political élite such as
Amir Kabir and Moshir al-Douleh; as well as the intellectual writings of the
period, including travel accounts, social and political writings, books and
newspapers.

181 **The role of the 'rebels' in the constitutional movement in Iran.**
Asghar Fathi. In: *International Journal of Middle East Studies*,
vol. 10, no. 1 (1979), p. 55–66.
An analytical study of the role played by a group of people from Tabriz,
described by the author as 'rebels', in the Iranian constitutional movement in
1908–09.

182 **Role of the traditional leader in modernization of Iran, 1890–1910.**
Asghar Fathi. In: *International Journal of Middle East Studies*,
vol. 11, no. 1 (1980), p. 87–98.
Examines the legitimization of change and modernization in Iran at the turn of
the century, sanctioned by the role played by the religious leaders and institutions
that enjoyed charismatic authority and legitimizing power.

183 **The Shah: the glittering story of Iran and its people.**
Edwin P. Hoyt. New York: Paul S. Eriksson, 1976. 233p. bibliog.
A somewhat superficial and journalistic narrative history of the Pahlavis in 20th-
century Iran, focusing on Mohammad Reza Shah since his ascending the throne in
1941. The volume is aimed at the general reader.

184 **Banking and empire in Iran: the history of the British Bank of the Middle East. Volume 1.**
Geoffrey Jones. Cambridge, England: Cambridge University Press, 1986. 340p. 5 maps. bibliog.

An authoritative history of the Imperial Bank of Persia which was founded in 1889 and changed its name several times before it was finally closed in 1952. The volume is arranged in three parts, detailing the foundation of the Bank; its growth; and finally its closure in the context of Iranian politics and economy as well as of British diplomacy in Iran. It includes some fascinating illustrations, and several relevant tables and appendixes.

185 **Nationalist trends in Iran, 1921–1926.**
Homayoun Katouzian. In: *International Journal of Middle East Studies*, vol. 10, no. 4 (1979), p. 533–51.

Studies a period of transformation and power politics in Iranian history during the years immediately following the First World War. It examines the Jangali movement and the establishment of the Gilan republic in 1920, the notorious 1919 Iran-Britain agreement, Reza Khan's 1921 coup d'état and the consequent five years of dual sovereignty.

186 **The assassination of the Amin al-Sultān (Atābak-i A'zam), 31 August 1907.**
Nikki R. Keddie. In: *Iran and Islam*. Edited by C. E. Bosworth. Edinburgh: Edinburgh University Press, 1971. p. 315–29.

Attempts to cast light on a mysterious political event which took place during the Iranian constitutional movement of 1905–09, namely the assassination of the eminent Qajar vizier Amin al-Sultan.

187 **Iran under the Pahlavis.**
Edited by George Lenczowski. Stanford, California: Stanford University Press, 1978. 475p. map. bibliog. (Hoover Institution Publication 164).

A collection of twelve articles focusing on the changes introduced in 20th century Iranian society by the Pahlavi monarchs. The articles cover various aspects of the Iranian social, political and economic structure.

188 **The origins of modern reform in Iran, 1870–80.**
Guity Nashat. Urbana, Illinois; Chicago; London: University of Illinois Press, 1982. 169p. map. bibliog.

The decade under examination is one of the turning-points in modern Iranian history. However, the author analyses the events of this period within the context of the 19th century as a whole. The book is based on Nashat's PhD thesis (University of Chicago, 1973), and examines the introduction of reforms in such areas as the judicial system, the military, and the political and economic settings. It also examines the cultural innovations.

History. The age of constitutionalism, secularism and modernism
(late 19th and 20th centuries)

189 **Women in pre-revolutionary Iran: an historical overview.**
Guity Nashat. In: *Women and revolution in Iran.* Edited by
Guity Nashat. Boulder, Colorado: Westview Press, 1983. p. 5–35.

An historical account of the status and position of women in Iranian society. The
study begins with a brief sketch of pre-Islamic Iran, followed by the mediaeval
Islamic times, the 19th-century Qajars and the age of the constitution in the
20th century up to women's participation in the 1979 Islamic Revolution.

190 **The history of modern Iran, an interpretation.**
Joseph M. Upton. Cambridge, Massachusetts: Harvard
University Press, 1961. 2nd ed. 158p. bibliog. (Centre for Middle
Eastern Studies).

A socio-political examination of Iranian history from the beginning of the
19th century to the late 1950s. The volume is divided into seven chapters: the first
is a brief introduction to the history of 19th-century Iran up to the granting of the
constitution in 1906; the following four discuss various social and political aspects
of Iranian society in the following period, focusing on the emergence of Reza
Khan in 1921, and his reign, 1925–41; chapter six outlines the developments from
1941 to the late 1950s; and the final chapter examines the events of 1958 and their
effects.

Iran: past, present and future.
See item no. 11.

Iran: past and present.
See item no. 19.

Migration and problems of development: the case of Iran.
See item no. 229.

The social sciences and problems of development.
See item no. 302.

Modernization and changing leadership in Iran.
See item no. 343.

The politics of Iran . . .
See item no. 345.

Persian oil: a study in power politics.
See item no. 346.

Capitalism and revolution in Iran.
See item no. 351.

Aspects of militancy and quietism in Imami Shi'ism.
See item no. 353.

Countercoup: the struggle for the control of Iran.
See item no. 357.

History. The age of constitutionalism, secularism and modernism
(late 19th and 20th centuries)

The communist movement in Iran.
See item no. 364.

Roots of Revolution . . .
See item no. 381.

The Iranian structure for liberation . . .
See item no. 386.

Militant Islam.
See item no. 398.

Iraq and Iran: roots of conflict.
See item no. 466.

The Iran-Iraq conflict.
See item no. 470.

Political process and institutions in Iran . . .
See item no. 482.

The army.
See item no. 489.

The political economy of modern Iran . . .
See item no. 504.

The Gulf in the early 20th century . . .
See item no. 505.

Development of the Iranian oil industry . . .
See item no. 516.

**Finance and foreign exchange for industrialization in Iran, 1310–1319
(1931/32–1940/41).**
See item no. 523.

Industrialization in Iran, 1900–1941.
See item no. 524.

**A micro-analysis approach to modernization process: a case study of
modernity and traditional conflict.**
See item no. 527.

The Persian Railway Syndicate and British railway policy in Iran.
See item no. 547.

Education and social awakening in Iran: 1850–1968.
See item no. 574.

Iran: from religious dispute to revolution.
See item no. 576.

The mantle of the prophet.
See item no. 577.

Biographies, Diaries and Memoirs

191   **'Ali Shari'ati ideologue of the Iranian Revolution.**
Ervand Abrahamian.   *MERIP Reports*, vol. 12, no. 1 (Jan. 1982),
p. 24–28.
An account of the life of the modernist Western-educated Islamic sociologist 'Ali
Shari'ati, who was politically active in the 1960s and 1970s until his sudden death
in London in 1977. It also outlines his political theory, his attitude towards
Marxism, his critical view of the traditional *'olamā* and conservative clerical
Islam.

192   **The vanished Imam: Musā al-Sadr and the Shia of Lebanon.**
Fouad Ajami.   London: I. B. Tauris, 1986. 288p.
A narrative of the political life of an Iranian *mullah* (priest), Musa Sadr, who
emigrated to Lebanon in 1959 and disappeared under mysterious circumstances in
1978 while on a visit to Libya. The author attempts to show how Musa Sadr
established himself as a charismatic leader of the Muslim Shi'ite sect in south
Lebanon. Along with a portrayal of his character, the revolutionary traits of the
Lebanon Shi'ite community have also been examined.

193   **Mirza Malkum Khān: a study in the history of Iranian modernism.**
Hamid Algar.   Berkeley, California; London: University of
California Press, 1973. 308p. bibliog.
A critical analysis of the Qajar period (1794–1925) with specific reference to its
intellectual aspects, focusing on the political biography of the 19th-century Iranian
reformist Malkom Khan. Three appendixes are included: the first examines the
attribution of four comedies to Malkom Khan; the second is an English rendering
of one of his essays 'A Traveller's Narrative'; and the last is a specimen of his
political journalism, taken from the journal *Qanun* (Law) which was edited and
published by Malkom Khan in London in the 1890s.

194 **Twenty-three years: a study of the prophetic career of Mohammad.**
'Ali Dashti, translated from the Persian by
F. R. C. Bagley.   London: Allen & Unwin, 1985. 218p.
Assesses the 'career' of the prophet Mohammad against a background of topical
issues such as humanity, economics and women in Islam.

195 **Mohammad Mossadegh: a political biography.**
Farhad Diba.   London; Sydney; Dover, New Hampshire: Croom
Helm, 1986. 210p. bibliog.
The 1951–53 premier Mohammad Mosaddeq is a key figure in the modern history
of Iran. He played a major part in Iranian politics during the post-war period,
until 1953 when he was deposed by a CIA coup. The nationalization of the
Iranian oil industry in this period was engineered and led by him. The present
volume provides his biography, based in part on his own writings, as well as on
documents in the British and American archives. The book is arranged in five
chronological parts and includes six informative appendixes.

196 **Reza Shah the Great: founder of the Pahlavi dynasty.**
L. P. Elwell-Sutton.   In: *Iran under the Pahlavis.*   Edited by
George Lenczowski. Stanford, California: Stanford University
Press, 1978. p. 1–50. bibliog.
Reza Shah (1877–1944), the founder of the Pahlavi dynasty, was, in the author's
view, solely responsible for the transformation of Iranian society in the 1920s and
1930s. This article outlines the conditions in Iran before he rose to power, the
1921 coup d'état, the foundation of the Pahlavi dynasty, Reza Shah's campaigns,
his introduction of many reforms into Iranian society and his abdication in 1941.

197 **The fall of the Shah.**
Fereydoun Hoveyda, translated from the French by Roger
Liddel.   London: Weidenfeld & Nicolson, 1980. 160p.
From the Tehran riots of 1963 which resulted in the exile of Ayatollah Ruhollah
Khomeini, to his return to Iran and the foundation of the Islamic Republic in
1979, public opinion changed, no longer supporting modernization and the secular
monarchy, but favouring instead an Islamic Republic which was against
modernization. An assessment of how and why this change of opinion took place
is the main concern of the author, who himself was a leading figure in the Shah's
régime. His brother, Amir 'Abbas Hoveyda, was the Shah's Prime Minister for a
large part of the period under consideration (1965–77). This work has more value
as a memoir, having little documentary support. It includes eight pages of
illustrations.

198 **Isfahan is half the world: memories of a Persian boyhood.**
Sayyed Mohammad 'Ali Jamalzadeh, translated by
W. L. Heston.   Princeton, New Jersey: Princeton University
Press, 1983, 286p. 2 maps. bibliog.
A translation of Jamalzadeh's *Sar-o tah-e yek karbas* (Cut from the same cloth)
which first appeared in Farsi (Persian) in 1956. The book narrates the author's

Biographies, Diaries and Memoirs

melancholic remembrance of his childhood at the beginning of the 20th century in Isfahan. It is a valuable source of social study although most of its Persian eloquence is lost in translation. The English translation's title, chosen by Princeton University Press, does not correspond to the book's original title; it is actually an exact translation of the title of a travelogue written by Jamalzadeh's contemporary, Sadeq Hedayat.

199 **Iran's men of destiny.**
Jamal Kashani.   New York; Washington; Atlanta, Georgia; Los Angeles; Chicago: Vantage Press, 1985. 171p. bibliog.

This book is an apologetic response to the accusations made by Westerners against Iran following the Iranian Revolution and American hostage crisis in 1979. The author attempts to bring about a better understanding of the Iranian nation, and its services to the world's history and civilization. The volume presents biographical sketches of thirty-five Iranian personalities, beginning with the pre-Islamic prophet of Iran, Zarathustra, followed by a number of kings, politicians, scientists and philosophers, including the two Pahlavi monarchs Reza Shah and Mohammad Reza. The volume ends with the biography of Khomeini and his role in the Islamic Revolution.

200 **Imam 'Ali: source of light, wisdom and might.**
Sulayman Kattani, translated from the Arabic by I. K. A. Howard.   London: Muhammadi Trust of Great Britain and Northern Ireland, 1983. 148p.

Provides an historical biography of Imam 'Ali (the fourth caliph after the prophet Mohammad, and the first Shi'ite Imam (656–61)) and his campaigns to promote Islamic belief. It includes a detailed foreword by Al-Ustadh Ja'far Khalili.

201 **Sayyid Jamal ad-Din 'al-Afghani': a political biography.**
Nikki R. Keddie.   Berkeley, California; Los Angeles; London: University of California Press, 1972. 423p. bibliog.

Provides an objective and detailed biography of the 19th-century Islamic thinker and politician Sayyid Jamal al-Din Afghani, 1838–97, concentrating in particular on his political involvement at a time when the integrity of the Islamic world was on the verge of collapse. It includes a list of books and articles by Sayyid Jamal al-Din himself.

202 **The American task in Persia.**
Arthur Chester Millspaugh.   New York: Middle East Collection, 1973. 318p. 2 maps.

The post-First World War American Financial Mission arrived in Persia in late 1922 to rescue Iran from her grave financial problems. The Mission was headed by Arthur C. Millspaugh who, in the present volume, reveals the story of his task from the beginning till 1925. He also covers the country's agriculture, manufacturing industry, transport and commerce. The book is a reprint of the original first published in 1925 in New York.

58

203 **Diary of HM the Shah of Persia, during his tour through Europe in AD 1873.**
Nāser al-Din Shāh Qājār, translated by J. W. Redhouse.
London: John Murray, 1874. 427p.
A literal translation of Naser al-Din Shah's fascinating diary kept during his tour to Europe through Russia.

204 **Faces in a mirror: memoirs from exile.**
Ashraf Pahlavi. Englewood Cliffs, New Jersey: Prentice-Hall, 1980. 221p.
The author is the daughter of Reza Khan (Reza Shah Pahlavi), the founder of the Pahlavis, and the twin sister of Mohammad Reza, the second and the last ruler of that dynasty. The book tells her own, and her family's, defensive story, beginning at the time when she was merely the daughter of an ordinary soldier, to the period when she was forced into exile in 1978 as the sister of a monarch.

205 **The Shah's story.**
Mohammad Reza Pahlavi, translated from the French by Teresa Waugh. London: Michael Joseph, 1980. 229p.
As indicated by its title, the book reveals the story of the Shah, Mohammad Reza Pahlavi, with reference to historical and political events, or rather reflects the Shah's version of the events. Contains four parts. Part one is a background study of the past against which the glory of the Pahlavi dynasty is attempted to be portrayed in part two. Part three deals with the so-called White Revolution, launched by the Shah himself in the early 1960s, and finally the last part deals with the destruction of the 'Pahlavi glory' by the 1979 Revolution.

206 **The pride and the fall: Iran 1974–1979.**
Anthony Parsons. London: Jonathan Cape, 1984. 156p.
The author served as the British ambassador to Tehran from autumn 1973 to the turbulent days of late January 1979. The book is a personal record of what he considers to have been 'the most absorbing and compelling experience' of his diplomatic life. The book contains seven parts. The first is a brief introductory note about his mission; part two is a slim record of the 1974–75 period; and parts three and four contain some historical remarks on the Pahlavi régime and the embassy. The events of 1976–79 form the next two parts. Finally, the author presents a retrospective view of these events.

207 **In the service of the peacock throne: the diaries of the Shah's last ambassador to London.**
Parviz C. Radji. London: Hamish Hamilton, 1983. 328p.
The author served as the Shah's ambassador to London from early June 1976 to late January 1979. This volume covers his diaries for the entire period of his service in one of the most turbulent periods of Iranian history. The book is, however, a typical example of how distant the Shah's régime and its key politicians were from reality.

208 **Mary Bird in Persia.**
Clara C. Rice.   London: Church Missionary Society, 1916. 194p.
map.

Presents a biographical picture of Mary Bird (1859–1914) as a pioneer missionary, a medical worker, a teacher and an inspiration to those friends who worked with her. Mary Bird went to Iran in the late 19th century, and whilst there she became known as both Khanom Maryam and Hakim Maryam. The book provides a background introduction to the ancient history of Iran and its contemporary social conditions and cultural traditions, followed by Mary Bird's life story. It includes a few colourful line-drawings of Iran's countryside.

209 **Mohammed.**
Maxime Rodinson, translated from the French by Anne
Carter.   Harmondsworth, England: Penguin, 1973. 324p. 2 maps.
bibliog.

A biography of the prophet Mohammad's life and the events of the time. The book is based on major sources of tradition and historical facts, yet it benefits from an eloquent narration which makes the book highly readable. The book was first printed in the original French in 1961 and in English translation in 1971.

210 **The strangling of Persia: story of the European diplomacy and oriental intrigue that resulted in the denationalization of twelve million Mohammedans, a personal narrative.**
W. Morgan Shuster.   New York: Greenwood Press, 1968
(Reprint). 334p. map.

Amidst the heat of the rivalry between the British and Russians in Iran, the Iranian government in 1911 employed five American financial experts supervised by W. Morgan Shuster. Although the contract between the Iranian government and the Americans was agreed to last a period of three years, they had to leave Iran following the Russian ultimatum later in the same year. Morgan's account of his brief service in Iran is a revealing document of internal intrigues and foreign influence of the time.

211 **Mission to Iran.**
William H. Sullivan.   London; New York: W. W. Norton. 287p.
map.

The author served as United States ambassador to Iran from June 1977 to April 1979. The volume is a subjective narrative of his service at this time, and has chapters on various aspects of Iranian society and political affairs.

212 **The spirit of Allah: Khomeini and the Islamic Revolution.**
Amir Taheri.   Bethesda, Maryland: Adler & Adler, 1986. 313p.
bibliog.

A political biography of Ayatollah Ruhollah Khomeini combined with a study of the 1979 Islamic Revolution. The book includes a chronology of major political events in Iran from 1902 when Khomeini was born to 1984–85. It also contains the

English translation of two poems by Khomeini, slogans of the Islamic Revolution, and a diagram showing who, in the author's view, rules the Islamic Republic.

213 **Riza Shah Pahlavi: the resurrection and reconstruction of Iran, 1878–1944.**
   Donald N. Wilber.   Hicksville, New York: Exposition Press, 1975. 268p. map. bibliog.
Examines the rise of Reza Khan, later Reza Shah, through the ranks of the Iranian army until 1920; his coup d'état and political involvement in 1921–25; the foundation of the Pahlavi dynasty; and modernization of Iran until the end of his reign in 1941 when the country was occupied by foreign forces and he was forced to leave the country. His years in exile (1941–44) are also outlined.

214 **The Persians amongst the English: episodes in Anglo-Persian history.**
   Denis Wright.   London: I. B. Tauris, 1985. 215p. bibliog.
An account of Anglo-Persian relations during the period of the Qajars (1787–1925) focusing on a variety of Persians who visited England as students, diplomats, refugees and reigning monarchs. Included in the volume are five appendixes, including a list of Persian envoys in England and British envoys in Iran, and an Anglo-Persian chronology up to 1925.

215 **Observations on Nasir al-Din Shah.**
   Ehsan Yar-Shater.   In: *Qajar Iran: political, social and cultural change, 1800–1925.*   Edited by E. Bosworth, C. Hillenbrand. Edinburgh: Edinburgh University Press, 1983. p. 3–13.
An account of the character and conduct of Naser al-Din Shah Qajar (1848–96) focusing on his concern for the country's prestige, modern administration and reforms. It also deals with the Shah's personal interests, including his passion for women.

History of Shah 'Abbas the Great.
See item no. 154.

On the sociology of Islam.
See item no. 312.

Islam and ownership.
See item no. 488.

The life and works of Jalal-ud-din Rumi.
See item no. 610.

Four eminent poetesses of Iran . . .
See item no. 611.

Modern Persian prose literature.
See item no. 615.

Biographies, Diaries and Memoirs

The life and works of Amir Khusrau.
See item no. 621.

Gholam-Hoseyn Sa'edi: a voice of the poor.
See item no. 627.

Nasir-i Khusraw: forty poems from the *Divan*.
See item no. 652.

The rose-garden of Sheikh Moslihu'd-din Sadi of Shiraz.
See item no. 662.

Bride of acacias.
See item no. 672.

M. A. Jamālzāda: *Once upon a time*.
See item no. 677.

Calligraphers and painters.
See item no. 754.

Bio-bibliographies de 134 savants . . . (Bio-bibliographies of 134 experts.)
See item no. 782.

Population

216   General information on the population of Iran and its growth rate.
Bank Markazi Iran.   In: *The population of Iran*.   Edited by
Jamshid Momeni. Honolulu: East-West Centre, 1977. p. 64–73.
A study of the population in Iran, with regard to its growth-rate and geographical
pattern of distribution.

217   Population.
Jamshid Behnam.   In: *The Cambridge history of Iran, vol. I: the
land of Iran*. Edited by W. B. Fisher. Cambridge, England:
Cambridge University Press, 1968. p. 468–85. 2 maps.
This population study considers its growth since 1956, and its distribution and
variations in density in the urban and rural areas. The article also deals with
marriage and its varied characteristics within the ethnic communities, and fertility.

218   The growth of towns and villages in Iran, 1900–66.
Julian Bharier.   In: *The population of Iran*. Edited by Jamshid
Momeni. Honolulu: East-West Centre, 1977. p. 331–41.
A sketch of the rural-urban structure of population growth in Iran during the 20th
century.

219   Iran: changing population patterns.
B. D. Clark.   In: *The population of Iran*. Edited by Jamshid
Momeni. Honolulu: East-West Centre, 1977. p. 83–111. 3 maps.
bibliog.
A study of population in Iran concerning its growth and distribution, and specific
characteristics such as age, sex, manpower charateristics and population trends. It
also investigates the tribal and nomadic population, urbanization and urban

population, mobility and migration, and so on. Supportive tables and figures are included.

220 **Factors affecting Moslem natality.**
Dudley Kirk. In: *The population of Iran*. Edited by Jamshid Momeni. Honolulu: East-West Centre, 1977. p. 146–51.
A study of some distinctive characteristics of Muslim natality. The author argues that Islam has been a more effective barrier to the diffusion of family planning than Catholicism. The paper includes a table on the population, birth and gross reproduction rates in Muslim countries, including Iran, taken from United Nations sources.

221 **Some demographic aspects of a rural area in Iran.**
Mohammad B. Mashayekhi, Pauline A. Mead, Guy S. Hayes. In: *The population of Iran*. Edited by Jamshid Momeni. Honolulu: East-West Centre, 1977. p. 195–211.
Analyses the demographic data derived from a survey of 173 agricultural villages in the south-west of Tehran. Amongst the aspects discussed are marital status, health, pregnancies and infant deaths. Also included are comparative data on both pregnancy and fertility rates.

222 **The population of Iran: a selection of readings.**
Edited by Jamshid A. Momeni. Shiraz, Iran: Pahlavi University; Honolulu: East-West Centre, 1977. 424p.
Attempts to provide a comprehensive text of readings on the population of Iran for students at undergraduate and graduate levels and a source of reference for researchers, demographers, government officials, policy makers and libraries both inside and outside Iran. Includes thirty-six articles under nine topics: 1, 'Demographic data in Iran'; 2, 'General'; 3, 'Fertility and nuptiality'; 4, 'Mortality'; 5, 'Migration'; 6, 'Family planning'; 7, 'Population, manpower and labour force'; 8, 'Urbanization and modernization'; and 9, 'Projections, forecasts and problems'.

223 **Population and family planning in Iran.**
Richard Moore, Khalil Asayesh, Joel Montague. In: *The population of Iran*. Edited by Jamshid Momeni. Honolulu: East-West Centre, 1977. p. 282–94. bibliog.
Offers a background introduction to the population in Iran, concerning its growth and distribution, and followed by population programmes and plannings introduced in the 1960s and 1970s.

224 **Sociocultural correlates of fertility among tribal, rural and urban population in Iran.**
Ali A. Paydarfar. In: *The population of Iran*. Edited by Jamshid Momeni. Honolulu: East-West Centre, 1977. p. 171–91.
A study of the determinant factors and variables concerning the fertility

differences among Iranian women in tribal, rural and urban environments. Supportive tables are included.

225 **Pastoralism, nomadism and the social anthropology of Iran.**
E. Sunderland. In: *The Cambridge history of Iran, Vol. I: the land of Iran.* Edited by W. B. Fisher. Cambridge, England: Cambridge University Press, 1968. p. 611–83. 2 maps. bibliog.
The author argues that population distribution in Iran is uneven and dictated by geographical characteristics, and, more specifically, water scarcity, as a result of which the nation is heavily divided. Nevertheless, he traces a certain social mobility in Iranian society. He examines the features of rural population, tribal communities and urban societies in modern times.

Iran almanac and book of facts.
See item no. 9.

Historical gazetteer of Iran . . .
See item no. 23.

Baluchestan: its political economy and history.
See item no. 26.

Notes on the toponymy of the Persian Makran.
See item no. 50.

Village ethnoarchaeology: rural Iran in archaeological perspective.
See item no. 83.

Archaeological ethnography of western Iran.
See item no. 89.

Geographical distribution guide to endemic diseases of Iran.
See item no. 335.

Iran's foreign policy 1941–1973 . . .
See item no. 425.

Security in the Persian Gulf 1 . . .
See item no. 433.

Cities and trade . . .
See item no. 511.

Agriculture.
See item no. 532.

Human resources development: problems and prospects.
See item no. 551.

Iran: developments during the last fifty years.
See item no. 564.

Population

Development of Iran: a statistical note.
See item no. 566.

Tehran: an urban analysis.
See item no. 569.

Planning for social change.
See item no. 573.

Iran: a bibliographic research survey.
See item no. 776.

Emigration and Migration

226 **The Iranian 'brain drain'.**
George B. Baldwin. In: *Iran faces the seventies*. Edited by Ehsan
Yar-Shater. New York; Washington; London: Praeger, 1971.
p. 260–83.
A survey of the excessive migration of Iranian educated manpower to Western
countries in the 1960s. The article also examines the educational characteristics of
those Iranian students who returned to their country after the completion of their
studies.

227 **The international migration of high-level manpower: its impact on
the development process.**
Committee on the International Migration of Talent. New York;
Washington; London: Praeger, 1970. 725p.
Examines the problem of the international brain drain, concerning itself,
primarily, with the impact of this phenomenon on the less-developed countries.
To this end, attempts have been made to study educational development in these
areas. In general, Iran is mentioned frequently in connection with various
problems discussed throughout the book. In particular, however, Iran is the
subject of a case-study presented by George B. Baldwin (p. 374–96). The paper is
called 'Four studies on the Iranian brain drain' and emphasizes the impact of
modern education, examining the experience at Pahlavi University, Shiraz.

228 **Migration in Iran: a quantitative approach.**
Mohammad Hemmasi. Shiraz, Iran: Pahlavi University
Publications (48), 1974. 120p. bibliog.
Investigates population redistribution and migration in Iran. The author argues
that the growth of the urban population and the flow of migration in Iran follow
the United Nations' estimates for the less-developed nations. These suggest that

rapid urban growth is mainly due to the migration of rural small-town populations to urban areas. The book is substantiated by a number of tables and figures.

229 **Migration and problems of development: the case of Iran.**
Mohammad Hemmasi.   In: *The social sciences and problems of development*. Edited by Khodadad Farmanfarmaian. Princeton, New Jersey: Princeton University Program in Near Eastern Studies, 1976. p. 208–25.
The author examines the determinants of labour migration to Tehran based on the national censuses of population and housing in 1956 and 1966, and concludes that the balance of socio-economic development in Iran was disturbed by the massive migration of rural, small-town population in Iran.

230 **Poverty and revolution in Iran: the migrant poor, urban marginality and politics.**
Farhad Kazemi.   New York; London: New York University Press, 1980. 156p. bibliog.
An empirical study of the poor rural migrants who were forced, by the social and economic changes of the 1960s, to leave their villages and reside in the city slums. The participation of the migrants in politics in general, and the Islamic Revolution in particular, and their place in the social class structure of Iran, are discussed in chapters four and five, while preceding chapters are concerned with background studies and social developments.

231 **Differential life-styles between migrants and nonmigrants: a case study of the city of Shiraz, Iran.**
Ali A. Paydarfar.   In: *The population of Iran*. Edited by Jamshid Momeni. Honolulu: East-West Centre, 1977. p. 220–31.
Argues that migration to the city of Shiraz in the south differs from the general pattern of migration observed in cities of other developing nations. These migrants are largely educated and come from other cities rather than from rural areas. The study examines the life-styles of non-migrants, rural migrants and urban migrants, noting their social, cultural, demographic and economic characteristics.

232 **Physician migration to the United States; one country's transfusion is another country's hemorrhage.**
Hossain A. Ronaghy, Kathleen Cahill, Timothy D. Baker.   In: *The population of Iran*. Edited by Jamshid Momeni. Honolulu: East-West Centre, 1977. p. 215–19. map.
An analytical investigation of the migration of Iranian physicians to the United States, and its social and environmental consequences. The study is based on the US migration influx from Tehran, Mashhad, Tabriz, Isfahan and Shiraz in the 1960s.

Some aspects of the labour market in the Middle East, with special reference to the Gulf States.
See item no. 553.

Labour migration to the Arabian Gulf . . .
See item no. 556.

Nationalities and
Minorities

General

233 **The Mandaeans of Iraq and Iran: their cults, customs, magic,
     legends, and folklore.**
     E. S. Drower (Stevens).   Oxford: Clarendon Press, 1937. 436p.
     bibliog.

The author, Lady Drower, spent many years observing the customs, beliefs, cults
and magic of the Mandaeans. She has written several books on their way of life,
and this work provides an exhaustive account of the religion and traditions of the
Mandaean peoples. The work is supported by illustrations. A further work on the
same subject is *The handbook of classical and modern Mandaic* by Rudolph
Macuch (Berlin, FRG: Walter de Gruyter, 1965. 463p. bibliog.) which presents a
study of the traditional and colloquial pronunciations of Mandaic. The volume
also deals with its morphology and syntax, concentrating on the phonetics. A
classical text, followed by its transliteration, translation and some notes, a
vocabulary of the vernacular, and some further useful materials are also provided
in the book's appendix.

234 **The Yomut Turkmen: a study of social organization among a
     Central Asian Turkic-speaking population.**
     William Irons.   Ann Arbor, Michigan: University of Michigan,
     1975. map. bibliog. (Anthropological Papers, Museum of
     Anthropology, University of Michigan, No. 58).

A monograph based on the author's research, conducted in Iran among the
Yomut Turkmen in 1965–67 and 1970. The Yomut, a large ethnic minority of
Turkmen, occupy a contiguous region in the south-eastern corner of the Caspian
Sea in Iran, and the adjacent area in the south-western region of Soviet Central
Asia and in Afghanistan. Major topics covered include the ecology, political and

social structure, domestic and family pattern, production and the distribution of wealth. Numerous figures, tables and plates are included, as well as linguistic charts.

235 The Armenians: a people in exile.
David Marshall Lang. London: Allen & Unwin, 1981. 190p.
2 maps. bibliog.

As a companion to the author's earlier work *Armenia: cradle of civilisation* (London: Allen & Unwin, 1970), this volume portrays the historical background and presents an account of the contribution of the Armenian people to the political, social, artistic and literary life of the Near East, including Iran. It contains thirty photographs.

236 Outcast: Jewish life in southern Iran.
Laurence D. Loeb. New York; London; Paris: Gordon & Breach, 1977. 273p. 2 maps. bibliog.

Based on the author's PhD dissertation, written for Columbia University, Ohio in 1970, this is a descriptive and analytical study of Iranian Jews in Shiraz. Even though the author kept in contact with some local informants, the book is based mainly on his field-work study, carried out between 1967 and 1968. A number of relevant appendixes and photographs are included.

237 The Kurdish revolt, 1961–1970.
Edgar O'Ballance. London: Faber, 1973. 178p. 2 maps.

The Kurdish revolt, although confined to northern Iraq, played a considerable role in the domestic policy of Iran concerning the Kurdish minority's nationalist tendencies and most significantly in the Iran-Iraq relations which culminated in the 1975 Algair's Agreement between the Shah and the Iraqi leader, Saddam Hosein, when the dispute between the two countries was settled. The book has a chapter on the Kurds and two chapters on Kurdish nationalism. The history of the revolt is discussed in the following five chapters, leaving the final chapter to an assessment of retrospect and prospect. It also includes two appendixes. The first provides a brief synopsis of the twelve-point programme for peace with the Kurds, broadcast by the Iraqi premier of the time, Abdul Rahman al-Bazzaz, on 29 June 1966. The second is a chronological summary.

238 The English amongst the Persians during the Qajar period, 1787–1921.
Denis Wright. London: Heinemann, 1977. 185p. map. bibliog.

A record of the activities of English subjects in Persia during the 19th century, in the context of British diplomatic relations, and the subsequent rivalry with Russia, over Iran. Included are appendixes providing the lists of British envoys to Persia and British residents in Bushehr, on the Persian Gulf, in this period.

A chronicle of the Carmelites in Persia . . .
See item no. 151.

Jews in Iran.
See item no. 287.

Christians in Persia . . .
See item no. 288.

The structure of Christian-Muslim relations in contemporary Iran.
See item no. 311.

Women and the family in Iran.
See item no. 321.

The Iranian Revolution of 1978–79 . . .
See item no. 374.

The wrath of Allah . . .
See item no. 387.

An index of articles in Western journals.
See item no. 784.

Nomads and pastoral settlers

239 **Tribes and state in Iran: from Pahlavi to Islamic Republic.**
G. Reza Fazel. In: *Iran: a revolution in turmoil.* Edited by Haleh
Afshar. London: Macmillan, 1985. p. 80–98. bibliog.
Demonstrates how isolated the pastoral tribes were from national politics and the
institutions instigated by the Pahlavi régime which sought to strengthen its central
government at the expense of non-Farsi-speaking minorities and pastoral tribes.
The author argues that the Revolution provided an opportunity for the new
régime to make contact with and enjoy the support of the pastoral tribes.
However, while the Shi'ite tribes identify themselves with the Shi'ite clergy who
rule the country, the five million Sunni nomads have found little difference
between the policies of the two régimes.

240 **The Qashqa'i nomads of Fars.**
Pierre Oberling. The Hague; Paris: Mouton, 1974. 221p. 4 maps.
bibliog.
An historical study of the Qashqa'i nomads of Fars province. The social structure
of the Qashqa'i and their political role in past and modern times are investigated
objectively.

241　**Geography of settlement.**

X. de Planhol. In: *The Cambridge history of Iran, vol. I: the land of Iran.* Edited by W. B. Fisher. Cambridge, England: Cambridge University Press, 1968. p. 409–67. bibliog.

Argues that while Iranian society, divided as it is between the nomadic peoples and those who are settled, has been determined by ecological conditions, the distribution of the largest nomadic groups is contrary to the demands made by the natural environment. The author tries to establish which human and historical factors have contributed to such a state of affairs.

242　**Tribalism and society in Islamic Iran, 1500–1629.**

James J. H. Reid. Malibu, California: Undena Publications, 1983. 153p. map. bibliog.

Argues that prior to the 10th century, when new waves of invaders entered Iran, the population structure of the country was dependent on a village economy in which pastoralism served only as an adjunct to the main economic task of cultivation. The Turko-Mongol invaders, however, brought with them a new concept of property organization and a new method of organizing production. Thus, a dualistic system of land utilization, and a new system of state and economic organization were created. The author examines these issues, and their effects on the Iranian life and value systems from the 10th to the 15th centuries.

243　**Multi-resource nomadism in Iranian Baluchistan.**

Philip C. Salzman. In: *Perspectives on nomadism.* Edited by William Irons, Neville Dyson-Hudson. Leiden, The Netherlands: E. J. Brill, 1972. p. 60–68. map. bibliog.

Studies the major features of two Baluch tribes, the Yarahmadzai and the Gamshadzai, on the Sarhad plateau of Iranian Baluchestan and the adjoining eastern lowlands of the Hamun-e Moshkel.

244　**Who are the Baluch? A preliminary investigation into the dynamics of an ethnic identity from Qajar Iran.**

Brian Spooner. In: *Qajar Iran: political, social and cultural change, 1800–1925.* Edited by E. Bosworth and C. Hillenbrand. Edinburgh: Edinburgh University Press, 1983. p. 93–110.

The author states that the Baluch community was ethnographically a product of the 19th-century Qajar period and that, although Baluchestan was then divided among Iran, Afghanistan and India, the area has remained culturally homogeneous. To justify his argument, Spooner examines the social diversity of Baluchestan, and the cultural homogeneity of the Baluch society with reference to the natural conditions of the area and the political conditions of the Qajar period.

Nationalities and Minorities. Nomads and pastoral settlers

Islam and its cultural divergence.
See item no. 17.

Persian diary 1939–1941.
See item no. 58.

Iran: changing population patterns.
See item no. 219.

Sociocultural correlates of fertility . . .
See item no. 224.

Pastoralism, nomadism and the social anthropology of Iran.
See item no. 225.

Religion and society today . . .
See item no. 313.

Tribal rugs: an introduction to the weaving of the tribes of Iran.
See item no. 721.

The Qashqa'i of Iran: World of Islam Festival 1976.
See item no. 745.

Language

Grammars and linguistic studies

245 'To be' as the original of syntax: a Persian framework.
Iraj Bashiri.   Minneapolis, Minnesota: Bibliotheca Islamica, 1973.
146p. bibliog. (Middle Eastern Languages and Linguistics, no. 2).
Based on material taken from Persian literature, this work systematically studies
the theory of syntax. Insights from modern linguistic theory are, therefore, combined with and supported by mediaeval Iranian observations. The grammatical
model thus provided is applicable to both Persian and other languages. Two
appendixes are included: one dealing with verb compounding and the other
providing a useful terminology for those not familiar with modern linguistics.

246 Elementary Persian grammar.
L. P. Elwell-Sutton.   Cambridge, England: Cambridge University
Press, 1983. 238p.
Aims primarily to provide a simple framework for modern written Persian,
though most lessons are supplemented by paragraphs teaching spoken Persian.
Since its first publication in 1936 the book has undergone two revisions: once in
1969 when it was reprinted with corrections and additions; and again in 1972 when
a key to the language was provided. The work includes appendixes on various
types of Arabic script and their history, and two rather brief Persian-English and
English-Persian vocabularies.

247 Iranian words containing -ān-.
Ilya Gershevitch.   In: *Iran and Islam*. Edited by C. E. Bosworth.
Edinburgh: Edinburgh University Press, 1971. p. 267–91.
An etymological and linguistic analysis of Old Persian words containing 'ān'.

75

248 **Lārestāni studies 1 – Lari basic vocabulari -.**
Koji Kamioka, Minoru Yamada.   Tokyo: Institute for the Study
of Languages and Cultures of Asia and Africa, 1979. 35 + 227p.
(Studia Culturae Islamicae, no. 10).

A linguistic study of Larestani, a Persian dialect of south Iran. The volume
contains one thousand vocabulary entries, with indexes in Lari, Persian and
English.

249 **Old Persian: grammar, texts, lexicon.**
Roland G. Kent.   New Haven, Connecticut: American Oriental
Society, 1950. 216p.

A manual for the Old Persian inscriptions, dealing with grammatical elements,
syntax and style, texts, and lexicon.

250 **Persian grammar.**
Ann K. S. Lambton.   Cambridge, England: Cambridge
University Press, 1953. 265p.

This grammar is aimed primarily at the student of modern Persian, although
Arabic elements and examples of classical Persian are also included to help those
wanting to read the classics. Appendixes on irregular verbs, interjections, the
calendar, currency, weights and measures, the Abjad alphabet, and intonation are
also included.

251 **Modern Persian.**
John Mace.   London: English Universities Press, 1962. 216p.
(Teach Yourself books).

A simple teach-yourself book for modern Persian with only a little attention paid to
the Arabic element. The book includes a key to the exercises, and a brief Persian-
English and English-Persian vocabulary.

252 **The Masal dialect of Talishi.**
T. Nawata.   *Acta Iranica*, vol. VIII, no. 22 (1982), p. 93–117.

A descriptive analysis of the Masal dialect of Taleshi, examining its phonology
and morphology, and providing a short text and some vocabulary.

253 **Principles of Persian bound phraseology.**
Mansour Shaki.   Prague: Oriental Institute in Academia,
Publishing House of the Czechoslovak Academy of Science, 1967.
111p.

Examines the theory and various features of bound phraseology in the Persian
language. The work investigates the general relevant concepts and various formal
and stylistic features, and includes a classification of Persian bound phraseology,
drawn up on the basis of the semantic-lexical and grammatical correspondence of
Persian.

Language. Grammars and linguistic studies

254 **Studies in the kinship terminology of the Indo-European languages, with special references to Indian, Iranian, Greek and Latin.**
O. Szemerenyi. *Acta Iranica*, vol VII, no. 16 (1977). p. 5–240. bibliog.
An analytical study of kinship terms in Indo-European languages examining consanguineals, affinals and groups.

255 **An introduction to Persian.**
Wheeler McIntosh Thackston, Jr. Tehran: Soroush Press, 1978. 223p.
A basic grammar which is intended to serve as an introduction on an elementary level to modern Persian. The book is arranged into three parts with an additional supplement. The first and largest part comprises the grammar of modern written Persian, although it has evidently been influenced by the spoken Tehrani dialect. Elements of classical literature and the modern spoken idiom are given in the following sections.

256 **Studies in the phonetics and phonology of modern Persian: intonation and related features.**
Jalil Towhidi. Hamburg, FRG: Helmut Buske Verlag, 1974. 237p. bibliog.
A theoretical study of Persian intonation, together with a survey of previous studies on this subject; an investigation of the functional use of pitch, prosodic and paralinguistic features; and a study of some areas of correlation between the intonation and grammar of Persian. It contains two appendixes: the first provides a guide to the tones covered in the book; and the second consists of two texts, together with their translations, giving examples based on issues studied in the main part of the book.

257 **The verbal category of inference in Persian.**
G. Windfuhr. *Acta Iranica*, vol. VIII, no. 22 (1982), p. 263–87. bibliog.
A discussion of two forms of the perfect in modern Persian normally overlooked by the grammarians.

258 **Modern Persian.**
Gernot Windfuhr, Hassan Tehranisa. Ann Arbor, Michigan: University of Michigan, 1981. 3 vols. (Department of Near Eastern Studies).
Aims to present an outline of the grammatical structure of contemporary formal Persian primarily for the English-speaking student. It discusses the basic points of Persian grammar with equal emphasis on four principal language skills, i.e., speaking, comprehension, reading and writing. The text provides the student with examples to aid writing and reading, while recorded texts and dialogues are included for use in a language laboratory. The book is arranged in elementary and intermediate levels in separate volumes.

259   **A grammar of southern Tati dialects.**
Ehsan Yar-Shater.   The Hague; Paris: Mouton, 1969. 274p.

Presents a descriptive grammatical sketch of nine closely-related Iranian dialects spoken in the regions to the south and south-west of Qazvin and in the south-east corner of Azarbaijan. It deals with both the phonology and morphology of the Tati dialects.

Islam and its cultural divergence.
See item no. 17.

Readers

260   **Modern Persian reader.**
Amir Abbas Haidari.   London: School of Oriental and African Studies, 1975. 37 + 165p.

Designed to provide reading material for the student of the Persian language. It includes fourteen short pieces in Farsi, followed by a lengthy vocabulary in Persian alphabetical order. An introduction on the development of modern Farsi in the last two centuries, and notes on writers and difficult points are provided in English in a different section, with separate pagination.

261   **A modern Persian prose reader.**
Hassan Kamshad.   Cambridge, England: Cambridge University Press, 1968. 249p.

A collection of twenty-seven language texts from eighteen modernist writers, designed to accompany the author's *Modern Persian prose literature* (q.v.). The texts are given in their original form with some minor alterations. Each writer's work is preceded by a brief introductory note in English. A list of words in Persian alphabetical order is also included.

262   **Persian letters: a manual for students of Persian.**
Collected and edited by H. D. Graves Law.   London: Iran Society. [n.d.]. 100p.

Contains forty-eight private letters, mainly written during the first half of the 1940s, by members of the Iranian élite to the editor or others, apparently British. The letters are given in both their original manuscript form and in print. The English translation, vocabulary, some notes and the book's introduction, which describes the technique of various scripts and a guide for reading them, are useful tools for the student.

263 **Social and cultural selections from contemporary Persian.**
Michael M. Mazzaoui, William G. Millward. Delmar, New York:
Caravan Books, 1973. 128p.
Contains sixteen selections from two Tehran dailies, *Keyhan* and *Ettela'at* with
linguistic notes, exercises and an alphabetical word list, designed to help the
English-speaking student of Persian.

Dictionaries

264 **The English-Persian collegiate dictionary.**
Abbas Aryanpur-Kashani, Manoochehr
Aryanpur-Kashani. Tehran: Amir Kabir, 1975. 2 vols.
This modern and comprehensive dictionary contains over 200,000 vocabulary
entries and expressions, including colloquialisms and slang. Illustrations are also
included.

265 **The concise Persian-English dictionary.**
Abbas Aryanpur-Kashani, Manoochehr
Aryanpur-Kashani. Tehran: Amir Kabir, 1978. 1440p.
This dictionary is designed to provide a comprehensive list of Persian words based
on a number of reliable Persian lexicographical works, including *Loghatnameh* by
'Ali Akbar Dehkhoda (et al.). Archaic and obsolete words, especially those of
Arabic and other foreign origins have been excluded and replaced by new Persian
coinages and scientific terms.

266 **The new unabridged English-Persian dictionary.**
Abbas Aryanpur-Kashani, Jahan Shah Saleh. Tehran: Amir
Kabir in association with the Printing Institution, 1963. 5 vols.
Provides a valuable source of reference for Persian studies. It is based on
Webster's International Dictionary, and the *Shorter Oxford Dictionary* attempting
to give the Persian equivalents of all the words in the Oxford and all the key-
words in Webster. A pronunciation key for difficult Persian words is included.

267 **A dictionary of scientific terms.**
Edited by Parviz Shahryari. Tehran: Franklin Book Programs,
1970. 613 + 163p. (Entesharat-e Bonyad-e Farhang-e Iran, 100;
Farhang-ha-ye Elmi va Fanni, 3).
Based on a number of up-to-date and reliable English, French and Persian lexicographical works, this is a dictionary of scientific terms, covering mathematics,
astronomy, physics, chemistry, geology, zoology and botany. The definitions are
given in Persian, and the equivalent words are listed in Persian, English and
French. The arrangement for the main part of the work, which includes the

Persian definitions, is according to the Persian alphabetical system. The terms are also given according to the English-French alphabetical system.

268 **A comprehensive Persian-English dictionary.**
F. Steingass.   London: Kegan Paul, Trench, Trübner, 1947. 1539p.

A useful and authoritatively prepared lexicographical source of reference for students of the Persian language and literature. It includes numerous Persian terms considered to be obsolete in the day-to-day language but which are to be found in classical texts. A large number of Arabic words which may seem to be foreign to Persian literature, but which can still be found in it are included, as well as words from other foreign languages such as Greek, Hindi, Mongolian, Turkish and Russian. However, it lacks all modern terms as it was first printed in 1892, and has never been revised.

269 **Technical dictionary of oil industry terms.**
Jalāloddin Tavana.   Tehran: Tehran University, 1967. 2 vols.

Provides a list of technical terms used in the oil industry, in English, French, German and Persian. The arrangement is in English alphabetical order, and the Persian equivalents are given in both transliteration and in Farsi script. The book is illustrated.

Religion

Islam

270 **Religion in the Timurid and Safavid periods.**
B. S. Amoretti.   In: *The Cambridge history of Iran, vol. 6: the Timurid and Safavid periods*. Edited by Peter Jackson. Cambridge, England: Cambridge University Press, 1986. p. 610–55. bibliog.
Offers a brief overview of religious developments and their characteristics in the 14th–18th centuries. It discusses the state of religion in Iran during the pre-Safavid period, examining the Horufis (a religious movement founded by Sayyid Fazalallah in the 14th century) and the Mosha'shah' movement (a similar contemporary movement with a great social significance, used as a model for the modern Babi offshoot of Shi'ism), and the recognition of Shi'ism and its development in the Safavid era.

271 **Islam in transition: Muslim perspectives.**
Edited by John J. Donohue, John L. Esposito.   New York; Oxford: Oxford University Press, 1982. 322p.
A collection of essays on Islam placing emphasis on the varying currents of thought of the Islamic world. It is divided into four parts: part one deals with the 19th-century Islamic movements in search of identity, and includes a study on Jamal al-Din Afghani. Part two analyses the relationship between Islam and the modern issues of nationalism, socialism and secularism. Part three discusses the topics of modernization and reform; and the re-emergence of Islam is studied in the final part, which deals with Sheikh Hosein Na'ini, Sheikh Fazlollah Nuri, 'Ali Shari'ati, Mortaza Motahhari and Ayatollah Khomeini.

272 **The religion of the Sufis.**
Sheikh Mohammad Mohsen Fani, translated by David Shea and
Anthony Troyer. London: Octagon Press, 1979. 87p.

A translation of the *Dabestan* attributed to the 11th-century Sufi, Sheikh
Mohammad Mohsen Fani. A resident of Kachmir, which once belonged to Iran
and which is now an area of dispute betwen India and Pakistan, the author refers
to the shores of Persia as his homeland. Sufism, according to the *Dabestan*,
appears to be the rationalism of any sort of doctrine and, therefore, seems to
belong to all religions. The text consists of three sections on the religious tenets of
the Sufis, the open interpretation of their open confessions and some individuals
among them. The text is preceded by a preliminary discourse, by Anthony
Troyer, on the author and his work. A brief introduction by Idris Shah is also
included.

273 **Changes in charismatic authority in Qajar Shi'ism.**
D. M. MacEoin. In: *Qajar Iran: political, social and cultural
change, 1800–1925*. Edited by E. Bosworth and C. Hillenbrand.
Edinburgh: Edinburgh University Press, 1983. p. 148–76.

Studies the characteristics of 19th-century Islamic religious attitudes, which were
influenced by contemporary socio-political developments. It also outlines the consequent theological interpretations of religious authority preached by Ayatollah
Khomeini in the 1979 Islamic Revolution.

274 **Islam and the plight of modern man.**
Seyyed Hossein Nasr. London; New York: Longman, 1975. 150p.
bibliog.

A study of some major modern issues that, in the author's view, disturb both
Western man and the present-day Muslims. The purpose of the book is to
familiarize the disturbed Western man with some Islamic teachings which provide
solace. It also aims to provide guidelines for the modernized Muslim whose
Islamic identity is threatened by forces of Western modernism.

275 **Sadr al-Din Shirazi and his transcendent theosophy: background,
life and works.**
Seyyed Hossein Nasr. Tehran: Imperial Iranian Academy of
Philosophy, 1978. 97p. bibliog.

Attempts to study the works of Molla Sadra in relation to the Islamic tradition,
and to analyse the most important aspects of his doctrine. The book is, however,
based mainly on the author's views, which were formed by his knowledge of the
contemporary expositors of the school of Molla Sadra. The life of the philosopher
and his intellectual background form the first two chapters, followed by studies on
the *Asfar*, the sources of his doctrines and ideas, and the investigation of the issue
of transcendent theosophy.

276 **Islamic life and thought.**
Seyyed Hossein Nasr.   Albany, New York: State University of
New York Press, 1981. 217p.
A collection of several essays, most of which had been printed previously in
various reviews and collections. The main themes of the volume are the integral
Islamic tradition, and the Iranian role in the development of Islamic civilization.
This is especially the case in the chapters on the sciences and philosophy.

277 **Spiritual movements, philosophy and theology in the Safavid period.**
S. H. Nasr.   In: *The Cambridge history of Iran, vol. 6: the
Timurid and Safavid periods.* Edited by Peter Jackson. Cambridge,
England: Cambridge University Press, 1986. p. 656–97. bibliog.
Examines the intellectual and spiritual history of Iran in the 16th–18th centuries.
It describes the revival of religious learning, focusing on the Shi'ite scholars and
the state of Sufism. Sheikh Bahaoddin 'Ameli, Mir Damād, Mir Fendereski, and
Sadr al-Din Shirazi (Molla Sadra) are the prominent scholars discussed
individually. It also examines the *akhbari-osuli* (theological) debates which were
continued into the 19th-century Qajar period.

278 **The path of God's bondsmen from origin to return.**
Najm al-Din Rāzi, translated by Hamid Algar.   Delmar, New
York: Caravan Books, 1982. 497p. bibliog. (Persian Heritage
Series, No. 35).
A translation of *Mersad al-ebad men al-mabda ela'l-ma'ad*, a major work on
Islamic mysticism written during the turbulent Mongol period. The translation is
supported by introductory notes and a comprehensive name, place and subject
index.

279 **Islam in the world.**
Malise Ruthven.   Harmondsworth, England: Penguin Books,
1984. 375p. 5 maps. bibliog.
A general examination of the Muslim's view of God and mankind's duties in the
world, with reference to the application of these views by Muslims throughout the
history of Islam. The author, although a non-Muslim layman, says that neither
English works written by Muslims, nor those by specialists, satisfactorily explain
how Islam has become a political force in the modern world, and that by writing
this book he has attempted to fill the gap in the market. Frequent reference is
made to Iran from the pre-Islamic period to the present day.

280 **The legacy of Islam.**
Edited by Joseph Schacht, C. E. Bosworth.   Oxford: Clarendon
Press, 1974. 505p.
A collection of eighteen articles which pays particular attention to Islam's
contribution to science and civilization. The papers come under ten topic
headings, including art and architecture, literature, mysticism and science. Iran is
referred to throughout the book in connection with various historical, religious,

literary, and economic issues, and the volume also covers the country's architecture, mysticism, science, politics, astronomy and music.

281 **A guide to the contents of the Qur'an.**
Faruq Sherif. London: Ithaca Press, 1985. 147p. bibliog.

Provides a subject guide to the contents of the Qur'an (Koran), leaving out all the dogma and laws of Islam which do not appear within its text. An index to the verses and a brief bibliography are included, along with a long list of errata.

282 **The book of Sufi chivalry.**
Muhammad ibn al-Husayn al-Sulami, translated from the Arabic by Sheikh Bayrak al-Jerrahi al-Halveti. London; The Hague: East-West Publications, 1983. 110p.

This is a translation of *Ketab al-Futuwat* (The book of chivalry), a Sufi text originally in Arabic even though it was written by a native of Nishapur who was influenced by the Iranian Sufi movements of his time.

283 **Shi'ite Islam.**
'Allamah Sayyid Muhammad Husayn Tabataba'i, translated by Seyyed Hossein Nasr. London: Allen & Unwin, 1975. 222p. bibliog. (Persian Studies Series, no. 5).

A general introduction to Shi'ism written by a contemporary leading Shi'ite authority and based on traditional Shi'ite methods of presentation, redressed for the world outside that religion. The work deals with its historical background, Shi'ite religious thought, and Islamic beliefs from the Shi'ite point of view. It also contains four appendixes on *taqiyah* or dissimulation, temporary marriage, ritual practices and a note on the *jinn*.

284 *Rawdatu't-taslim*: **commonly called** *tasawwurat*.
Nasir al-Din Tusi, translated by W. Ivanow. Leiden, The Netherlands: E. J. Brill, 1950. 204 + 160p. (Ismaili Society Series A, no. 4).

An English translation of a treatise on Isma'ilism long recognized as the work of Nasir al-Din Tusi, the 13th-century Persian philosopher, astronomer and theologian. The original Persian text, which is attached to the back of the volume under independent page numbers, was printed separately in Bombay. It contains a detailed section analysing the technical terms used by the author.

285 **God's caliph: Qur'ānic interpretations and Umayyad claims.**
W. Montgomery Watt. In: *Iran and Islam*. Edited by C. E. Bosworth. Edinburgh: Edinburgh University Press, 1971. p. 565–74.

A philological study of the root and original meaning of *khalifeh* (caliph) in two Qur'anic passages, and an interpretative commentary on the secular denotation of this word as a title for Abubakr when he became the first head of the Islamic State in succession to the prophet Mohammad. It also discusses Umayyad claims to the caliphate.

The legacy of Persia.
See item no. 2.

Iran: continuity and variety.
See item no. 5.

Iran: religion, politics and society.
See item no. 12.

The glory of the Shia world . . .
See item no. 59.

A history of Persia.
See item no. 97.

The Cambridge history of Iran, vol. 3 . . .
See item no. 115.

Religion in the Saljuq period.
See item no. 116.

Religion under the Mongols.
See item no. 117.

The Ismaili state.
See item no. 126.

The occultation of the Twelfth Imam . . .
See item no. 127.

The prophet and the age of Caliphates . . .
See item no. 130.

The Shu'ubiyah controversy and the social history of early Islamic Iran.
See item no. 133.

The shadow of God and the Hidden Imam . . .
See item no. 145.

Religion and politics in contemporary Iran . . .
See item no. 173.

Role of the traditional leader in modernization of Iran, 1890–1910.
See item no. 182.

'Ali Shari'ati ideologue of the Iranian Revolution.
See item no. 191.

The vanished Imam . . .
See item no. 192.

Twenty-three years . . .
See item no. 194.

Imam 'Ali: source of light, wisdom and might.
See item no. 200.

Religion. Islam

Sayyid Jamal ad-Din 'al-Afghani': a political biography.
See item no. 201.

Mohammed.
See item no. 209.

Factors affecting Moslem natality.
See item no. 220.

Misconceptions regarding the juridical status of the Iranian *'ulama.*
See item no. 300.

Islam and capitalism.
See item no. 309.

On the sociology of Islam.
See item no. 312.

Religion and society today . . .
See item no. 313.

The bazaar as a case study of religion and social change.
See item no. 315.

Sexuality and Shi'i social protest in Iran.
See item no. 317.

Women of Iran: the conflict with fundamentalist Islam.
See item no. 318.

Women and the family in Iran.
See item no. 321.

Women in the Shi'i *fiqh*: images through the *hadith*.
See item no. 322.

Fatimeh as a role model in the works of Ali Shari'ati.
See item no. 324.

The position of women in Shi'a Iran: views of the *'ulama*.
See item no. 326.

Women and revolution in Iran.
See item no. 329.

Status of women in the Qur'an.
See item no. 330.

In the shadow of Islam . . .
See item no. 333.

Mysticism and dissent . . .
See item no. 344.

Modern Islamic political thought . . .
See item no. 347.

Aspects of militancy and quietism in Imami Shi'ism.
See item no. 353.

Islam and politics.
See item no. 354.

Marxism and other Western fallacies: an Islamic critique.
See item no. 360.

The Islamic movement: a system's approach.
See item no. 361.

Roots of Revolution . . .
See item no. 381.

The Islamic Revolution in Iran.
See item no. 391.

Religion and politics in the Middle East.
See item no. 393.

Iran: Khumaini's concept of the 'guardianship of the jurisconsult'.
See item no. 394.

Islam and development . . .
See item no. 395.

Religious ritual and political struggle in an Iranian village.
See item no. 397.

Militant Islam.
See item no. 398.

The nature of the Islamic Revolution.
See item no. 401.

Society and economics in Islam . . .
See item no. 403.

Islam and ownership.
See item no. 488.

Islamic banking . . .
See item no. 501.

Work and Islam.
See item no. 552.

Iran: from religious dispute to revolution.
See item no. 576.

Of piety and poetry: the interaction of religion and literature in the life and works of Hakim Sanā'i of Ghazna.
See item no. 597.

The sense of unity: the Sufi tradition in Persian architecture.
See item no. 691.

International Journal of Middle East Studies (IJMES).
See item no. 763.

Christianity and Judaism

286 **Christians in Iran.**
J. P. Asmussen. In: *The Cambridge history of Iran, vol. 3: the Seleucid, Parthian and Sasanian periods.* Edited by Ehsan Yar-Shater. Cambridge, England: Cambridge University Press, 1983. p. 924–48. bibliog.
Studies the emergence of Christianity in Iran and traces the development of the Christian Church during the Sasanian period (224–651).

287 **Jews in Iran.**
J. Neusner. In *The Cambridge history of Iran, vol. 3: the Seleucid, Parthian and Sasanian periods.* Edited by Ehsan Yar-Shater. Cambridge, England: Cambridge University Press, 1983. p. 909–23. bibliog.
A brief study of Judaism and the Jewish settlement in Iran in the pre-Islamic era, focusing on the Sasanian period and the Jewish autonomous government.

288 **Christians in Persia: Assyrians, Armenians, Roman Catholics and Protestants.**
Robin E. Waterfield. London: Allen & Unwin, 1973. 176p. map. bibliog.
Studies Christianity and Christians in Iran. It is divided into three chapters: Christianity in Iran before Islam, the Roman Catholic era, and 19th- and 20th-century developments. An appendix on the Bible is included in Persian.

A chronicle of the Carmelites in Persia . . .
See item no. 151.

Outcast: Jewish life in southern Iran.
See item no. 236.

The structure of Christian-Muslim relations in contemporary Iran.
See item no. 311.

Religion and politics in the Middle East.
See item no. 393.

Zoroastrianism

289 **The letter of Tansar.**
Translated by Mary Boyce. Rome: Istituto Italiano per il Medio ed Estremo Oriente (IsMEO), 1968. 70p. (Persian Heritage Series, Literary and Historical Texts from Iran, 1).
A translation of a 6th-century treatise commonly attributed to Tansar, a great Zoroastrian *herbad* (priest). The volume contains an objective introduction on the treatise, its author and relevant studies.

290 **A Persian stronghold of Zoroastrianism.**
Mary Boyce. Oxford: Oxford University Press, 1977. 270p. bibliog. (Ratanbai Katrak Lectures, 1975).
A collection of ten essays based on the author's study and observations made when she lived, for twelve months during 1963–64, with a community of Zoroastrians in a little village in the northern part of the Yazd region.

291 **Textual sources for the study of Zoroastrianism.**
Edited and translated by Mary Boyce. Manchester, England: Manchester University Press, 1984. 160p. map. bibliog. (Textual Sources for the Study of Religion).
A publication from the Textual Sources for the Study of Religion series which provides a reliable translation of major texts for the study of religion. This work is intended for students in higher education as well as for Zoroastrians and those who have a basic knowledge of Zoroastrianism.

292 **The Avestan hymn to Mithra.**
Translation and commentary by Ilya Gershevitch. Cambridge, England: Cambridge University Press, 1959. 299p.
A critical translation of *Mehr Yasht* in *Avesta* with a reproduction of the readings of the original text in transliteration by the German scholar and specialist in Old Iranian languages, Karl Friedrich Geldner. The text and its translation are followed by a commentary which also includes alternative interpretations. In his commentary the author attempts to seek a meaningful record of Mithra's character in each hymn. It includes introductory notes on Zoroastrianism in general, with the emphasis on Mithra, the god of light.

293 **Parsism: the religion of Zoroaster.**
Sven S. Hartman. Leiden, The Netherlands: E. J. Brill, 1980. 30p. bibliog. (Institute of Religious Iconography, State University at Groningen: Iconography of Religions XIV, 4).
Contains forty-eight plates, mainly photographs taken in India in 1972, the main theme being Parsism and Zoroastrianism. The plates are preceded by thirty pages of introductory notes and explanations.

294 *Rivāyat-i hēmīt-i asawahistān*: a study in Zoroastrian law.
Nezhat Safa-Isfahani. Cambridge, Massachusetts: Harvard
University Press, 1980. 290p. (Harvard Iranian Series, vol. 2).

A translation of a Pahlavi text dating from the late 9th or early 10th century and
containing a collection of religious, social, and civil laws based on the Zoroastrian
religious codes.

295 **Zurvan: a Zoroastrian dilemma.**
R. C. Zaehner. Oxford: Oxford University Press, 1955. 451p.
bibliog.

Attempts to collect from all available sources the texts relevant to the ancient
Iranian god Zurvan, with the objective of co-ordinating Zoroastrian ideas on the
issue. It consists of two parts. The first is an analytical study of Zoroastrianism in
relation to other beliefs and faiths, and Zurvan has been discussed in this part as a
fourfold god. Part two contains a number of texts, with a translation and some
notes from *Avesta* and other Zoroastrian sources. This part also includes some
unfavourable texts from non-Zoroastrian sources.

296 **The teachings of the Magi: a compendium of Zoroastrian beliefs.**
R. C. Zaehner. London: Allen & Unwin; New York: Macmillan,
1956. 150p. bibliog.

Provides the general reader with basic information concerning the Zoroastrian
religion as practised in the later Sasanian period and reflected in the Pahlavi
literature of the post-Islamic period.

297 **The dawn and twilight of Zoroastrianism.**
R. C. Zaehner. London: Weidenfeld & Nicolson, 1961. 337p.
bibliog.

Presents an historical investigation of Zoroastrianism, combined with an
interpretative study of the religion. It is based mainly on Zoroastrian literature
and is aimed at the student of comparative religions and also at the general
reader. Numerous illustrations are included.

Études mithriaques.
See item no. 92.

A history of Zoroastrianism.
See item no. 100.

The Western response to Zoroaster.
See item no. 105.

Zoroaster's time and homeland . . .
See item no. 110.

The *Gāthās* of Zarathustra.
See item no. 609.

Zoroastrian Pahlavi writings.
See item no. 617.

The Zoroastrian houses of Yazd.
See item no. 693.

Social Structure and Social Change

General

298 **Faces of Persian youth: a sociological study.**
A. Reza Arasteh. Leiden, The Netherlands: E. J. Brill, 1970.
268p.

The author's objective seems to have been to study the problems of Iranian youth in a period of transition, and the excess of the generation gap envisaged by resistance for continuity and a search for self identity. The end result is, however, a readable, narrative type of study for the general public, but with little to recommend it as a sociological study.

299 **Man and society in Iran.**
A. Reza Arasteh, in collaboration with Josephine
Arasteh. Leiden, The Netherlands: E. J. Brill, 1970. 2nd ed.
193p.

Attempts to show that man is the central issue and the only guarantee for such orientations as religion, science, law and the social system in the destiny of mankind, through an analytical examination of man and culture in Iran. It is divided into three sections: 1, 'Man in traditional Iranian society'; 2, 'Man in contemporary Iranian society'; 3, 'A measure for the future'.

300 **Misconceptions regarding the juridical status of the Iranian 'ulama.**
Joseph Eliash. In: *International Journal of Middle East Studies*,
vol. 10, no. 1 (1979), p. 9–25.

Argues that the studies concerning the political power of the Shi'ite 'olama in modern Iran cover either their historical role in political affairs; outline the ways in which they exploit different aspects of popular religion for their political ends;

or examine their status based on juridical sources and their interpretations. This work also states that studies discussing this last issue provide only a misconception.

301 **Old and new values in changing cultural patterns.**
Hormoz Farhat. In: *Iran: past, present and future.* Edited by Jane W. Jacqz. New York: Aspen Institute for Humanistic Studies, 1976. p. 433–37.

Argues that traditional values, although not necessarily things of worth or beauty, have to be preserved as they are elements of identity. He is, therefore, in favour of reviving the pre-Islamic Zorastrian code of 'Good Thought, Good Works and Good Deeds'. Amongst the topics briefly touched upon is Persian music.

302 **The social sciences and problems of development.**
Edited by Khodadad Farmanfarmaian. Princeton, New Jersey: Princeton University Program in Near Eastern Studies, 1976. 332p. bibliog.

A collection of some seventeen articles which initially contributed to a conference held in June 1974 at Persepolis in Iran, focusing on various aspects and problems of development. The articles are arranged into two parts: part one is discipline-oriented, outlining general aspects of development in Iran; while part two includes papers on the more specific problems.

303 **Contributions to the anthropology of Iran.**
Henry Field. New York: Kraus Reprint Company, 1968. 507p. 14 maps. bibliog.

A reprint of the Field Museum of Natural History's Anthropological Series, volume 29, nos 1–2, December 1939. No. 1 (up to p. 507) contains the main text, which is an anthropological report based on observations and data obtained during August and September 1934, concerned with the physical characteristics of Iranians. No. 2 contains eight relevant appendixes, glossary, bibliography, indexes and numerous portraits and photographs.

304 **The sociology of development: Iran as an Asian case study.**
Norman Jacobs. New York; Washington; London: Praeger, 1966. 532p. bibliog.

Attempts to provide an answer to the following questions: Why has Iran as an Asian case-study failed to develop as successfully as the European and Japanese societies? and How the situation can be improved? The political, economic and social conditions in Iran are investigated; the facts are based on a model for the study of Iranian problems, which is presented in chapter ten.

305 **Polygyny and social status in Iran.**
Merle K. Miller, Charles Windle. In: *The population of Iran*.
Edited by Jamshid Momeni. Honolulu: East-West Centre, 1977.
p. 133–37.

A study of polygyny as a foundation for social status in Iran, based on observations made by the Iranian Oil Refining Company.

306 **Iran's cultural identity and the present day world.**
Ehsan Naraghi. In: *Iran: past, present and future*. Edited by
Jane W. Jacqz. New York: Aspen Institute for Humanistic Studies,
1976. p. 421–32.

A general overview of Iranian culture. Some of the topics covered include Shi'ite Islam, the Persian language and the pre-Islamic history of Iran as elements of Iranian identity and unity. It also discusses the modern ideas concerning cosmopolitanism, nationalism, modernism and Westernism in a period of change.

307 **Social change in a southern province of Iran.**
Ali Paydarfar. Chapel Hill, North Carolina: University of North
Carolina at Chapel Hill, 1974. 150p. 7 maps. bibliog.

A comparative analysis of the social, cultural and demographic characteristics of the tribal, rural and urban populations of Fars province, based on information collected during a research survey in 1967–69. The work deals with the differences and similarities of various social settings in terms of the impact of the forces of modernization. It includes topics such as exposure to formal education, non-agricultural occupations, mass communications, and urban life-style.

308 **Income distribution in Iran: income distribution and its major determinants in Iran.**
M. H. Pesaran. In: *Iran: past, present and future*. Edited by
Jane W. Jacqz. New York: Aspen Institute for Humanistic Studies,
1976. p. 267–86.

Investigates the relationship of growth and distribution in the Iranian economy in the 1960s and 1970s. The topics examined include a brief review of the trends of income distribution; the socio-economic and demographic characteristics of households by expenditure classes; and the determinants of income inequality. Also included are ten relevant statistical tables.

309 **Islam and capitalism.**
Maxime Rodinson, translated from the French by Brian
Pearce. Harmondsworth, England: Penguin Books, 1977. 296p.

A sociological study which aims to help intellectuals in the Muslim world understand their situation, and which provides a theoretical study for a better understanding of the problems facing an important section of the Third World. The major issues it discusses include the teachings of Islam concerning social justice; feudalism; and the Asiatic mode of production and capitalism in Muslim countries. Iran, as a Muslim country, is referred to constantly throughout the book. Particular emphasis is placed on trade and the state's investment role.

310 **Social development in Iran during the Pahlavi era.**
Roger M. Savory. In: *Iran under the Pahlavis*. Edited by George Lenczowski. Stanford, California: Stanford University Press, 1978. p. 85–127. bibliog.

The author argues that Iran, in the 19th century, was one of the most backward countries in the world and that the foundations for social development were laid by Reza Shah and continued by his son Mohammad Reza Shah. Savory discusses the social developments, and reforms in education, public health, industry and so on. He also studies the emergence of a bureaucratic middle class and an industrial working class.

311 **The structure of Christian-Muslim relations in contemporary Iran.**
Richard Merrill Schwartz. Washington, DC: Washington University, PhD thesis, call no. 74–7066. 1973. 182p. bibliog.

Provides an anthropological analysis of ethnic relations in the city and region of Rezaiyeh, the provincial capital of West Azarbaijan in north-west Iran. Amongst the topics dealt with are: missionaries in Rezaiyeh; institutional and individual issues in the context of ethnic relations; languages and women.

312 **On the sociology of Islam.**
'Ali Shari'ati, translated by Hamid Algar. Berkeley, California: Mizan Press, 1979. 125p.

An English translation of eight lectures by 'Ali Shari'ati, a Paris-educated scholar in sociology with a deep concern for the role of Islam in modern politics. The translation is preceded by a biographical sketch of Shari'ati's life and a detailed bibliography of his works by Gholam Abbas Tavassoli.

313 **Religion and society today: an anthropological perspective.**
Brian Spooner. In: *Iran faces the seventies*. Edited by Ehsan Yar-Shater. New York; Washington; London: Praeger, 1971. p. 166–88.

Studies the religious institutions in the cities and villages, and of the pastoral tribes. It also examines the authority of the *'olama* over different social groups in the 1960s.

314 **Iran: precapitalism, capitalism and revolution.**
Edited by Georg Stauth. Saarbrücken, FRG: Verlag Breitenbach Publishers, 1980. 161p. (Bielefeld Studies on Sociology of Development, vol. 9).

A collection of four articles reflecting diverse views on Iranian society and the 1979 Revolution. The authors of the first three articles discuss the processes of change prior to the Islamic Revolution, and the last examines the social and ideological characteristics of the Revolution. The titles of articles are as follows:

Social Structure and Social Change. General

1, 'The character of the organization of production in Iranian agriculture, 1891–1925' by Abbas Vali; 2, 'Capitalism and feudalism in Iran, 1502–1979' by Bryan S. Turner; 3, 'Functional changes of political power in Iran – a hypothesis' by Georg Stauth; and 4, 'On the ideological and class character of Iran's anti-imperialist revolution' by James D. Cockcroft.

315 **The bazaar as a case study of religion and social change.**
Gustav Thaiss. In: *Iran faces the seventies*. Edited by Ehsan Yar-Shater. New York; Washington; London: Praeger, 1971.
p. 189–216.
A social-anthropological study of the role of religious institutions and the function of the *'olama* in the traditional bazaar, based on the author's research in the bazaar in Tehran and his further studies.

316 **Sociology of the Middle East: a stocktaking and interpretation.**
Christoffel A. O. Van Nieuwenhuijze. Leiden, The Netherlands: E. J. Brill, 1971. 819p. (Social, Economic and Political Studies of the Middle East, vol. I).
An interpretative and scholarly work studying the Middle East as a cultural area. This issue is, in particular, projected in the first of the book's four parts. Part two is a comparative study of the sub-areas: the Fertile Crescent, Egypt, the Arabian Peninsula, the Iranian Plateau, Turkey and North Africa. Such morphological characteristics as the family, tribal society, the village and city structure, minorities, the Islamic community and the state-nation relationships are discussed in part three. The fourth and final part of the book examines social order and authority, public affairs, and the perception of change and its social impact.

317 **Sexuality and Shi'i social protest in Iran.**
Nahid Yeganeh, Nikki R. Keddie. In: *Shi'ism and social protest*. Edited by Juan R. I. Cole, Nikki R. Keddie. New Haven, Connecticut; London: Yale University Press, 1986. p. 108–36.
Examines the place of sexuality in Shi'ite social and political protest. The essay begins with Yeganeh's brief investigative introduction to the contemporary Shi'ite text and its treatment of sexuality. This is followed by Keddie's contribution to the essay which is on the general theory of sexuality in Islam. A third section on variations in past ideology and practice was written jointly.

Iran: continuity and variety.
See item no. 5.

Persia.
See item no. 14.

Islam and its cultural divergence.
See item no. 17.

Historical gazetteer of Iran . . .
See item no. 23.

Yazd and its hinterland . . .
See item no. 30.

Semnan: Persian city and region.
See item no. 33.

Iranian cities.
See item no. 38.

A year amongst the Persians . . .
See item no. 53.

Checkmate: fighting tradition in central Asia.
See item no. 55.

Persian diary 1939–1941.
See item no. 58.

Vakil Abad, Iran: a survivor's story.
See item no. 60.

The rise of the Achaemenids and the establishment of their empire.
See item no. 102.

Media.
See item no. 104.

The socio-economic condition of Iran under Il-Khans.
See item no. 134.

The shadow of God and the Hidden Imam . . .
See item no. 145.

Qajar Iran, political, social and cultural change, 1800–1925.
See item no. 150.

The fall of the Safavi dynasty and the Afghan occupation of Persia.
See item no. 163.

Karim Khan Zand: a history of Iran, 1747–1779.
See item no. 164.

Iran between two revolutions.
See item no. 172.

Role of the traditional leader in modernization of Iran, 1890–1910.
See item no. 182.

Iran under the Pahlavis.
See item no. 187.

The history of modern Iran, an interpretation.
See item no. 190.

'Ali Shari'ati ideologue of the Iranian Revolution.
See item no. 191.

Social Structure and Social Change. General

Mary Bird in Persia.
See item no. 208.

Population.
See item no. 217.

Some demographic aspects of a rural area in Iran.
See item no. 221.

Pastoralism, nomadism and the social anthropology of Iran.
See item no. 225.

Poverty and revolution in Iran . . .
See item no. 230.

Differential life-styles between migrants and nonmigrants . . .
See item no. 231.

The Yomut Turkmen: a study of social organization . . .
See item no. 234.

Tribes and state in Iran . . .
See item no. 239.

The Qashqa'i nomads of Fars.
See item no. 240.

Tribalism and society in Islamic Iran, 1500–1629.
See item no. 242.

Multi-resource nomadism in Iranian Baluchistan.
See item no. 243.

A Persian stronghold of Zoroastrianism.
See item no. 290.

Social work in Iran since the White Revolution.
See item no. 338.

Social mobilization and participation in Iran.
See item no. 341.

The politics of Iran . . .
See item no. 345.

Revolutions and military rule in the Middle East.
See item no. 349.

Islam and politics.
See item no. 354.

An analysis of Fida'i and Mujahidin positions on women's rights.
See item no. 359.

Marxism and other Western fallacies: an Islamic critique.
See item no. 360.

The political elite of Iran.
See item no. 367.

Iran: a revolution in turmoil.
See item no. 368.

The reign of the ayatollahs . . .
See item no. 370.

Iran: from monarchy to republic.
See item no. 371.

Roots of Revolution . . .
See item no. 381.

The Iranian structure for liberation . . .
See item no. 386.

The Iranian Revolution.
See item no. 392.

The revolutionary character of the Iranian *ulama* . . .
See item no. 396.

Society and economics in Islam . . .
See item no. 403.

Iran's foreign policy 1941–1973 . . .
See item no. 425.

Income distribution and taxation laws of Iran.
See item no. 477.

Impact of the oil technology on Iran: 1901–1951.
See item no. 519.

Agricultural and rural development in Iran . . .
See item no. 528.

Agriculture.
See item no. 532.

The Persian land reform: 1962–1966.
See item no. 536.

Land reform and the rural cooperative societies.
See item no. 537.

The development of large-scale farming in Iran: the case of the province of Gorgan.
See item no. 539.

Dam construction in Iran.
See item no. 544.

Social Structure and Social Change. General

An assessment of agricultural development policies in Iran.
See item no. 549.

The impact of urban income per capita on agricultural output . .
See item no. 550.

Employee-supervisor attitudes in banks . . .
See item no. 555.

Labour unions, law and conditions in Iran (1900–1941).
See item no. 559.

Tehran: an urban analysis.
See item no. 569.

The effect of development on the urban family.
See item no. 570.

Planning for social change.
See item no. 573.

Education and social awakening in Iran: 1850–1968.
See item no. 574.

Some socio-religious themes in modern Persian fiction.
See item no. 635.

The school principal.
See item no. 665.

Plague by the West (*Gharbzadegi*).
See item no. 666.

Bride of acacias.
See item no. 672.

The Zoroastrian houses of Yazd.
See item no. 693.

Living tradition of Iran's crafts.
See item no. 715.

International Journal of Middle East Studies (IJMES).
See item no. 763.

MERIP Reports.
See item no. 771.

Iran's politics and government under the Pahlavis . . .
See item no. 779.

Women

318 **Women of Iran: the conflict with fundamentalist Islam.**
Edited by Farah Azari. London: Ithaca Press, 1983. 225p.

Contains six chapters on the question of Iranian women, prepared by Iranian women who were among the founders of the London-based Iranian Women's Solidarity Group. The chapters are as follows: 1, 'Islam's appeal to women in Iran: illusion and reality', by Farah Azari; 2, 'The economic base for the revival of Islam in Iran', by Soraya Afshar; 3, 'Sexuality and women's oppression in Iran', by Farah Azari; 4, 'The attitude of the Iranian left to the women's question', by Soraya Afshar; 5, 'A historical background to the women's movement in Iran', by Sima Bahar; and 6, 'The post-revolutionary women's movement in Iran', by Farah Azari.

319 **Poor women and social consciousness in revolutionary Iran.**
Janet Bauer. In: *Women and revolution in Iran*. Edited by Guity Nashat. Boulder, Colorado: Westview Press, 1983. p. 141–69. bibliog.

A study of women from the poor neighbourhoods, the growth of feminist consciousness, and their active role in the Islamic Revolution.

320 **To veil or not to veil: a matter of protest or policy.**
Anne H. Betteridge. In *Women and revolution in Iran*. Edited by Guity Nashat. Boulder, Colorado: Westview Press, 1983. p. 109–28.

This article's mock-Shakespearean title reveals its content, focusing on the women's veil in the years immediately prior to, and after, the Islamic Revolution as a determinant issue in women's social status, and their role in the Revolution. The study is based on the author's personal observations in Shiraz in the mid- to late 1970s.

321 **Women and the family in Iran.**
Edited by Asghar Fathi. Leiden, The Netherlands: E. J. Brill, 1985. 236p. (Social, Economic and Political Studies of the Middle East, vol. 38).

A collection of thirteen essays on the position of women and the family in Iran. The essays are divided into three parts, namely cultural, historical, and social and case-studies. The situation of women before and after the Islamic Revolution; their status and rights under the secular and religious states; their movements and their place in the modern history of Iran; their position at home and at work; and women of religious minorities are the major themes discussed.

Social Structure and Social Change. Women

322   **Women in Shi'i** *fiqh*: **images through the** *hadith*.
Adele K. Ferdows, Amir H. Ferdows.   In: *Women and revolution in Iran*. Edited by Guity Nashat. Boulder, Colorado: Westview Press, 1983. p. 55–68.
Studies the purported sayings of the prophet Mohammad and those of the twelve Shi'ite Imams, known as *hadith*, to help a better understanding of the origins of the position of women in the contemporary Islamic Republic of Iran.

323   **State ideology and village women.**
Erika Friedl.   In: *Women and revolution in Iran*. Edited by Guity Nashat. Boulder, Colorado: Westview Press, 1983. p. 217–30.
Discusses the views held by a group of peasants, labourers, craftsmen and, in particular, women, from a village in western Iran on the Islamic government's ideology concerning the liberation of the nation from the 'evil yoke' of Western decadence. The article is based on data gathered in 1981.

324   **Fatimeh as a role model in the works of Ali Shari'ati.**
Marcia K. Hermansen.   In: *Women and revolution in Iran*. Edited by Guity Nashat. Boulder, Colorado: Westview Press, 1983. p. 87–96.
A study of Islamic modernist thought and ideas about the role of women and their identity as expressed in *Fātemeh Fātemeh ast* (Fatemeh is Fatemeh) and *Zan-e Mosalmān* (The Muslim woman) by the Islamic sociologist 'Ali Shari'ati (1933–77).

325   **Aliabad women: revolution as religious activity.**
Mary E. Hooglund.   In: *Women and revolution in Iran*. Edited by Guity Nashat. Boulder, Colorado: Westview Press, 1983. p. 171–94. bibliog.
Argues that the majority of women who took part in the Islamic Revolution did not consider their actions to be contradictory to the social and traditional religious norms. Neither did they expect to gain anything or benefit themselves as women. The article is based on a field-work study undertaken in a village near Shiraz, and on interviews with women in Shiraz and elsewhere in Iran from June 1978 to December 1979.

326   **The position of women in Shi'a Iran: views of the** *'ulama*.
Shireen Mahdavi.   In: *Women and the family in the Middle East: new voices of change*. Edited by Elizabeth Warnock Fernea. Austin, Texas: University of Texas Press, 1985. p. 255–68.
Examines the interpretations of the Islamic concept of women by the *'olama*, and presents a picture of the social position of women in Islamic Iran.

327 **Social and economic change in the role of women, 1956–1978.**
S. Kaveh Mirani. In: *Women and revolution in Iran.* Edited by
Guity Nashat. Boulder, Colorado: Westview Press, 1983. p. 69–86.
A study of the social and economic position of women under the period of
economic development between 1956–78. The time-span chosen for the study
relates to the second-fifth medium-term development programmes, the first of
which was launched in 1949 by the Plan and Budget Organization.

328 **Women in the ideology of the Islamic Republic.**
Guity Nashat. In: *Women and revolution in Iran.* Edited by Guity
Nashat. Boulder, Colorado: Westview Press, 1983. p. 195–216.
Attempts to study the ideology of the Islamic Republic towards women, the
policies introduced and women's compliance with these reforms.

329 **Women and revolution in Iran.**
Edited by Guity Nashat. Boulder, Colorado: Westview Press,
1983. 289p.
A collective effort examining the status of Iranian women prior to, and after the
Islamic Revolution. It consists of fifteen essays in three parts. Part one, containing
three essays, covers the historical and religious background of the present status
of women. Part two, with seven essays, is concerned with the social, political and
economic changes affecting the life and position of women during the 20th
century, and the role played by them in the Islamic Revolution. Part three
examines the condition of women since the Revolution and the relevant policies
introduced by the Islamic government.

330 **Status of women in the Qur'an.**
Fazlur Rahman. In: *Women and revolution in Iran.* Edited by
Guity Nashat. Boulder, Colorado: Westview Press, 1983. p. 37–54.
Attempts to demonstrate analytically that the inferior status of women in Muslim
societies is as a result of the prevailing social conditions rather than of the moral
teachings of the Qur'an (Koran), which in the author's view tries to promote their
position.

331 **The women's rights movement in Iran: mutiny, appeasement, and
repression from 1900 to Khomeini.**
Eliz Sanasarian. New York: Praeger, 1982. 156p. bibliog.
The volume was inspired and influenced by the views and attitudes of Iranian
feminists, and analyses the status of women and their rights in 20th-century Iran.
The author tries to identify the earliest stages of the women's rights movement in
Iran, and presents its features in the context of cultural diversity. The volume
contains eight chapters on chronological developments of the women's movement.

332 **The role of women in Iranian development: dynamics of women's condition in Iran.**
Hamideh Sedghi, Ahmad Ashraf. In: *Iran: past, present and future.* Edited by Jane W. Jacqz. New York: Aspen Institute for Humanistic Studies, 1976. p. 201–10.
Studies the role of Iranian women in a period of rapid transition and development during the 1960s and 1970s. The essay looks at the place of women and their conditions in Iranian society, their role in production, and their concern for education and modern politics.

333 **In the shadow of Islam: the women's movement in Iran.**
Azar Tabari, Nahid Yeganeh. London: Zed Press, 1982. 230p.
Examines the position of women in Iranian society in the light of the events and ideas which contributed to the course of the Iranian Revolution. It contains three parts. Part I includes three essays: 1, 'Islam and the struggle for emancipation of Iranian women', by Azar Tabari; 2, 'Women's struggles in the Islamic Republic of Iran', by Nahid Yeganeh; and 3, 'Khomeini's teachings and their implications for Iranian women', by Haleh Afshar. Part II deals with various topics of importance to women, including religious, social and political issues, supported by relevant documents. Part III deals with the women's organizations in Iran which emerged after the 1979 Revolution. A final section offers a chronology of events from 1905–81 with a direct bearing on women's issues, to provide the reader with a general background. There are no indexes.

Behind the veil in Persia and Turkish Arabia . . .
See item no. 56.

Women in pre-revolutionary Iran: an historical overview.
See item no. 189.

Shi'ism and social protest.
See item no. 373.

Iran: essays on a revolution in the making.
See item no. 380.

Women imprisoned in the kingdom of the *mullahs*.
See item no. 407.

Conformity and confrontation . . .
See item no. 619.

Social Services, Health and Welfare

334 **Medical change and the doctor-patient relationship in an Iranian provincial town.**
Byron Joseph Good.   In: *The social sciences and problems of development*. Edited by Khodadad Farmanfarmaian. Princeton, New Jersey: Princeton University Program in Near Eastern Studies, 1976. p. 244–60.
Examines the relationship, or rather the absence of relationship, between the modern doctors and their patients who, in most cases, come from traditional backgrounds. Argues that communication, except for the most simple information about basic symptoms and prescribed medication, is not being achieved between the two.

335 **Geographical distribution guide to endemic diseases of Iran.**
Moosa Hekmat.   Miami, Florida: Field Research Projects, 1970. 43p. 33 maps.
As late as 1970 such endemic diseases as malaria, bilharzia and trachoma still constituted a problem for Iran. This slim volume provides a detailed description of the distribution of these and other endemic diseases in Iran through a number of maps. The density of the population, and tribal movements throughout Iran are also shown.

336 **An Iranian experiment in primary health care, the West Azerbaijan project.**
Edited by Maurice King.   Oxford: Oxford University Press, 1983. 164p. map. (School of Public Health, Tehran, Ministry of Health and Social Welfare, Tehran, and the World Health Organization).
This book is the result of the co-operation of a number of individuals and

105

institutes who, in the early 1970s, investigated social services, health and welfare in Iran, focusing in particular on West Azarbaijan. Other primary health care projects throughout Iran are also investigated, however, and the general achievements are analysed.

337 Family planning in Iran: results of a survey and a mass media campaign.
Samuel S. Lieberman. In: *The population of Iran*. Edited by Jamshid Momeni. Honolulu: East-West Centre, 1977. p 244–74.

A report of a general investigation into family-planning practices in the city and province of Isfahan, based on material collected in the early 1970s. It assesses the family planning services, fertility and birth control, and the campaign of the mass media.

338 Social work in Iran since the White Revolution.
Charles S. Prigmore. Montgomery, Alabama: University of Alabama Press, 1976. 188p. bibliog.

An assessment in four parts of social change in Iran during a period of rapid transition. It reveals the nature of the change, which was neither indigenous nor gradual, but was imposed 'overnight' by the Shah's régime, and is documented mainly by material presented by the students of the Tehran School of Social Work and publications either provided or controlled by the government.

Behind the veil in Persia and Turkish Arabia . . .
See item no. 56.

A medical history of Persian and the eastern Caliphate . . .
See item no. 93.

Safavid medical practice . . .
See item no. 153.

Iran in the service of world peace.
See item no. 179.

Mary Bird in Persia.
See item no. 208.

Factors affecting Moslem natality.
See item no. 220.

Some demographic aspects of a rural area in Iran.
See item no. 221.

The population of Iran: a selection of readings.
See item no. 222.

Population and family planning in Iran.
See item no. 223.

Sociocultural correlates of fertility . . .
See item no. 224.

Social change in a southern province of Iran.
See item no. 307.

Social development in Iran during the Pahlavi era.
See item no. 310.

The Iranian family protection law of 1967 . . .
See item no. 473.

Family planning in post-revolutionary Iran.
See item no. 484.

Family laws of Iran.
See item no. 486.

The effect of development on the urban family.
See item no. 570.

Planning for social change.
See item no. 573.

MERI Report: Iran.
See item no. 770.

Politics

339 The crowd in Iranian politics, 1905–53.
Ervand Abrahamian.   In: *Iran: a revolution in turmoil*. Edited by
Haleh Afshar. London: Macmillan, 1985. p. 121–48.

Demonstrates the historical alliance of the traditional bazaar and the clergy in the
first half of the 20th century. The author argues that the merchant class
mobilized, whenever necessary, the smaller bazaar-traders and craftsmen, while
the clergy enjoyed the support of the poverty-stricken inhabitants of the city
slums.

340 The guerrilla movement in Iran, 1963–77.
Ervand Abrahamian.   In: *Iran: a revolution in turmoil*. Edited by
Haleh Afshar. London: Macmillan, 1985. p. 149–74.

A study of the guerrilla movement in Iran during the 1960s and 1970s focusing on
two major groups – the Mojahedin, which was composed of Shi'ite students from
a traditional middle-class background; and the Fada'iyan, organized by the
educated youth from a modern middle-class background. Two tables are included,
giving the number of guerrillas who died in the period under consideration, their
affiliations, how they died and their occupations.

341 Social mobilization and participation in Iran.
Gholamreza Afkhami, Cyrus Elahi.   In: *Iran: past, present and
future*. Edited by Jane W. Jacqz. New York: Aspen Institute for
Humanistic Studies, 1976. p. 227–41.

An overview of the pattern of the political system and its environment evolved by
the simultaneous operations of the traditional culture and the new political
consciousness. The work also includes a brief examination of the Shah's one-party
system and his Rastakhiz Party which was proclaimed the sole party in the winter
of 1975.

108

342 **Politics in the Gulf.**
M. S. Agwani. New Delhi: Vikas, 1978. 199p. bibliog.
Analyses the political conflicts in the Persian Gulf, including the anti-British riots of the early 1970s. This area, as an oil-producing region, is of particular significance for Iran.

343 **Modernization and changing leadership in Iran.**
Amin Alimard, Cyrus Elahi. In: *Iran: past, present and future.*
Edited by Jane W. Jacqz. New York: Aspen Institute for
Humanistic Studies, 1976. p. 217–25.
A brief, superficial discussion of political leadership and socio-political change in Iran in an historical context. The essay is concerned with the country's political system, its pattern of leadership, the modern administration and the élite in the 1960s and 1970s.

344 **Mysticism and dissent: socioreligious thought in Qajar Iran.**
Mangol Bayat. Syracuse, New York: Syracuse University Press,
1982. 211p. bibliog.
The author argues that, contrary to commonly-held views, Shi'ite political dissent in 19th-century Iran was far less important than popular and intellectual dissent. The book examines the tradition of dissent in Islamic thought in general, and its radicalization in Shi'ite thought, focusing on Sheikhism and Babism for its socialization and politicization. The book concludes with a discussion on the secularization of political dissent and its eventual victory.

345 **The politics of Iran: groups, classes and modernization.**
James Alban Bill. Columbus, Ohio: Charles E. Merrill, 1972.
156p. bibliog.
An objective investigation of the political structure of Iran in the 1960s and 1970s, during a period of transition and modernization. The volume begins with an analysis of the traditional Islamic system of authority, followed by that of the role played by the newly-emerged professional-bureaucratic intelligentsia. In the following chapters the issue of alienation and the structure of the new modernized political system are studied. The book's bibliography includes public documents, unpublished material and Persian sources.

346 **Persian oil: a study in power politics.**
L. P. Elwell-Sutton. London: Lawrence & Wishart, 1955. 335p.
A study of the Persian government's relations with the Anglo-Iranian Oil Company, in an attempt to illuminate the disastrous policies adopted by the British government, while providing a guideline to prevent the disruption of relations elsewhere. It discusses in some detail the role played by Premier Mosaddeq in the Iranian oil nationalization campaign in the 1940s and early 1950s.

347 **Modern Islamic political thought: the response of the Shi'i and Sunni Muslims to the twentieth century.**
Hamid Enayat. London: Macmillan, 1982. 212p.

Studies the major political ideas among Muslims in the 20th century, focusing on those expressed by the Egyptians and Iranians. The introduction attempts to interpret the impact of the traditional heritage on the development of modern thought. The book is then divided into five chapters: 1, 'Shi'ism and Sunnism: conflict and concord'; 2, 'The crisis over the Caliphate'; 3, 'The concept of the Islamic State'; 4, 'Nationalism, democracy and socialism'; and 5, 'Aspects of Shi'i modernism'.

348 **Politics during the sixties: a historical analysis.**
Hafez F. Farmayan. In: *Iran faces the seventies*. Edited by Ehsan Yar-Shater. New York; Washington; London: Praeger, 1971. p. 88–116.

An analytical study of the political history of Iran in the 1960s, focusing on the steps taken by the Shah to modernize and strengthen his system of authority.

349 **Revolutions and military rule in the Middle East.**
George M. Haddad. New York: Speller, vol. I, 1965. 251p.

Presents a comprehensive study of the phenomena of revolution, reform and military rule, covering Iran as well as the three neighbouring countries of Turkey, Afghanistan and Pakistan. Two further volumes were printed in 1971 and 1973 under the same title dealing with revolutionary movements in other Middle Eastern countries in the period between 1936 and 1969.

350 **The Iranian bulletins: the news bulletins of the Committee for the Defence of Political Prisoners in Iran.**
Index on Censorship. London: Index on Censorship, 1979. 119p. map.

A translation of fourteen bulletins, which were originally published in Farsi in Tehran during the turbulent period between April 1978 and January 1979, concerning the condition of human rights in Iran. It includes a preface by Edward Mortimer, a contemporary foreign specialist and leader writer on *The Times* (London).

351 **Capitalism and revolution in Iran.**
Bizhan Jazani. London: Zed Press, 1980. 151p.

Translates a collection of the political writings of Jazani, a revolutionary activist and theoretician who was murdered in prison in the early 1970s while allegedly attempting to escape. The topics included are: 1, 'The history of contemporary Iran'; 2, 'Land reform in modern Iran'; 3, 'Dependent capitalism'; and 4, 'The revolutionary forces'. Also included are a foreword, concerning the history of the Organization of Iranian People's Fada'iyan Guerillas, and a postscript on 'Iran after the fall of the Shah'.

352 **The mind of a monarch.**
R. K. Karanjia. London: Allen & Unwin, 1977. 265p.
A series of interviews with the Shah on various topics of modern politics,
providing at the same time a superficial picture of the history of 20th-century Iran.

353 **Aspects of militancy and quietism in Imami Shi'ism.**
Denis McEoin. In: *British Society for Middle Eastern Studies*
Bulletin, vol. 11, no. 1 (1984), p. 18–27.
A study of the contradictory but co-existing forces of political militancy and
quietism in Shi'ism, with reference to the relevant expressions in religious
literature and movements throughout the history of Islam to the present day.

354 **Islam and politics.**
Middle East Research and Information Project. In: *MERIP*
Reports, vol. 12, no. 1 (Jan. 1982), p. 3–30.
Three interesting articles with 'Islam and politics' as the central theme: 'Iraq's
underground Shi'i movement' by Hanna Batatu; 'Religious ritual and political
struggle in an Iranian village' by Mary Hooglund; and "Ali Shari'ati: ideologue of
the Iranian Revolution' by Ervand Abrahamian. The issue also includes an
interview with Mohammad Sid Ahmed entitled: 'The masses speak the language
of religion to express themselves politically'.

355 **Iran: the new imperialism in action.**
Bahman Nirumand, translated from the German by Leonard
Mins. London; New York: Monthly Review Press, 1969. 189p.
Examines the loss of sovereignty as a result of the policies implemented by the
Shah's régime and the American administration. The new fronts in world politics,
Iran's oil and industry, the Shah's relation with America, the country's business
boom, the police state, and the roots of violence are all covered in detail. A
chronology of political history of Iran since 1900 is also included.

356 **Reza Shah's court minister: Teymourtash.**
Miron Rezun. In: *International Journal of Middle East Studies*,
vol. 12, no. 2 (1980), p. 119–37.
Assesses the political role played by Abdol Hosein Khan Teymourtash, the
powerful court minister of Reza Shah, in introducing progressive social changes
into Iran for which, in the author's view, the illiterate Shah has been wrongly
credited. Teymourtash was dismissed from his position in late 1932, and shortly
after that he was murdered in prison.

357 **Countercoup: the struggle for the control of Iran.**
Kermit Roosevelt. New York; St. Louis, Missouri; San
Francisco; Düsseldorf, FRG; London; Mexico; Sydney; Toronto:
McGraw-Hill, 1979. (Actual date of circulation 1980). 210p.
A narrative account of the 1953 British-engineered and CIA-operated coup which
brought down the nationally-elected government of Mosaddeq, the hero of oil

nationalization in Iran, and reinstated the second Pahlavi monarch as an American puppet. The author, who was in charge of the operation, presented a surprisingly objective view, but the book was withdrawn from sale soon after its publication. A second edition of the volume was released in 1980 with many of the names altered and the more revealing details modified.

358 The rise and fall of the Shah.
Amin Saikal.   Princeton, New Jersey; Guildford, Surrey: Princeton University Press, 1980. 246p. 3 maps. bibliog.

Examines the domestic and foreign policy objectives of the Shah, and the characteristics he exhibited during the course of his rule, focusing on the period from the fall of Mosaddeq in 1953 to the collapse of his régime in 1979. The dependence of the Shah's régime for survival on the United States in the 1950s, and his attempts in the 1970s to transform Iran into a major pro-Western regional power are also analysed in some depth. Divided into two parts and eight chapters, it studies 'The Shah and Iran: between dependence and oil power', and 'The emergence of Iran as a regional power'. Fifteen illustrations are included.

359 An analysis of Fida'i and Mujahidin positions on women's rights.
Eliz Sanasarian.   In: *Women and revolution in Iran.* Edited by Guity Nashat. Boulder, Colorado: Westview Press, 1983. p. 97–108.

A brief sketch of the women's rights issue in Iran, focusing on the attitues of two political groups, the Fada'iyan and the Mojahedin organizations, which operated as guerrilla units in the 1970s in opposition to the Pahlavi régime.

360 Marxism and other Western fallacies: an Islamic critique.
'Ali Shari'ati, translated by R. Campbell.   Berkeley, California: Mizan Press, 1980. 122p.

Consists of a series of lectures by 'Ali Shari'ati on modern political and social issues. The first lecture (p. 15–31) is the translation of a text which was first printed in the state-controlled Tehran daily, *Keyhan*, and later published abroad as a book entitled *Man, Islam and Western schools of thought*. The other lectures included are entitled: 'Modern calamities' (p. 32–48); 'Humanity between Marxism and religion' (p. 49–96); and 'Mysticism, equality and freedom' (p. 97–122).

361 The Islamic movement: a system's approach.
Kalim Siddiqui.   London: Open Press in association with the Muslim Institute, 1980. 24p.

The author argues that as the Muslim community is supposedly a united body called 'the Ummah', it should not be as divided and fragmented as it is. The answer to this, in his view, is a single Islamic movement.

362 **Capital development and land reform in Khuzistan, Iran.**
Susan P. Silsby. In: *RIPEH: Review of Iranian Political
Economy and History*, vol. 4, no. 1 (Spring 1980) p. 34–67. map.

Attempts to fill the gap that, in the author's view, was created by the absence of
unbiased literature and reports in the American press concerning the involvement
of the US government in the political and economic affairs of Iran during the
Shah's reign after the overthrow of Premier Mosaddeq in 1953. It concentrates on
the American involvement in capital development and mechanized agriculture in
Khuzestan province in Iran.

363 **Land reform and politics: a comparative analysis.**
Hung-Chao Tai. Berkeley, California; Los Angeles; London:
University of California Press, 1974. 479p. 2 maps.

A comparative and objective analysis of the primarily political aspects of the land-
reform programmes in eight developing countries. Rural political participation,
political stability and the relationship between reform and communism are studied
generally, while in the case of Iran, the idea that the initiation of land reform
depends upon the perceived need of the élite for political legitimacy is a major
topic discussed in depth. The other countries studied are Taiwan, the Philippines,
India, Pakistan, Egypt, Colombia and Mexico. Following three introductory and
informative chapters, the book includes a further eleven chapters in two parts.
Part one deals with the political processes and part two investigates the political
effects of land reform. The volume contains some useful appendixes, including
the 1962 Land Reform Law of Iran and the 1964 implementation regulations
(p. 494–99).

364 **The communist movement in Iran.**
Sepehr Zabih. Berkeley, California; Los Angeles: University of
California Press, 1966. 259p. bibliog.

Assesses the development of communism in Iran prior to the mid-1960s, firstly as
a case-study of the communist doctrine of social and national revolution in the
East, and secondly as an indigenous phenomenon which influenced Iranian
politics. By investigating the development of communism in Iran, the interplay
between traditional and modern forces, such as Islamic religion and nationalism,
are brought into light as impediments or catalysts of communism. The role played
by the Tudeh Party in Iranian politics claims a large proportion of the book.

365 **The Mossadegh era: roots of the Iranian Revolution.**
Sepehr Zabih. Chicago: Lake View Press, 1982. 169p.

This book focuses on the role of Premier Mosaddeq (1951–53) in modern politics
and the history of Iran. The author examines Mosaddeq in power and the
domestic problems his country faced at that time. The volume also includes a
postscript in which Mosaddeq's legacy for the 1979 Revolution is discussed.

Politics

366 The left in contemporary Iran.
Sepehr Zabih. Beckenham, Kent, England: Croom Helm, 1986. 207p. bibliog.

Outlines the emergence and development of the left in 20th-century Iran. It examines the historical perspective, the Soviet connection and different leftist movements divided into the old – the Tudeh Party; the new – the Mojahedin and the Fada'iyan; and the militant – the League of Iranian Communists.

367 The political elite of Iran.
Marvin Zonis. Princeton, New Jersey: Princeton University Press, 1971. 361p.

A sociological analysis of Iran's political élite under the Shah and their inter-relations. The composition of the political élite and the counter-élite, their social backgrounds and orientations, and the role played by the Shah in such an environment, are some of the major topics investigated.

Iran: religion, politics and society.
See item no. 12.

Area handbook for Iran.
See item no. 16.

An historical geography of Iran.
See item no. 27.

Atlas of geographical maps and historical documents on the Persian Gulf.
See item no. 47.

British interests in the Persian Gulf, 1747–1780.
See item no. 144.

The shadow of God and the Hidden Imam . . .
See item no. 145.

Russia and Iran, 1780–1828.
See item no. 146.

An enquiry into the outbreak of the second Russo-Persian war, 1826–28.
See item no. 147.

Persia and the Persian question.
See item no. 152.

The fall of the Safavi dynasty and the Afghan occupation of Persia.
See item no. 163.

Iran between two revolutions.
See item no. 172.

Religion and politics in contemporary Iran . . .
See item no. 173.

The modernization of Iran: 1921–1941.
See item no. 175.

The Persian revolution of 1905–1909.
See item no. 177.

Nationalist trends in Iran, 1921–1926.
See item no. 185.

The assassination of the Amin al-Sultān . . .
See item no. 186.

Iran under the Pahlavis.
See item no. 187.

The history of modern Iran, an interpretation.
See item no. 190.

The vanished Imam . . .
See item no. 192.

Mizra Malkum Khān . . .
See item no. 193.

Mohammad Mossadegh: a political biography.
See item no. 195.

The fall of the Shah.
See item no. 197.

Sayyid Jamal ad-Din 'al-Afghani': a political biography.
See item no. 201.

The Shah's story.
See item no. 205.

The pride and the fall: Iran 1974–1979.
See item no. 206.

In the service of the peacock throne . . .
See item no. 207.

Mission to Iran.
See item no. 211.

Riza Shah Pahlavi . . .
See item no. 213.

Poverty and revolution in Iran . . .
See item no. 230.

The English amongst the Persians during the Qajar period, 1787–1921.
See item no. 238.

Tribes and state in Iran . . .
See item no. 239.

Politics

Islam in transition: Muslim perspectives.
See item no. 271.

Islam and the plight of modern man.
See item no. 274.

Islam in the world.
See item no. 279.

The legacy of Islam.
See item no. 280.

On the sociology of Islam.
See item no. 312.

Iran: precapitalism, capitalism and revolution.
See item no. 314.

Fatimeh as a role model in the works of Ali Shari'ati.
See item no. 324.

Women and revolution in Iran.
See item no. 329.

The role of women in Iranian development . . .
See item no. 332.

In the shadow of Islam . . .
See item no. 333.

Iran: a revolution in turmoil.
See item no. 368.

The reign of the ayatollahs . . .
See item no. 370.

The Iranian Revolution: triumph or tragedy?
See item no. 376.

Iran – the continuing struggle for power.
See item no. 377.

Roots of Revolution . . .
See item no. 381.

Revolution in Iran . . .
See item no. 383.

Economic origins of the Iranian Revolution.
See item no. 384.

The Iranian structure for liberation . . .
See item no. 386.

The wrath of Allah . . .
See item no. 387.

116

Religion and politics in the Middle East.
See item no. 393.

Islam and development . . .
See item no. 395.

The revolutionary character of the Iranain *ulama* . . .
See item no. 396.

Religious ritual and political struggle in an Iranian village.
See item no. 397.

Militant Islam.
See item no. 398.

Security in the Persian Gulf 1 . . .
See item no. 433.

The United States and Iran: a documentary history.
See item no. 440.

The United States-Iranian relationship 1948–1978 . . .
See item no. 443.

Security in the Persian Gulf 4 . . .
See item no. 444.

The USSR in Iran . . .
See item no. 447.

Iran's international position . . .
See item no. 449.

Debâcle: the American failure in Iran.
See item no. 453.

Russia and the West in Iran . . .
See item no. 454.

The United States and Iran . . .
See item no. 455.

The Iranian crisis of 1941 – the actors: Britain, Germany and the Soviet Union.
See item no. 456.

Iran: the impact of United States interests and policies 1941–1954.
See item no. 458.

International and legal problems of the Gulf.
See item no. 459.

The Gulf and the search for strategic stability . . .
See item no. 462.

Politics

The Gulf War.
See item no. 468.

Rim of prosperity. The Gulf: a survey.
See item no. 469.

The problems encountered in establishing an Islamic republic in Iran . . .
See item no. 481.

Political process and institutions in Iran . . .
See item no. 482.

Iran's armed forces under the Pahlavi dynasty.
See item no. 491.

Iran: economic development under dualistic conditions.
See item no. 495.

Economics of oil.
See item no. 499.

The political economy of modern Iran . . .
See item no. 504.

The Gulf in the early 20th century . . .
See item no. 505.

Expenditure of oil revenue . . .
See item no. 508.

Economic development and revolutionary upheavals in Iran.
See item no. 509.

The political environment of economic planning in Iran, 1971–1983 . . .
See item no. 510.

Development of the Iranian oil industry . . .
See item no. 516.

Iran's petroleum policy . . .
See item no. 518.

Shahanshah of Iran on oil: Tehran agreement – background and perspectives.
See item no. 521.

The evolution of Iranian oil policy, 1925–1975.
See item no. 522.

The Persian land reform: 1962–1966.
See item no. 536.

The Persian Railway Syndicate and British railway policy in Iran.
See item no. 547.

Workers say no to the Shah . . .
See item no. 560.

High level manpower in Iran: from hidden conflict to crisis.
See item no. 561.

Iran: from religious dispute to revolution.
See item no. 576.

Higher education and social change: problems and prospects.
See item no. 578.

Technical assistance in theory and practice . . .
See item no. 579.

Transfer of technology and development . . .
See item no 582.

The political poetry of modern Persia.
See item no. 590.

The poetics of politics: commitment in modern Persian literature.
See item no. 594.

Protest and perish . . .
See item no. 616.

Power, prudence, and print: censorship and Simin Daneshvar.
See item no. 620.

British Society for Middle Eastern Studies Bulletin (BRISMES).
See item no. 761.

International Journal of Middle East Studies (IJMES).
See item no. 763.

Iranian Studies . . .
See item no. 765.

Khamsin.
See item no. 766.

MERI report: Iran.
See item no. 770.

MERIP Reports.
See item no. 771.

Middle East Newsletters . . .
See item no 772.

The Iranian opposition to the Shah.
See item no. 775.

Iran's politics and government under the Pahlavis . . .
See item no. 779.

Ayatollah Khomeini and the Iranian Revolution, 1979– .

General

368 **Iran: a revolution in turmoil.**
Edited by Haleh Afshar. London: Macmillan, 1985. 253p.

A collection of ten articles divided into three parts, dealing with the Islamic Revolution in its historical context of national discontent. Part one includes five articles focusing on economic developments; part two, containing three articles, examines the expression of political discontent, the forces of opposition and the Iranian armed troops used against the rebels. The last section contains two articles, the first of which is an English translation of a selection of speeches by Ayatollah Mortaza Motahhari, the theoretician of the Islamic Revolution. The final chapter is an assessment of the policies and shortcomings of the Islamic government.

369 **Tell the American people: perspectives on the Iranian Revolution.**
Edited by David H. Albert. Philadelphia: Movement for a New Society, 1980. 2nd ed. 210p.

A collection of essays on various aspects of the 1979 Islamic Revolution, dealing mainly with the internal conditions before and after the Revolution. It includes articles on political, economic, social, religious and historical topics, as well as arms and the Shah, human rights and international law. Most of the essays have previously been printed elsewhere. The volume's first edition appeared only a few months earlier, in June 1980.

370 **The reign of the ayatollahs: Iran and the Islamic Revolution.**
Shaul Bakhash. London: Unwin, 1986. 2nd ed. 276p.

An account of the Islamic Revolution based on the author's personal observation and study of events. He examines the fall of the Shah's régime in 1979, the establishment of the Islamic Republic, Premier Bazargan's provisional government, the election of the first president, Banisadr, and his loss of power in June 1981. Bakhash also examines the social, political and economic issues of the period.

371   **Iran: from monarchy to republic.**
Edited by Günter Barthel.   Berlin, GDR: Akademie-Verlag, 1983. 144p. bibliog. (Asia, Africa, Latin America, special issue 12).
A collection of ten articles concentrating on contradictory developments in Iranian society prior to, and after, the 1979 Islamic Revolution. The authors are mainly employed at the Academy of Sciences of the GDR in Berlin, the Academy for State and Law in Potsdam-Babelsberg, the Humboldt University in Berlin and the Karl Marx University in Leipzig. They present here, in addition, the results of their research, which was based on a materialist social analysis.

372   **The state and revolution in Iran, 1962–1982.**
Hossein Bashiriyeh.   London: Croom Helm; New York: St. Martin's Press, 1984. 185p.
Studies the rise of Islamic nationalism in the 1960s, 1970s and 1980s. It assesses the structure of the old régime, the rise of revolutionary ideology, and the outbreak of a revolution stimulated by the liberalization of the Shah's economically and dictatorially weak régime. The author also deals with the new régime's attempt to reconstitute the state, and the rule of the fundamentalist clergy.

373   **Shi'ism and social protest.**
Edited by Juan R. I. Cole, Nikki R. Keddie.   London; New Haven, Connecticut: Yale University Press, 1986. 301p. map.
A collection of eleven articles on Shi'ism, focusing on the widespread involvement of the Shi'ia in contemporary movements of social protest throughout the Islamic world. While Iran is referred to generally throughout the book, three articles are exclusively concerned with the Iranian Revolution, her foreign policy and the status of women in the Islamic government.

374   **The Iranian Revolution of 1978–79: potential implications for major countries in the area.**
Robert Ghobad Darius.   In: *Revolution in Iran: a reappraisal.* Edited by Enver M. Koury, Charles G. MacDonald. Hyattsville, Maryland: Institute of Middle Eastern and North African Affairs, 1982. p. 30–48.
Examines the roots of the Islamic Revolution and its effect on major domestic and foreign policies, including its potential implications for the Middle Eastern countries such as Afghanistan, Egypt, Saudi Arabia, Iraq and Turkey. The volume also analyses the impact of the Revolution on the ethnic minorities, on OPEC and on the PLO.

375 **Hostage to Khomeini.**
Robert Dreyfuss. New York: New Benjamin Franklin House
Publishing Company, 1980. 232p.
A pro-American interpretation of the Iranian Revolution. In the author's view it
was instigated by British Military Intelligence, who installed Khomeini by a
carefully-orchestrated operation, relying on the support of Iran's unfortunate
peasant population and the nation's youth. The author finds similarity between
the mythical Wizard of Oz and the 'turbaned magician' Khomeini, and suggests
that the 'Khomeini disease' will destroy the countries of the Muslim world. Its
prevention, he says, depends 'on the will of the American citizenry'. He would
like every American citizen to buy two copies of this book, and send one to their
representative in Congress!

376 **The Iranian Revolution: triumph or tragedy?**
L. P. Elwell-Sutton. In: *The security of the Persian Gulf*. Edited
by Hossein Amirsadeghi. London: Croom Helm, 1981. p. 231–54.
The author states that Iran has undergone three revolutions during the present
century: the 1906 constitutional revolution; the 1963 White Revolution; and the
1979 Islamic Revolution. But, he argues, none of them fit the pattern of a
revolution in its conventional sense. To justify his argument, he examines the
conditions leading up to the Islamic Revolution, relates these events to earlier
conditions, and briefly studies the achievements and failures of the Islamic
government.

377 **Iran – the continuing struggle for power.**
Hugo Gordon. Wisbech, Cambridgeshire, England: Menas Press,
1984. 69p. map.
Examines developments in post-revolutionary Iran, focusing on the political and
economic structure, and the country's foreign affairs. Amongst the sensitive topics
included are the succession of Khomeini and the war with Iraq. A study of the
forces of opposition is also included.

378 **Revolution in Iran: the politics of countermobilization.**
Jerrold D. Green. New York: Praeger, 1982. 151p. bibliog.
A range of contradictions began to develop in Iranian society under the régime of
the Shah, and it is this set of contradictions which the author believes to have
been the cause of the disintegration of the long-lasting Iranian monarchy. The
work includes an appendix on the chronology of the Iranian Revolution
(p. 152–65).

379 **The return of the Ayatollah: the Iranian Revolution from Mossadeq
to Khomeini.**
Mohamed Heikal. London: André Deutsch, 1981. 209p.
A leading Middle Eastern journalist and confidant of Jamal Abd al-Naser, Heikal
was in contact with the key protagonists of the Shah's régime. He also interviewed
the Ayatollah Khomeini in Paris and in Iran. In this volume he provides a
narrative account, for the general reader, of Iran's modern history, focusing in

particular on the Islamic Revolution. A second imprint of this book was published in 1982 by Pantheon Books in New York, entitled *Iran: the untold story*.

380 **Iran: essays on a revolution in the making.**
Edited by Ahmad Jabbari, Robert Olson.   Lexington, Kentucky: Mazda Publishers, 1981. 214p.
A collection of seven articles presented to a symposium entitled 'Iran: a revolution in the making' held at the Centre College of Kentucky in mid-June 1979. The articles provide a background to the Revolution and are entitled: 1, 'Background to the Iranian Revolution: imperialism, dictatorship, and nationalism, 1872 to 1979', by Thomas Ricks; 2, 'Development of political institutions in Iran and scenarios for the future', by G. Hossein Razi; 3, 'A critical assessment of 'Ali Shari'ati's theory of revolution', by Soheyl Amini; 4, 'Women in Islam', by Shahin Etezadi Tabatabai; 5, 'Revolution, Islam, and contemporary Persian literature', by Michael Hillmann; 6, 'Revolutionary struggle over economy: some experienced benchmarks', by Allan N. Williams; and 7, 'Economic factors in Iran's Revolution: poverty, inequality, and inflation', by Ahmad Jabbari.

381 **Roots of Revolution: an interpretative history of modern Iran.**
Nikki R. Keddie.   London; New Haven, Connecticut: Yale University Press, 1981. 298p. map. bibliog.
The volume includes nine chapters, of which the first seven are based on the author's previous studies on religion and society in Iran. The eighth chapter was contributed by the French scholar Yann Richard and analyses the emergence and development of modernism in Iran with reference to intellectual and literary trends till 1960, and the revival of Shi'ite thought in the following decades. The final chapter deals with forces of opposition (secular, religious and guerrilla) and the Revolution.

382 **The Ayatollah revolution: lack of consensus on fundamentals.**
Enver M. Koury.   In: *Revolution in Iran: a reappraisal*. Edited by Enver M. Koury, Charles G. Macdonald. Hyattsville, Maryland: Institute of Middle Eastern and North African Affairs, 1982. p. 61–87. map.
Attempts to show that while the Iranians were once united in their anti-Pahlavi Islamic Revolution, the community is now deeply divided and is proving a serious threat to Iran's integrity. The author analyses the composition of Iranian society and post-revolutionary communal interests, and includes two tables showing the construction of the Iranian social system and its population.

383 **Revolution in Iran: a reappraisal.**
Edited by Enver M. Koury, Charles G. MacDonald.   Hyattsville, Maryland: Institute of Middle Eastern and North African Affairs, 1982. 110p.
A collection of six articles examining the 1979 Islamic Revolution. 1, 'Iran's

foreign policy: perspectives and projections', by Rouhollah K. Ramazani; 2, 'The Iranian Revolution of 1978–79: potential implications for major countries in the area', by Robert Ghobad Darius; 3, 'Iran as a political variable: patterns and prospects', by Charles G. MacDonald; 4, 'The Ayatollah Revolution: lack of consensus on fundamentals', by Enver M. Koury; 5, 'US security in the Persian Gulf: an assessment', by Lisa deFilippis; 6, 'Reactions to Iran's Revolution: the search for security', by Charles G. MacDonald. Articles are given separately.

384 **Economic origins of the Iranian Revolution.**
Robert E. Looney. New York; Oxford; Toronto; Sydney; Paris; Frankfurt, FRG: Pergamon Press, 1982. 284p. bibliog.
Following his earlier forecast about the economic situation in *Iran at the end of the century* (q.v.), the author seeks to identify the economic origins and political dimensions of the upheaval in Iran before the establishment of the Islamic Republic. He includes sections on the historical background, some areas of development and economic conditions, plans and policies.

385 **Iran as a political variable: patterns and prospects.**
Charles G. MacDonald. In: *Revolution in Iran: a reappraisal.* Edited by Enver M. Koury, Charles G. MacDonald. Hyattsville, Maryland: Institute of Middle Eastern and North African Affairs, 1982. p. 49–60.
Investigates the Iranian revolutionary policy through an examination of the present political relationships in the Persian Gulf. It also deals with the militant ideology of revolution instigated by the Islamic government of Iran.

386 **The Iranian structure for liberation: socio-historical roots to the Islamic Revolution.**
Ali-Akbar Mahdi. In: *RIPEH: Review of Iranian Political Economy and History*, vol. 4, no. 1 (Spring 1980), p. 1–33.
Examines the social, political and economic roots of the 1979 Islamic Revolution in Iran in general, and the reinstatement of the Shah following the 1953 American coup in particular. The author focuses on the Shah's so-called White Revolution, the land-reform policy and the subsequent religious riots in 1963. Social life and culture, social class structure, economy and industry, agriculture and bureaucracy are some of the issues covered.

387 **The wrath of Allah: Islamic Revolution and reaction in Iran.**
Ramy Nima. London; Sydney: Pluto Press, 1983. 170p.
This book on the Islamic Revolution is divided into three parts, starting with a brief background to foreign domination and economics, and the major social and political developments of modern Iran. Part two examines the consolidation of the Shah's dictatorship, the social forces of opposition, the Revolution and the overthrow of the Pahlavi régime. Part three is concerned with Khomeini's Islamic order and theocracy, the revolutionary government's economic chaos, the struggle of national minorities and the Iran-Iraq war. A chronology of political events in Iran from 1891–1982 is included.

388 **The Islamic Revolution: achievements, obstacles and goals.**
Kalim Siddiqui, Iqbal Asaria, Abd al-Rahim Ali, Ali
Afrouz. London: Open Press in association with the Muslim
Institute, 1980. 48p.

A collection of four essays on the Islamic Revolution in Iran assessing its
achievements and problems, its impact on the Muslim political awakening and on
the Islamic movements, and its treatment of the counter-revolutionary forces.

389 **Inside the Iranian Revolution.**
John D. Stempel. Bloomington, Indiana: Indiana University
Press, 1981. 332p.

Examines the progress of political opposition in Iran during the last few years of
the Shah's reign; the dawn of the Islamic era; and the significance of the Iranian
Revolution. The author was in Iran during that period, and personally observed
the development of events in 1975–79. Amongst the topics discussed are the role
played by Americans in Iran in the 20th century, the hostage crisis, and the Gulf
War.

Religion and politics in contemporary Iran . . .
See item no. 173.

Women in pre-revolutionary Iran: an historical overview.
See item no. 189.

The fall of the Shah.
See item no. 197.

Iran's men of destiny.
See item no. 199.

The Shah's story.
See item no. 205.

The pride and the fall: Iran 1974–1979.
See item no. 206.

Mission to Iran.
See item no. 211.

The spirit of Allah . . .
See item no. 212.

Poverty and revolution in Iran . . .
See item no. 230.

Tribes and state in Iran . . .
See item no. 239.

Iran: precapitalism, capitalism and revolution.
See item no. 314.

Women of Iran: the conflict with fundamentalist Islam.
See item no. 318.

Women in Shi'i *fiqh*: images through the *hadith*.
See item no. 322.

State ideology and village women.
See item no. 323.

The position of women in Shi'a Iran: views of the *'ulama*.
See item no. 326.

Women and revolution in Iran.
See item no. 329.

The Mossadegh era . . .
See item no. 365.

Iranian foreign policy since 1979 . . .
See item no. 419.

Iran since the Revolution . . .
See item no. 428.

The security of the Persian Gulf.
See item no. 431.

Security in the Persian Gulf 1 . . .
See item no. 433.

Oil and security in the Arabian Gulf.
See item no. 434.

The Gulf in the 1980s.
See item no. 439.

Debâcle: the American failure in Iran.
See item no. 453.

The United States and Iran: the patterns of influence.
See item no. 455.

Paved with good intentions . . .
See item no. 457.

The Gulf and the search for strategic stability . . .
See item no. 462.

Conflict in the Persian Gulf.
Se item no. 463.

The Middle East from transition to development.
See item no. 464.

Revolution and war in the Persian Gulf.
See item no. 467.

Constitution of the Islamic Republic of Iran.
See item no. 472.

The Islamic consultative assembly of the Islamic Republic of Iran.
See item no. 476.

The problems encountered in establishing an Islamic republic in Iran . . .
See item no. 481.

Family planning in post-revolutionary Iran.
See item no. 484.

The army.
See item no. 489.

Iran's armed forces under the Pahlavi dynasty.
See item no. 491.

Ravaged and reborn: the Iranian army, 1982.
See item no. 492.

Economic development and revolutionary upheavals in Iran.
See item no. 509.

The political environment of economic planning in Iran, 1971–1983 . . .
See item no. 510.

Revolution and energy policy in Iran . . .
See item no. 517.

Iran's petroleum policy . . .
See item no. 518.

Land and revolution in Iran, 1960–1980.
See item no. 535.

High level manpower in Iran: from hidden conflict to crisis.
See item no. 561.

Iranian oilworkers in the 1978–79 Revolution.
See item no. 563.

Iran: from religious dispute to revolution.
See item no. 576.

The mantle of the prophet.
See item no. 577.

Sorraya in a coma.
See item no. 673.

Religious ideology

390 The Iranian theocracy.
Haleh Afshar. In: *Iran: a revolution in turmoil*. Edited by Haleh Afshar. London: Macmillan, 1985. p. 220–43.

A critical analysis of the views expressed by Ayatollah Khomeini on various issues facing the Islamic government, paying particular attention to economic matters.

391 The Islamic Revolution in Iran.
Hamid Algar, edited by Kalim Siddiqui. London: Open Press 1980. 69p. (Muslim Institute, London).

Contains a four-lecture course given by Hamid Algar in July 1979 at the Muslim Institute in London. It examines the background to the understanding of the Islamic movement in the past, present and future. The titles of the lectures are as follows: 1, 'Iran and Shi'ism'; 2, 'Ayatollah Khomeini: the embodiment of a tradition'; 3, 'Islam as ideology: the thought of Ali Shari'ati'; 4, '1398–1399 H: the year of revolution'. Each lecture is followed by the text of a recorded discussion.

392 The Iranian Revolution.
Richard W. Cottam. In: *Shi'ism and social protest*. Edited by Juan R. I. Cole, Nikki R. Keddie. New Haven; London: Yale University Press, 1986. p. 55–87.

Investigates the social and ideological aspects of the Iranian Revolution against its historical background. The author attempts to analyse and see how justifiable the term 'revolution' is for the change of ruling élite in Iran.

393 Religion and politics in the Middle East.
Edited by Michael Curtis. Boulder, Colorado: Westview Press, 1981. 362p. bibliog.

Contains twenty-four articles investigating various Islamic and political issues in general (articles 1–5) and the major problems of each Middle Eastern country in particular. Emphasis is placed on the different ethnic and religious divisional bodies, and on attempts being made by them to overcome the diversities between modern government and traditionalist practices. The revival of Islam, nationalism and a comparison of the political characters of Judaism and Islam are among the major issues discussed in the general part of the book. Iran is covered in Part III, with two articles concerning the problem of sovereignty in a Shi'ite state and Khomeini's Islamic republic.

394 Iran: Khumaini's concept of the 'guardianship of the jurisconsult'.
Hamid Enayat. In: *Islam in the political process*. Edited by James P. Piscatori. Cambridge, England: Cambridge University Press, 1983. p. 160–80.

Examines the nature of the régime set up by the 1979 Islamic Revolution in Iran, dealing with the issue of authority which is believed by some *'olama* to be the legitimate right of only those *'olama* who have attained the highest theological position. According to Shi'ite doctrine, such an *'alem* is the only person legitimately allowed to act as ultimate ruler in an Islamic community.

395 **Islam and development: religion and sociopolitical change.**
Edited by John L. Esposito. Syracuse, New York: Syracuse University Press, 1980. 254p.

Studies the role of Islam in a period of change. The work contains eleven papers covering a range of Islamic issues in different countries. The paper on Iran is entitled 'Islam in Pahlavi and post-Pahlavi Iran: a cultural revolution?' by Mangol Bayat, p. 87–106.

396 **The revolutionary character of the Iranian *ulama*: wishful thinking or reality.**
Willem M. Floor. In: *International Journal of Middle East Studies*, vol. 12, no. 4 (1980), p. 501–24.

An analytical study of the Shi'ite religious leaders' perception of the social, political and economic structure of Iranian society. This perception, in the author's view, does not differ basically from that of the secular power élite, and Floor proposes that the revolutionary character ascribed to the Shi'ite *'olama* in Iran is only a myth.

397 **Religious ritual and political struggle in an Iranian village.**
Mary Hooglund. *MERIP Reports*, vol. 12, no. 1 (Jan. 1982). p. 10–17.

A social investigation of the part played by religious activities and rituals in the political struggles of a village outside Shiraz in south-west Iran. The article is based on the author's field-research, undertaken in Iran from June 1978 to December 1979. It assesses the increasing consolidation of power by the Shah's central government, and the decline of the significance of religious rituals and activities after the land reform of the early 1960s. These are seen as contributory factors to the change of conditions in the village, and in the villagers' attitudes during and after the Islamic Revolution.

398 **Militant Islam.**
G. H. Jansen. London; Sydney: Pan Books, 1981. 3rd ed. 213p.

Assesses the militant role of Islam during the last two centuries and discusses the idea that the 1970s marked the resurgence of Islamic militancy. Jansen attempts to illustrate the role played by such traditionalists as the Ayatollah Khomeini and General Zia in the new wave of Islamic movement.

399 **Islam and Revolution: writings and declarations of Imam Khomeini.**
Ruhollah Khomeini, translated and annotated by Hamid Algar. Berkeley, California: Mizan Press, 1981. 434p.

An English-language anthology of the writings and speeches of Ayatollah Khomeini on the Islamic Revolution and government. Two interviews which the translator, a converted British Muslim, was granted by Khomeini in 1978 and 1980 are also included.

400 A clarification of questions: an unabridged translation of *'Resaleh Towzih al-Masael'*.
Ruhollah Mousavi Khomeini, translated by J. Borujerdi.
Boulder, Colorado; London: Westview Press, 1984. 414p.

This is a translation of Ayatollah Khomeini's treatise which is meant to guide the Shi'ite believers in their religious duties and to provide answers to all aspects of life's questions and needs. The translation includes some introductory notes and supporting appendixes. There is also a useful subject index.

401 The nature of the Islamic Revolution.
Morteza Motahhari. In: *Iran: a revolution in turmoil*. Edited by Haleh Afshar. London: Macmillan, 1985. p. 201–19.

Extracts from the Ayatollah Motahhari's speeches, highlighting the theoretical ideology of the Islamic Revolution presented by the clergy. The author argues that the Islamic Revolution in Iran was supported by people from different social classes because of its Islamic nature, which is formulated to serve the interests of all.

402 Islamic values and world view: Khomeyni on man, the state and international politics.
Farhang Rajaee. New York; Lanham, Maryland; London: University Press of America, 1983. 129p. bibliog. (Exxon Education Foundation funded series (American Values Viewed Through Other Cultures), vol. 13).

An objective analysis of the origins and development of Khomeini's view of man, the state and international politics. The volume examines all Khomeini's works in order to ascertain his deliberate intention viewed in the context of his overall philosophy. It also includes a chapter on the political biography of Khomeini.

403 Society and economics in Islam: writings and declarations of Ayatullah Sayyid Mahmud Taleghani.
Sayyid Mahmud Taleghani, translated by R. Campbell.
Berkeley, California: Mizan Press, 1982. 218p. (Contemporary Islamic Thought, Persian Series).

An English-language anthology of the writings of Ayatollah Taleghani, a religious leader of the 1979 Islamic Revolution in Iran. It includes an introduction by Hamid Algar, and a bibliography of Taleghani's works.

Changes in charismatic authority in Qajar Shi'ism.
See item no. 273.

Women in the ideology of the Islamic Republic.
See item no. 328.

The Islamic movement: a system's approach.
See item no. 361.

Human rights

404 **Law and human rights in the Islamic Republic of Iran.**
Amnesty International.   London: Amnesty International Index,
1980. 216p.
A human rights report covering the events which took place during the first seven
months after the Islamic Revolution in February 1979. The Islamic law on human
rights, the International Human Rights Law, the Universal Declaration of Human
Rights, and the International Covenant on Civil and Political Rights are outlined
in the introduction, which also presents some useful background information.
Post-revolutionary events form the bulk of the book, and are categorized under
three headings: arrests; revolutionary tribunals; and offences and penalties. An
examination of the laws forms the final chapter, followed by five appendixes, of
which the first provides a list of 438 cases of executions.

405 **Iran: briefing.**
Amnesty International.   London: Amnesty International
Publications, 1987. 12p. map.
This briefing is part of Amnesty International's campaign for protecting human
rights, and is confined to human rights violation in Iran based on the United
Nations Declaration of Human Rights. It presents moving stories and pictures of
arbitrary arrests, torture and executions.

406 **Iran, violations of human rights: documents sent by Amnesty
International to the Government of the Islamic Republic of Iran.**
Amnesty International.   London: Amnesty International
Publications, 1987. 94p. map.
This special volume of Amnesty International Publications comprises three
chapters. The first two are the texts of memoranda sent by Amnesty International
on 8 August 1986 and on 20 November 1986 to the Government of the Islamic
Republic of Iran. They are concerned with political arrest and imprisonment,
torture, the right to a fair trial, judicial punishments, and the death penalty and
executions. The third chapter includes testimonies given to Amnesty International
representatives by former prisoners of conscience and political prisoners.

407 **Women imprisoned in the kingdom of the *mullahs*.**
Cynthia Brown Dwyer.   In: *Women and revolution in Iran*. Edited
by Guity Nashat. Boulder, Colorado: Westview Press, 1983.
p. 263–84.
Provides an account of the effect of the Iranian Revolution on a few hundred,
mostly political, women prisoners who were serving varying lengths of
imprisonment in Evin prison, Tehran.

Ayatollah Khomeini and the Iranian Revolution, 1979– .
The hostage crisis

408 **Iran's secret pogrom: the conspiracy to wipe out the Baha'is.**
Geoffrey Nash.   Suffolk, England: Neville Spearman, 1982. 136p.
A religious protest against the political attempts made by the Islamic Republic to rid Iran of Baha'ism. It is supported by numerous illustrations and three appendixes.

409 **A cry from the heart: the Baha'is in Iran.**
William Sears.   Oxford: George Ronald, 1982. 219p.
Provides an account of the sufferings of the Baha'is under the Islamic government in Iran.

Twenty-three years . . .
See item no. 194.

Human rights and the legal system in Iran.
See item no. 474.

The problems encountered in establishing an Islamic republic in Iran, 1979–1981.
See item no. 481.

The Iranian working class . . .
See item no. 558.

Labour unions and autocracy in Iran.
See item no. 562.

God's shadow: prison poems.
See item no. 667.

The hostage crisis

410 **The biggest deal.**
Roy Assersohn.   London: Methuen, 1982. 342p.
A narrative account of the 1979 Islamic Revolution, aimed at the general public. It includes a chronology of events from 1 January 1978, when the Shah received President Jimmy Carter in Tehran, to 20 January 1981, when the hostage crisis was over.

411 **The Iran-United States Claims Tribunal; 1981–1983.**
Edited by Richard B. Lillich.   Charlottesville, Virginia: University Press of Virginia, 1984. 156p.
A study of the arbitral Iran-United States Claims Tribunal, established in January

Ayatollah Khomeini and the Iranian Revolution, 1979– .
The hostage crisis

1981 following the Claims Settlement Agreement which was meant to secure the release of fifty-two American hostages being held by Iran. It includes seven chapters, originally delivered as papers at the Seventh Sokol Colloquium on Private International Law held at the University of Virginia School of Law in April 1983. The titles and authors are as follows: 1, 'Developments at the Iran-United States Claims Tribunal: 1981–1983' by David P. Stewart and Laura B. Sherman; 2, 'The Iran-United States Claims Tribunal: private rights and state responsibility' by David Lloyd Jones; 3, 'The Iran-United States Claims Tribunal: an interim appraisal' by Andreas F. Lowenfeld; 4, 'The Iran-United States Claims Tribunal: jurisprudential contributions to the development of international law' by Louis B. John; 5, 'The elaboration of substantive legal norms and arbitral adjudication: the case of the Iran-United States Claims Tribunal' by Thomas E. Carbonneau; 6, 'The Iran-United States Claims Tribunal: a practitioner's perspective' by Brice M. Clagett; 7, 'The hostage crisis and domestic litigation: an overview' by Michael F. Hertz.

412 **America held hostage: the secret negotiations.**
Pierre Salinger.   London: André Deutsch, 1982. 310p.
A journalistic account of the political events in Iran from the last day in December 1977 to the release of the American hostages on 20 January 1981. A chronology of events of the period of the hostage crisis is included.

413 **All fall down: America's tragic encounter with Iran.**
Gary Sick.   New York: Random House, 1985. 360p.
A chronicle of the Islamic Revolution as observed by Sick, who was the principal Presidential assistant for Iran during the Revolution and the hostage crisis. Sick assesses the developments made by the White House and the CIA. He deals with Iranian-US relations during the latter years of the Shah's reign, the Islamic Revolution, the hostage crisis and the other major issues of the 1978–81 period.

Inside the Iranian Revolution.
See item no. 389.

Iran since the Revolution . . .
See item no. 428.

The United States and Iran: a documentary history.
See item no. 440.

United States-Iranian relations.
See item no. 450.

133

Foreign Relations

General

414 **Bahrein islands, a legal and diplomatic study of the British-Iranian controversy.**
Fereydoun Adamiyat. New York: Praeger, 1955. 268p. bibliog.
Examines British diplomacy in the Persian Gulf since the beginning of the 19th century, with particular reference to the Persian claim to the Bahrein islands.

415 **The Persian Gulf.**
R. M. Burrell. Washington, DC: Center for Strategic and International Studies, Georgetown University; New York: Library Press, 1972. 81p. map. (Washington Papers, no. 1).
Analyses the course of events following the British withdrawal from the Gulf on 1 December 1971. It presents a superficial view of the factors and major issues which are of continuing importance in the region, including an account of the settlement of the Iranian claim to the Bahrein islands as a result of the United Nations mission to Bahrein in March 1970, and the consequent referendum.

416 **Recent trends in Middle East politics and Iran's foreign policy options.**
Shahram Chubin, Mohammad Fard-Saidi. Tehran: Institute for International, Political and Economic Studies, 1975. 97p. bibliog.
Examines the Arab-Israeli conflict and its impact on the region, including Iran, focusing on developments in the 1973–75 period. The security of Iran and the Indian Ocean is discussed in detail.

417 **The foreign relations of Iran: a developing state in a zone of great-power conflict.**
Shahram Chubin, Sepehr Zabih. Berkeley, California;
Los Angeles; London: University of California Press, 1974. 322p.
map. bibliog.
The authors examine Iran's foreign relations from the Second World War onwards, with reference to the country's strategic significance. The volume is divided into two parts: the first assesses Iran's foreign relations at international level, while the country's regional relations are discussed in the second part.

418 **Iran's foreign policy in the Pahlavi era.**
William Griffith. In: *Iran under the Pahlavis*. Edited by George Lenczowski. Stanford, California: Stanford University Press, 1978. p. 365–88. bibliog.
An account of Iran's foreign policy in the Pahlavi era, with particular emphasis on Mohammad Reza Shah's reign. The major topics included are the Shah's positive nationalism in the 1950s, and his global and regional policies from the early 1960s onwards. The author also assesses the impact of the 1973 oil price-increase, the Dhofar rebellion, the Iranian-Iraqi *rapprochement* and Iran's foreign policy towards the east.

419 **Iranian foreign policy since 1979: internationalism and nationalism in the Islamic Revolution.**
Fred Halliday. In: *Shi'ism and social protest*. Edited by Juan R. I. Cole and Nikki R. Keddie. New Haven, Connecticut; London: Yale University Press, 1986. p. 88–107.
Examines the different phases of Iranian foreign policy since the Islamic Revolution. It also outlines the ideology of Islamic internationalism, and the resurgence of nationalist tendencies.

420 **Iran in world and regional affairs.**
J. C. Hurewitz. In: *Iran faces the seventies*. Edited by Ehsan Yar-Shater. New York; Washington; London: Praeger, 1971. p. 117–42.
An assessment of Iran's foreign-policy objectives in the 1960s, and its international political setting in relation to the Superpowers and among its regional neighbours.

421 **Foreign powers' intervention in Iran during World War I.**
George Lenczowski. In: *Qajar Iran: political, social and cultural change, 1800–1925*. Edited by E. Bosworth and C. Hillenbrand. Edinburgh: Edinburgh University Press, 1983. p. 76–92.
An account of the political and military interventions of Russia, Turkey, Germany and Britain in Iran during the First World War. The German expedition to Afghanistan, the dissident government of Nezam al-Saltaneh in the western

city of Kermanshah, and the change of British policies following the Russian Revolution are discussed in detail.

422   **German-Persian diplomatic relations: 1873–1912.**
Bradford G. Martin.   The Hague: Mouton & Company, 1959.
212p. bibliog.
A pioneering study of diplomatic relations between Iran and Imperial Germany during the Bismarck (1873–90) and subsequent periods till just before the outbreak of the First World War.

423   **Anglo-Iranian relations during World War I.**
William J. Olson.   London: Cass, 1984. 275p. bibliog.
A critical study of relations between Iran and the British government during the First World War. The volume is arranged into six chapters, covering the crisis of war and its impact on Iran in the period which was characterized by political upheavals. The South Persian Rifles (an army division organized by the British in their zone of influence in southern Iran in the early 20th century) are discussed in the fifth chapter.

424   **The foreign policy of Iran: a developing nation in world affairs 1500–1941.**
Rouhollah K. Ramazani.   Charlottesville, Virginia: University Press of Virginia, 1966. 313p.
A chronological study of Iranian foreign policy from 1500 to 1941. The volume is divided into three parts, of which the first covers the 16th to the beginning of the 20th century, although the emphasis is mainly on Iran's foreign policy during the 19th-century Qajar period. Part two is concerned with the early constitutional period, that is, from 1905 to 1920. The final part, which is the most comprehensive section of the volume, discusses the country's foreign policy, manipulated by Reza Khan (later Reza Shah) from 1920–41.

425   **Iran's foreign policy 1941–1973: a study of foreign policy in modernizing nations.**
Rouhollah K. Ramazani.   Charlottesville, Virginia: University Press of Virginia, 1975. 454p. 3 maps. bibliog.
An analytical investigation of the interaction between Iran's political modernization and its foreign policy during the 1941–73 period. Ramazani examines the régime's 'third-power strategy' in the early days followed by its 'negative equilibrium', 'positive nationalism' and 'independent national policy'. The work contains a number of tables, including demographic and military indicators, as well as the national income, oil production and world trade figures. It also includes comparative statistics on Iran's social, economic, and military capabilities throughout the period.

426 **The instruments of Iranian foreign policy.**
Rouhollah K. Ramazani. In: *Iran: past, present and future.*
Edited by Jane W. Jacqz. New York: Aspen Institute for
Humanistic Studies, 1976. p. 387–96.
An overview of the problems and prospects of Iran's foreign policy in 1970–75.
The topics covered include the military, diplomacy, economics, trade and oil.

427 **Iran's foreign policy: perspectives and projections.**
Rouhollah K. Ramazani. In: *Revolution in Iran: a reappraisal.*
Edited by Enver M. Koury, Charles G. MacDonald. Hyattsville,
Maryland: Institute of Middle Eastern and North African Affairs,
1982. p. 9–29.
A study of Iran's foreign policy from the 1905 constitutional revolution to the
1979 Islamic Revolution. It is divided into several historical sections, covering the
periods of crisis (1905–14, 1914–21, 1941–51, 1951–53, and 1961–64) and those of
relative peace (1921–41, 1954–61, 1964–78). The country's relations with the
United States and the Soviet Union are given additional attention.

428 **Iran since the Revolution: internal dynamics, regional conflicts, and
the superpowers.**
Edited by Barry M. Rosen. New York: Social Science
Monograph, Boulder, 1985. 147p. 4 maps. (Brooklyn College
Studies on Society in Change, no. 47).
Contains a selection of papers which were presented to the Brooklyn College
Conference in the spring of 1983. The volume provides a response to the
questions asked in America during the hostage crisis, namely what happened,
what went wrong and what was going on. Following an introduction on the
question of ideology in the Iranian Revolution the book is divided into three parts
dealing with: 1, 'The Islamic Revolution in Iran'; 2, 'Iran and the balance of
power in the Middle East'; and 3, 'Iran and the strategic rivalry in the region',
each containing three papers. The volume includes an appendix of twenty-three
posters from the Revolution.

Iran almanac and book of facts.
See item no. 9.

The Shatt al-Arab river dispute in terms of law.
See item no. 24.

**Comment on the Iranian claims concerning the Iraqi-Iranian Frontier
Treaty . . .**
See item no. 41.

European contacts with Persia, 1350–1736.
See item no. 132.

Russia and Iran, 1780–1828.
See item no. 146.

History of Shah 'Abbas the Great.
See item no. 154.

The fall of the Safavi dynasty and the Afghan occupation of Persia.
See item no. 163.

Indo-Persian relations . . .
See item no. 165.

Iran in the service of world peace.
See item no. 179.

Banking and empire in Iran . . .
See item no. 184.

Nationalist trends in Iran, 1921–1926.
See item no. 185.

Mohammad Mossadegh: a political biography.
See item no. 195.

The strangling of Persia . . .
See item no. 210.

The Persians amongst the English: episodes in Anglo-Persian history.
See item no. 214.

The English amongst the Persians during the Qajar period, 1787–1921.
See item no. 238.

Persian oil: a study in power politics.
See item no. 346.

Iran: the new imperialism in action.
See item no. 355.

The rise and fall of the Shah.
See item no. 358.

Shi'ism and social protest.
See item no. 373.

Iran – the continuing struggle for power.
See item no. 377.

Revolution in Iran: a reappraisal.
See item no. 383.

Inside the Iranian Revolution.
See item no. 389.

Iran in the world economic setting.
See item no. 507.

Oil and world power.
See item no. 520.

MERI Report: Iran.
See item no. 770.

With the Gulf States

429 **Persian Gulf oil in Middle East and international conflicts.**
Mordechai Abir. Jerusalem: Leonard Davis Institute for
International Relations, Hebrew University of Jerusalem, 1976.
35p. 2 maps. (Jerusalem Papers on Peace Problems, no. 20).
Assesses the significance of the Gulf's oil-producing nations in maintaining the
stability and balance of power in that region, as well as their effect on regional, or
even world, peace.

430 **The Persian Gulf and Indian Ocean in international politics.**
Edited by Abbas Amirie. Tehran: Institute for International
Political and Economic Studies, 1976. 417p.
Includes thirteen papers presented to an international conference held in Tehran
in March 1975 to determine the role of the Persian Gulf and the Indian Ocean in
international politics.

431 **The security of the Persian Gulf.**
Edited by Hossein Amirsadeghi. London: Croom Helm, 1981.
294p. 2 maps. bibliog.
A collection of twelve, mainly general, essays focusing on the security of the
Persian Gulf. Because of its strategic position, Iran is discussed generally
throughout the book, while six essays concentrate particularly on the country.
The titles of the relevant essays are: 4, 'The United States-Iranian relationship
1948–1978: a study in reverse influence' by C. D. Carr (p. 57–84); 6, 'The Iranian
military: political symbolism versus military usefulness' by Steven L. Canby
(p. 100–30); 7, 'Arms transfers, indigenous defence production and dependency:
the case of Iran' by Stephanie G. Neuman (p. 131–50); 8, 'Saudi Arabia and Iran:
the twin pillars in revolutionary times' by Richard Haass (p. 151–69); 11, 'The
Iranian Revolution: triumph or tradgedy?' by L. P. Elwell-Sutton (p. 231–54);
and 12, 'Revolution and energy policy in Iran: international and domestic
implications' by Fereidun Fesharaki (p. 255–80).

432 **The politics of oil and revolution in Iran.**
Shaul Bakhash. Washington, DC: Brookings Institution, 1982.
37p.
Investigates the role of the Islamic government in Iran as a Persian Gulf oil

Foreign Relations. With the Gulf States

producer; and the relations and hostilities with Iraq in determining oil policy and its effect on Iran, the countries of the region and the international market.

433 **Security in the Persian Gulf 1: domestic political factors.**
Edited by Shahram Chubin. Hampshire, England: Gower, 1981. 90p. map. (International Institute for Strategic Studies).
Contains four papers focusing on the issue of Persian Gulf security in general. Iran is referred to throughout the book, with such issues as population (including migration), foreign workers, housing, land reform, modernization, religious and ethnic groups, and revolution.

434 **Oil and security in the Arabian Gulf.**
Edited by Abdel Majid Farid. London: Croom Helm (in association with the Arab Research Centre, London), 1981. 158p.
A collection of articles focusing on the oil and the security of the Persian Gulf. The Iranian Revolution and the Gulf War are two major themes running throughout the book, and the Iranian Revolution is examined in further detail by Fred Halliday in chapter two (p. 18–35). A summary of the views and debate presented in a discussion about the Gulf War, held at the Arab Research Centre in London in December 1980, is also presented in chapter fifteen (p. 141–52).

435 **Saudi Arabia and Iran: the twin pillars in revolutionary times.**
Richard Haass. In: *The security of the Persian Gulf.* Edited by Hossein Amirsadeghi. London: Croom Helm, 1981. p. 151–69.
Argues that Iran and Saudi Arabia, influenced by international parameters and individual politicians rather than developed political institutions, became the 'twin pillars' of the region. With the outbreak of the Revolution a new era in their relationship began. How this change of circumstances in one of the 'pillars' affects the other is discussed in this essay.

436 **Reactions to Iran's Revolution: the search for security.**
Charles G. MacDonald. In: *Revolution in Iran: a reappraisal.* Edited by Enver M. Koury, Charles G. MacDonald. Hyattsville, Maryland: Institute of Middle Eastern and North African Affairs, 1982. p. 98–110.
Assesses the impact of the 1979 Islamic Revolution on the region's security, focusing on the internal stability of Saudi Arabia, Iraq, and Egypt.

437 **Oil supply disruption in the 1980s.**
Karim Pakravan. Stanford, California: Hoover Institution Press, 1982. 77p. bibliog.
A general analysis of the dynamic aspects of the oil security-problem, the international inter-relationships, and the stakes of various groups of Gulf nations in the security of oil supplies.

438 **The Persian Gulf: Iran's role.**
Rouhollah K. Ramazani. Charlottesville, Virginia: University
Press of Virginia, 1972. 118p. 2 maps. bibliog.

A policy-oriented investigation of the Persian Gulf, concentrating on the role of
Iran in the patterns of continuity and change in that area from ancient times to
the present day. It deals with Iran's political and economic interests, and the
problems facing the country from 1941 to the early 1970s. It also studies Persian
Gulf security, and contains a series of relevant tables and five appendixes on
various issues, including the 1937 Iran-Iraq Boundary Treaty.

439 **The Gulf in the 1980s.**
Valerie Yorke. London: Royal Institute of International Affairs,
1980. 80p. map. (Chatham House Papers, no. 6).

Attempts to forecast the consequences of the Islamic Revolution on the countries
of the Gulf. The author suggests the likelihood of an adventurist policy adopted
by Iran against neighbouring countries, the growth of instability and the
enforcement of external pressures.

Iran in world and regional affairs.
See item no. 420.

International and legal problems of the Gulf.
See item no. 459.

Iraq and Iran: roots and conflict.
See item no. 466.

The Iran-Iraq conflict.
See item no. 470.

The Arabian Gulf states . . .
See item no. 471.

Development of the Iranian oil industry . . .
See item no. 516.

With the Superpowers

440 **The United States and Iran: a documentary history.**
Edited by Yonah Alexander, Allan Nanes. Frederick, Maryland:
University Publications of America, 1980. 522p.

A primary source of reference on the development of United States-Iranian
relations which provides informative material for researchers. The volume also
provides essential background information for the general reader. The work

covers relations between the two countries from 1856, when the initial Treaty of Friendship and Commerce was signed at Constantinople, to the seizure of the American Embassy in Tehran by Iranians in 1979, and the hostage crisis.

441 **Conflict and intervention in the Third World.**
Edited by Mohammed Ayoob. London: Croom Helm, 1980. 252p.

Deals with a highly controversial issue of 20th-century politics, namely the political and economic trends of the relationship between the Superpowers and the Third World. It includes nine papers, of which the first and the last analyse the issue in general terms. Other essays are more concerned with particular cases. Iran is referred to throughout the book, but is most closely studied in the fourth paper, 'The Middle East', by Robert Springborg, p. 73–106.

442 **Recent United States policy in the Persian Gulf (1971–82).**
C. Paul Bradley. Grantham, New Hampshire: Tompson & Rutter. 1982. 141p. map. bibliog.

Provides a report of the United States policy in the Persian Gulf in the 1970s and early 1980s, dealing with US relations with Iran and Saudi Arabia, as well as regional relations between Iran and Saudi Arabia, the Carter administration and its new directions in Persian Gulf policy, and the Reagan administration's Persian Gulf policy.

443 **The United States-Iranian relationship 1948–1978: a study in reverse influence.**
C. D. Carr. In: *The security of the Persian Gulf*. Edited by Hossein Amirsadeghi. London: Croom Helm, 1981. p. 57–84.

The author refuses to agree with the widely-held view that the Shah was a dutiful puppet of the United States, and argues instead that relations between the two nations, especially on security matters, were dictated by the authorities in Tehran and not those in Washington. He examines the Iranian control system and American policy from the 1950s to the 1970s.

444 **Security in the Persian Gulf 4: the role of outside powers.**
Shahram Chubin. Hampshire, England: Gower, 1982. 180p. (International Institute for Strategic Studies).

Investigates the volatility of politics in the Persian Gulf and the dependence of Western powers on the region, which, the author believes, is reflective of the international environment in the 1980s. The influence of the United States on Iran and Saudi Arabia during the 1973–80 period is analysed in the first chapter, along with that of the USSR in Iraq from 1968 to 1980. In the next three chapters the Superpower contribution to regional co-operation and conflict, and the arms transfer and its influence are studied. The role of Iran in the security of the Persian Gulf is also analysed. The work is heavily based on Western media sources, and does not include a bibliography, maps or tables.

445   **Iran: diplomacy in a regional and global context.**
       Alvin J. Cottrell.   Washington, DC: Centre for Strategic and
       International Studies, Georgetown University, 1975. 21p. map.
Examines the relations between Iran and the United States in the world context.
Covers the period from 1960 to Iran's agreement with Iraq in March 1975.

446   **US security in the Persian Gulf: an assessment.**
       Lisa deFilippis.   In: *Revolution in Iran: a reappraisal*. Edited by
       Enver M. Koury, Charles G. MacDonald. Hyattsville, Maryland:
       Institute of Middle Eastern and North African Affairs, 1982.
       p. 88–97.
A superficial assessment of the role played by the US in the security of the
Persian Gulf. The author's suggestion for preserving American interests in the
Persian Gulf, is to further militarize the region and exercise tighter control over
the oil-producing nations.

447   **The USSR in Iran: the background history of Russian and Anglo-
       American conflict in Iran, its effects on Iranian nationalism, and the
       fall of the Shah.**
       Faramarz S. Fatemi.   London: Thomas Yoseloff; Cranbury, New
       Jersey; New York: A. S. Barnes, 1980. 191p. map. bibliog.
As the book's informatively long title implies, the author examines the relations
between Iran and the USSR during the occupation of Iran by the allies in
1941–46.

448   **The Iranian Revolution: its impact on economic relations with the
       United States.**
       Khosrow Fatemi.   In: *International Journal of Middle East
       Studies*, vol. 12, no. 3 (1980), p. 303–17.
Investigates the consequences of the fall of Mohammad Reza Shah and the
establishment of the Islamic Republic of Iran on Iran's economic and trade
relations with the United States.

449   **Iran's international position: an interpretation.**
       Ahmad Ghoreyshi, Cyrus Elahi.   In: *Iran, past, present and
       future*. Edited by Jane W. Jacqz. New York: Aspen Institute for
       Humanistic Studies, 1976. p. 369–86.
An overview of Iran's political position in the region, and its historical relations
with Britain, Russia and the US, focusing in particular on the post-Second World
War period. The article includes a number of statistical tables concerning, for
example, foreign capital and investors in Iran, and the country's importation of
goods and defence articles.

Foreign Relations. With the Superpowers

450 **United States-Iranian relations.**
Benson Lee Grayson. Washington, DC: University Press of
America, 1981. 177p. bibliog.
Outlines the relations between Iran and the United States from 1830, when early
contacts were made by the Americans for potential missionary activities, until the
release of the American hostages in 1981. The author was himself, for a long
time, a Foreign Service Officer of the Department of State.

451 **Threat from the East: Soviet policy from Afghanistan and Iran to
the Horn of Africa.**
Fred Halliday. Harmondsworth, England: Penguin Books, 1982.
2nd ed. 129p.
Discusses the political developments in a region known as the 'Arc of Crisis', and
considers the effect of Soviet policy in the area. Because of its geographical
position and its political characteristics, post-revolutionary Iran plays a major part
in the book.

452 **Politics, polemics and pedagogs: a study of United States technical
assistance in education to Iran, including negotiations, political
considerations in Iran and the United States, programming,
methods, problems, results, and evaluation.**
Clarence Hendershot. New York; Washington; Atlanta, Georgia;
Hollywood, Los Angeles: Vantage Press, 1975. 344p. map. bibliog.
Covers the history of US aid to Iran over a sixteen-year period and provides an
outline, from an American point of view, of the numerous strands, such as
economics, politics and education, that tied together the two governments for a
time.

453 **Debâcle: the American failure in Iran.**
Michael Ledeen, William Lewis. New York: Alfred A. Knopf,
1981. 248p.
Investigates the nature of American foreign policy during the 1978–79 Iranian
Revolution. The volume is divided into seven chapters dealing with the Shah and
his relationship with the Americans, focusing on President Carter's administration;
the different stages of crisis; and the Revolution and the Ayatollah. A conclusion
on the prospect of America's foreign policy is also included.

454 **Russia and the West in Iran, 1918–1948: a study in big-power
rivalry.**
George Lenczowski. New York: Cornell University Press, 1949.
315p. map.
A study of Superpower rivalry in Iran between 1918 and 1948, concentrating on
political matters and also emphasizing Iran's external relations with foreign
powers. The volume is arranged in eleven chapters. It was followed by a twelfth
chapter, which was published separately, dealing with the events of the following

years, and taking the study up to the nationalization of oil and the severance of Iran's diplomatic relations with Great Britain.

455 **The United States and Iran: the patterns of influence.**
Rouhollah K. Ramazani. New York: Praeger, 1982. 170p. bibliog.

An examination of United States-Iranian relations during the Shah's régime, from his accession to the throne in 1941 to his downfall in 1979. The work studies the different areas of influence including oil influence and other economic issues, and the security and arms transfer issue. Also examines the close identification of the Shah and the US and its impact on Iranian society, the decline of the Shah's influence, and the growth of the power of the revolutionary forces, as well as the events which immediately followed the collapse of both the Shah's régime and US influence.

456 **The Iranian crisis of 1941 – the actors: Britain, Germany and the Soviet Union.**
Miron Rezun. Cologne; Vienna: Böhlau Verlag, 1982. 105p. bibliog.

An historical account of the political rivalry among the Great Powers in Iran, culminating in the 1941 occupation of Iran and the abdication of Reza Shah, who was taken into British custody.

457 **Paved with good intentions: the American experience and Iran.**
Barry Rubin. Oxford; New York: Oxford University Press, 1980. 401p. bibliog.

A study of Iranian-United States relations from early 1943 to 1980 when the friendship was destroyed by the Islamic Revolution. The author suggests that the 1979 Islamic Revolution was the second stage of a revolution which was first generated in the affairs of oil nationalization in the early 1950s. He has used classified archival materials and interviewed a number of Americans as well as both pro- and anti-Shah Iranians. Two appendixes are included. The first outlines the role of the media, and the second presents a chronology of events from 1 January 1978 to 27 July 1980 when the Shah died in exile in Egypt.

458 **Iran: the impact of United States interests and policies 1941–1954.**
Michael Kahl Sheehan. Brooklyn, New York: Theo Gaus' Sons, 1968. 81p. bibliog.

A journalistic account of relations between Iran and the United States in one of the most turbulent periods of Iranian history. The chapters are arranged chronologically, and the volume includes a brief account of the nationalization of the oil industry.

Capital development and land reform in Khuzistan, Iran.
See item no. 362.

Iran in world and regional affairs.
See item no. 420.

Foreign Relations. With the Superpowers

Iran's foreign policy: perspectives and projections.
See item no. 427.

Technical assistance in theory and practice . . .
See item no. 579.

Technical cooperation with Iran . . .
See item no. 580.

The Gulf War, 1980– .

459 **International and legal problems of the Gulf.**
Sayed Hassan Amin.   Cambridge, England: Middle East and
North African Studies Press; Boulder, Colorado: Westview Press,
1981. 235p. 8 maps. bibliog.
Studies the major legal problems of the Persian Gulf (a focal point is the question
of rights of passage through the Strait of Hormuz) and of the Iran-Iraq War.
Fisheries and pollution control are also included in the investigation. In addition,
the author analyses the relevant political and economic arguments. Primary
sources in Arabic and Farsi (Persian) have been used, and supportive appendixes
and a separate subject index on legal issues are provided.

460 **The Iraq-Iran conflict: questions and discussions.**
Tareq Aziz, translated by Naji al-Hadithi.   London: Third World
Centre for Research and Publishing, 1981. 89p.
Presents a pro-Iraqi picture of the Gulf War, its causes and repercussions. The
author, a former journalist, was a leader of the Ba'ath Socialist Party in Iraq, and
is now Foreign Affairs Minister and Deputy Premier in the Iraqi government.

461 **The Arab Gulf economy in a turbulent world.**
Hazem Beblawi.   London: Croom Helm, 1984. 288p.
Examines the effects on Iran of the fall in oil revenues and the subsequent
recession in the industrialized countries. Also studies the Gulf War in the context
of its financial burden on the country.

The Gulf War, 1980– .

462 **The Gulf and the search for strategic stability: Saudi Arabia, the military balance in the Gulf, and trends in the Arab-Israeli military balance.**
Anthony H. Cordesman.   Boulder, Colorado: Westview Press; London: Mansell, 1984. 987p. 44 maps. bibliog.
An analytical study of the security problem in the Persian Gulf region, concentrating on the United States' military relations with, and strategic ties to, the Gulf states, following the collapse of the Shah's régime in 1979 and the outbreak of the Gulf War in 1980. The Iranian Revolution and Gulf War are constantly referred to throughout the book, but are studied in further detail in chapter seventeen (p. 725–75), which includes tables concerning the military build-up in Iran from 1972 to 1983, and the nuclear weapons in the region.

463 **Conflict in the Persian Gulf.**
Edited by Murray Gordon.   London: Macmillan; Kingsport, Tennessee: Kingsport Press, 1981. 167p. 7 maps.
Discusses a number of issues in the region which pose a problem to the West in general and to the United States in particular. The role of the Soviet Union in the area is also touched upon. The position of Iran in local and world politics before and after the Revolution is a key issue, and the Iran-Iraq War is analysed in detail. The discussions are not documented and there is no bibliography.

464 **The Middle East from transition to development.**
Edited by Sami G. Hajjar.   Leiden, The Netherlands: E. J. Brill, 1985. 152p. map.
A collection of ten papers studying various economic, social and political developments in the Middle East. Some of the major topics investigated include oil, modernization, Islamic and other ideological issues, and foreign relations. Iran is referred to throughout the volume, with particular emphasis on the Islamic Revolution and the Gulf War.

465 **Iraq: eastern flank of the Arab world.**
Christine Moss Helms.   Washington, DC: Brookings Institution, 1984. 208p. 8 maps.
An overview of the fundamental development of the policies in Iraq which have been influenced by the latest regional events, including the Iranian Revolution and the Gulf War. The war and its consequences are studied in further detail in chapter six (p. 163–94). This chapter also assesses Iraqi goals and assumptions, and its military strategy.

466 **Iraq and Iran: roots of conflict.**
Tareq Y. Ismael.   Syracuse, New York: Syracuse University Press, 1982. 219p. 6 maps. bibliog.
Investigates the complex historical background to the Iran-Iraq conflict. The book is divided into two parts. The first is an introduction to the legal dimensions and ideological facets of the conflict. The second part, forming the bulk of the book, is

further subdivided into two valuable sections, containing twenty-nine documents, covering the legal-historical background (1847–1975), and the more recent ideological and political aspects (1963–80). The book presents a balanced and objective assessment, based mainly on first-hand documents, offering a rich source of reference, much of which is not available elsewhere in English.

467 **Revolution and war in the Persian Gulf.**
S. Kassicieh, Jamal R. Nassar. In *Management International Review*, vol. 26 (Fall 1983), p. 88–99.
A brief study of the impact of the Islamic Revolution and the Iran-Iraq War on the multinational oil companies.

468 **The Gulf War.**
Jabr Muhsin. In: *Saddam's Iraq: revolution or reaction?*
Committee against Repression and for Democratic Rights in Iraq (CARDRI). London: Zed Books, 1986. p. 227–44.
The author suggests that the Gulf War is not simply a border disagreement, nor is it caused by the long-lasting hostility between the Arabs and Iranians. He argues that it has been caused by far-reaching political, economic and social problems. He first reviews the developments preceding the war, and this is followed by a discussion of its political, economic and social consequences.

469 **Rim of prosperity. The Gulf: a survey.**
The Economist, special report (13 Dec. 1980). 84p.
A special report on the economic and political conditions of the Persian Gulf, particularly in relation to oil and the effects of the Iran-Iraq war.

470 **The Iran-Iraq conflict.**
Christopher Rundle. In: *Asian Affairs: Journal of the Royal Society for Asian Affairs*, vol. 17 (old series vol. 73), part 2 (June 1986), p. 128–33.
Following an outline of the historical background to the two countries and their conflicts, the article attempts to examine, briefly, the outbreak of war, the aims of each government, the effects of the conflict and the future prospects.

Iran – the continuing struggle for power.
See item no. 377.

The wrath of Allah . . .
See item no. 387.

Inside the Iranian Revolution.
See item no. 389.

The politics of oil and revolution in Iran.
See item no. 432.

The Gulf War, 1980– .

Oil and security in the Arabian Gulf.
See item no. 434.

Oil supply disruption in the 1980s.
See item no. 437.

The army.
See item no. 489.

Economic development and revolutionary upheavals in Iran.
See item no. 509.

Oil and world power.
See item no. 520.

Constitution and the Legal System

471 The Arabian Gulf states: their legal and political status and their international problems.
Husain M. Albaharna. Beirut: Librairie du Liban, 1975. 2nd rev. ed. 428p. 9 maps. bibliog.

A revised and updated version of the author's *The legal status of the Arabian Gulf states* (Manchester, England: Manchester University Press, 1968.). It includes five monographs, the first of which deals with the settlement of the Bahrein-Iran dispute.

472 Constitution of the Islamic Republic of Iran.
Translated by Hamid Algar. Berkeley, California: Mizan Press, 1980. 91p.

An English translation of the text of the Constitution of the Islamic Republic of Iran, drafted by the Revolutionary government and approved in a referendum held on 2–3 December 1979.

473 The Iranian family protection law of 1967: a milestone in the advance of women's rights.
F. R. C. Bagley. In: *Iran and Islam*. Edited by C. E. Bosworth. Edinburgh: Edinburgh University Press, 1971. p. 47–64.

An historical and analytical study of the secular Iranian family protection law of 1967 which restricted polygamy and divorce. A translation of the law, brought into force on 15 July 1967, is included.

474 Human rights and the legal system in Iran.
William J. Butler, Georges Levasseur. Geneva: International Commission of Jurists, 1976. 70p. bibliog.

Includes two reports on human rights and the legal system in Iran, prepared by the International Commission of Jurists. The first report, by William J. Butler, is concerned with human rights conditions in Iran during the period 1953–75, gives brief historical background information on pre-1953 conditions, and includes an English translation of the establishment of the Security Organization Act (SAVAK, 1957). The second report, by Professor Georges Levasseur, analyses the organization of the judicial system in Iran, Iranian criminal law and its procedure, and the prison system.

475 Judicial authority in Imami Shi'i jurisprudence.
Norman Calder. In: *British Society for Middle Eastern Studies Bulletin*, vol. 6, no. 2 (1979), p. 104–08.

A preliminary study of judicial authority in Imami Shi'ite jurisprudence, in contrast to the Sunni tradition and distinct from non-sacred profane practices.

476 The Islamic consultative assembly of the Islamic Republic of Iran.
Council for Ten Days Dawn Celebration. Tehran: Council for Ten Days Dawn Celebration, 1984. 46p.

A record of the major procedures concerning the making of the Constitution and the functioning of the Islamic Consultative Assembly, the Majles.

477 Income distribution and taxation laws of Iran.
Ferydoon Firoozi. In: *International Journal of Middle East Studies*, vol. 9, no. 1 (1978), p. 73–97.

Examines the development of taxation laws in Iran since the early 20th century, and the amended legislation of the latter days of the Shah's régime. It also discusses the objective of the distribution of income through the taxation system, and the classification of families by income.

478 Change and development in the judicial system of Qajar Iran (1800–1925).
Willem Floor. In: *Qajar Iran: political, social and cultural change, 1800–1925*. Edited by E. Bosworth and C. Hillenbrand. Edinburgh: Edinburgh University Press, 1983. p. 113–47.

Examines the 19th-century dual judicial system of Iran, where the religious courts were run by the clergymen and the secular courts were administered by government officials. It also deals with various developments and cases, including the position of foreigners, during this period and the first three decades of the 20th century.

479 The institution of *mut'a* marriage in Iran: a formal and historical perspective.
Shahla Haeri. In: *Women and revolution in Iran*. Edited by Guity Nashat. Boulder, Colorado: Westview Press, 1983. p. 231–51. bibliog.

Describes the *mut'a*, a temporary form of marriage, which, since the Islamic Revolution, has gained a revived popularity and received the support of the current régime. It includes an appendix briefly discussing the motives of men and women for contracting such a marriage.

480 Shahanshah: a study of the monarchy of Iran.
E. Burke Inlow. Delhi: Motilal Banarsidass, 1979. 274p. map. bibliog.

A book overtaken by events, providing a study in political and legal theory concerning the power of the Shah, its nature, its tradition and the exercise of its function. It consists of seven chapters. Chapters one, two and three deal with the ancient pre-Islamic structure of kingship. The historic relationship in Iran between politics and religion is the subject of the fourth chapter. The last three chapters are concerned with the means of the Shah's authority, the government, the armed forces and the judicial system.

481 The problems encountered in establishing an Islamic republic in Iran, 1979–1981.
C. M. Lake. In: *British Society for Middle Eastern Studies Bulletin*, vol. 9, no. 2 (1982), p. 141–70. bibliog.

A study of the Constitution of the Islamic Republic of Iran with the objective of ascertaining why the country's revolutionary leaders had to resort to oppression in order to establish their 'government of righteousness'. It examines the application of the Constitution in theory and in practice.

482 Political process and institutions in Iran: the second Pahlavi kingship.
George Lenczowski. In: *Iran under the Pahlavis*. Edited by George Lenczowski. Stanford, California: Stanford University Press, 1978. p. 433–75. bibliog.

Provides a brief history of Iran's institutional framework, the 1906 Constitution, and the parliament (Majles). It also deals with amendments to the Constitution and the changing role of parliament, focusing on the post-war period. Other major topics covered include the government-sponsored parties and their political ideologies, the modernizing monarchy, and the style of leadership.

483 An introduction to Shi'i law: a bibliographical study.
Hossein Modarressi Tabātabā'i. London: Ithaca Press, 1984. 215p. bibliog.

Presents a general outline of Shi'ite law. The volume is arranged into two parts. Part one includes four chapters focusing on the contents of the law and jurisprudence, its sources, and a brief discussion of its historical development. Part two, which forms the bulk of the book, is divided into two parts providing a list of some Shi'ite comprehensive legal works and monographs.

484 **Family planning in post-revolutionary Iran.**
Yasmin L. Mossavar-Rahmani. In: *Women and revolution in Iran.* Edited by Guity Nashat. Boulder, Colorado: Westview Press, 1983. p. 253–62.

Examines the effects of the legal aspects of the Islamic Revolution on family planning in Iran. As a comparison, the policies adopted by the Shah's régime towards the same issue are also given briefly.

485 **Iranian approaches to decentralization.**
M. Bagher Namazi. In: *Iran, past, present and future.* Edited by Jane W. Jacqz. New York: Aspen Institute for Humanistic Studies, 1976. p. 243–56.

Examines the government's efforts to reorganize its pattern of administration, and its new policy concerning the local governments and regional systems of authority in the 1960s and early 1970s.

486 **Family laws of Iran.**
Sayyid Ali Reza Naqavi. Islamabad, Pakistan: Islamic Research Institute, 1971. 308p.

Presents a critical and comparative study of the Family Laws of Iran which were passed between 1928 and the late 1960s. The volume contains the texts of the laws in both Persian and English. Comments and assessments are made, in particular when the modern law departs from classical Shar'iah law. Comparison has also been made, though briefly, between these laws and the family laws in force in Pakistan.

487 **The Iranian Constitution with amendments.**
Translated by Ali Pasha Saleh. New York: Oceana Publications, 1971. 29p.

This is the third, revised, translation of the amended Iranian Constitution. The translation also forms the second section of the *Constitution of the countries of the world: Iran* by Abolghasem Sedeh: (Oceana Publications, 1971. 15p. + 29p.), the first part of which includes a brief chronology of the Iranian Constitution and its subsequent amendments from 1906–1971.

488 **Islam and ownership.**
Seyyed Mahmood Taleghani, translated by Ahmad Jabbari and Farhang Rajaee. Lexington, Kentucky: Mazda Publishers, 1983. 200p. (Iran-e No Literary Collection, book no. 4).

This translation provides a major text in English by a leading Shi'ite theologian on economics and ownership in the modern world. The translation is based on the

fourth and final edition of the original, and includes a brief introduction on
Taleghani's life and works.

Iran: past and present.
See item no. 19.

The Persian revolution of 1905–1909.
See item no. 177.

The origins of modern reform in Iran, 1870–80.
See item no. 188.

Misconceptions regarding the juridical status of the Iranian *'ulama*.
See item no. 300.

Modern Islamic political thought . . .
See item no. 347.

Land reform and politics: a comparative analysis.
See item no. 363.

The state and revolution in Iran, 1962–1982.
See item no. 372.

Law and human rights in the Islamic Republic of Iran.
See item no. 404.

International and legal problems of the Gulf.
See item no. 459.

Iraq and Iran: roots of conflict.
See item no. 466.

Islamic banking . . .
See item no. 501.

Impact of the oil technology on Iran: 1901–1951.
See item no. 519.

The Persian land reform: 1962–1966.
See item no. 536.

Labour unions, law and conditions in Iran (1900–1941).
See item no. 559.

Workers say no to the Shah . . .
See item no. 560.

Education and social awakening in Iran: 1850–1968.
See item no. 574.

The Military
and Defence

489 The army.

Haleh Afshar. In: *Iran: a revolution in turmoil*. Edited by Haleh Afshar. London: Macmillan, 1985. p. 175–98.

The author argues that the army in pre-revolutionary Iran acted as the pivot of the Shah's régime inside the country, and was a symbol of his prestige and authority at international level. It lacked, however, a coercive power due to its nature of conscription. Debilitated by the Khomeini régime's fear of a military coup, the army was to be built up again following the Iraqi invasion.

490 The Iranian military: political symbolism versus military usefulness.

Steven L. Canby. In: *The security of the Persian Gulf*. Edited by Hossein Amirsadeghi. London: Croom Helm, 1981. p. 100–30.

Argues that sophistication in weapons, except for the major powers, bears little relationship to military usefulness and that the consequent military and political power is more apparent than real. The essay examines the strategy of the Shah's régime, which favoured technological superfluity, and its effectiveness in a potential confrontation with the Russians.

491 Iran's armed forces under the Pahlavi dynasty.

Alvin J. Cottrell. In: *Iran under the Pahlavis*. Edited by George Lenczowski. Stanford, California: Stanford University Press, 1978. p. 389–431. bibliog.

An historical account of the modern military in Iran during the Pahlavi era, focusing on the post-war period. The essay deals with the alliance of Iran and the United States, the growth of the country's interest in the Persian Gulf, its relations with Iraq, and its intervention in Oman.

492　**Ravaged and reborn: the Iranian army, 1982.**
William F. Hickman.　Washington, DC: Brookings Institution,
1982. 33p.

Analyses the statements and actions of the leaders of the Islamic Republic of Iran
concerning the role and position of the army, its continuity and the changes
imposed upon it. The author states that the Iranian army has been reborn as an
effective and Islamic force.

493　**Arms transfers, indigenous defence production and dependency: the
case of Iran.**
Stephenie G. Neuman.　In: *The security of the Persian Gulf.*
Edited by Hossein Amirsadeghi. London: Croom Helm, 1981.
p. 131–50.

An analytical study of the dependency of the Third World countries on the states
which supply them with arms. It deals with the inevitable stages of a development
pattern in arms transfer, focusing on the rapid modernization of the Iranian Air
Force between 1964–78. Particular reference is made to Iran in the 1960s and
1970s.

Arms trade registers, the arms trade with the Third World.
See item no. 565.

Economy

494 **Capital formation and development finance.**
Jahangir Amuzegar.   In: *Iran faces the seventies*. Edited by Ehsan
Yar-Shater. New York; Washington; London: Praeger, 1971.
p. 66–87.
Studies the nature of capital formation in Iran during the post-war period.
Amuzegar focuses on the country's 'third plan' (1962–68) and 'fourth plan'
(1968–72), and emphasizes the trends in the structure of development, and the
patterns of product use.

495 **Iran: economic development under dualistic conditions.**
Jahangir Amuzegar, M. Ali Fekrat.   Chicago; London: University
of Chicago Press, 1971. 163p.
Studies the interaction between the oil industry and other sectors of Iranian
economy during the Pahlavi era, with the objective of providing, at the same
time, a case-study, or rather a generalized model for similar dualistic economies
elsewhere.

496 **Iran: an economic profile.**
Jahangir Amuzegar.   Washington, DC: Middle East Institute,
1977. 265p. map. bibliog.
Investigates and describes the details of Iran's rapid economic growth during the
1963–76 period. The author discusses the basic features and socio-economic
structure of the country; describes the economic sectors and activities; examines
national objectives and policies; and finally presents an overall review of the
economic performance.

497 **Economic development in Iran: 1900–1970.**
Julian Bharier. London; New York; Toronto: Oxford University
Press, 1971. 279p. map. bibliog.

An objective description and analysis of the Iranian economy, its structure and its
growth in a period of great change and frequent upheavals. While the first chapter
studies the start of a modern economy in 1900, the fourth and final chapter
analyses its development up to 1970, and assesses its prospects. Part two is
concerned with the economy as a whole, while part three deals with the individual
economic sectors. Numerous supporting tables and a comprehensive bibliography
are included.

498 **Private enterprise and socialism in the Middle East.**
Howard S. Ellis. Washington, DC: American Enterprise
Institute, 1970. 126p.

Dealing with the Middle East Reseach Project of the American Enterprise
Institute, this book covers Iran as well as Egypt, Iraq, Lebanon and Turkey. Each
country has been studied individually, but comparative estimates and observations
are also given.

499 **Economics of oil.**
R. Fallah. In: *Iran: past, present and future.* Edited by Jane W.
Jacqz. New York: Aspen Institute for Humanistic Studies, 1976.
p. 291–300.

Assesses the place of oil in the international economy of the 1970s, paying
subservient homage to the last Pahlavi monarch (1941–79). The author discusses
the role of the industrialized nations, the price of crude oil, the energy crisis and
how to surmount it, and the problems facing the Third and even the 'Fourth'
World (sic).

500 **Iran's petrodollars: surplus or deficit? An examination of
alternative Iranian policies.**
Fereidun Fesharaki. In: *Iran: past, present and future.* Edited by
Jane W. Jacqz. New York: Aspen Institute for Humanistic Studies,
1976. p. 301–27.

Describes how Iran dealt with the superfluous oil revenue of 1974–75; how it
could change her expenditure policy in the face of declining oil revenues; and how
far the country's investment strategy can help her future foreign exchange
requirements. Eleven relevant statistical tables are included.

501 **Islamic banking: the adaptation of banking practice to conform with
Islamic Law.**
Sami Hassan Hamoud. London: Arabian Information, 1985.
259p. bibliog.

Attempts to throw light on the original basis of the Islamic attitude towards
problems affecting banking and commercial activities, especially in connection
with the issue of interest, which is forbidden by Shari'ah law. It aims to expound

Economy

both the theoretical and the applied bases for banking operations with a view to their compatibility with contemporary international requirements and needs. The work was first presented to the School of Law, Cairo University as a PhD thesis, and is based on several primary Islamic sources. There are no indexes.

502 **The economy: an assessment of performance.**
Charles Issawi. In: *Iran faces the seventies*. Edited by Ehsan Yar-Shater. New York; Washington; London: Praeger, 1971. p. 44–65.

Examines the performance of the Iranian economy in terms of growth, stability, structural development, international balance and social justice during the 1950s and 1960s.

503 **The Iranian economy 1925–1975: fifty years of economic development.**
Charles Issawi. In: *Iran under the Pahlavis*. Edited by George Lenczowski. Stanford, California: Stanford University Press, 1978. p. 129–66. bibliog.

Surveys the Iranian economy under the Pahlavis, and is divided into periods covering the reign of Reza Shah (1925–41), war and the nationalization of oil (1941–52), recovery and imbalance (1954–62), the White Revolution (1962–71), and the multiplication of oil revenues (1972–75). Discusses employment, the labour force and GNP (Gross National Product) as well as agriculture, industry, transport and finance.

504 **The political economy of modern Iran: despotism and pseudo-modernism, 1926–1979.**
Homa Katouzian. London: Macmillan, 1981. 373p.

Studies the political economy of the Pahlavi dynasty from its accession in 1925 to its demise in 1979. The volume is divided into four chronological parts. The first part deals briefly with 19th-century developments and the constitutional movement till the end of the First World War. Part two covers the period of Reza Shah, the founder of the Pahlavi dynasty, from 1921 when he was involved in a British-instigated coup till 1941 when he was forced to abdicate. The following two sections are concerned with the reign of the second and last Pahlavi monarch, Mohammad Reza. The third part covers the 1941–61 period, leaving the period of the Shah's absolute despotism and his so-called White Revolution to the fourth and final part.

505 **The Gulf in the early 20th century: foreign institutions and local responses.**
Edited by R. I. Lawless. Durham, England: Centre for Middle Eastern and Islamic Studies, 1986. 215p. map. (Occasional Paper series, no. 31).

A collection of seven papers initially presented to the 'Conference/workshop on the Gulf region during the first half of the twentieth century', sponsored by the Centre for Middle Eastern and Islamic Studies, University of Durham, England, and held in April 1985. The articles cover a variety of economic aspects, focusing on the impact of foreign institutions (oil companies, banks and trading companies) in the region during the period in question. Iran is studied in general, while two articles are devoted to the country in particular: 'Finance and foreign exchange for industrialization in Iran, 1310–1319 (1931/32–1940/41)' by Patrick Clawson and Willem Floor (q.v.); and 'The Persian Railway Syndicate and British railway policy in Iran' by Paul Luft (q.v.).

506 **Iran at the end of the century: a Hegelian forecast.**
Robert E. Looney. Lexington, Massachusetts; Toronto: Lexington Books, 1977. 140p. bibliog.

A forecast of the social and economic position of Iran at the end of this century which was undertaken prior to the Islamic Revolution and the onslaught of the Gulf War. The author attempts to establish a systematic relationship between logic and the realities in Iran based on Hegel's dialectical logic. However, Looney adopts a non-Marxist approach, for he believes that Marxist theory is capable only of dealing 'with situations of growth growing out of growth' and not with the situation which existed in Iran in the mid-1970s which, he claims, falls into one of the areas ignored by Marx (sic). Looney makes recommendations which, he asserts, will help Iran sustain a steady economic growth rate to the end of the century when oil will cease to be a major contributor to growth.

507 **Iran in the world economic setting.**
Hassan Ali Mehran. In: *Iran: past, present and future.* Edited by Jane W. Jacqz. New York: Aspen Institute for Humanistic Studies, 1976. p. 339–45.

An official view of Iran's place in the world economic setting and the role played by the Organization of Petroleum Exporting Countries (OPEC) to change what the author calls 'imbalances and inequities'. The article assesses Iran's international economic relations in the 1960s and 1970s, and discusses the country's relations with international financial organizations.

508 **Expenditure of oil revenue: an optimal control approach with application to the Iranian economy.**
Homa Motamen. London: Frances Pinter, 1979. 178p. bibliog.

Assesses the long-running problems facing the oil-producing countries that engage in undisciplined spending and rely on a single income which is unlikely to last long. The Iranian economy provides an example and serves as a model. A number of tables and figures are included.

509 **Economic development and revolutionary upheavals in Iran.**
M. H. Pesaran. In: *Iran: a revolution in turmoil.* Edited by Haleh Afshar. London: Macmillan, 1985. p. 15–50. bibliog.

An assessment of the growing alienation of most Iranians by the Shah's modernization policies and the penetration of Western capital and culture. The author provides an outline of the realities of Iranian society which is contradictory to the image projected by the state's propaganda machine. He argues that the nationwide discontent was used by the clergy and that the opposition forces were

Economy

manipulated to achieve the aims of Islamic Revolution. However, in his view, the
new régime has equally failed to deal with the basic social and economic
problems, and Pesaran believes that a counter-revolution is being prevented only
by the Gulf War.

510 **The political environment of economic planning in Iran, 1971–1983:
     from monarchy to Islamic Republic.**
     Hossein Razavi, Firuz Vakil. Boulder, Colorado; London:
     Westview Press, 1984. 154p. bibliog.
Presents an analysis of the operation of Iran's economy before and after the
Islamic Revolution as a result of the changing political conditions. The authors
investigate the nature of the Shah's economic plans in relation to his unstable
régime, discuss the problems facing the Islamic government and finally outline the
future prospects for economic planning in Iran.

The Persian Gulf states, a general survey.
See item no. 7.

Iran almanac and book of facts.
See item no. 9.

Iran: religion, politics and society.
See item no. 12.

Area handbook for Iran.
See item no. 16.

Baluchestan: its political economy and history.
See item no. 26.

Semnan: Persian city and region.
See item no. 33.

Checkmate: fighting tradition in central Asia.
See item no. 55.

The rise of the Achaemenids and establishment of their empire.
See item no. 102.

The socio-economic condition of Iran under the Il-Khans.
See item no. 134.

British interests in the Persian Gulf, 1747–1780.
See item no. 144.

Social and internal economic affairs.
See item no. 156.

The economic history of Iran, 1800–1914.
See item no. 158.

The case of Hajjī 'Abd al-Karim . . .
See item no. 161.

The fall of the Safavi dynasty and the Afghan occupation of Persia.
See item no. 163.

Iran under the Safavids.
See item no. 168.

Iran in the service of world peace.
See item no. 179.

Banking and empire in Iran . . .
See item no. 184.

Iran under the Pahlavis.
See item no. 187.

The origins of modern reform in Iran, 1870–80.
See item no. 188.

Twenty-three years . . .
See item no. 194.

The American task in Persia.
See item no. 202.

The strangling of Persia . . .
See item no. 210.

Migration and problems of development: the case of Iran.
See item no. 229.

Poverty and revolution in Iran . . .
See item no. 230.

The legacy of Islam.
See item no. 280.

The sociology of development: Iran as an Asian case study.
See item no. 304.

Income distribution in Iran . . .
See item no. 308.

Islam and capitalism.
See item no. 309.

The bazaar as a case study of religion and social change.
See item no. 315.

Women of Iran: the conflict with fundamentalist Islam.
See item no. 318.

Social and economic change in the role of women, 1956–1978.
See item no. 327.

Iran: the new imperialism in action.
See item no. 355.

Economy

Capital development and land reform in Khuzistan, Iran.
See item no. 362.

Iran: a revolution in turmoil.
See item no. 368.

The reign of the ayatollahs: Iran and the Islamic Revolution.
See item no. 370.

Iran – the continuing struggle for power.
See item no. 377.

Iran: essays on a revolution in the making.
See item no. 380.

Economic origins of the Iranian Revolution.
See item no. 384.

The Iranian structure for liberation . . .
See item no. 386.

The wrath of Allah . . .
See item no. 387.

The Iranian theocracy.
See item no. 390.

The revolutionary character of the Iranian *ulama* . . .
See item no. 396.

Society and economics in Islam . . .
See item no. 403.

Iran's foreign policy 1941–1973 . . .
See item no. 425.

The instruments of Iranian foreign policy.
See item no. 426.

Conflict and intervention in the Third World.
See item no. 441.

The Iranian Revolution . . .
See item no. 448.

Politics, polemics and pedagogs . . .
See item no. 452.

The United States and Iran: the patterns of influence.
See item no. 455.

International and legal problems of the Gulf.
See item no. 459.

The Arab Gulf economy in a turbulent world.
See item no. 461.

Revolution and war in the Persian Gulf.
See item no. 467.

Rim of prosperity. The Gulf: a survey.
See item no. 469.

Income distribution and taxation laws of Iran.
See item no. 477.

Islam and ownership.
See item no. 488.

Iran's international economic outlook.
See item no. 514.

Development of the Iranian oil industry . . .
See item no. 516.

Revolution and energy policy in Iran . . .
See item no. 517.

Iran's petroleum policy . . .
See item no. 518.

Impact of the oil technology on Iran: 1901–1951.
See item no. 519.

Shahanshah of Iran on oil: Tehran agreement – background and perspectives.
See item no. 521.

Finance and foreign exchange for industrialization in Iran . . .
See item no. 523.

Strategies of industrial development in Iran.
See item no. 526.

The agricultural development of Iran.
See item no. 530.

The impacts of large-scale farms on development in Iran . . .
See item no. 531.

Land reform and the rural cooperative societies.
See item no. 537.

Land reform in Iran.
See item no. 538.

The development of large-scale farming in Iran: the case of the province of Gorgan.
See item no. 539.

Dam construction in Iran.
See item no. 544.

Economy

The Persian Railway Syndicate and British railway policy in Iran.
See item no. 547.

The impact of the urban income per capita on agricultural output . . .
See item no. 550.

Employment and income policies for Iran.
See item no. 554.

Employee-supervisor attitudes in banks . . .
See item no. 555.

High level manpower in Iran: from hidden conflict to crisis.
See item no. 561.

Iran: developments during the last fifty years.
See item no. 564.

Development of Iran: a statistical note.
See item no. 566.

Iran's basic macroeconomic problems: a 20-year horizon.
See item no. 567.

Tehran – a demographic and economic analysis.
See item no. 571.

Planning for social change.
See item no. 573.

Technical assistance in theory and practice . . .
See item no. 579.

British Society for Middle Eastern Studies Bulletin (BRISMES).
See item no. 761.

Country Report: Iran.
See item no. 762.

International Journal of Middle East Studies (IJMES).
See item no. 763.

Iranian Studies . . .
See item no. 765.

MERI Report: Iran.
See item no. 770.

MERIP Reports.
See item no. 771.

Middle East Newsletters.
See item no. 772.

The economy of Iran, 1940–1970: a bibliography.
See item no. 774.

Iran: a bibliographic research survey.
See item no. 776.

Iran's politics and government under the Pahlavis . . .
See item no. 779.

Economic history of the Middle East to 1914.
See item no. 781.

Trade

511   **Cities and trade: Consul Abbott on the economy and society of Iran 1847–1866.**
Edited by Abbas Amanat.   London: Ithaca Press (for the Board of the Faculty of Oriental Studies, Oxford University), 1983. 98p.
A selection of reports by K. E. Abbott providing information on trade, production, agriculture, revenue, prices, population and military activity, and covering most provinces and centres of activity in Iran during the mid-19th century. It includes a number of informative appendixes.

512   **Major companies of Iran.**
Edited by Giselle C. Bricault.   London: Graham & Trotman, 1977. 170p.
Contains general information on the major Iranian commercial and industrial firms. It is a revised and expanded edition of the Iran section of the *Major companies of the Arab World and Iran* issued in 1975 by the same publisher.

513   **Technology trade with the Middle East.**
James J. Emery, Norman A. Graham, Michael F. Oppenheimer.   London: Westview Press, 1986. 271p. bibliog.
A general overview of the commercial technology trade relationships between the industrial countries of the West and the Middle East. The volume discusses the trends of technology trade, the factors affecting the trade, future patterns and the policies adopted by the US. Iran, as a major Middle Eastern country, is dealt with throughout the volume.

168

514 **Iran's international economic outlook.**
Mohsen A. Fardi. In: *Iran: past, present and future*. Edited by
Jane W. Jacqz. New York: Aspen Institute for Humanistic Studies,
1976. p. 347–65.
Provides a brief outline of Iran's performance in the foreign-trade sector mainly in
the 1960s and early 1970s, and attempts to forecast the country's future foreign-
trade outlook. The necessity to expand non-oil exports is one of the topics
discussed. Twelve statistical tables are included.

515 **The trade from the mid-14th century to the end of the Safavid
period.**
Ronald Ferrier. In: *The Cambridge history of Iran, vol. 6: the
Timurid and Safavid periods*. Edited by Peter Jackson. Cambridge:
Cambridge University Press, 1986. p. 412–90. bibliog.
A survey of Iranian economics, focusing on trade, during the period of the
Timurids and their Turkmen successors in the 14th and 15th centuries, and in the
Safavid era from the 16th to the mid-18th centuries.

Persian metal technology . . .
See item no. 80.

British interests in the Persian Gulf, 1747–1780.
See item no. 144.

The economic history of Iran, 1800–1914.
See item no. 158.

The case of Hajjī 'Abd al-Karim . . .
See item no. 161.

The American task in Persia.
See item no. 202.

Islam and capitalism.
See item no. 309.

The bazaar as a case study of religion and social change.
See item no. 315.

The Iranian Revolution of 1978–79 . . .
See item no. 374.

Iran's foreign policy 1941–1973 . . .
See item no. 425.

The instruments of Iranian foreign policy.
See item no. 426.

The Iranian Revolution . . .
See item no. 448.

Trade

Iran's international position . . .
See item no. 449.

Expenditure of oil revenue . . .
See item no. 508.

Strategies of industrial development in Iran.
See item no. 526.

Impetus for change: the transformation of peasant marketing in Mazandaran, Iran.
See item no. 540.

Communications, transport, retail trade and services.
See item no. 548.

Iran: developments during the last fifty years.
See item no. 564.

Arms trade registers . . .
See item no. 565.

Development of Iran: a statistical note.
See item no. 566.

Iran's basic macroeconomic problems: a 20-year horizon.
See item no. 567.

The house building market in the Middle East.
See item no. 568.

Felt-making craftsmen of the Anatolian and Iranian plateaux.
See item no. 719.

Country Report: Iran.
See item no. 762.

Oil, Industry and Industrialization

Oil

516 **Development of the Iranian oil industry: international and domestic aspect.**
Fereidun Fesharaki. New York; Washington; London: Praeger, 1976. 296p. 2 maps. bibliog.
Investigates the economics and politics of the oil industry as a regional determinant factor, with special focus on Iran. It contains three parts: the first is concerned with the early oil-concessions in the 1901–51 period; the role of Iran, through the oil industry, in international affairs is dealt with in part two; and part three discusses the domestic activities of the Oil Company.

517 **Revolution and energy policy in Iran: international and domestic implications.**
Fereidun Fesharaki. In: *The security of the Persian Gulf*. Edited by Hossein Amirsadeghi. London: Croom Helm, 1981. p. 255–80.
Examines the impact of Iran's oil-supply interruption, caused by the Revolution, on the industrial countries and OPEC, and assesses the inevitable changes in the oil price. The essay also studies Iran's domestic energy policy with regard to the oil industry, gas, and atomic energy.

518 **Iran's petroleum policy: how does the oil industry function in revolutionary Iran?**
Fereidun Fesharaki. In: *Iran: a revolution in turmoil*. Edited by Haleh Afshar. London: Macmillan, 1985. p. 99–117.
Investigates the resilience of the oil industry in Iran after the fall of the Shah. The article examines the potential oil resource of Iran, its fall in price, oil production

Oil, Industry and Industrialization. Oil

and the effects of incomplete projects, investment requirements, Iran's export strategy and her position in OPEC, and the role of the potential oil revenue for the country's economy.

519 **Impact of the oil technology on Iran: 1901–1951.**
Mohammad Moghari. Ames, Iowa: Committee on Technology and Social Change in Foreign Cultures, 1975. 132p.

Studies the impact of the oil industry on economic life, the political system, and the social and cultural institutions in Iran during the first half of the 20th century. The first chapter discusses the effect of Westernization on Iran, while the oil concessions prior to the nationalization of oil in Iran are covered in chapter two. An investigation of the oil industry's impact on politics, economics and society is undertaken in the next three chapters. The texts of the 1901 D'Arcy Oil Concession and the new concession of 1933 are presented in appendixes one and two (p. 138–66), and appendix three covers the text of the laws concerning the nationalization of the oil industry in 1951 (p. 167–69).

520 **Oil and world power.**
Peter R. Odell. Harmondsworth, England: Penguin Books, 1983. 7th ed. 270p. 12 maps. bibliog.

A descriptive study of the world's oil industry. The book, which was first printed in 1970, has been revised several times, and the present issue was more or less up-to-date for its date of publication. Iran is discussed in detail throughout the book, and the major issues include: the role of Iran in the region as a member of CENTO (Central Treaty Organization); the development of non-oil interests; foreign relations, including those with the USSR; and the Gulf War.

521 **Shahanshah of Iran on oil: Tehran agreement – background and perspectives.**
Mohammad Reza Pahlavi. London: Transorient, 1971. 57p.

Contains the major statements of the Shah and important documents relating to the Tehran Oil Agreement (15 February 1971).

522 **The evolution of Iranian oil policy, 1925–1975.**
Robert B. Stobaugh. In: *Iran under the Pahlavis.* Edited by George Lenczowski. Stanford, California: Stanford University Press, 1978. p. 201–52. bibliog.

A descriptive account of the oil industry from 1925, when the Pahlavi dynasty was founded, until 1975, focusing on the period following nationalization of the oil industry, and the 1953 CIA coup.

Iran in the service of world peace.
See item no. 179.

Mohammad Mossadegh: a political biography.
See item no. 195.

172

The American task in Persia.
See item no. 202.

Technical dictionary of oil industry terms.
See item no. 269.

Politics in the Gulf.
See item no. 342.

Persian oil: a study in power politics.
See item no. 346.

Iran: the new imperialism in action.
See item no. 355.

The Mossadegh era . . .
See item no. 365.

The Iranian Revolution of 1978–79 . . .
See item no. 374.

Iran's foreign policy 1941–1973 . . .
See item no. 425.

The instruments of Iranian foreign policy.
See item no. 426.

The security of the Persian Gulf.
See item no. 431.

The politics of oil and revolution in Iran.
See item no. 432.

Oil and security in the Arabian Gulf.
See item no. 434.

Oil supply disruption in the 1980s.
See item no. 437.

The United States and Iran . . .
See item no. 455.

Revolution and war in the Persian Gulf.
See item no. 467.

Iran: economic development under dualistic conditions.
See item no. 495.

Economics of oil.
See item no. 499.

Iran's petrodollars . . .
See item no. 500.

The Iranian economy 1925–1975 . . .
See item no. 503.

Iran at the end of the century: a Hegelian forecast.
See item no. 506.

Iran in the world economic setting.
See item no. 507.

Expenditure of oil revenue . . .
See item no. 508.

Major companies of Iran.
See item no. 512.

Labour migration to the Arabian Gulf . . .
See item no. 556.

Iranian oilworkers in the 1978–79 Revolution.
See item no. 563.

Iran: developments during the last fifty years.
See item no. 564.

Development of Iran: a statistical note.
See item no. 566.

Energy policy in Iran . . .
See item no. 581.

Industry and industrialization

523 **Finance and foreign exchange for industrialization in Iran, 1310–1319 (1931/32–1940/41).**
Patrick Clawson, Willem Floor. In: *The Gulf in the early 20th century: foreign institutions and local responses*. Edited by R. I. Lawless. Durham, England: Centre for Middle Eastern and Islamic Studies, 1986. p. 125–57.

A study of the Iranian economy in the 1930s, concentrating on the development programme, and focusing in particular on the means by which the industrial development was financed internally and through securing the foreign exchange.

524 **Industrialization in Iran, 1900–1941.**
Willem Floor. Durham, England: Centre for Middle Eastern and Islamic Studies, University of Durham, 1984. 44p. bibliog.

A study of the emergence and development of industry in Iran from the beginning of the 20th century to the downfall of Reza Shah. It includes two lists of the factories open and working in Iran in 1932 and in 1940.

525 **Industrial activities.**
A. Melamid. In: *The Cambridge history of Iran, vol. I: the land of Iran.* Edited by W. B. Fisher. Cambridge, England: Cambridge University Press, 1968. p. 517–51. 2 maps. bibliog.

A general survey of industrial activities in Iran. It concentrates on the mining industries (and in particular the petroleum industry), electricity, food processing and other resource-based industries, and the arts and crafts.

526 **Strategies of industrial development in Iran.**
F. Najmabadi. In: *Iran: past, present and future.* Edited by Jane W. Jacqz. New York: Aspen Institute for Humanistic Studies, 1976. p. 105–21.

An overview of the Shah's attempt to industrialize Iran. It examines, for example, the emergence of private-sector enterprises, the financing of industrial projects, taxation, trade policy, consumer protection and price control, and foreign investment.

527 **A micro-analysis approach to modernization process: a case study of modernity and traditional conflict.**
M. Reza Vaghefi. *International Journal of Middle East Studies,* vol. 12, no. 2 (1980), p. 181–97.

The Iranian appliance industry is explored as a case-study for a micro-analysis of the modernization process. The field-research for the study was carried out in the early 1970s, followed up by a re-examination during the period 1974–77 when the growth of the country's revenue from oil allowed the industrialization process to progress at a faster pace.

Persian metal technology . . .
See item no. 80.

The economic history of Iran, 1800–1914.
See item no. 158.

Iran in the service of world peace.
See item no. 179.

Social development in Iran during the Pahlavi era.
See item no. 310.

Iran: the new imperialism in action.
See item no. 355.

The Iranian structure for liberation . . .
See item no. 386.

Major companies of Iran.
See item no. 512.

Oil, Industry and Industrialization. Industry and industrialization

Iran: developments during the last fifty years.
See item no. 564.

The house building market in the Middle East.
See item no. 568.

MERI Report: Iran.
See item no. 770.

Middle East Newsletters . . .
See item no. 772.

Agriculture and Irrigation

Agriculture

528 **Agricultural and rural development in Iran: agrarian reform, modernization of peasants and agricultural development in Iran.**
Ismail Ajami. In: *Iran: past, present and future.* Edited by Jane W. Jacqz. New York: Aspen Institute for Humanistic Studies, 1976. p. 131–56.

Investigates the problem of modernizing traditional agriculture in the 1960s. Ajami describes the agrarian structure and its development, the 1962 land-reform programme and its socio-economic and political implications, and the farmers' response to change.

529 **Land reform and modernization of the farming structure in Iran.**
Ismail Ajami. In: *The social sciences and problems of development.* Edited by Khodadad Farmanfarmaian. Princeton, New Jersey: Princeton University Program in Near Eastern Studies, 1976. p. 189–207.

Examines the farming structure of Iran under the impact of the 1962 land-reform programme, and the introduction of modernization with reference to the agrarian situation prior to reform.

530 **The agricultural development of Iran.**
Oddvar Aresvik. New York; Washington; London: Praeger, 1976. 246p. 5 maps. bibliog.

Analyses the effects of the agricultural changes made after the 1962 White Revolution, against an historical background. The author, fascinated by the favourable economic potential of the mid-1970s, studies the changes introduced into Iranian agriculture, and generally concludes that the traditional idea of using long-term programmes, which require patience and time, has to be abandoned in favour of rapid agricultural development, for which Iran is a case in point.

531   **The impacts of large-scale farms on development in Iran: a case study of certain aspects of the Iranian agrarian reform.**
Herbert Bergman, Nasser Khademadam.   Saarbrücken, FRG: Verlag der SSIP-Schriften Breitenbach, 1975. 179p. bibliog.
(Research Centre for International Agrarian Development, 4).

Contains a report of the results of an empirical study carried out by the Research Centre of International Agrarian Development in Heidelberg, in co-operation with the Institute for Rural Sociology at the University of Giessen. The study is supported by tables, some from Iranian sources but mostly prepared by authors in the course of their field-work. The socio-economic impact of large-scale farming is one of the major themes discussed.

532   **Agriculture.**
H. Bowen-Jones.   In: *The Cambridge history of Iran, vol. I: the land of Iran*. Edited by W. B. Fisher. Cambridge, England: Cambridge University Press, 1968. p. 565–98. 2 maps. bibliog.

An overview of agriculture and agricultural problems in Iran, concentrating on agricultural geography, land utilization in agricultural regions and the annual water balance. References are also made to population distribution, as well as to the social and economic factors.

533   **Land reform of the Shah and people.**
D. R. Denman.   In: *Iran under the Pahlavis*. Edited by George Lenczowski. Stanford, California: Stanford University Press, 1978. p. 253–301. bibliog.

A descriptive account of the 1962 land-reform programme, its three-phase implementation, and the subsequent social and economic reforms, including the introduction and role of the co-operatives. Several relevant tables and an account of the background history of land reform are included.

534   **Modernization of rural economy in Iran.**
R. Doroudian.   In: *Iran: past, present and future*. Edited by Jane W. Jacqz. New York: Aspen Institute for Humanistic Studies, 1976. p. 157–68.

The 1962 land-reform programme in Iran, and the subsequent disappearance of the landlords, created a financial and managerial gap. This and other problems, particularly the scarcity of water sources, required large-scale projects for land consolidation, land levelling, a modern irrigation system, and new management for large-scale operations. To solve these problems four models were adopted: rural co-operative societies; agribusiness; farm corporations; and production co-operatives. These four models are briefly examined in this paper.

535   **Land and revolution in Iran, 1960–1980.**
      Eric Hooglund.   Austin, Texas: University of Texas Press, 1982.
      171p. bibliog. (Modern Middle East Studies series, no. 7).
A study of the 1962 land reform programme. It is divided in two parts: the first deals with the background of land reform, looking at the rural setting, the origins of land reform and the land reform programme; part two is concerned with the effects of land reform, that is, the land tenure after redistribution and rural socio-economic changes. It also covers the effects of the Revolution.

536   **The Persian land reform: 1962–1966.**
      Ann K. S. Lambton.   Oxford: Oxford University Press, 1969.
      366p. map.
Provides an account of the 1962 land-reform programme in Iran, the way it was put into operation, the problems it encountered, and its achievements. The work presents a solid general background to the rural structure in Iran; its political, social and economic characteristics; the execution of land reform in various stages, and its social and economic impact. The Land Reform Law of 9 January 1962 is also included.

537   **Land reform and the rural cooperative societies.**
      Ann K. S. Lambton.   In: *Iran faces the seventies*. Edited by Ehsan Yar-Shater. New York; Washington; London: Praeger, 1971.
      p. 5–43.
The first stage of the Iranian land-reform programme was introduced in 1962, followed by the introduction of rural co-operative societies, and still further stages throughout the decade. These events are objectively studied by the author, who also makes some preliminary remarks about the physical setting of the land reform, the pre-1962 tenurial system of landownership, and the social and economic background.

538   **Land reform in Iran.**
      K. S. McLachlan.   In: *The Cambridge history of Iran, vol. I: the land of Iran*. Edited by W. B. Fisher. Cambridge, England: Cambridge University Press, 1968. p. 684–713. bibliog.
The traditional relationship between landlord and peasant in Iran was changed in the 1960s following the introduction of the Shah's White Revolution, which included land reform. This reform also altered the pattern of economic and social life throughout the country. The article examines several aspects of agriculture and the landlord-peasant relationship prior to the implementation of land reform in 1962, and the subsequent impact of the reform on the pattern of Iranian life, focusing on social and economic factors.

539   **The development of large-scale farming in Iran: the case of the province of Gorgan.**
      Shōkō Okazaki.   Tokyo: Institute of Asian Economic Affairs, 1968. 51p. 4 maps. (IAEA Occasional Paper).
Investigates the conditions of the establishment and development of large-scale

farming operations in the Gorgan area of north-east Iran. The author surveyed fourteen farms in the area and also analysed the effects of the introduction of large-scale mechanized agriculture upon the traditional agricultural structure and the national economy.

540 **Impetus for change: the transformation of peasant marketing in Mazandaran, Iran.**
C. T. Thompson.   In: *The social sciences and problems of development.* Edited by Khodadad Farmanfarmaian. Princeton, New Jersey. Princeton University Program in Near Eastern Studies, 1976. p. 226–43.
Argues that the structure of the rural marketing system of Iran underwent basic changes in the 1960s. The article examines some rural markets in the northern province of Mazandaran and looks at their historical background.

Semnan: Persian city and region.
See item no. 33.

Checkmate: fighting tradition in central Asia.
See item no. 55.

The economic history of Iran, 1800–1914.
See item no. 158.

The American task in Persia.
See item no. 202.

Iran: precapitalism, capitalism and revolution.
See item no. 314.

Capital development and land reform in Khuzistan, Iran.
See item no. 362.

Land reform and politics: a comparative analysis.
See item no. 363.

Economic origins of the Iranian Revolution.
See item no. 384.

The Iranian structure for liberation . . .
See item no. 386.

Security in the Persian Gulf 1 . . .
See item no. 433.

An assessment of agricultural development policies in Iran.
See item no. 549.

The impact of the urban income per capita on agricultural output . . .
See item no. 550.

Iran: developments during the last fifty years.
See item no. 564.

Development of Iran: a statistical note.
See item no. 566.

Living with the desert: working buildings of the Iranian plateau.
See item no. 692.

The traditional crafts of Persia . . .
See item no. 728.

MERI Report: Iran.
See item no. 770.

Irrigation

541 **Water use in north-east Iran.**
J. Flower. In: *The Cambridge history of Iran, vol. I: the land of Iran*. Edited by W. B. Fisher. Cambridge, England: Cambridge University Press, 1968. p. 599–610.
The article examines in some detail the conditions of water supply and irrigation in the rural zone surrounding Mashhad city in north-east Iran. It deals with three different types of water supply: wells, underground water canals known as *qanat*, and rivers and streams.

542 **Irrigation in the Zagros mountains: Iran.**
H. Lister. Newcastle upon Tyne, England: University of Newcastle upon Tyne, 1978. 66p. 3 maps. bibliog. (Department of Geography Research Series, no. 12).
Offers the results of a multi-disciplinary programme of observation, carried out by a team of Iranian and British students. Their aim was to present a geographical picture of the Khorram-rud valley, 2000 metres up in the Zagros mountains, where the small villages use irrigation for crop production. This work studies the region, its vegetation, the catchment, irrigation channels, water seepage, permeability, and so on, and analyses the data.

543 **The water-supply system in the margin of Dasht-e-Kawir (central Iran).**
Masud Mahdavi, E. W. Anderson. *British Society for Middle Eastern Studies Bulletin*, vol. 10, no. 2 (1983), p. 131–47. 2 maps.
Studies the system of water supply in the arid basin of Dasht-e Kawir, i.e., the extraction of underground water through slightly sloping tunnels called *qanat*, which are dug into the water table.

544 **Dam construction in Iran.**
Plan Organization. Tehran: Plan Organization, Bureau of
Information and Reports, 1969. 87p.

This state publication provides an account of the historical background and
progress of dam construction in Iran prior to 1969. The technical specification of
all existing dams and their social and economic effects are discussed. The volume
contains a number of illustrations.

545 **Agricultural change and rural society in southern Iran.**
Cyrus Salmanzadeh. Cambridge, England: Middle East and
North African Studies Press, 1980. 272p. 5 maps.

An objective investigation of the process of change in a relatively small rural area
of Khuzestan following the construction of a dam. The area was also affected by
the government's introduction of the Dez Irrigation Project in the 1960s, which
shifted away from peasant farming to the establishment of large-scale commercial
agriculture. The work is supported by numerous tables, figures and plates.

546 **Water and irrigation in Iran.**
Manuchehr Vahidi, translated from the Persian by Roger
Cooper. Tehran: Plan Organization, 1968. 79p. 2 maps.

Examines the natural and geographical features of Iran in connection with the
problems of water supply and irrigation, and recommends ways in which a
balance between supply and demand can be preserved. Vahidi also discusses the
economic factors surrounding reservoir dams, whether built at the time, under
construction or under consideration. The book is illustrated and includes a
number of tables and figures.

Semnan: Persian city and region.
See item no. 33.

Geomorphology.
See item no. 49.

Blind white fish in Persia.
See item no. 63.

Transport

547 **The Persian Railway Syndicate and British railway policy in Iran.**
Paul Luft. In: *The Gulf in the early 20th century: foreign
institutions and local responses*. Edited by R. I. Lawless. Durham,
England: Centre for Middle Eastern and Islamic Studies, 1986.
p. 158–215.
A detailed study of the role played by Iranian railway construction in
international power politics up until the 1920s, Luft focuses on several issues of
foreign investment, relevant political aspects and the leading policy which British
institutions like the Anglo-Persian Oil Company and the Imperial Bank of Persia
adopted in setting up the Persian Railway Syndicate (1911–39).

548 **Communications, transport, retail trade and services.**
A. Melamid. In: *The Cambridge history of Iran, vol. I: the land
of Iran*. Edited by W. B. Fisher. Cambridge, England: Cambridge
University Press, 1968. p. 552–64. bibliog.
A brief record of the roads, transport and internal trade in Iran. It also covers sea
and air transport, and the system of communications.

The economic history of Iran, 1800–1914.
See item no. 158.

The American task in Persia.
See item no. 202.

Transport

The Iranian economy 1925–1975 . . .
See item no. 503.

The Gulf in the early 20th century . . .
See item no. 505.

Tehran: an urban analysis.
See item no. 569.

Employment and
Manpower

549 An assessment of agricultural development policies in Iran.
Haleh Afshar.   In: *Iran: a revolution in turmoil*. Edited by Haleh
Afshar. London: Macmillan, 1985. p. 58–79.

The author argues that the Shah's régime was wrong to encourage the migration
of illiterate villagers to cities in search of employment, since the sophisticated
modern technology demanded only a skilled labour force. The peasants'
migration was a blow to agriculture, and their poor conditions in the city slums
forced the government to keep the price of agricultural production low – hence a
further blow. The author points out that, in spite of its promises for rural
development, the Khomeini régime, too, is following its predecessor's disastrous
agricultural policy.

**550 The impact of the urban income per capita on agricultural output: a
case study of pre-1975 Iran.**
Kamran Afshar.   In: *Iran: a revolution in turmoil*. Edited by
Haleh Afshar. London: Macmillan, 1985. p. 51–57.

A brief theoretical analysis of the Shah's development policies concerning the
labour force in Iran's agricultural sector. Afshar argues that the planners of these
policies were wrong to organize a six-day working week of eight hours a day
throughout the year for the agricultural labour force, and to encourage the labour
surplus to join the industrial labour force in the cities.The reasoning behind his
argument is that the agricultural labour requirement is seasonal and the peak of
the harvest season, as a result, suffered from labour shortage.

185

551 **Human resources development: problems and prospects.**
F. Aminzadeh. In: *Iran: past, present and future*. Edited by
Jane W. Jacqz. New York: Aspen Institute for Humanistic Studies,
1976. p. 179–94.

An overview of the development of human resources from the mid-1950s to the
early 1970s. Some statistical tables on demography, education, occupation and
employment, and human resources are included.

552 **Work and Islam.**
Mehdi Bazargan, translated by M. Yasefi, Ali A. Behzadnia and
Najpu Denny. Houston, Texas: Free Islamic Literatures, n.d.
(ca. 1979). 62p.

Mehdi Bazargan was the first Prime Minister of the Islamic Republic of Iran in
1979. He has been involved in Iranian politics since the 1950s, and has written a
number of apologetic pamphlets, attempting to find a reconciliation between
Islamic issues and modern scientific achievements. The present volume is a case-
study on work in Iran with a general background and some Islamic explanations.

553 **Some aspects of the labour market in the Middle East, with special
reference to the Gulf States.**
J. Stace Birks, Clive A. Sinclair. *Journal of Developing Areas*,
vol. 13, no. 3 (April 1979), p. 301–18.

Studies manpower mobilization in the capital-rich Arab states. Amongst the non-
national labour force, the migrant Iranians form a noticeable group in this study.

554 **Employment and income policies for Iran.**
International Labour Office. Geneva: ILO, 1973. 100p.

A report which was prepared by the International Labour Office during
November 1971–June 1972, offering practical advice to Iranian planners and
policy-makers on various labour issues. The major policy recommendations are
listed, and then analytically developed.

555 **Employee-supervisor attitudes in banks: a comparative study
between the Netherlands and Iran.**
Reza Najafbagy. Leiden, The Netherlands: E. J. Brill, 1970.
304p. bibliog.

A cross-cultural comparative study of employee-supervisor attitudes, and the
related subject of personnel management. The study is based mainly on personal
interviews and questionnaires.

556 **Labour migration to the Arabian Gulf: evolution and characteristics
1920–1950.**
Ian J. Seccombe. *British Society for Middle Eastern Studies
Bulletin*, vol. 10, no. 1 (1983), p. 3–20.

An historical and analytical study of labour migration to the Gulf States, and the impact of the oil industry on the regional and international labour market. Reference is made to the national composition, skill levels and recruitment of migrant labour forces in the earliest period of oil exploitation. Iranian work-forces are frequently analysed and included in the tables.

Artisans and guild life in the later Safavid period . . .
See item no. 160.

The population of Iran: a selection of readings.
See item no. 222.

The international migration of high-level manpower . . .
See item no. 227.

Migration and problems of development: the case of Iran.
See item no. 229.

Social change in a southern province of Iran.
See item no. 307.

The role of women in Iranian development . . .
See item no. 332.

Security in the Persian Gulf 1 . . .
See item no. 433.

The Iranian economy 1925–1975 . . .
See item no. 503.

High level manpower in Iran: from hidden conflict to crisis.
See item no. 561.

Development of Iran: a statistical note.
See item no. 566.

Higher education and social change: problems and prospects.
See item no. 578.

Technical cooperation with Iran . . .
See item no. 580.

Labour Movement
and Trade Unions

557   **Workers and Revolution in Iran: a Third World experience of
      workers' control.**
      Assef Bayat.   London; New Jersey: Zed Books, 1987, 207p.
      bibliog.
Based on the author's PhD thesis, the volume examines analytically the growth
of the industrial working class in Iran and the role they played in the 1979 Islamic
Revolution. The politics of industrial relations in post-Revolutionary Iran are also
discussed in detail.

558   **The Iranian working class: a survey of conditions, repression and
      struggles.**
      Committee against Repression in Iran.   London: Committee
      against Repression in Iran, 1977. 28p. map.
Briefly investigates the composition of the labour force and the industries in Iran,
the labour laws, trade unions, and the conditions of the working class and their
movement. Photographs and statistics are included.

559   **Labour unions, law and conditions in Iran (1900–1941).**
      Willem Floor.   Durham, England: Centre for Middle Eastern and
      Islamic Studies, University of Durham, 1985. 118p. bibliog.
Examines the emergence and development of the labour unions, the labour laws,
and the occupational and social conditions of the working class throughout the
20th century.

560 **Workers say no to the Shah: labour law and strikes in Iran.**
Ahmad Ghotbi.   London: Campaign for the Restoration of Trade
Union Rights in Iran, 1978. 2nd ed. 104p.

Provides an introduction to the conditions of the Iranian labour force. Special
emphasis is placed on the oppression of the workers, and on their protests and
campaigns for obtaining their trade union rights. The text of Iran's Labour Law is
given in the first appendix, p. 105–24.

561 **High level manpower in Iran: from hidden conflict to crisis.**
Gail Cook Johnson.   New York: Praeger, 1980. 104p.

An interdisciplinary study of the economic, social and political factors of pre-
Revolutionary Iran. The main focus is on the labour market and organizational
development, and the objective is to prove that the country's high-level
manpower was an underlying cause of revolution.

562 **Labour unions and autocracy in Iran.**
Habib Ladjevardi.   Syracuse, New York: Syracuse University
Press, 1985. 304p. map. bibliog.

Studies the emergence of labour unions in Iran in the context of the political
developments of the 1906–63 period. Chapters are chiefly divided according to the
political epochs. The 1941–53 period receives, for obvious reasons, a lengthier
and more detailed assessment. The 1963–78 and post-Revolution periods are
covered only briefly in the epilogue.

563 **Iranian oilworkers in the 1978–79 Revolution.**
Terisa Turner.   In: *Oil and class struggle*. Edited by Petter Nore,
Terisa Turner. London: Zed Press, 1980. p. 272–90. map.

During the course of the Iranian Revolution in 1978–79 the oil-workers played a
highly significant role in overthrowing the Shah's régime by seizing and shutting
down the national oil installations, and only reactivating them after the
establishment of the new régime. The article examines the organization of the
Iranian oil industry, the class composition of the oil-workers and their role in the
Revolution, with reference to the history of working-class struggle in Iran.

Artisans and guild life in the later Safavid period . . .
See item no. 160.

Iran between two revolutions.
See item no. 172.

Social development in Iran during the Pahlavi era.
See item no. 310.

The bazaar as a case study of religion and social change.
See item no. 315.

The communist movement in Iran.
See item no. 364.

Labour Movement and Trade Unions

The left in contemporary Iran.
See item no. 366.

Protest and perish . . .
See item no. 616.

MERIP Reports.
See item no. 771.

Statistics

564 **Iran: developments during the last fifty years.**
Manouchehr Ganji, Abbas Milani.   In: *Iran: past, present and future*. Edited by Jane W. Jacqz. New York: Aspen Institute for Humanistic Studies, 1976. p. 33–55.

A brief review of Iran's development under the Pahlavis. It is supported by a number of statistical tables concerning the population, the Gross National Product (GNP), varying levels of education, the literacy campaign, agriculture and land ownership, industry, economic and foreign trade.

565 **Arms trade registers, the arms trade with the Third World.**
Eva Grenbäck.   Cambridge, Massachusetts; London: MIT Press; Stockholm: Almqvist and Wiksell International, 1975. 130p. (A Stockholm International Peace Research Institute Publication).

Casts a statistical light on the issue of arms deals with ninety-seven Third World countries in the mid-1970s by presenting a register of deals in major arms. The information is as complete as the open literature allows up to 1 January 1974, and is substantiated by tables, charts and figures. Arms supplies to Iran are given in detail on pages 46–50.

566 **Development of Iran: a statistical note.**
Firouz Tofigh.   In: *Iran: past, present and future*. Edited by Jane W. Jacqz. New York: Aspen Institute for Humanistic Studies, 1976. p. 57–67.

A brief multi-disciplinary note on Iran's social conditions in the 20th century, with particular emphasis on the 1970s. It covers population, urbanization, labour force and manpower, education and literacy, national income, industry, agriculture and foreign trade. Statistical tables are included.

191

567 **Iran's basic macroeconomic problems: a 20-year horizon.**
F. Vakil.   In: *Iran: past, present and future*. Edited by
Jane W. Jacqz. New York: Aspen Institute for Humanistic Studies,
1976. p. 83–104.

A brief statistical examination of the major macro-economic problems that the
author anticipates will occur in Iran in the following twenty years. It is mainly
concerned with the role of oil revenues, inflation as a short-term loss of resources
with longer-term consequences, the urban-rural income gap, and the strategy of
export promotion with a view to the role of non-oil exports. Relevant statistical
tables are included.

Historical gazetteer of Iran . . .
See item no. 23.

Income distribution in Iran . . .
See item no. 308.

Iran's foreign policy 1941–1973 . . .
See item no. 425.

Iran's petrodollars . . .
See item no. 500.

Iran's international economic outlook.
See item no. 514.

Human resources development: problems and prospects.
See item no. 551.

MERI Report: Iran.
See item no. 770.

MERIP Reports.
See item no. 771.

Urbanization and Planning

568 **The house building market in the Middle East.**
B. Al-Alak, I. D. Ford.   London: Graham & Trotman, 1979.
178p. bibliog.

Proposes that the Middle East has become a far more important market for many construction firms than a number of industrialized countries. It also argues that the Middle East market has been under-explored internationally and that it is steadily growing. The countries are discussed individually and include Iran, Iraq, Jordan, Kuwait, Saudi Arabia, Syria and Egypt.

569 **Tehran: an urban analysis.**
H. Bahrambeygui.   Tehran: Sahab Books Institute, 1977. 180p.
15 maps. bibliog.

A study of Tehran in contrast with the rest of Iran. The book is based on the author's MA dissertation, which was presented to the University of Durham, England in 1972. The physical setting of Tehran, its development up to the Second World War, and an analysis of its demographic characteristics are given in the first three chapters. Chapter four, forming the major part of the book, analyses the most important functions and activities of Tehran, and examines its interaction with physical development. Chaper five deals with transportation and communication, while land use and land values are discussed in the seventh and final chapter.

570 **The effect of development on the urban family.**
Constance Cronin.   In: *The social sciences and problems of development*. Edited by Khodadad Farmanfarmaian. Princeton, New Jersey: Princeton University Program in New Eastern Studies, 1976. p. 261–72.

Assesses the impact of development programmes in Iran and some of the

193

traditional upper-class families in Tehran. The author claims that she studied this group in Iranian society because Iran was a rapidly developing country in the early 1970s, and because the individuals in his selected group were assumingly the most affected by development.

571 **Tehran: a demographic and economic analysis.**
Ferydoon Firoozi. In: *The population of Iran*. Edited by Jamshid Momeni. Honolulu: East-West Centre, 1977. p. 342–58.

A survey of the development of Tehran from a small rural area in the later 18th century, when it was chosen by the newly-established Qajar dynasty as their place of residence and the country's capital, to a large 20th-century metropolitan centre.

572 **Development and planning in Iran after World War II.**
Harald Mehner. In: *Iran under the Pahlavis*. Edited by George Lenczowski. Stanford, California: Stanford University Press, 1978. p. 167–99. bibliog.

An overview of planning in modern Iran focusing on its aims and objectives, its methods, and the way it was financed. The article also covers the implementation of the plans and problems caused by this implementation.

573 **Planning for social change.**
Shahpour Rassekh. In: *Iran faces the seventies*. Edited by Ehsan Yar-Shater. New York; Washington; London: Praeger, 1971. p. 143–65. bibliog.

The first Iranian development programme acceptable to the World Bank for financial assistance was concluded in 1947 and put into action in 1948 for a period of seven years. The next two development programmes were carried out in the 1955–62 and 1962–68 periods, with the fourth, 1968–73, being in progress in 1971 when the present article was printed. The author examines these programmes with reference to changes in the demographic situation, educational institutions, public health and environmental sanitation, urbanization, social welfare, the White Revolution, economic growth and the need for administrative reforms.

Yazd and its hinterland . . .
See item no. 30.

The Iranian city of Shiraz.
See item no. 31.

Kermanshah: an Iranian provincial city.
See item no. 32.

The first cities.
See item no. 90.

Elam.
See item no. 103.

Media.
See item no. 104.

The population of Iran: a selection of readings.
See item no. 222.

Poverty and revolution in Iran . . .
See item no. 230.

Income distribution in Iran . . .
See item no. 308.

Security in the Persian Gulf 1 . . .
See item no. 433.

Economic development and revolutionary upheavals in Iran.
See item no. 509.

Development of Iran: a statistical note.
See item no. 566.

Education

574 **Education and social awakening in Iran: 1850–1968.**
A. Reza Arasteh. Leiden, The Netherlands: E. J. Brill, 1971.
rev. ed. 236p.

Includes twelve chapters on various aspects and historical developments of the educational system in ancient and modern times, and in relation to continuity and change. The impact of education in modern socio-political issues; the role and position of women on modern education; the role of education in the reconstruction of Iran; and the social awakening of the nation are some of the other major topics investigated. Several important laws affecting education in Iran are included in the appendix.

575 **Educational and cultural development in Iran during the Pahlavi era.**
Wilhelm Eilers. In: *Iran under the Pahlavis*. Edited by George Lenczowski. Stanford, California: Stanford University Press, 1978.
p. 303–31. bibliog.

A descriptive account of the system of education in Iran during the Pahlavi era, and the reforms introduced by the Pahlavi kings. Eilers deals with elementary, secondary and higher education, and the administration, as well as foreign and special schools and the campaign against illiteracy. He also provides an account of cultural activities, including publications and libraries, museums and excavations, theatre, art and music, as well as sports and youth organizations.

576 **Iran: from religious dispute to revolution.**
Michael M. J. Fisher. Cambridge, Massachusetts; London: Harvard University Press, 1980. 244p. bibliog.

Examines the transformation of culture and common sense (or 'the underlying assumptions of everyday life') in Iran, focusing on religious education, and in

196

particular on its function in moulding character and thereby reinforcing common sense. The work includes six chapters: 1. 'Culture, history, and politics'; 2. 'Rise and decline of the *madrasa*'; 3. '*Madrasa*: style and substance'; 4. 'Qum: arena of conflict'; 5. 'Discourse and mimesis: Shi'ism in everyday life'; 6. The revolutionary movement of 1977–1979'. The content is substantiated by first-hand information, appendixes, notes and tables.

577 **The mantle of the prophet.**
Roy Mottahedeh.   London: Chatto & Windus, 1986. 390p. bibliog.

A discursive study of Iranian cultural life in narrative style, based on fact, but with fictionalized characters. A cleric, 'Ali Hashemi, is the central figure, and the reader is taken with him on a cultural tour through a religious school in the holy city of Qom from 1953 to the confusions and challenges of more recent Iranian history. Hashemi's life story is set against a rich background of Iranian culture, interwoven with the characteristics of Islam and yet distinct from the Islamic Revolution.

578 **Higher education and social change: problems and prospects.**
Marvin Zonis. In: *Iran faces the seventies*. Edited by Ehsan Yar-Shater. New York; Washington; London: Praeger, 1971. p. 217–59. bibliog.

A survey of higher education in the 1960s as a modern institution and as a manpower producer. It also covers the role of modern education in shaping political attitudes and values.

The forces of modernization in nineteenth century Iran . . .
See item no. 180.

Mary Bird in Persia.
See item no. 208.

The Iranian 'brain drain'.
See item no. 226.

The international migration of high-level manpower . . .
See item no. 227.

Physician migration to the United States . . .
See item no. 232.

Social change in a southern province of Iran.
See item no. 307.

Social development in Iran during the Pahlavi era.
See item no. 310.

The role of women in Iranian development . . .
See item no. 332.

Education

Politics, polemics and pedagogs . . .
See item no. 452.

Iran: developments during the last fifty years.
See item no. 564.

Development of Iran: a statistical note.
See item no. 566.

Planning for social change.
See item no. 573.

The role of information and communication in national development.
See item no. 758.

MERI Report: Iran.
See item no. 770.

Science and Technology

579 **Technical assistance in theory and practice: the case of Iran.**
Jahangir Amuzegar.   New York; Washington; London: Praeger,
1966. 269p.

Studies the United States' Point IV programme (launched by President Truman in
1949 with the objective of providing poorer nations with American technical
assistance) as an example of foreign technical assistance, and Iran as a model of
an aid-receiving country since 1949. The main purpose is to explore the
possibilities and limitations of foreign assistance, its social and economic impacts
on the aid-receiving nations and their views concerning the aid. The work includes
a list of US aid projects from 1950 to 1965.

580 **Technical cooperation with Iran: a case study of opportunities and
policy implications for the United States.**
Lewis M. Branscomb. Washington, DC: Agency for International
Development, 1972. 116p.

Following the termination of the United States' programme of concessional
assistance to Iran in 1967, the US-Iran economic and industrial relationship was
organized by a new body: the Agency for International Development (AID). In
January 1972 AID sent a team of American specialists to Iran to carry out a case-
study for general guidance and to identify Iran's needs for American technology
and expertise. The book provides the team's subsequent report and includes
fourteen relevant appendixes.

581 **Energy policy in Iran: domestic choices and international
implications.**
Bijan Mossavar-Rahmani.   New York; Oxford; Toronto; Sydney;
Paris; Frankfurt: Pergamon Press, 1981. 140p.

Analyses the patterns of energy demand-and-supply sources and prepares a

Science and Technology

guideline for Iran's oil production which, if put into action, the author suggests, will achieve the best and most efficient energy policy. Oil has received the most attention as the primary source of energy, but other sources, such as natural gas, hydropower, solid fuel, electricity and nuclear power, have also been studied. Petrochemicals are covered in a separate section.

582   **Transfer of technology and development: a framework and some observations from Iran.**
Taghi Saghafi-Nejad.   In: *The social sciences and problems of development*. Edited by Khodadad Farmanfarmaian. Princeton, New Jersey: Princeton University Program in Near Eastern Studies, 1976. p. 143–70. bibliog.

Examines the introduction of modern technology by the multi-national enterprises into Iran, its impact on the local manufacturing activities and the subsequent instability.

The exact sciences in Timurid Iran.
See item no. 129.

Persian science in Safavid times.
See item no. 170.

A dictionary of scientific terms.
See item no. 267.

The legacy of Islam.
See item no. 280.

Politics, polemics and pedagogs . . .
See item no. 452.

The Iranian military . . .
See item no. 490.

Technology trade with the Middle East.
See item no. 513.

Land reform and modernization of the farming structure in Iran.
See item no. 529.

Persian medical manuscripts . . .
See item no. 740.

An annotated bibliography of Islamic science.
See item no. 783.

Literature

Literary history and criticism

583 Life and works of Abdul Qadir Bedil.
  Abdul Ghani. Lahore, Pakistan: Publishers United, 1960. 285p.
Investigates the life and works of the Persian poet Abdul Qadir Bedil, who was
born and lived in India during the reign of Shah Jahan and the following period
when the Mongol Empire was crumbling under Mohammad Shah. Famous in
Afghanistan and Central Asia as a literary pioneer, Bedil's work centred round an
anti-feudalist theme.

584 The formation of *sabk-i Hindi*.
  Aziz Ahmad. In: *Iran and Islam*. Edited by C. E. Bosworth.
  Edinburgh: Edinburgh University Press, 1971. p. 1–9.
Traces the origins and development of the complex and intellectualized Persian
literary style of poetry, especially the form known as *ghazal* employed in the
literary school *sabk-e Hendi* (Indian style), in India from the 16th to the 18th
century.

585 Ahmad Shamlu: the rebel poet in search of an audience.
  Leonardo P. Alishan. *Iranian Studies*, vol. 18, no. 2–4 (Spring–
  Autumn 1985), p. 375–422.
A critical study of the poetry of the modernist contemporary poet Ahmad Shamlu
as a means of communication between the artist and his audience.

586 **Rumi the Persian, the Sufi.**
A. Reza Arasteh. London: Routledge & Kegan Paul, 1974. 194p.
bibliog.

A study of Persian culture and character, as reflected in the works of the 13th-century Sufi poet Jalal al-Din Rumi. The book consists of four parts: 1, 'An analysis of Persian culture'; 2, 'Rebirth in love and creativity: an analysis of Rumi'; 3, 'The human situation and self realization'; and 4, 'The contribution of Rumi to the situation of modern man'.

587 **Classical Persian literature.**
A. J. Arberry. London: Allen & Unwin, 1958. 450p. bibliog.

Investigates the chronological development of classical Persian literature from the middle of the 9th century to the 15th century, covering a number of works by Iranian and European scholars. The chapters are divided according to historical epochs and the ruling dynasties in Iran, although the principal poets, such as Sa'di, Rumi, Hafez and Jami are each given a full chapter.

588 **The Kūfic inscription in Persian verses in the court of the royal palace of Mas'ūd III at Ghazni.**
Alessio Bombaci. Rome: Istituto Italiano per il Medio ed
Estremo Oriente (IsMEO), 1966. 42p. bibliog.

Attempts to introduce, translate and analyse a Persian inscription in verse which was found by the Italian Archaeological Mission in Afghanistan during its excavations between 1959 and 1964. It is claimed that the inscription is as old as the palace which was completed in March 1112 and was the residence of the Ghaznavid ruler Mas'ud III. The book is concluded by 742 plates.

589 **Parthian writings and literature.**
Mary Boyce. In: *The Cambridge history of Iran, vol. 3: the
Seleucid, Parthian and Sasanian periods*. Edited by Ehsan
Yar-Shater. Cambridge, England: Cambridge University Press,
1986. p. 1151–65. bibliog.

A study of the writings and literature in the pre-Islamic Parthian language, of which little has survived in its original form. The author's study is, therefore, based on later redactions and on Persian or Georgian versions of Parthian literature.

590 **The political poetry of modern Persia.**
Compiled and translated by Edward G. Browne. Cambridge,
England: Cambridge University Press, 1914. 308p.

A reprint of the second part of the author's *Press and poetry of modern Persia*, thus omitting the translation of Tarbiyat's alphabetical list of newspapers, as well as the prefaces and indexes which constitute the first part. The illustrations of the complete work are placed together at the end.

591 **Mithra on the lotus.**
Martha L. Carter. *Acta Iranica*, vol. VII, no. 21 (1981), p. 74–98.
A study of the imagery of Mithra, the sun god, in the pre-Islamic Sasanian era, emphasizing its relationship to the early Indian Buddhist imagery of the lotus.

592 **The literary genres in modern Iran.**
Peter Chelkowski. In: *Iran under the Pahlavis*. Edited by George Lenczowski. Stanford, California: Stanford University Press, 1978. p. 333–64. bibliog.
Relates the emergence of modernism in literature to the rise of Reza Khan, later Reza Shah (1925–41), and his campaign against traditionalism. Deals with the departure of poetry from classical forms, and the emergence and development of modern poetry, the novel, the short story and drama.

593 **The *Divan* of Manuchehri Damghani: a critical study.**
Jerome W. Clinton. Minneapolis, Minnesota: Bibliotheca Islamica, 1972. 154p. bibliog.
Studies court poetry in classical Persian literature through a critical investigation of the works of Manuchehri Damghani. The characteristics, content and composition of his poetry are discussed. The general aspects and tradition of court poetry in Iran are also studied.

594 **The poetics of politics: commitment in modern Persian literature.**
Hamid Dabashi. *Iranian Studies*, vol. 18, nos 2–4. (Spring–Autumn 1985), p. 147–88.
A study of the problem of commitment in modern Persian literature. To this end, the author attempts to trace the emergence and development of the intelligentsia in Iran.

595 **In search of Omar Khayyam.**
Ali Dashti, translated by L. P. Elwell-Sutton. London: Allen & Unwin, 1971. 249p. bibliog. (Persian Studies Monographs).
Studies the reminiscences and judgements of Khayyam's contemporaries, and assesses the work which is known without doubt to be that of Khayyam. Dashti's purpose is to establish a framework for determining which of the *ruba'is* (the most ancient essentially Persian verse-form) are likely to be authentic so that those which do not conform can be eliminated. It consists of three parts: 1, 'In search of Khayyam'; 2, 'In search of quatrains'; and 3, 'Random thoughts'.

596 **The influence of Arabic poetry on the development of Persian poetry.**
Umar Muhammad Daudpota. Bombay: Fort Printing Press, 1934. 192p. bibliog.
Traces the influence of Arabic poetry on the development and growth of Persian poetry and investigates in turn how far Arabic poetry itself has been influenced by

Literature. Literary history and criticism

elements of Persian culture and poetry. The work is based on a large number of parallel passages from the poetical literature of both the Arabs and Persians.

597   **Of piety and poetry: the interaction of religion and literature in the life and works of Hakim Sanā'i of Ghazna.**
J. T. P. De Bruijn.   Leiden, The Netherlands: E. J. Brill, 1983. 279p. bibliog. (Publication of 'De Goeje Fund', No. 25).

The life and works of Hakim Sana'i, as a poet during a period of change, are the subjects of this volume. A history of his life, and a textual history and literary analysis of his works are provided. The author claims that Sanā'i is the forerunner, or rather founder, of a literary school and that his work shows, for the first time in Persian poetry, elements of interaction between poetry and religion.

598   **The influence of folk-tale and legend on modern Persian literature.**
L. P. Elwell-Sutton.   In: *Iran and Islam.* Edited by C. E. Bosworth. Edinburgh: Edinburgh University Press, 1971. p. 247–54.

Traces the influence of Persian folk-literature on the post-First World War literature of Iran. The article was first read under the general theme 'Legends and Mythologies as a source of inspiration in Arts and Literature' at the XXXV International PEN Congress, Abidjan, Ivory Coast, in August 1967.

599   **Persian poetic metres.**
Mas'ud Farzad.   Leiden, The Netherlands: E. J. Brill, 1967. 127p.

A synthetic study of Persian poetic metres in ten sections, including one on the metre of the *ruba'i* (Khayyamian quatrain). Ninety-four tables, of various metres, are included.

600   **Prophets of doom: literature as a socio-political phenomenon in modern Iran.**
Mohammad Reza Ghanoonparvar.   Lanham, New York; London: University Press of America, 1984. 199p.

Attempts to study the modern literature of Iran, i.e. that which is regarded as the *engagé* or committed literature of the Pahlavi era, with emphasis on post-Second World War period.

601   **The idea of constitutionalism in Persian literature prior to the 1906 revolution.**
Abdul-Hadi Hairi.   In: *Akten des VII Kongresses für Arabistik und Ismalwissenschaft.* Edited by Albert Dietrich. Göttingen, FRG: Vendenhoeck & Ruprecht, 1976. p. 189–207.

A study of Persian literature in the second half of the 19th century, with reference to the emergence of new tendencies in theme and style.

602 **Formal elements in the Persian popular romances.**
William L. Hanaway. *Review of National Literatures*, vol. 2,
no. 1 (1971), p. 139–60.
An investigation of the broad formal characteristics and narrative elements
apparent in some Persian popular romances.

603 **Popular literature in Iran.**
William Hanaway. In: *Iran, continuity and variety*. Edited by
Peter J. Chelkowski. New York: Centre for Near Eastern Studies,
New York University, 1971. p. 59–75.
A critical study of the literary and social characteristics of traditional Persian folk-
tales. The author discusses the idea that the modernist trend in Persian literature
preserved certain elements of traditional folklore and did not break from past
traditions as sharply as has been suggested by most critics.

604 **The rhythmic structure of Persian verse.**
Bruce Hayes. *Edebiyat: a Journal of Middle Eastern Literature*,
vol. 4, no. 2 (1979), p. 193–242.
An analytical study of the rhythmic structure of Persian verse. Hayes shows how
the structure of a poem determines the organized system of metrical groups and
the relationship between the metres.

605 **Folk tales of ancient Persia.**
Retold by Forough Hekmat. Delmar, New York: Caravan
Books, 1974. 119p. (Persian Heritage Series, no. 18).
Relates ten folk-tales from Shiraz, which have been handed down from
generation to generation in the Persian oral tradition. The classical style of
recounting is preserved, and accompanied by striking illustrations.

606 **Unity in the *ghazals* of Hafez.**
Michael C. Hillmann. Minneapolis, Minnesota; Chicago:
Bibliotheca Islamica, 1976. 169p. bibliog.
It is a popular view that the *ghazal* (ode) verse-form in mediaeval Persian
literature lacks unity. The author controversially attempts to seek unity in the
Hafezian *ghazals*.

607 **Hedāyat's *The blind owl* forty years after.**
Edited by Michael C. Hillmann. Austin, Texas: University of
Texas at Austin, 1978. 197p. bibliog. (Centre for Middle Eastern
Studies, Middle East Monographs, no. 4).
A collection of critical studies on the life and works of Sadeq Hedayat. Particular
emphasis is on his *Buf-e Kur* (The blind owl) which was written in 1937. A list of
Hedayat's major works is included in the bibliography.

608 **Sociology of the Iranian writer.**
Edited by Michael Craig Hillmann. *Iranian Studies*, vol. 18, no. 2–4 (Spring–Autumn 1985), p. 131–460.

This issue of Iranian studies is confined to the sociology of the Iranian writer, focusing on a number of writers from the Pahlavi and post-Revolution period. Several articles covering the major literary events, trends and writers are included. The volume is dedicated to the writer Gholam Hosein Sa'edi (1935–85), whose death delayed the publication date of the issue until early 1986. Sa'edi's brief autobiography in Farsi, dated 1976, is also included.

609 **The *Gāthās* of Zarathustra.**
S. Insler. Leiden, The Netherlands: E. J. Brill; Tehran; Liège, Belgium: Bibliothèque Pahlavi, 1975. 334p. bibliog. (Acta Iranica, 8).

A critical commentary on the Gathas (the oldest of the five sections of the *Avesta*) outlining the problems of the text and its grammar, vocabulary and syntax. Contains the original text, in transliteration, and its translation on alternate pages.

610 **The life and works of Jalal-ud-din Rumi.**
Afzal Iqbal. London: Octagon Press, 1983. 314p. bibliog.

A study for the general reader of Rumi's contributions to literature and thought, and an appreciation of his achievements. The author first describes the conditions of the 13th century when Rumi lived and worked. This provides a setting for a detailed biography of Rumi, which is given in the second chapter. The appearance of *Shams-e Tabriz* and the poet's revolutionary change are dealt with in the next three chapters. Chapter six is concerned with the thoughts and philosophy of Rumi. The seventh and final chapter gives an English translation of that portion of *Masnavi* which had been omitted by Nicholson in his translation.

611 **Four eminent poetesses of Iran: with a brief survey of Iranian and Indian poetesses of neo-Persian.**
M. Ishaque. Calcutta, India: Iran Society, 1950. 95p.

Sheds some light on the life and literary works of four Iranian women poets, Rābi'ah of Quzdar; Mahsatī of Ganja; Qurratu'l-'Ayn; and Parvin-i I'tasāmī. Several poems are presented, and are given in both Persian and English. The book ends with a brief survey of ninety-six other women poets based on scant references in thirteen literary collections.

612 **History of Persian literature.**
Edited by Yunus Jaffery. Delhi: Triveni Publications, 1981. 152p.

A collection of some twelve articles on various aspects of the Persian language and literature, focusing on the pre-Islamic period.

613 **Matthew Arnold's** *Sohrab and Rustum* **and its Persian original.**
Hasan Javadi. *Review of National Literatures*, vol. 2, no. 1
(Spring 1971), p. 61–73.
A review of Matthew Arnold's interest in oriental literature and his version of
Ferdousi's *Sohrab and Rustum* which appeared in 1853. Reference is also made to
the Persian original.

614 **Recent Persian literature: observation on themes and tendencies.**
Mohammad Ali Jazayery. *Review of National Literatures*, vol. 2,
no. 1 (Spring 1971), p. 11–28. bibliog.
Provides a brief sketch of the emergence, general pattern and development of the
modernist trend in contemporary Persian literature since its beginning in the late
19th century.

615 **Modern Persian prose literature.**
Hassan Kamshad. Cambridge, England: Cambridge University
Press, 1966. 210p. bibliog.
Although the title gives an impression of generality, the work is in fact confined to
modern intellectual prose fiction. Drama gets scant attention, as do journalism,
belles lettres, and other areas. Nevertheless, Kamshad's volume has been a major
source of reference on modern Persian fiction since it was published. The book is
divided into two parts. Part one is rather fragmentary, moving from 19th-century
linguistic reformism to social attitudes in post-constitutional literature. This forms
a background for part two which deals with the works of Sadeq Hedayat, the
leading writer of the 1930s and, to a lesser extent, the 1940s. It contains a
comprehensive list of Hedayat's works.

616 **Protest and perish: a history of the Writers' Association of Iran.**
Ahmad Karimi-Hakkak. *Iranian Studies*, vol. 18, no. 2–4
(Spring–Autumn 1985), p. 189–229.
An account of the formation of the Writers' Association of Iran in 1968 and its
campaigns against both the Pahalvi régime and the revolutionary government of
the Islamic Republic.

617 **Zoroastrian Pahlavi writings.**
Jean P. de Menasce. In: *The Cambridge history of Iran, vol. 3:
the Seleucid, Parthian and Sasanian periods*. Edited by Ehsan
Yar-Shater. Cambridge, England: Cambridge University Press,
1983. p. 1166–95. bibliog.
Although based on the pre-Islamic Sasanian material, Zoroastrian Pahlavi
writings are the products of the 9th and 10th centuries when the scholar-priests
made an effort to record the oral, predominantly religious, literature which was
threatened by the decline of the Zoroastrian community. The article examines
some of these texts.

618 **Revitalization: some reflections on the works of Saffar-Zadeh.**
Farzaneh Milani. In: *Women and revolution in Iran.* Edited by
Guity Nashat. Boulder, Colorado: Westview Press, 1983.
p. 129–40.
Studies the literary works of the contemporary poetess Saffarzadeh. The author
compares the literary aspects and social and political reflections in her poetry of
pre-Revolutionary Iran with those after the Revolution in which she finds her
goals for identity fulfilled.

619 **Conformity and confrontation: a comparison of two Iranian women
poets.**
Farzaneh Milani. In: *Women and the family in the Middle East:
new voices of change.* Edited by Elizabeth Warnock Fernea.
Austin, Texas: University of Texas Press, 1985. p. 317–30.
Attempts to study, through their literary works, the struggle for freedom of two
contemporary women poets, Forugh Farrokhzad and Tahereh Saffarzadeh, in an
environment which is depicted as treating women as subordinate to men.

620 **Power, prudence, and print: censorship and Simin Daneshvar.**
Farzaneh Milani. *Iranian Studies*, vol. 18, no. 2–4
(Spring–Autumn 1985), p. 325–47.
A study of censorship in modern Iran with special emphasis on self-censorship
and other unofficial modes of suppression. Simin Daneshvar's fictional works, the
first of which appeared in 1948, and particularly her novel *Suvashun* (1969), are
examined in this study as an example of censorship emphasizing the male-female
relationship.

621 **The life and works of Amir Khusrau.**
Mohammad Wahid Mirza. Lahore, Pakistan: Panjab University
Press, 1962. 240p. bibliog.
Provides a biographical sketch of Amir Khosrou. Born in India in the mid-13th
century, he is considered to be one of the best classical Persian writers of the
sabk-e Hendi (Indian style). The invention of the originally three-stringed
instrument *seh-tār* (sitar) has also been attributed to him.

622 **History of Persian literature from the beginning of the Islamic
period to the present day.**
Edited by G. Morrison. Leiden, The Netherlands; Cologne,
FRG: E. J. Brill, 1981. 206p.
A collection of four articles on the Persian literature of the last twelve centuries,
dealing mainly with published works. The first article, by the editor, is a study of
classical Persian literature from its emergence in the 9th century to the time of its
last great poet, Jami, in the 15th century. The subsequent developments, from the
time of Jami to the emergence of modern attitudes in literature in the
20th century and its characteristics till the mid-1950s, is the subject of the last

article by Mohammad Reza Shafi'i Kadkani. The other two articles, both by Julian Baldick, deal with the mediaeval Sufi literature in prose and in poetry.

623 **The Iranian national epic.**
Theodor Nöldeke. Translated from the German by L. Bogdanov. Bombay: British India Press, Mazgaon, 1925. 161p. (Journal of the K. R. Cama Oriental Institute, no. 6)

An English translation of Nöldeke's contribution to the Iranian national epic in general, and to Ferdousi's *Shahnameh* (Book of Kings) in particular. The book includes two chapters, namely 'The traces of epic narratives' and 'Formation of the national tradition', as a background to the author's main interest, the *Shahnameh*, which forms the bulk of the work.

624 **Post-revolution Persian verse.**
Munibur Rahman. Aligarh, India: Institute of Islamic Studies, Muslim University, 1955. 188p. bibliog.

A critical study of Persian poetry in the years after the constitutional revolution of 1905–09. It assesses the impact of European literature and modernizing influences, and the introduction of social and political themes. It also examines the characteristics of the traditional verse-forms and the popular ballads. The works of the prominent poets, such as Bahar, Lāhuti, 'Aref, Iraj, Eshqi and Parvin E'tesami are examined in more detail.

625 **Persian mysticism in Goethe's *West-östlicher Divan*.**
Ernst Rose. *Review of National Literatures*, vol. 2, no. 1 (1971), p. 92–111.

Studies the mystic influences traced in Goethe's *West-östlicher Divan* which was originally published in 1819. At the beginning of the 19th century Goethe's writing seemed not to have been affected by the storming of the Bastille in 1789 and the events which followed. However, his view towards the realities of life, and, subsequently, the pure classical values in literature, was gradually changed by the emergence of Napoleonic imperialism and modern European individualism. He began to read the Persian poet Hafez and entered the phase in his life which is the subject of this study.

626 **Poets and prose writers of the late Saljuq and Mongol periods.**
J. Rypka. In: *The Cambridge history of Iran, vol. 5: the Saljuq and Mongol periods*. Edited by J. A. Boyle. Cambridge, England: Cambridge University Press, 1968. p. 550–625. bibliog.

Surveys the literary developments in Iran from the mid-12th to the mid-14th centuries, focusing on poetry. It covers the different schools, court patrons and the great poets of the period, and briefly examines both literary and non-literary prose works.

627 **Gholam-Hoseyn Sa'edi: a voice of the poor.**
G. R. Sabri-Tabrizi. In: *Index on Censorship*, 4 (1986). p. 11–13.
Presents an overview of the life and works of the contemporary writer and
playwright, Gholam Hosein Sa'edi, who died in exile in Paris in November 1985.

628 **Persian poets of Sind.**
H. I. Sadarangani. Karachi, Pakistan: Ahmed A. Jivaji at Aage
Kadam Printery, 1956. 319p. bibliog. (Sindhi Adabi Board).
This is the first book to be published under an ambitious scheme introduced by
the Sindhi Adabi Board, forming a contribution towards the development of a
national history and literature. A four-year period (1956–59) was set for the
execution of the scheme: the intention was to publish as many as 114 books, of
which six works should have been in English and eighty-seven works in the field
of Persian poetry and historical works in Persian. The present book, which was
originally prepared in 1946 as a PhD thesis, is divided into five chronological
chapters covering the period from the 15th to the 20th centuries. Many quotations
in Persian script (some with a translation) are included.

629 **Persian literature in the Safavid period.**
Zabihollah Safa. In: *The Cambridge history of Iran, vol. 6: the
Timurid and Safavid periods*. Edited by Peter Jackson. Cambridge,
England: Cambridge University Press, 1986. p. 948–64.
Surveys Persian poetry in the Safavid period (1501–1736). The impact of the
recognition of Shi'ism and its active propagation by the Safavid shahs is assessed.
The subsequent influence of the Arabic language, the centralization of the
government and the political and economic cohesion of the country are also
regarded as having had some influence on the development of literature.

630 **Persian literature in the Timurid and Turkmen periods,
(782–907/1380–1501).**
Zabihollah Safa. In: *The Cambridge history of Iran, vol. 6: the
Timurid and Safavid periods*. Edited by Peter Jackson. Cambridge,
England: Cambridge University Press, 1986. p. 913–28. bibliog.
A brief examination of the character of Persian literature, and its development in
a period of complex linguistic evolution and historical change under the Timur
and Turkmen dynasties of the late 14th and the 15th centuries.

631 **The triumphal sun: a study of the works of Jalāladdin Rumi.**
Annemarie Schimmel. London: Fine Books; The Hague: East-
West Publications, 1978. 480p. bibliog. (Persian Studies series,
no. 8).
An interpretative study of Rumi's poetical language and his mystical thought,
with the purpose of casting some light on the poet's personality and his influence
in the East and the West. The author shows how certain key images and works
play a significant symbolic role in the understanding of Sufi literature and that of

the 13th-century poet Rumi. The volume includes some introductory historical and biographical notes, and a number of illustrations.

632 **Hāfiz and his contemporaries.**
Annemarie Schimmel. In: *The Cambridge history of Iran, vol. 6: the Timurid and Safavid periods*. Edited by Peter Jackson. Cambridge, England: Cambridge University Press, 1986. p. 929–47. bibliog.
An overview of the celebrated Persian poet Hafez of Shiraz (ca. 1319/20–1389) and his poetry, with reference to his contemporaries and to social and political developments of his time.

633 **Persian literature (belles-lettres) from the time of Jami to the present day.**
Mohammad Reza Shafi'i Kadkani. In: *History of Persian literature from the beginning of the Islamic period to the present day*. Edited by George Morrison. Leiden, The Netherlands; Cologne, FRG: E. J. Brill, 1981. p. 133–206.
Presents an analytical study of post-classical Persian literature since the early 15th century, focusing on the Indian style in the 16th–18th centuries, the revival of the classical style in the 19th century, and the emergence of modernism in literature and its development in the 20th century.

634 **A manual of classical Persian prosody.**
Finn Thisen. Wiesbaden, FRG: Otto Harrassowitz, 1982. 225p. bibliog.
This volume presents a general introduction to classical Persian prosody for the general reader, as well as reference materials for scholars in Persian, Urdu and Turkish. It contains three parts: part one discusses the basic rules of classical Persian prosody, supported by relevant examples; chapter two describes the common rhythms occurring in classical Persian poetry; and the last chapter in the volume shows how classical Persian prosody was adapted to Urdu, Ottoman Turkish, and Karakanidic, a purer East-Turkish language spoken in Sinkiang around Kashghar.

635 **Some socio-religious themes in modern Persian fiction.**
Girdhari L. Tikku. In: *Islam and its cultural divergence: studies in honour of Gustave E. von Grunebaum*. Edited by Girdhari L. Tikku. Urbana, Chicago; London: University of Illinois Press, 1971. p. 165–79.
Examines the social and religious themes reflected in modern Persian fiction (that which was published between 1921 and 1960) focusing on characters of religious significance in the works of writers from various generations and styles.

636 **The outsider in the life and work of Jalāl Āl-e Ahmad.**
Robert Wells. *British Society for Middle Eastern Studies Bulletin*,
vol. 8, no. 2 (1981), p. 108–14.
Studies the issue of alienation in the modernist intellectual literature of Iran. The
writings of Jalal Al-e Ahmad in the 1950s and 1960s form a central part of the
study.

637 **Persian literature as an affirmation of national identity.**
G. M. Wickens. *Review of National Literatures*, vol. 2, no. 1
(Spring 1971), p. 29–60.
Discusses the idea that while most other Middle Eastern nations have attained a
sense of their national identity only during the 19th and 20th centuries, the
classical Persian literature is evidence of the Iranians' centuries old cultural self-
awareness and their concern for royalist nationalism.

638 **The modern literary idiom.**
Ehsan Yar-Shater. In: *Iran faces the seventies*. Edited by Ehsan
Yar-Shater. New York; Washington; London: Praeger, 1971.
p. 284–320.
Surveys the key characteristics of modernist Persian literature, focusing on the
works produced in the 1960s. Reference is also made to the modernist works of
previous decades, as well as to some traditional elements of Persian classics.

639 **Persian poetry in the Timurid and Safavid periods.**
Ehsan Yar-Shater. In: *The Cambridge history of Iran, vol. 6: the
Timurid and Safavid periods*. Edited by Peter Jackson. Cambridge,
England: Cambridge University Press, 1986. p. 965–94.
Examines the development and nature of two important phases in Persian
literature. The first phase, known as the Iraqi school, which started in the 12th
century and reached its zenith with Hafez in the 14th century, is renowned for its
lyrico-mystical poetry. The second phase, stretching from the 15th to the mid-
18th century, is called the Indian style, or *sabk-e Hendi*.

The legacy of Persia.
See item no. 2.

Iran and Islam: in memory of the late Vladimir Minorsky.
See item no. 3.

Persia: history and heritage.
See item no. 4.

Iran: continuity and variety.
See item no. 5.

Studies in art and literature of the Near East.
See item no. 6.

Iranica: twenty articles.
See item no. 13.

Islam and its cultural divergence.
See item no. 17.

Cultural development in Iran.
See item no. 21.

Alamut and Lamasar . . .
See item no. 42.

A year amongst the Persians . . .
See item no. 53.

The Cambridge history of Iran, vol. 3 . . .
See item no. 115.

The medieval history of Iran, Afghanistan and Central Asia.
See item no. 120.

Toward a theory of historical narrative . . .
See item no. 142.

The fall of the Safavi dynasty and the Afghan occupation of Persia.
See item no. 163.

Mirza Malkum Khān . . .
See item no. 193.

The legacy of Islam.
See item no. 280.

Iran: essays on a revolution in the making.
See item no. 380.

Roots of Revolution . . .
See item no. 381.

British Society for Middle Eastern Studies Bulletin (BRISMES).
See item no. 761.

International Journal of Middle East Studies (IJMES).
See item no. 763.

Iranian Studies . . .
See item no. 765.

Life and Letters, vol. 63, no. 148.
See item no. 767.

The Literary Review . . .
See item no. 768.

Literature. Classical literary works

A bibliography of Iran . . .
See item no. 780.

Iran: bibliographical spectrum.
See item no. 787.

Classical literary works

640 **Immortal rose: an anthology of Persian lyrics.**
Translated by A. J. Arberry. London: Luzac, 1948. 174p.
Contains a selection of lyrical poems (*ghazal*) by some of the greatest Persian
poets: Hafez, Rumi, Sanai, Sa'di and Attar. The notes on each individual poet
are helpful, if rather brief.

641 **The conference of birds.**
Farid ud-Din Attar, translated from the Persian by Afkham
Darbandi and Dick Davis. Harmondsworth, England; New York;
Victoria, Australia; Ontario, Canada; Auckland, New Zealand:
Penguin Classics, 1984. 229p.
A complete verse translation of a Persian literary masterpeice, *Manteq al-teir*, by
Attar, the 12th-century Sufi poet. The co-operation of the two translators – one a
native Persian speaker with a good sense for literature and the other an English
poet with a sound knowledge of Persian – has produced a sound and accurate
rendering of Attar's mystical and allegorical Sufi poems. Included in the volume is
an introduction on the author and his work, emphasizing its Sufi concepts.

642 **The collected Persian poems: the golden pomegranate.**
John Charles Edward Bowen. London: John Baker, 1966. 120p.
Translates thirty-five poems from the 16th-century Moghul Empire in India, most
of which were originally in Farsi (Persian). Biographical introductions and
illustrations are incorporated into the text. The volume is aimed at the general
reader.

643 **The collected Persian poems: poems from the Persian.**
John Charles Edward Bowen. Warminster, England: Aris &
Phillips, 1976. 119p.
Contains the Persian text and accompanying translation of fifty poems by the
major poets from the 10th to 15th centuries. The selections are very short, but are
illustrated with line drawings. The volume also includes an introduction and some
notes, and is aimed at the general reader.

644   **The epic of the kings: shāh-nāma, the national epic of Persia by Ferdowsi.**
A. Ferdowsi Tusi, translated by Reuben Levy.   London: Routledge & Kegan Paul, 1967. 423p. (Persian Heritage series).

A prose translation of Ferdousi's *Shahnameh*, although with many passages omitted or abbreviated. The text is preceded by the translator's brief introductory notes on the *Shahnameh*, its origins, its contents, its character and its author.

645   **Vis and Ramin.**
Fakhr al-Din Gorgani, translated by George Morrison.   London; New York: Columbia University Press, 1972. 357p. (Persian Heritage series).

A prose translation of an 11th-century romantic tale by Fakr al-Din Gorgani. It tells the story of two lovers, Vis and Ramin, and the conflicts, intrigues and adventures which beset them. The translation is preceded by an informative introduction by Morrison on the poet and his narrative poetry. The translator also briefly compares *Vis and Ramin* with the Celtic tale of *Tristan and Isolde*.

646   **Fifty poems of Hafiz.**
Hafiz Shirazi, selected and translated by Arthur J. Arberry.   Cambridge, England: Cambridge University Press, 1953. 183p.

Contains a collection of selected poems by Hafez in their original Arabic script, followed by the translations. The volume includes an introduction on the poet's life and work, as well as a set of explanatory notes on each poem's difficult or controversial points, and metre.

647   **Ibn Yamin.**
Ibn Yamin, translated by E. H. Redwell.   London: Kegan Paul, Trench, Trübner, 1933. 45p.

Contains one hundred short poems by the 14th-century poet, Ibn Yamin. The layout of the book is in two columns with the original Persian poems in one column in alphabetical order according to the final letter corresponding with the English translation in the opposite column. The translation is not of the highest quality, resulting in some cases in misreadings or misunderstandings.

648   *Yusuf and Zulaikha*: **an allegorical romance.**
Hakim Nuruddin Abdurrahman Jami, translated from the Persian by David Pendlebury.   London: Octagon Press, 1980. 185p.

A prose translation of a late 15th-century Persian literary work, the original of which is a verse narrative. The work contains rich Sufi elements which inevitably pose semantic problems for its rendering into a European language. However, this is undoubtedly a brave and successful attempt.

649 **A new selection from** *The rubaiyat* **of Omar Khayyām.**
Omar Khayyam, edited by John Charles Edward
Bowen. Warminster, England: Aris & Phillips, 1976. 136p.
Contains sixty illustrated *ruba'is* (four-lined stanzas) attributed to Khayyam in
Arabic script, each accompanied by the corresponding well-known verse
translation of Edward FitzGerald and a prose translation by A. J. Arberry. The
volume contains an introduction, by J. C. E. Bowen, on Khayyam and his works,
focusing in particular on his poems.

650 *The rubā'iyāt* **of 'Umar Khayyām.**
'Umar Khayyām, translated by Parichehr Kasra. Delmar, New
York: Scholar's Fascimiles and Reprints, 1977. 178p. bibliog.
(UNESCO Collection of Representative Works, Persian series;
Persian Heritage series, no. 21).
Contains 178 *ruba'is* attributed to Khayyam in fine Arabic script accompanied by
a literal prose translation. The relevant information on Persian culture and history
is given in a series of footnotes. References, for each *ruba'i*, to parallel *ruba'is* in
two Persian editions, and to seven translations, including that of Edward
FitzGerald, are also provided. The text is preceded by a comprehensive
introduction on Khayyam and his time, his thought, the structure of *ruba'i*, and
the manuscripts.

651 **Heart's witness: the Sufi quatrains of Awhaduddin Kirmani.**
Awhaduddin Kirmani, edited by Bernd Manuel Weischer,
translated by the editor and Peter Lamborn Wilson. Tehran:
Imperial Iranian Academy of Philosophy, 1978. 179p.
The volume contains 120 quatrains about thirteen different Sufi topics, in both the
original Farsi and English on alternate pages. It includes a brief introduction by
the editor.

652 **Nasir-i Khusraw: forty poems from the** *Divan.*
Nasir-i Khusraw, translated with introduction and notes by Peter
Lamborn Wilson, Gholam Reza Aavani. Tehran: Imperial
Iranian Academy of Philosophy, 1977. 138p.
The volume is a joint attempt, containing translations of forty poems on six
various topics, including philosophy. The volume also contains the author's
biography, and two introductions studying Isma'ilism, the author's life, his works
in general and his *Divan* in particular. It has been edited by Seyyed Hossein Nasr
and funded by the Agha Khan family.

653 **The book of government or rules for kings.**
Nezām al-Mulk, translated by Hubert Đrake. London: Routledge
& Kegan Paul, 1960. 252p.
A translation of the *Siyasat-nameh ya Siyar al-Moluk* which was initially written
by the Saljuq chief Vizier Nezam al-Mulk as a manual of rulership, and has been
considered ever since to be a fine example of penmanship.

654 **The *haft paikar*: the seven beauties.**
Nezāmi Ganjavi, translated from the Persian with a commentary
by C. E. Wilson. London: Probsthain, 1924. 2 vols.
The first of these two volumes is a translation of the original text containing the
life and adventures of Shah Bahram Gur, and the seven stories revealed to him by
his seven queens. The second volume contains the commentary by C. E. Wilson.

655 **Discourses of Rumi.**
Jalal al-Din Rumi, translated by A. J. Arberry. London: John
Murray, 1961. 276p.
This is a literal translation of Badi' al-Zaman Foruzanfar's 1952 Persian edition of
seventy of Rumi's discourses. Further comments on the difficult areas are
provided at the end of the book.

656 **Tales from the Masnavi.**
Jalal al-Din Rumi, translated by A. J. Arberry. London: Allen &
Unwin, 1961. 300p.
A selected prose translation of the *Masnavi* by the 13th-century poet Rumi for
students of Persian studies, and also for the general reader. The volume includes
a short informative introduction on Rumi and his work.

657 **Mystical poems of Rumi: first selection, poems 1–200.**
Jalal al-Din Rumi, translated by A. J. Arberry. London;
Chicago: University of Chicago Press, 1968. 202p. (Persian
Heritage series, no. 3).
Consists of a readable translation of 200 selected odes and lyrics. The system of
selection and the choice of themes included is, however, left unclear.

658 **Selected poems from the *Divāni Shamsi Tabrīz*.**
Jalal al-Din Rumi, edited and translated by Reynold A.
Nicholson. Cambridge; London; New York; Melbourne:
Cambridge University Press, 1977. 330p. bibliog.
An accurate prose translation of forty-eight selected poems. The volume includes
an introduction on Rumi and his works with an emphasis on the collection of
poems know as *Divan-e Shams*. The translation of the poems is followed by
explanatory notes, and the original Persian poems are also included.

659 *Masnavi i ma'navi*: **the spiritual couplets of Maulana Jalālu-'d-Din
Muhammad i Rumi.**
Jalal al-Din Rumi, translated and abridged by
E. H. Whinfield. London: Octagon Press, 1979. 330p.
This readable collection of poems, preceded by a brief introduction by Idris Shah,
is aimed at the general public and concentrates on Sufi themes.

660   **Mystical poems of Rumi: second selection, poems 201–400.**
       Jalal al-Din Rumi, translated by A. J. Arberry.   Boulder,
       Colorado: Westview Press, 1979. 177p. bibliog. (Persian Heritage
       series, no. 23).

A second selection in a readable translation of 200 poems selected from Rumi's
Divan, edited and annotated by Hasan Javadi.

661   **Morals pointed and tales adorned:** *The bustān of Sa'di.*
       Sheikh Mosleh al-Din Sa'di, translated by
       G. M. Wickens.   Toronto; Buffalo, New York: University of
       Toronto Press, 1974. 310p. (Persian Heritage series, no. 17).

A translation of the collection of poems entitled *The bustan of Sa'di* based on the
editions by Mohammad 'Ali Foroughi and Karl Heinrich Graf, and the latter's
German translation. A concordance of lines in this volume with the three
mentioned editions is provided. It also contains several explanatory notes, by the
translator, on difficult points.

662   **The rose-garden of Sheikh Moslihu'd-din Sadi of Shiraz.**
       Sheikh Moslihu'd-din Sa'di, translated by Edward B.
       Eastwick.   London: Octagon Press, 1979. 243p.

A translation of the well-known classic *Golestan* (Rose-garden) of Sa'di,
composed in 1487 and comprising eight chapters of prose and poetry of Sa'di. The
volume also contains Sa'di's biography in translation from the 18th-century *Atesh-
kadeh* (Fire-temple), by Lotf Ali Beg Azar, a preface by the translator and an
introduction by Idris Shah.

663   **The Nasirean ethics.**
       Nasir ad-Din Tusi, translated from the Persian by
       G. M. Wickens.   London: Allen & Unwin, 1964. 333p.

Renders an English translation of *Akhlaq-e Naseri*, a well-known mediaeval
Persian ethical work. The text is supported by introductory notes on the merits of
the original work and its translation, and on the author. Supplementary notes on
the text and a comprehensive index are also included.

Artisans and guild life in the later Safavid period . . .
See item no. 160.

The letter of Tansar.
See item no. 289.

Modern literary works

664   The prison papers of Bozorg Alavi.
Bozorg Alavi, translated by Donné Raffat.   Syracuse, New York: Syracuse University Press, 1985. 246p.

This book is divided into three parts. Part one is a political biography of Bozorg Alavi, along with an interview and a number of photographs. These provide a background to the second, main part of the book, which is a translation of Alavi's *Varaq-pareh-ha-ye zendan* (Scrap papers from prison). Part three, entitled 'The return', forms a record of Alavi's life and the relevant events in 1978 in Berlin and in 1979–80 in Iran.

665   The school principal.
Jalal Al-e Ahmad, translated from the Persian by John K. Newton, with an introduction and notes by Michael C.
Hillmann.   Minneapolis, Minnesota; Chicago: Bibliotheca Islamica, 1974. 135p. (Studies in Middle Eastern Literatures, no. 4).

Jalal Al-e Ahmad (1923–69) was a leading intellectual writer in the 1960s, and his novel *The school principal* (Modir-e madreseh), published in 1958, is a widely-read work of fiction, although it owes its popularity to a strong blend of social criticism rather than its literary characteristics. Michael Hillmann's introduction (p. 7–32) and the book's glossary (p. 136–44) contribute to a better understanding of this novel in the context of its cultural and socio-political background. The introduction also includes the translation of a short story and part of another novel by the same author.

666   Plague by the West (*Gharbzadegi*).
Jalal Al-e Ahmad, translated by Paul Sprachman.   Delmar, New York: Caravan Books, 1982. 111p.

A translation of Al-e Ahmad's pamphlet in socio-political criticism. Gharbzadegi, a term coined by the contemporary Iranian philosopher Ahmed Fardid, was adopted by Al-e Ahmad both as a socio-political term and the title of his book. Since its appearance in 1962 its title *Gharbzadegi* has become a catch-phrase, referring the roots of social and political problems in modern Iranian society to Western influences. A more appropriate translation of the book's title would be *Plagued by the West*.

667   God's shadow: prison poems.
Reza Barahani.   Bloomington, Indiana; London: Indiana University Press, 1976. 103p.

This collection of poems, translated into English by the poet himself, represents Barahani's personal experience and feelings while in prison in 1973. An introduction describing his arrest, cross examination and torture is also included.

219

668   **The little black fish and other modern Persian stories by Samad Behrangi.**
Samad Behrangi, translated by Eric Hooglund, Mary Hooglund.
Washington, DC: Three Continents Press, 1976. 126p. bibliog.
Translates a collection of fictional works by Samad Behrangi, with a 'Biblio-graphical-historical essay' by Thomas Ricks and an English translation, by Azad, of Gholam Hosein Sa'edi's memorial essay on Behrangi, 'It is night, yes night'. The bibliography includes a selected list of works by, and about, Behrangi.

669   **Sadeq Chubak: an anthology.**
Sadeq Chubak, introduced and edited by
F. R. C. Bagley.   Delmar, New York: Caravan Books, 1982.
282p. (Modern Persian Literature Series, no. 3).
An anthology of one of the leading post-Second World War writers, Sadeq Chubak. It contains the translation of his novel *Tangsir*, four short stories, and a one-act play, *Tup-e lastiki* (Rubber ball). *Tangsir*, one short story, and the play were translated by the editor, who has also written the book's introduction. Another of the short stories, 'The glass eye', has been translated by the writer's son, Babak Chubak.

670   **A nightingale's lament: selections from the poems and fables of Parvin E'tesami (1907–41).**
Parvin E'tesami, translated by Heshmat Moayyad, A. Margaret
Arent Madelung.   Lexington, Kentucky: Mazda Publishers, 1985.
227p.
The volume includes the English rendering of eighty-two poems by Parvin E'tesami. She introduced contemporary social ideas into her poetry, which is otherwise traditional in style. The volume also includes an introduction: 'Parvin's personality and poetry' by Heshmat Moayyad (p. XI–XXXVIII), and a 'Commentary' by the co-editor, Margaret Arent Madelung (p. 202–27). The titles of some of the poems have been changed in translation.

671   **Another birth: selected poems of Forugh Farrokhzad.**
Forugh Farrokhzad, translated by Hasan Javadi and Susan
Sallee.   Emeryville, California: Albany Press, 1981. 135p. bibliog.
(Modern Eastern Series, no. 1).
A representative anthology of Forugh Farrokhzad (1935–67), one of the outstanding poets of the 1950s and 1960s. The volume consists of the translation of poems from her various collections, though a higher proportion is selected from her *Tavallodi digar* (Another birth). The authors provide a literal translation, and this sets the book in contrast with *Bride of acacias* (q.v.), which more or less consists of the same poems. It includes introductory notes on Forugh and her works, some letters by Forugh and interviews with her, as well as two other informative articles.

672 **Bride of acacias.**
Forugh Farrokhzad.   Selected poems, translated by Jascha Kessler and Amin Banani. Delmar, New York: Caravan Books, 1982. 152p. (Modern Persian Literature Series, no. 5).

Forugh Farrokhzad was one of the leading poets and artists in modern Iran. She was both a woman intellectual in a male-dominated environment, and a politically-committed individual in an autocratic state. As such, her poetry reflects the socio-political pressure of her time and environment. The background to her poetry is presented in Banani's introduction and Farzaneh Milani's afterword. An attempt has been made to preserve the originality of the language and style of Forugh's poetry, and the translation is thus fluent and poetic.

673 **Sorraya in a coma.**
Esmail Fassih, translated from the Persian.   London: Zed Books, 1985. 287p.

Written during the Iranian Revolution (1979) and the Iran-Iraq War, this novel presents a contrast between the imaginative world of the alienated Iranian intellectuals living in self-exile at Paris, and the harsh realities of the Abadan war-zone. The work includes an introduction about the novel and the author.

674 **The blind owl.**
Sadeq Hedayat, translated by D. P. Costello.   London: John Calder, 1957. 134p.

This is the second European translation of Hedayat's *Buf-e Kur* (1937), since it was preceded by Roger Lescot's translation of the novel into French, entitled *La chouette aveugle* (Paris: Libraire Jose Corti, 1953). Costello's English translation was also published in New York in 1957 by Grove Press, who also published a paperback edition in 1969. It remains, however, in need of emendation.

675 **Sādeq Hedāyat: an anthology.**
Sadeq Hedayat edited by Ehsan Yar-Shater.   Boulder, Colorado: Westview Press, 1979. 217p. (Modern Persian Literature Series, no. 2, UNESCO Collection of Representative Works).

This is a representative anthology of the work of Sadeq Hedayat, the eminent Persian writer of the 1930s and 1940s, consisting of the translation of sixteen short stories and a novelette. The translations are generally close to the text in an attempt to preserve the works' originality.

676 **Major voices in contemporary Persian literature.**
Edited by Michael C. Hillmann.   Austin, Texas: Literature East and West, 1980. 327p. bibliog. (Literature East and West, vol. XX, nos. 1–4, Jan.–Dec. 1976, actual date of publication 1980).

Mainly contains translations of modern Persian novels and short stories (thirteen pieces from ten writers) and poems (forty-one pieces from five poets), as well as a number of essays, plays, plot summaries and book reviews. The translations vary in quality and accuracy, and are almost all prefaced by the editor's bibliographical

221

notes. The work's detailed bibliography is a major source of reference for the modern history and literature of Iran.

677 **M. A. Jamālzāda:** *Once upon a time.*
M. A. Jamalzadeh, translated by Heshmat Moayyad and Paul Sprachman. New York: Bibliotheca Persica, 1985. 107p. (Modern Persian Literature Series, no. 6).

The first edition of Jamalzada's *Once upon a time* was published in Berlin in 1922 by Kaviani Press. It is a collection of six satirical sketches, portraying clashes between the old and new institutions caused by that period of social transition. In addition to the translation of the sketches, the volume includes an introduction on Jamalzada's life and works, and some notes concerning the problems of translation.

678 **An anthology of modern Persian poetry.**
Selected and translated by Ahmad Karimi-Hakkak. Boulder, Colorado: Westview Press, 1978. 197p. (Modern Persian Literature Series, no. 1).

This is a collection of eighty-three poems by twenty-six modernist poets (including two women). The work of each poet is preceded by a brief biography, accompanied in some cases by a photograph. The volume contains an introduction, by the editor, on the development of modernist poetry in Iran.

679 **The adventures of Hajji Baba of Ispahan.**
James Morier. London; New York: Macmillan, 1985. 456p.

Since its first appearance in 1824, *Hajji Baba* has remained a popular work, being reissued several times and translated into many languages, including Persian. It is a fictional 19th-century portrait of Persian manners and life as observed by a European.

680 **False dawn: Persian poems by Nāder Nāderpour.**
Nader Naderpour, translated by Michael C. Hillmann. Austin, Texas: Literature East and West, 1986. 110p. bibliog.

A translation of forty poems by the modernist contemporary poet Naderpour, who is now living in exile in Paris. The volume also includes an introduction by the translator on the poet, his life and his works, and a critical study of his works by Leonardo Alishan.

The forces of modernization in nineteenth century Iran . . .
See item no. 180.

Isfahan is half the world . . .
See item no. 198.

Iranian writers, the Iranian cinema and the case of *Dash Akol*.
See item no. 712.

The Arts

Visual arts

681 Modern Persian artists.
Karim Emami. In: *Iran faces the seventies*. Edited by Ehsan Yar-Shater. New York; Washington; London: Praeger, 1971. p. 349–64. bibliog.
A survey of the characteristics of modern art and the attitudes of modernist artists. It focuses on experimentation and the search for new ways of expression, and deals with the enduring elements of tradition.

682 An introduction to modern Persian painting.
Richard Ettinghausen. In: *Iran faces the seventies*. Edited by Ehsan Yar-Shater. New York; Washington; London: Praeger, 1971. p. 341–48.
A brief account of modern Persian painting, the influence of tradition, and the contemporary revolutionary aspects prevailing in the arts. It also covers the role played by the government and the Shah's wife in supporting the modern arts.

683 Highlights of Persian art.
Edited by Richard Ettinghausen, Ehsan Yar-Shater. Boulder, Colorado: Westview Press, 1979. 377p. (Persian Art Series, no. 1).
A collection of fifteen papers on Persian art, covering topics from the late second millennium and early first millennium BC. The papers study Amlash pottery and Luristan bronzes; Scythian art of the Eurasian steppes; Achaemenid art; and the court silver of the Sasanians. They also deal with topics such as pottery, painting, calligraphy, and architecture, which flourished in the Islamic period. The style of painting in more recent times is also assessed in the last two chapters.

684 **Qajar paintings: Persian oil paintings of the 18th & 19th centuries.**
S. J. Falk.   London: Faber, in association with Sotheby Parke-
Bernet Publishers, 1972. 54p.

An introduction to Qajar oil-paintings, with an examination of the works of seven
artists, namely Mirza Baba, Muhammad Sadiq, Mihr 'Ali, Abu'l-Qasim,
Muhammad Hasan, Sayid Mirza, and an unknown painter referred to as 'The
Shirin painter', including examples of their paintings. Also included are sixty-
three magnificent colour paintings, originally from the Amery collection
(assembled by Major Harold and the Rt. Hon. Leopold Amery) which, in 1969,
were passed into the possession of Farah Pahlavi.

685 **The visual arts, 1050–1350.**
O. Grabar.   In: *The Cambridge history of Iran, vol. 5: the Saljuq
and Mongol periods*. Edited by J. A. Boyle. Cambridge, England:
Cambridge University Press, 1968. p. 626–58. bibliog.

A survey of the major characteristics of the arts from the 11th to the 14th
centuries, concentrating on mosque architecture, objects from the 12th to the 14th
centuries, and the paintings of the 14th century.

686 **Persian painting in the fourteenth century, a research report.**
Ernest J. Grube.   Naples, Italy: Istituto Orientale di Napoli. 1978.
54p.

A survey of the developments and principal elements of Persian painting in the
14th century. The volume contains 101 black-and-white miniature paintings with
their annotations printed on glossy paper at the end of the book.

687 **Shiraz painting in the sixteenth century.**
Grace Dunham Guest.   Washington, DC: Freer Gallery of Art,
1949. 56p. bibliog. (Oriental Studies, no. 4).

Studies and presents the characteristics particular to the Shiraz school of painting
in the 16th century. Fifty black-and-white illustrations of miniatures are included
at the back of the volume.

688 **A survey of Persian art, from prehistoric times to the present.**
Edited by Arthur Upham Pope, Phyllis Ackerman.   Oxford:
Oxford University Press, 1938–39. 6 vols.

A magnificently-illustrated six-volume work (three of text and three of plates),
presenting an unusual blend of architecture, painting, metalwork, pottery,
carpets, textiles, etc. Although in major parts outdated, it is still the basic source
book for the historian of Iranian and Islamic art. It was reprinted in 1977 in
Japan.

689 **Islamic art and design: 1500–1700.**
J. M. Rogers.   London: British Museum Publications, 1983. 159p.
map. bibliog.

Examines the Islamic decorative arts between 1500 and 1700 in three great

Muslim empires: the Safavids, the Ottomans, and the Moghuls; and discusses their artistic inter-relations. Rogers includes numerous illustrated examples from painting, manuscript illumination and calligraphy, paper-cutting, textiles, pottery, metalwork and jewellery. The book's chapterization is thematic rather than geographical, although chapter ten (p. 122–40) is devoted entirely to Persian pottery.

690 **Persian art through the eyes of nineteenth-century British travellers.**
Jennifer Scarce.   In: *British Society for Middle Eastern Studies Bulletin*, vol. 8, no. 1 (1981), p. 38–50.
A description of 19th-century Persian art, and the collective impressions and observations of eight British travellers, namely James Morier, Sir William Ouseley, Sir Robert Ker Porter, James Baillie Fraser, Robert Murdoch Smith, Dr. C. Wills, Isabella Bishop and George Curzon.

Persia: history and heritage.
See item no. 4.

The Persian Gulf states, a general survey.
See item no. 7.

Iranica: twenty articles.
See item no. 13.

Old routes of western Iran.
See item no. 64.

The memorial volume of the Vth International Congress of Iranian Art and Archaeology.
See item no. 85.

The king and kingship in Achaemenid art . . .
See item no. 113.

The Cambridge history of Iran, vol. 3 . . .
See item no. 115.

The fall of the Safavi dynasty and the Afghan occupation of Persia.
See item no. 163.

Iran under the Safavids.
See item no. 168.

The legacy of Islam.
See item no. 280.

Iranische Kunst in deutschen Museen.
See item no. 732.

The royal hunter: art of the Sasanian empire.
See item no. 733.

The Arts. Architecture

The arts of Islam.
See item no. 734.

Catalogue of the ancient Persian bronzes in the Ashmolean Museum.
See item no. 735.

Ancient Persian bronzes in the Adam collection.
See item no. 737.

Masterpieces of Persian art.
See item no. 739.

A descriptive catalogue of the Persian paintings in the Bodleian Library.
See item no. 741.

Persian paintings in the India Office Library . . .
See item no. 742.

Sports and pastimes: scenes from Turkish, Persian and Mughal paintings.
See item no. 743.

Persian miniature painting . . .
See item no. 744.

British Society for Middle Eastern Studies Bulletin (BRISMES).
See item no. 761.

International Journal of Middle East Studies (IJMES).
See item no. 763.

An index of articles in Western journals.
See item no. 784.

Architecture

691 **The sense of unity: the Sufi tradition in Persian architecture.**
Nader Ardalan, Laleh Bakhtiar.   Chicago; London: University of
Chicago Press, 1973. 137p. bibliog.
Islamic architecture is studied in its traditional setting and the authors attempt to
trace the reflection in architecture of God's oneness and unity. The relationship
between the elements of architecture, such as space and form is studied
analytically and supported by illustrations. The volume consists of three parts: the
first deals with space, form, colour and matter; the second discusses traditional
forms; and the final part is concerned with the system of natural, geometric and
harmonic orders. Several colour plates and numerous other illustrations are
included.

692 **Living with the desert: working buildings of the Iranian plateau.**
Elizabeth Beazlay, Michael Harverson, with a contribution by
Susan Roaf. Wiltshire, England: Aris & Phillips, 1982. 116p.
2 maps. bibliog.

This is based on several field-work surveys made between 1961 and 1977. The
work is initially concerned with the architectural characteristics of the buildings in
the area, followed by a discussion of the function of those buildings, focusing on
the purpose-built ones such as ice-houses and windmills. The work contains eight
chapters: 1, 'The plateau'; 2, 'Buildings'; 3, 'Water'; 4, 'Ice-houses'; 5, 'Wind-
catchers'; 6, 'Watermills'; 7, 'Windmills'; and 8, 'Pigeon towers'. The content is
supported by a large number of illustrations and drawings.

693 **The Zoroastrian houses of Yazd.**
Mary Boyce. In: *Iran and Islam*. Edited by C. E. Bosworth.
Edinburgh: Edinburgh University Press, 1971. p. 125–47.

A functional analysis of Zoroastrian architecture in the light of its social and
religious characteristics. Three figures and three plates are also included.

694 **New Julfa: the Armenian churches and other buildings.**
John Carswell. Oxford: Clarendon Press, 1968. 69p. bibliog.

Following an historical introduction, the book presents a descriptive study of
Armenian churches and other buildings in New Julfa at Isfahan. The book is
substantiated by colour photographs and drawn figures, and includes, in a final
section, ninety-six black-and-white plates on glossy pages.

695 **Isfahān: Masǧid-i ǧum'a.** (Isfahan: Friday Mosque.)
Eugenio Galdieri. Rome: Istituto Italiano per il Medio ed
Estremo Oriente (IsMEO), 1972. 379p.

This is basically a book of illustrations about the Masjed-e Jom'eh (Friday
Mosque) of Isfahan which is one of the greatest monumental complexes of Iran.
The illustrations, forming the bulk of the book, are followed by a section entitled
'Preliminary reports' which state that the building as it stands now is a Saljuq
stratum, under which traces of a far more ancient structure, perhaps of Sasanian
age, are hidden. This assumption is supported by drawings and further
illustrations.

696 **Safavid architecture.**
Robert Hillenbrand. In: *The Cambridge history of Iran, vol. 6:
the Timurid and Safavid periods*. Edited by Peter Jackson.
Cambridge, England: Cambridge University Press, 1986.
p. 759–842.

Demonstrates the characteristics of the function-oriented Safavid architecture.
The author suggests that, in this period, at least three religious, palatial and
otherwise secular styles coexisted. The political context of Safavid architecture;
the distribution of the buildings; their types, style and chronology; and the
craftsmen and their resistance to external influences, are amongst the topics
discussed.

697 **Islamic architecture: Iran 1.**
Antony Hutt, Leonard Harrow. London: Scorpion Publications, 1977. 192p. map.
A pictorial introduction to the Islamic architecture of Iran, covering the period of the Saljuqs, beginning in the 11th century, to the end of the Mongols in the mid-14th century. It contains numerous colour and black-and-white photographs with brief informative captions, supported by an introduction and a time chart. The chronological material is continued in a second volume by the same authors (*Islamic architecture: Iran 2*, 1978. 172p.) which covers the period from the 14th to the 19th centuries.

698 **Isfahān, New Julfa: the houses of the Armenians.**
Karapet Karapetian. Rome: Istituto Italiano per il Medio ed Estreme Oriente (IsMEO), 1974. 378p. 9 maps.
An historical study of the architecture of the Armenian houses in Julfa, at Isfahan, during the Safavid dynasty and in particular of the reign of Shah 'Abbas I (1585–1629), built under the influence of an Islamic environment. Hence the significance of the subtitle 'houses of Armenians' rather than 'Armenian houses'. The historical study forms the first part of the book. The second part includes an examination of thirteen houses supported by an architectural analysis, figures and drawings.

699 **The pictorial tile cycle of Hašt Behešt in Isfahān and its iconographic tradition.**
Ingeborg Luschey-Schmeisser. Rome: Istituto Italiano per il Medio ed Estreme Oriente (IsMEO), 1978. 212p.
A study of a small palace, the Hasht Behesht (Eight paradises), which was built in Isfahan by the order of Shah Soleiman in ca. 1670 AD. The study is divided into four parts: 1, 'The tile cycle'; 2, 'The pictorial objects in their iconography: origin and significance'; 3, 'The position of the iconographic tile cycle of Hašt Behešt within Safavid art'; and 4, 'Summary'. It contains a descriptive catalogue, an iconographic study, and an estimation of the cycle of the Hasht Behesht from the viewpoint of the history of Safavid art. The book is concluded by 218 interesting figures.

700 **Timurid architecture.**
R. Pinder-Wilson. In: *The Cambridge history of Iran, vol. 6: the Timurid and Safavid periods*. Edited by Peter Jackson. Cambridge, England: Cambridge University Press, 1986. p. 728–58. bibliog.
A survey of architectural achievement under the Il-Khans (13th–14th centuries), and its development in western and southern Persia under successive dynasties in the 14th and 15th centuries.

701 **Persian architecture.**
Arthur Upham Pope. Shiraz, Iran: Asia Institute, 1969. 115p. (Library of Introductions to Persian Art).
A chronological survey of Persian architecture, beginning with the rise of the

Achaemenids, covered in the first chapter, and followed by other pre-Islamic dynasties in the second. The Islamic period is discussed in the next six chapters. Numerous illustrations, some in colour, and some drawings are included.

702　**The architecture of Islamic Iran: the Il Khanid period.**
　　Donald N. Wilber.　Princeton, New Jersey: Princeton University
　　Press, 1955. 191p. bibliog.
Discusses, from a political rather than a stylistic viewpoint, the architecture of the Il-Khanid period in Iran during the 13th and 14th centuries. The volume consists of two parts. Part one provides an historical sketch of the period under question, which helps towards a better understanding of the main topic. Historical documents and materials are also frequently studied as a background to the monuments. The work contains a catalogue, which includes, amongst the 119 chronologically ordered items, architectural monuments, architectural elements, and inscriptions. Even though the country covered a much larger area during the Il-Khanid period, the present boundaries of Iran have set the geographical limits. The work also contains figures as well as 217 illustrations.

703　**The Masjid-i 'Atiq of Shiraz.**
　　Donald N. Wilber.　Shiraz, Iran: Asia Institute, 1972. 75p.
　　(Monograph no. 2).
The Masjid-i 'Atiq, dating from the end of the 10th century, is believed to be the most ancient mosque in Shiraz. This volume builds up a picture of the mosque from the literary and epigraphical sources available, and this is followed by a study of its architectural history. A description of the mosque and its inscriptions is provided in two appendixes, and forty-eight illustrations and twelve drawings are also included.

Persia: history and heritage.
See item no. 4.

The road to Oxiana.
See item no. 54.

Isfahan, pearl of Persia.
See item no. 68.

The Islamic city of Gurgan.
See item no. 82.

Ionians in Pasargadae: studies in old Persian architecture.
See item no. 112.

Highlights of Persian art.
See item no. 683.

A survey of Persian art . . .
See item no. 688.

Music

704 **The music of professional musicians of northwest Iran (Azerbaijan).**
Charlotte Fey Albright Farr. Washington, DC: University of
Washington, PhD dissertation, 1976. 261p. bibliog.

Attempts to define the status of the traditional music of Azarbaijan in terms of its
historical antecedents in classical Persian and Turkish musical theory. This is in
contrast with the present styles in the same area, as well as with present-day
Persian and Turkish classical music.

705 **The Persian doctrine of *dastga*-composition: a phenomenological
study in the musical modes.**
Edith Gerson-Kiwi. Tel-Aviv, Israel: Israel Music Institute
(IMI), 1963. 43p. bibliog.

A contribution to Persian music, focusing on instrumental art music, and
describing the conception of the *maqam* or *dastgah* (mode) system. Two *dastgahs*,
shur and *abu-ata* are dealt with in detail.

706 ***Daramad of chahargah*: a study in the performance practice of
Persian music.**
Bruno Nettl, Bela Foltin, Jr. Detroit, Michigan: Information
Coordination, 1972. 84p. (Detroit Monographs in Musicology,
no. 2).

Attempts to investigate the use of improvisation and performance practices in
Persian music based upon a collection of some forty presentations of the *dastgah*,
or mode, known as *chahargah*.

707 **A modal system of Arab and Persian music – AD 1250–1300.**
O. Wright. Oxford: Oxford University Press, 1978. 269p. bibliog.
(London Oriental Series, vol. 28).

The author argues that musical contact between Persia and Arabia goes back to
pre-Islamic times. In the Islamic period a parallel development was encouraged
by the cantillation of the Qur'an (Koran), which became an art in itself. In the
late 13th century, Arab and Persian art-music shared the same modal system. The
latter half of the 13th century, in the author's view, constitutes one of the most
important periods in the history of Arab and Persian musical theory. It witnessed
the emergence of a corpus of theoretical writing which has originality and a
guiding significance, while the post-13th century texts show a certain lack of
originality. The volume is arranged in four parts, covering the scales, modes,
examples of notation, and commentary.

708 **Classical Persian music today.**
Ella Zonis. In: *Iran faces the seventies*. Edited by Ehsan Yar-
Shater. New York; Washington; London: Praeger, 1971.
p. 365–80. bibliog.
Surveys classical Persian music, its traditional charateristics, and the way it has
been presented and developed by contemporary musicians. Also included is a
short list of selected readings in English, French and German as well as some
recordings.

709 **Classical Persian music: an introduction.**
Ella Zonis. Cambridge, Massachusetts: Harvard University Press,
1973. 201p. map. bibliog.
Aims to study classical Persian music in the context of its historical and cultural
background. The reader is, however, expected to have a basic knowledge of
musical terminology. The book contains thirty-two photographs, and some
explanatory notes and figures. An attempt has also been made to show the
relationship between Persian music and poetry. The work is divided into seven
chapters, and covers, for example, the historical background, theoretical and
technical explanations, the impact of the traditional Persian music, and Persian
musical instruments. It also contains two appendixes: 1, 'The medieval rhythmic
modes'; and 2, 'Excerpts from the Bahjat al Ruh'' (sic).

Old and new values in changing cultural patterns.
See item no. 301.

The life and works of Amir Khusrau.
See item no. 621.

Theatre and film

710 **Dramatic and literary aspects of *Ta'zieh-Khani*, Iranian passion
play.**
Peter Chelkowski. *Review of National Literatures*, vol. 2, no. 1
(1971), p. 121–38.
A general study of the origins of the *Ta'zieh*, its religious significance and its
literary characteristics. The author refers to the *Ta'zieh* as the only form of
indigenous drama to be developed in Iran. He is, therefore, pleased to see that
after a period of decline it was revived in the 1960s and was shown on television
during the Islamic month of Muharram and at the Shiraz Art Festival.

711 *Ta'ziyeh*: **ritual and drama in Iran.**
Edited by Peter J. Chelkowski. New York: New York University
Press, Soroush Press, 1979. 268p.

Contains twenty studies by Iranian and Western scholars, on the subject of the
Ta'zieh, or passion play, which, it is claimed, is the only form of drama
indigenous to the world of Islam. The studies are, therefore, not totally confined
to Iran, though most of them are about the various characteristics of the *Ta'zieh*
as it is performed in Iran or influenced by Shi'ism or Iranian culture. The editor's
study, entitled 'Bibliographical spectrum' (p. 255–68), provides a critical assessment of the various materials available on the subject.

712 **Iranian writers, the Iranian cinema and the case of *Dash Akol*.**
Hamid Nafici. *Iranian Studies*, vol. 18, no. 2–4 (Spring–Autumn
1985), p. 231–51.

The author suggests that since the first Iranian feature film was made in 1930, the
Iranian cinema has always had a close connection with Persian literature. He
attempts to show that the cinema, especially during the period from the mid-1960s
to the late 1970s, provides ample material for a study of the development of
Persian fiction and the sociological role of the Iranian writer. The article focuses
on a comparative study of Sadeq Hedayat's story *Dash Akol* (1932) and its film
version, which was produced in 1971 and bore the same title.

Iran: continuity and variety.
See item no. 5.

Folk art, customs and handicrafts

713 **The undiscovered *kilim*.**
David Black, Clive Loveless. London: David Black Oriental
Carpets, 1977. 24p.

Following a brief, commercially-oriented introduction which describes what a
kilim is, the book contains fifty-five magnificently printed *kilim* illustrations, in
colour, from Anatolia, the Caucasus and Iran.

714 **Iranian festivals.**
Mary Boyce. In: *The Cambridge history of Iran, vol. 3: the
Seleucid, Parthian and Sasanian periods*. Edited by Ehsan Yar-
Shater. Cambridge, England: Cambridge University Press, 1983.
p. 792–815. bibliog.

A survey of the pre-Islamic festivals, their origins, the services and celebrations
performed, and the significance attached to them.

The Arts. Folk art, customs and handicrafts

715 **Living tradition of Iran's crafts.**
Jasleen Dhamija.   New Delhi: Vikas Publishing House, 1979. 75p.
bibliog. (Farabi University, Tehran).
Describes the range of handicrafts in contemporary Iran. The author's objective is
to show that this particular art form is a direct expression of the culture and the
traditions of the people. She provides an analytical study of the symbolic meaning
of the designs and motifs used in the various crafts, and tries to show the
importance of the role of rhythm. An introduction presents an historical
perspective, and background information concerning the development of
handicrafts and the relevant socio-economic organizations. The volume contains
numerous colour illustrations and black-and-white photographs.

716 **Persian designs and motifs for artists and craftsmen.**
Ali Dowlatshahi.   New York: Dover Publications, 1979. 109p.
Numerous designs taken from textiles, ceramics, book-illustrations, calligraphy
and miscellaneous ornaments are presented in this volume. The patterns range
from those used in prehistoric pottery-painting to those expressed in 20th-century
calligraphy. Eight colour plates are included.

717 **Sasanian silver and history.**
R. N. Frye.   In: *Iran and Islam*. Edited by C. E. Bosworth.
Edinburgh: Edinburgh University Press, 1971. p. 255–62.
A study of pre-Islamic decorative silver objects. The author argues that silver, as
a metal used for ornamental purposes, occupied a more prominent place in
Sasanian art than gold. A few plates are included.

718 **Iranian carpets: art, craft and history.**
E. Gans-Ruedin.   London: Thames & Hudson, 1978. 525p. map.
bibliog.
This magnificently-printed volume contains 254 carpet illustrations in colour, with
introductory notes (in English and Persian) on the art of carpet-weaving in Iran,
the major carpet centres, and the illustrated carpets.

719 **Felt-making craftsmen of the Anatolian and Iranian plateaux.**
Michael Gervers, Veronika Gervers.   *Textile Museum Journal*,
vol. 4, no. 1 (1974), p. 14–29. bibliog.
A study of the methodology of felt-making and the ornamentation of felt rugs,
with reference to the social and cultural significance of such skills in Turkey and
Iran. The development of rug production in recent decades and its new market is
also discussed.

720 **A survey of Persian handicraft.**
Edited by Jay Gluck, Sumi Hiramoto Gluck,
Carl J. Penton.   Tehran; New York; London; Ashia, Japan: Bank
Melli Iran, 1977. 412p.
A lavish pictorial art-book which provides an introduction to the contemporary

folk art and crafts of modern Iran. It consists of a selection of essays, and is enriched by numerous high-quality illustrations of art objects.

721 **Tribal rugs: an introduction to the weaving of the tribes of Iran.**
Jenny Housego. London: Scorpion Publications, 1978. 172p.
map. bibliog.

This is an introductory survey of tribal weaving. It contains a brief technical analysis of a typical example from each of the nine principal weaving tribes or areas discussed in the volume. The bulk of the book constitutes numerous black-and-white and colour illustrations of woven objects, with brief introductory notes.

722 **Masterpieces of Persian carpet.**
Iran Carpet Company. Tehran: Pishgar, [n.d.]. 2 vols.

These two volumes, most probably printed in the late 1970s, present colour illustrations of two hundred magnificent carpets. Informative notes and technical details in English and Persian are also provided.

723 **The iconography of everyday life in nineteenth-century Middle Eastern rugs.**
Gerard A. Paquin. *Textile Museum Journal*, vol. 22 (1983). p. 5–18.

Examines the significance of designs which incorporate people, animals, combs, hands, architectural motifs, ewers, vases, and various amulets and signs. These all appear in Middle Eastern rugs, and reference is made to their cultural, social and artistic contexts. The article forms a thematic study, with frequent examination of Iranian designs and culture.

724 *Kilims*: **the art of tapestry weaving in Anatolia, the Caucasus and Persia.**
Yanni Petsopoulos. London: Thames & Hudson, 1979. 379p. map. bibliog.

Surveys the art of *kilim* weaving, the predominantly woollen, tapestry woven, weft-faced fabrics, from Anatolia, the Caucasus and Persia. The volume deals with each locality separately. Persian *kilims* and their development from the 16th century, and the art of *kilim* weaving in various major centres in Iran are discussed in the last part of the book (p. 271–379).

725 **Weaver of tales: Persian picture rugs.**
Karl Schlamminger, Peter Lamborn Wilson. München, FRG: Verlag Georg D. W. Callwey, 1980. 193p. bibliog.

An introduction, in English and German, to Persian tribal rugs. The author argues that Persian pictorial rugs convey, in a naïve and direct way, the popular ancient tales which are part of the Persian national consciousness. The volume contains magnificent colour illustrations with informative notes.

726 **Carpets and textiles.**
F. Spuhler.   In: *The Cambridge history of Iran, vol. 6: the Timurid and Safavid periods*. Edited by Peter Jackson. Cambridge, England: Cambridge University Press, 1986. p. 698–727. bibliog.

A study of the characteristics of Persian carpets and textiles from the 14th to the 18th centuries. It deals with the different fabrics of the carpets as well as with their technical and aesthetic developments. The study of pre-16th century carpets and Timurid textiles is based mainly on Timurid miniatures. The Safavid era, however, provides a wide variety of choice, and the author has had to confine himself to a few outstanding examples.

727 **Persian lustre ware.**
Oliver Watson.   London; Boston, Massachusetts: Faber, 1985. 175p. map. bibliog.

A study of Persian lustre ware, focusing on the lustre technique. It describes the ceramic used, the production sites and the various styles. Three appendixes on lustre patterns, lustre-decorated buildings and a list of dated Persian lustre ware are included.

728 **The traditional crafts of Persia: their development, technology, and influence on Eastern and Western civilizations.**
Hans E. Wulff.   Cambridge, Massachusetts; London: Massachusetts Institute of Technology Press, 1966. 304p. map. bibliog.

An introduction to Iranian crafts, divided into five sections and covering metalwork, woodwork, building crafts and ceramics, textile and leather, and agriculture and food-treating crafts. Some supportive illustrations are also included. Also included is a useful comprehensive glossary of Persian technical terms with their English equivalents.

Persia: history and heritage.
See item no. 4.

The Persian Gulf states, a general survey.
See item no. 7.

Persian metal technology . . .
See item no. 80.

The small finds.
See item no. 81.

History of Shah 'Abbas the Great.
See item no. 154.

Industrial activities.
See item no. 525.

The Arts. Folk art, customs and handicrafts

The influence of folk-tale and legend on modern Persian literature.
See item no. 598.

Popular literature in Iran.
See item no. 603.

Highlights of Persian art.
See item no. 683.

A survey of Persian art . . .
See item no. 688.

Islamic art and design: 1500–1700.
See item no. 689.

Iranian Collections in Foreign Libraries, Museums and Art Galleries

729 **Catalogue of the Library of the India Office, vol. 2, part 6, Persian books.**
A. J. Arberry.   London: Secretary of State for India, 1937. 571p.
Presents a catalogue of printed and lithographed Persian books held by the Library of the India Office. Its compilation follows the style of the other catalogues of Oriental books, prepared by the India Office. The main entries are given under the titles of books in alphabetical order.

730 **A catalogue of the Persian manuscripts in the library of the University of Cambridge.**
Edward G. Browne.   Cambridge, England: Cambridge University Press, 1896. 424p.
Offers a list of 336 manuscripts, which are wholly or partly in Persian and kept in the library of the University of Cambridge. They are arranged in subject order, the main subjects being history, lexicography and poetry.

731 **Sasanian stamp seals in the Metropolitan Museum of Art.**
Christopher J. Brunner.   New York: Metropolitan Museum of Art, 1978. 149p.
Provides an analysis of seal stones attributed to the Sasanian empire in the New York Metropolitan Museum of Art's collection. The catalogue is arranged according to the physical shape of the seals, which is to some extent useful in defining their chronology.

732 **Iranische Kunst in deutschen Museen.**
Hanna Erdmann, with an introduction by Annemarie Schimmel.   Wiesbaden, FRG: Franz Steiner, 1976. [n.p.].
This is basically a book of illustrations of art objects in German museums. It

includes seventy-five glossy pages of illustrations, with the appropriate notes in German and Persian. They are based on Professor Dr. Kurt Erdmann's works, and provide, although briefly, the available detailed information about the objects, including size, colour, material, place of origin, date, and so on. The book includes art objects belonging to ancient as well as Islamic Iran.

733   **The royal hunter: art of the Sasanian empire.**
Prudence Oliver Harper.   New York: Asia House Gallery, 1978.
173p. map. bibliog.
A catalogue of the Asia House Gallery exhibition which was organized by the Asia Society and held in New York in the winter of 1978. It includes objects of luxury, such as the royal silver plate and the patterned silks of the Sasanian design, as well as minor works of art, such as stucco, glass, ceramics, bronzes and seals. The catalogue also includes a section of informative texts written both by the author and by Carol Manson Bier, Jens Kröger and Martha L. Carter. Also included are introductory notes and a chronology of the Sasanian dynasty (224–651 AD), and the contemporary Eastern and Western nations.

734   **The arts of Islam.**
Edited by D. Jones, G. Mitchell.   London: Hayward Gallery, 1976. 396p. map. bibliog.
A catalogue of the exhibition of Islamic art held in London in April–July 1976. The topics included, by several contributors, are textiles and carpets; rock-crystal, jade, glass, ivory and ceramics; metalwork; wood; marble and stucco; calligraphy, miniatures and book-bindings; and architecture. Sixteen coloured plates and numerous other illustrations are also included.

735   **Catalogue of the ancient Persian bronzes in the Ashmolean Museum.**
P. R. S. Moorey.   Oxford: Oxford University Press, 1971. 309p. 2 maps. bibliog.
A catalogue of the Ashmolean collection of ancient Persian bronzes. They are categorized by the function of the objects listed, although their style and iconography are also described. Each main section in the catalogue is preceded by a brief review of the general category of object, with special reference to its artistic significance and its geographical location.

736   **Ancient bronzes from Luristan.**
P. R. S. Moorey.   London: British Museum Publications, 1974. 42p. 2 maps. bibliog.
Provides a brief but objective presentation of the British Museum's collection of bronzes from Luristan. It includes thirty-eight photographs of various objects.

737   **Ancient Persian bronzes in the Adam collection.**
P. R. S. Moorey.   London: Faber, 1974. 191p. map. bibliog.
A catalogue of Peter Adam's collection of bronze objects excavated in Luristan in

West Iran, and in Amlash on the shore of the Caspian Sea. The objects are arranged by their function. General introductions to each category, and further covering notes on each object are incorporated with their photographs.

738   **Ancient Iran.**
      P. R. S. Moorey.   Oxford: Ashmolean Museum, 1975. 47p.
      2 maps. bibliog.

Seeks to set the collection of antiquities from Iran which are on show in the Ashmolean Museum in their wider archaeological context, and to present a sketch of the prehistory and early history of Iran. Much of the material in this museum comes from the excavations carried out by British archaeologists in ten different sites in Iran, from 1948 until the operation was discontinued by the Iranian authorities in 1974.

739   **Masterpieces of Persian art.**
      Arthur Upham Pope.   New York: Dryden Press, 1945. 204p.

An introduction to early Persian art, commemorating and in part recording the Exhibition of Persian Art held in New York in 1940. It consists of 155 plates, each including one or more illustrations of art objects, divided into six sections, containing introductory notes.

740   **Persian medical manuscripts at the University of California,**
      Los Angeles: a descriptive catalogue.
      Lutz Richter-Bernburg.   Malibu, California: Undena Publications, 1978. 261p. (Centre for Medieval and Renaissance Studies, vol. 4).

Contains descriptions of Persian medical manuscripts in the collections at UCLA. Persian texts in predominantly Arabic medical manuscripts are also included. A total of 137 titles are discussed.

741   **A descriptive catalogue of the Persian paintings in the Bodleian**
      Library.
      B. W. Robinson.   Oxford: Oxford University Press, 1958. 190p.

A chronologically-arranged catalogue which provides comments on the style, quality and condition of the miniature illustrations in several manuscripts belonging to the Bodleian Library. It emphasizes the miniatures' subject matter, although particular stylistic features are also discussed. The selections are taken from the Mongol, Timurid, Safavid and post-Safavid periods. Numerous plates are included.

742   **Persian paintings in the India Office Library: a descriptive**
      catalogue.
      B. W. Robinson.   London: Sotheby Parke-Bernet, 1976. 256p.

A classified, indexed and descriptive catalogue of Persian paintings in the India Office Library in London. The catalogue is weighted towards the number of Safavid paintings held by the Library, although it also covers those from the

Mongol, Timurid, Zand and Qajar periods. It contains sixteen colour plates and several black-and-white photographs.

743 **Sports and pastimes: scenes from Turkish, Persian and Mughal paintings.**
Norah M. Titley.   London: British Library, 1979. 35p.

'Sports and pastimes' is the theme of this small book which is based on miniature paintings in manuscripts from Persia, as well as from Turkey and Moghul India, and which are now held by the British Library.

744 **Persian miniature painting and its influence on the art of Turkey and India: the British Library collections.**
Norah M. Titley.   London: British Library, 1983. 258p. map. bibliog.

Traces the antecedents and development of this style of Persian painting which, under Chinese influence, emerged in the 14th century. The illustrated manuscripts in the British Library collection form the basis of the book, which contains a selection of colour plates and black-and-white photographs. The less well-known miniatures are discussed in greater detail, and are thus brought to the attention of those already familiar with the subject. A subject index of several thousand miniature paintings is also provided.

745 **The Qashqa'i of Iran: World of Islam Festival 1976.**
Whitworth Art Gallery.   Manchester, England: Whitworth Art Gallery, University of Manchester, 1976. 95p. map.

A publication from the World of Islam Festival held in London and other major cities in Britain in 1976 in connection with the exhibition of Qashqa'i tribal art in Manchester. The bulk of the book comprises photographs of art and craft objects, portraits and local scenes. The photographs were catalogued by John Allgrove with the help of Sarah Drake and Linda Coleing. Further background information on the Qashqa'i tribe is provided in the introductory notes.

746 **Calligraphy from Iran.**
Khosrow Za'imi.   London: Commonwealth Institute, 1976. [n.p.].

Contains the work of twenty-four Iranian calligraphers which was presented at an exhibition in London in 1976. Each calligrapher is given a full page, which includes one or more examples of his work, as well as his photograph and a brief introductory caption in both English and Farsi.

Islamic bookbindings: in the Victoria and Albert Museum.
See item no. 753.

Union catalogue of Persian serials and newspapers in British libraries.
See item no. 786.

Book Production, Decoration and Calligraphy

747 **Mawarannahr book painting.**
Olympiada Galerkina, David Plaksin. Leningrad, USSR: Aurora Art Publishers, 1980. 32p.

An introduction, in English and Russian, to the 16th-century Persian art of book- and miniature-painting in Central Asia. The volume's introduction is followed by forty-eight magnificent colour miniatures and notes.

748 **Epic images and contemporary history: the illustrations of the great Mongol Shahnama.**
Oleg Grabar, Sheila Blair. Chicago; London: University of Chicago Press, 1980. 173p.

A critical and detailed examination of a magnificent 14th-century manuscript of the *Shahnameh*, which is renowned for its paintings. Since its rediscovery some years before the First World War, and especially since 1931 when the great exhibition of Iranian art was held in London, the manuscript has been associated with the name of its notorious dealer, Demotte, who mutilated it and sold its miniatures piecemeal. This volume contains fifty-eight miniatures known to have belonged to the Demotte *Shahnameh*, and includes the list of paginated folios and a reconstruction of the original manuscript.

749 **Persian miniatures: from ancient manuscripts.**
Basil Gray. Milan, Italy: Unesco, 1962. 24p. bibliog. (Fontana Unesco Art Books, 5).

A brief introduction to the miniatures of the two greatest periods of Persian art – the Timurid and the Safavid periods. The introduction includes a number of black-and-white examples of Persian miniatures, and also included in the volume is a separate section of twenty-eight colour illustrations.

750 **Persian painting.**
Basil Gray.   New York: Rizzoli International Publications, 1977.
171p. map. bibliog. (Treasures of Asia).

A study of Persian painting, focusing on calligraphy and book illustration. Following an introduction to the background of Persian painting, the author argues that the Mongol invasion of Iran, while devastating major centres of Persian civilization, encouraged the growth of artistic life, and particularly the arts of book illustration and calligraphy, which reached their peak in the 15th century. Various schools of painting during this period, the new style of the 16th century, and later Safavid paintings are examined.

751 **The arts in the Safavid period.**
Basil Gray. In: *The Cambridge history of Iran, vol. 6: the Timurid and Safavid periods.* Edited by Peter Jackson. Cambridge, England: Cambridge University Press, 1986. p. 877–912. bibliog.

An examination of the arts in the Safavid period, concentrating on book- and miniature-painting. This article is, in fact, a continuation of the author's study of the book in the late 14th and 15th centuries, which is published in the same volume of *The Cambridge history of Iran* (q.v.).

752 **The pictorial arts in the Timurid period.**
Basil Gray. In: *The Cambridge history of Iran, vol. 6: the Timurid and Safavid periods.* Edited by Peter Jackson. Cambridge, England: Cambridge University Press, 1986. p. 843–76. bibliog.

A study of the book in Iran during the late 14th and 15th centuries, focusing in particular on miniature painting. It deals with different book-production and printing centres and assesses the patronage necessary for the arts to flourish. Further areas of the arts which are briefly examined, are metalwork and the ceramics of the period.

753 **Islamic bookbindings: in the Victoria and Albert Museum.**
Duncan Haldane.   London: World of Islam Festival Trust
(in association with the Victoria and Albert Museum), 1983. 200p.
bibliog.

This is a magnificently-produced volume, covering in some detail the art of book-binding and sumptuous decoration as practised in the eastern territories of the Islamic world. It contains sections on Arab, Persian, Turkish and Indian bookbinding. A section on bookbinding tools is also included.

754 **Calligraphers and painters.**
Qazi Ahmad, translated from the Persian by Vladimir Minorsky.
Washington, DC: Freer Gallery of Art Occasional Papers, vol. 3,
no. 2, 1959. 201p. bibliog.

An English translation of a treatise by the 16th-century writer Qazi Ahmad on calligraphers and painters. The translation is preceded by a comparative and

objective investigation of the life and works of the author. The book includes
eight plates and useful indexes.

755 **Islamic painting: a survey.**
David Talbot Rice. Edinburgh: Edinburgh University Press,
1971. 179p. bibliog.
A general survey of book- and miniature-painting in the Islamic world from the
early Islamic time to the 18th century. Persian painting has received special
attention, with chapters on the Sasanian legacy, the Mongol school, the 15th
century and the Safavid age. The volume contains a selection of black-and-white
and some colour illustrations.

756 **Royal Persian manuscripts.**
Stuart Gary Welch. London: Thames & Hudson, 1976. 127p.
A collection of forty-eight delightful 16th-century book illustrations, with covering
notes on their history, the condition of the original manuscript, and some stylistic
remarks. The volume's introduction and its brief bibliography provide further
material which will be of use to the student of Persian art and those familiar with
the subject. The illustrations are from the *Shahnameh* of Ferdousi the collected
works of Mir 'Ali-Shir Nava'i, the *Divan* of Hafez, the *Khamseh* of Nezami and
Jami's *Haft Ourang*.

757 **The *Shāh-nāmah* of Firdausi: the book of the Persian kings.**
J. V. S. Wilkinson. London: India Society, 1931. 92p.
Contains twenty-four miniature paintings (six of which are in colour) from 15th-
century manuscripts. The narrative power of these illustrations is critically studied
by the author. The book includes an informative introduction, by Laurence
Binyon, on the artistic characteristics of the paintings, and an investigation, by the
author, on the manuscript of the *Shahnameh*.

Highlights of Persian art.
See item no. 683.

Islamic art and design: 1500–1700.
See item no. 689.

The arts of Islam.
See item no. 734.

Persian paintings in the India Office Library . . .
See item no. 742.

Calligraphy from Iran.
See item no. 746.

Mass Media

758 **The role of information and communication in national development.**
H. A. Anvari, Ghassem Khalizadeh Rezai. In: *The social sciences and problems of development*. Edited by Khodadad Farmanfarmaian. Princeton, New Jersey: Princeton University Program in Near Eastern Studies, 1976. p. 171–88.
A general assessment of the role played by the system of communication in social, cultural and educational development.

759 **The role of the mass media.**
Amin Banani. In: *Iran faces the seventies*. Edited by Ehsan Yar-Shater. New York; Washington; London: Praeger, 1971. p. 321–40.
A general historical survey of the evolution of the mass media in Iran since the mid-19th century. It examines the role of radio, television, newspapers and periodicals generally during the period of their active operation, but focusing in particular on the 1960s. The essay also deals with censorship.

760 **Iran media index.**
Hamid Nafici. Westport, Connecticut; London: Greenwood Press, 1984. 233p.
An annotated index of non-fiction films, filmstrips, and television news and public affairs programmes on Iran, produced in the major English-speaking countries.

Iran almanac and book of facts.
See item no. 9.

244

Mirza Malkum Khān . . .
See item no. 193.

Family planning in Iran: results of a survey and a mass media campaign.
See item no. 337.

Paved with good intentions . . .
See item no. 457.

Communications, transport, retail trade and services.
See item no. 548.

Union catalogue of Persian serials and newspapers in British libraries.
See item no. 786.

Professional
Periodicals

761 **British Society for Middle Eastern Studies Bulletin (BRISMES).**
Oxford: British Society for Middle Eastern Studies,
c/o St. Antony's College, 1973– . semi-annual.
An interdisciplinary periodical containing articles on the political, social and cultural history of the Middle Eastern countries. Book reviews are also included, as well as a list of the Middle Eastern studies carried out in British universities, and works in progress.

762 **Country Report: Iran.**
London: Economist Intelligence Unit, 1952– . quarterly.
The new title was adopted in April 1986, and was previously known as the *Quarterly Economic Review*. It provides up-to-date information on economic and business trends and includes charts, indicators, and so on. Other relevant publications from the EIU include the *EIU Regional Reviews* (annual), *The Middle East and North Africa* (annual), and *Country Profile: Iran* (annual).

763 **International Journal of Middle East Studies (IJMES).**
Cambridge, England: Cambridge University Press, 1969– .
quarterly.
Publishes research into the political, social and cultural history of the Middle East, ranging from the 7th century up to the present day. Book reviews are also included. Particular attention is paid to the history, politics, economics, anthropology, sociology, literature and folklore of the area, and to comparative religion, theology, law and philosophy.

764 **Iran: Journal of the British Institute of Persian Studies.**
London: British Institute of Persian Studies, 1963– . annual.
Concerned with Persian culture in the widest sense, but focuses on the development of archaeological techniques and historical issues.

765 **Iranian Studies: Journal of the Society for Iranian Studies.**
New York: Society for Iranian Studies, 1968– . irregular.
The journal was originally entitled *Iranian Studies: Bulletin of the Society for Iranian Cultural and Social Studies*, and briefly changed its title for the first time on number four of the first volume. The present title was adopted in 1970, from volume three onwards. The journal is concerned with various topics of Iranian culture and society, including the history, language, literature, and social, economic and political problems of Iran. Some issues, especially in recent years, have been thematically organized.

766 **Khamsin.**
London: Journal of Revolutionary Socialists of the Middle East.
irregular.
This journal is mainly concerned with the struggles to establish social and national movements in the Middle East. Each issue deals with a central theme, but articles on additional topics are also included. The first four issues were published in French, and the first English-language issue began with *Khamsin 5*, which appeared in 1978.

767 **Life and Letters, vol. 63, no. 148.**
Edited by Robert Herring. London: Life & Letters, 1949.
p. 190–270.
This issue of *Life and Letters*, a continuation of *The London Mercury*, is confined to Iran's modern literature. It contains three introductory essays on modern Persian prose, poetry, and Sadeq Hedayat, each followed by a number of relevant translations. The Persian authors appearing in the volume are: Al-e Ahmad, H. B. Jawan, R. Mostafavi, Mohammad Hejazi, Hamid Rahnoma, Sadeq Chubak, Iraj, Farzad, Tavallali, Ra'di, Khanlari, Eslami, Golchin, and Hedayat.

768 **The Literary Review: an international journal of contemporary writing, vol. 18, no. 11, Fall 1974.**
Edited by Thomas M. Ricks. Rutherford, New Jersey: *The Literary Review*, 1974. 144p.
This volume of *The Literary Review* is confined to the modern literature of Iran. It contains an introductory essay on the emergence of modern literature in Iran and on the translations in the volume, with a bibliography of general works on contemporary Iran and English translations of modern Persian literature. Other essays in the volume are translations of Jalal Al-e Ahmad's 'The old man was our eyes' and Mohammad 'Ali Jamalzadeh's Preface to *Yeki bud yeki nabud*. Short stories and poetry in translation are from Samad Behrangi, Sadeq Chubak, Ebrahim Golestan, Sadeq Hedayat, Bahram Sadeqi, Forough Farrokhzad, Nader Naderpour, Mehdi Akhavan Sales, Ahmad Shamlu and Nima Yushij.

Professional Periodicals

769 **MEED (Middle East Economic Digest).**
London: Middle East Economic Digest, 1957–   . weekly.
Contains regional news, analyses and forecasts, concentrating on the political and economic issues.

770 **MERI Report: Iran.**
Middle East Research Institute, University of Pennsylvania. London; Sydney: Croom Helm, 1985. 181p.
A handbook of current social, political and economic issues. It examines the causes and historical background of various developments, and their effects on Iran's immediate future. The topics covered include the political structure; external developments and foreign relations; Islamization and its consequences; economic analyses; the budget; and industry and agriculture. It also contains a comprehensive statistical appendix on various areas such as defence, economy, trade, industry and agriculture, communication, education, health and welfare.

771 **MERIP Reports.**
Washington, DC: Middle East Research and Information Project, 1970–   . Nine issues per year.
Focuses mainly on the political economy of the contemporary Middle East, and the political struggles in the region. Each issue adopts a central theme, but articles on additional topics are also included. The journal has so far published several issues on various Iranian economic and political topics.

772 **Middle East Newsletters: Gulf States, Iraq, Iran, Kuwait, Bahrain, Qatar, United Arab Emirates, Oman.**
London: ICI Publications, 1 Dec. 1980–   . fortnightly.
Previously known as the *Middle East Newsletter*, the journal deals mainly with issues such as politics, security, economics, energy, minerals, finance and banking.

248

Bibliographies

773 Fehrest-e maqalat-e Farsi (Index Iranicus).
Iraj Afshar. Tehran: Tehran University Press, 1961. 984p.

A subject listing of 5993 articles in Farsi, printed in 179 periodicals, journals, etc. during the period 1910–60. It includes all aspects of Iranian history and culture. A supplement to this bibliography entitled *Fehrest-e maqālāt-e Farsi: 1339–1345 (1960–1966)* contains a further 4,642 entries which cover the following six-year period.

774 The economy of Iran, 1940–1970: a bibliography.
William H. Bartsch, Julian Bharier. Durham, England: University of Durham, 1971. 104p. (Centre for Middle Eastern and Islamic Studies, no. 2).

Contains most English source materials on various aspects of the Iranian economy. It also includes a selection of Persian- and French-language sources, which are of particular value. The volume is arranged in thirteen chapters, and there are 1,200 entries.

775 The Iranian opposition to the Shah.
Wolfgang H. Behn. Berlin, FRG: Staatsbibliothek Preussischer Kulturbesitz, [n.d.].

This bibliography contains a list of over 700 anti-Pahlavi references, in both Farsi and other languages, published outside Iran between 1962 and 1979.

776 Iran: a bibliographic research survey.
Eckart Ehlers. München, FRG: New York; London; Paris: K. G. Saur, 1980. 411p.

This bibliography, with comments in German and English, is aimed especially at those who have a professional or general geographical interest in Iran and its population, although it also includes some archaeological-historical, and some economic literature. It includes titles in English, French and German, though it does not claim to be comprehensive.

777 **Bibliographic guide to Iran.**
Edited by L. P. Elwell-Sutton. Brighton, Sussex, England: Harvester Press; Totowa, New Jersey: Barnes & Noble Books, 1983. 425p.

A companion volume to the *Arab Islamic Bibliography* (Edited by D. Grimwood-Jones (et al.). Brighton, Sussex: Harvester Press, 1977), focused on Iran and designed to list a selective number of books on various topics for postgraduate students and scholars of Persian studies. Works in Persian and other European languages are included. The bibliography is arranged under fifteen headings.

778 **A bibliography of the works of L. P. Elwell-Sutton.**
L. P. Elwell-Sutton. In: *Qajar Iran: political, social and cultural change, 1800–1925.* Edited by E. Bosworth, C. Hillenbrand. Edinburgh: Edinburgh University Press, 1983. p. XVII–XXV.

The bibliography includes 134 entries in chronological order, covering the years from 1940 to 1983.

779 **Iran's politics and government under the Pahlavis, an annotated bibliography.**
Dariush Gitisetan. Metuchen, New Jersey; London: Scarecrow Press, 1985. 191p.

Contains material related to the politics and government in Iran during the Pahlavi dynasty. The sources are in major Western languages, although most are in English. It is divided into six parts, two on the rise and fall of the dynasty, a concluding section on general sources, and the three remaining on the political, economic and social conditions. It includes 1160 entries with brief, informative annotations.

780 **A bibliography of Iran: a catalogue of books and articles on Iranian subjects, mainly in European languages.**
Iranian Culture Foundation. Tehran: Iranian Culture Foundation, vol. I, 1969. 244p. (Publication no. 53); vol. II, 1971. 479p. (Publication no. 106).

Vol. I contains studies on the *Avesta*, Mani and Manichaeism, Old Persian, Pahlavi (Parsik and Parthian), the Parsis of India, and Zoroastrianism. Vol. II contains studies on the Persian language and literature. It is a subject listing, but has no indexes.

781 **Economic history of the Middle East to 1914.**
Charles P. Issawi. In: *Middle East Studies Association Bulletin*,
(New York), vol. 2, part II (1968), p. 1–14.

A bibliographical introduction to the material available on the economic history
of the Middle East, including a section on Iran. The general sections are
chronologically divided, starting with the Islamic period to 1500 AD, followed by
1500–1800 and, finally, 1800–1918, which challenges the date in the title.
Geographical sections other than Iran which are covered are the Ottoman
Empire, Egypt, Sudan and ArabAsia.

782 **Bio-bibliographies de 134 savants. Acta Iranica 20, répertoires,**
vol. 1. (Bio-bibliographies of 134 experts. Acta Iranica 20, index,
vol. 1.).
Edited by Pierre Lecoq, J. Duchesne-Guillemin, Jean
Kellens. Leiden, The Netherlands: E. J. Brill, 1979. 561p.

Provides the curricula vitae of 134 scholars of Persian studies, followed by a list
of their publications. Most entries are in English but some are in other European
languages.

783 **An annotated bibliography of Islamic science.**
Seyyed Hossein Nasr, with the collaboration of William C.
Chittick. Tehran: Offset Press, 1975–78. 2 vols. (Imperial Iranian
Academy of Philosophy, publication no. 1).

In 1975 the first volume of a five-volume project designed to provide a comprehensive annotated bibliography of Islamic science was printed. It was followed by the
second volume in 1978, leaving the subsequent three volumes still to appear. The
material assembled was systematically classified into twelve chapters, some
including a number of sub-chapters. The first volume covers the first two chapters
on general works and bibliographies. Chapters three to seven dealing with most
sciences and scientific texts, translation, encyclopaedias, bio-bibliographies,
cosmology and cosmography, and logic, are provided in the second volume.
Areas to be covered in the following volumes include mathematics and its
relevant branches of knowlege, natural philosophy, occult sciences, philosophy
and theology, and the influence of Islamic science.

784 **An index of articles in Western journals.**
V. Nersessian. London: Luzac, 1975. 95p.

Even though somewhat obsolete, it provides the student of Armenian studies with
a useful list of articles in eighty-nine Western journals. The list is divided into
eight headings: 1, 'Religion, church, monasticism, theology'; 2, 'History'; 3,
'Numismatics'; 4, 'Texts, folk-lore, mythology'; 5, 'Manuscripts, palaeography';
6, 'Philology, linguistics'; 7, 'Architecture, archaeology, arts, miniatures, music';
8, 'The Armenian dispersion'.

Bibliographies

785 **Bibliography on Qajar Persia.**
Edited by Shoko Okazaki, Kinji Eura.   Osaka, Japan: Osaka
University of Foreign Studies, 1985. 150p.

The bibliography contains literature on Qajar Persia (1796–1925) in English, German, French, Italian, Russian and Japanese, with English entries forming a considerable proportion of the work. The English titles of Japanese works are also given. The English lists of confidential papers relating to foreign affairs, and consular reports relating to Persia, 1861–1906, are included, as well as the list of the Iranian governors of different provinces throughout the period.

786 **Union catalogue of Persian serials and newspapers in British**
libraries.
Edited by Ursula Sims-Williams, with an introduction by John
Gurney.   London: Ithaca Press, 1985. 140p. bibliog. (Middle East
Libraries Committee).

Presents a list of Persian-language serials in national, university and government libraries in Great Britain. The details of periodicals and newspapers partially in Persian, as well as those in Dari or Tajik, are also included. The initial listing, which was completed by 1983, was updated by including holdings obtained immediately before the catalogue was printed. Contains 640 entries.

787 **Iran: bibliographical spectrum.**
Donald N. Wilber.   *Review of National Literatures*, vol. 2, no. 1
(1971), p. 161–81.

A review of the area and the material which, in the author's view, seems to be the essential starting point from which to develop an interest in classical Persian literature.

Studies in art and literature of the Near East.
See item no. 6.

Iran: religion, politics and society.
See item no. 12.

Iranica: twenty articles.
See item no. 13.

Islam and its cultural divergence.
See item no. 17.

Qajar Iran, political, social and cultural change, 1800–1925.
See item no. 150.

Sayyid Jamal ad-Din 'Al-Afghani': a political biography.
See item no. 201.

On the sociology of Islam.
See item no. 312.

Society and economics in Islam . . .
See item no. 403.

An introduction to Shi'i law . . .
See item no. 483.

Economic development in Iran: 1900–1970.
See item no. 497.

Major voices in contemporary Persian literature.
See item no. 676.

Iran media index.
See item no. 760.

Index

The index is a single alphabetical sequence of authors (personal and corporate), titles of publications and subjects. Index entries refer both to the main items and to other works mentioned in the notes to each item. Title entries are in italics. Numeration refers to the items as numbered.

A

Aavani, G. R. 652
'Abbas the Great, Shah 154
Abbasid caliphs 130
Abbasid rule 119
  Khurasan revolt 123
  politics 123
  society 123
Abbot, J. 1
Abbott, K. E. 511
'Abd al-Karim, Hajji 161
Abd al-Naser, Jamal 379
Abir, M. 429
Abjad alphabet 250
Abrahamian, E. 171-172, 191, 339-340, 354
Abu Moslem 123
Abubakr, Caliph 97, 285
Abu'l-Qasim 684
Academy of Sciences of the GDR, Berlin 371
Academy for State and Law, Potsdam-Babelsberg 371
Achaemenian period 98, 101-104, 108, 111-113
  administration 102
  arts 108, 112-113, 683
  culture 108, 113
  economy 102
  iconography 113

society 102, 114
Ackerman, P. 688
Actes du 2e Congrès International, Tehran, du 1er au 8 septembre 1975 92
Adam collection 737
Adam, Peter 737
Adamec, L. W. 23
Adamiyat, F. 174, 414
Administration 343
  Achaemenian period 102
  American 355, 442, 453
  decentralization 485
  education 575
  Islamic government 485
  mediaeval Islamic period 121, 131
  pre-Islamic era 115
  Qajar period 148-149, 215
  reforms 573
  Safavid period 169
  Saljuq period 131
  Sasanian period 107
  under Karim Khan Zand 164
  under Shah Isma'il Safavi 167
Admiralty War Staff, Naval Intelligence Division 14
Adventures of Hajji Baba of Ispahan 59, 679
Adventures of Hajji Baba of Ispahan in England 59
Afghan occupation 162-163

Afghani, Sayyid Jamal al-Din 271
    bibliography 201
    biography 201
Afghanistan 54
    Baluchestan 244
    German expedition 421
    Kufic inscription 588
    literature 583
    mediaeval period 120
    military rule 349
    policy of USSR 451
    Yomut Turkmen 234
Afkhami, G. 341
Afrouz, A. 388
Afshar, H. 239, 333, 339-340, 368, 390,
    401, 489, 509, 518, 549-550
Afshar, I. 773
Afshar, K. 550
Afshar, S. 318
Agency for International Development
    (AID) 580
Agha Khan 652
Agha Mohammad Khan 146
Agribusiness 534
*Agricultural change and rural society in
    southern Iran* 545
Agricultural development 528-531
Agricultural development of Iran 530
Agricultural geography 532
Agriculture 202, 386, 528-540, 770
    19th century 511
    19th-20th centuries 158
    co-operatives 533
    crop production 542
    early 20th-century 55, 529, 538
    and the economy 156, 503, 532,
        537-539
    effect of Islamic Revolution 535
    effect of migration 549
    history 530
    labour force 550
    large-scale farming 531, 534, 539,
        545
    mechanization 362, 539
    mediaeval Islamic period 134
    and modernization 528-530
    pastoralism 225, 242
    policies 549-550
    production organization 314
    and society 532
    statistics 564, 566, 770
    traditional crafts 728
    urban 33
    see also Irrigation, Land reform,
        Pastoral tribes
Agwani, M. S. 342
Ahmad, A. 584
Ahmad, Qazi 754
Ahmed, M. S. 354
AID (Agency for International
    Development) 580
Ajami, F. 192
Ajami, I. 528-529
Akhavan Sales, Mehdi 768
Akhavi, S. 173
akhbari-osuli debates 277
Akhlaq-e Naseri 663
*Akten des VII Kongresses für Arabistik
    und Ismalwissenschaft* 601
Al-Alak, B. 568
Alamara-ye 'Abbasi 154
Alamut 42
*Alamut and Lamasar: two medieval
    Ismaili strongholds in Iran* 42
Alavi, Bozorg
    biography 664
al-Aziz, K. 24
Albaharna, H. M. 471
al-Bazzaz, Abdul Rahman 237
Albert, D. H. 369
Alburz system 39
Al-e Ahmad, Jalal 636, 665-666, 767-
    768
Alexander the Great 98-99, 108
    conquest of Iran 98
    march to Asia 98
    military campaigns 98
Alexander Y. 440
Algair's Agreement (1975) 237
Algar, H. 193, 278, 312, 391, 399, 403,
    472
al-Hadithi, N. 460
al-Halveti, Sheikh B. al-Jerrahi 282
Ali, Abd al-Rahim 388
Ali, Caliph 97
'Ali, Mihr 684
Aliabad
    ethnoarchaeology 83
Alimard, A. 343
Alishan, L. P. 585, 680
*All fall down: America's tragic
    encounter with Iran* 413
Allan, J. W. 80
Allgrove, J. 745

Allied occupation (1941–46) 213, 447, 456
Alphabet, Abjad 250
al-Sulami, M. ibn al-Husayn 282
Amanat, A. 511
Ambassadors
  diaries 214
  Qajar period 214
Ambraseys, N. N. 25
'Ameli, Sheikh Bahaoddin 277
*America held hostage: the secret
  negotiations* 412
American Embassy, Tehran
  seizure, 1979 440
American Enterprise Institute, Middle
  East Research Project 498
American Financial Mission 202
American task in Persia 202
Americans
  in Iran 389
Amery collection 684
Amery, Major Harold 684
Amery, Rt. Hon. Leopold 684
Amin, A. A. 144
Amin, S. H. 459
Amin al-Douleh 149
Amin al-Sultān
  assassination 186
Amini, S. 380
Aminzadeh, F. 551
Amir Arjomand, S. 145
Amir Kabir, M. T. 180
Amirie, A. 430
Amirsadeghi, H. 376, 431, 435, 443,
  490, 493, 517
Amlash
  bronzes 737
  pottery 683
Amnesty International 404-406
Amoretti, B. S. 270
Amphibians 73
Amuzegar, J. 494-496, 579
Anatolia
  Kilims 713, 724
Ancient bronzes from Luristan 736
Ancient Iran 738
*Ancient Persian bronzes in the Adam
  collection* 737
Anderson, E. W. 543
Anderson, S. C. 73
Anglo–Iranian Oil Company 346
*Anglo–Iranian relations during World
  War I* 423

Anglo–Persian Oil Company 547
*Annotated bibliography of Islamic
  science* 783
Annual Round Table Series 5
*Another birth: selected poems of
  Forugh Farrokhzad* 671
Anthologies 640, 642-643, 646-647,
  649-652, 657-661, 667-672,
  675-676, 678
Anthology of modern Persian poetry
  678
Anthropology 35, 225, 303
  ethnic relations 311
  Makran area 50
  religion and society 313
  role of religious institutions 315
Anti-British riots 342
Antiquities 64
  Ashmolean Museum 738
Anvari, H. A. 758
Appliance industry 527
Aq Quyunlu 139
*Arab Gulf economy in a turbulent
  world* 461
Arab Islamic Bibliography 777
Arab–Israeli conflict 416, 462
Arab Research Centre, London 434
*Arabian Gulf states: their legal and
  political status and their
  international problems* 471
Arabian Peninsula 316
Arabic language 246, 250-251, 629
Arabic music 707
Arabic poetry 596
Arabs
  conflict with Shu'ubis 133
Arasteh, A. R. 298-299, 574, 586
Arasteh, J. 299
Arberry, A. J. 2, 587, 640, 646, 649,
  655-657, 660, 729
'Arc of Crisis' 451
*Archaeological ethnography in western
  Iran* 89
Archaeological sites 84
  Elam (Khuzestan) 103
  Gurgan 82
  Marlik (Cherāgh-Ali tape) 86
  Pasargade 87
  Persepolis 91
  Tape Nush-i Jan 81
Archaeology 22, 80-91, 108
  and ethnography 83, 89

Archaeology *contd.*
  expeditions 64
  guidebook 71
  Kirmanshah caves 88
  periodical 764
  Shiraz 88
Architecture 4, 280, 688, 691-703
  7th-14th century 697
  14th-19th century 697
  Armenian 694, 698
  desert buildings 692
  Gurgan 82
  Hasht Behesht 699
  history 701
  Il-Khanid period 700, 702
  Ionian 112
  Isfahan 68
  Islamic 54, 683, 697
  Masjid-i 'Atiq mosque 703
  mediaeval Islamic period 137
  mosques 685
  prehistoric 90
  pre-Safavid 68
  Safavid 696
  Timurid period 700
  traditional 691
  Zoroastrian 693
*Architecture of Islamic Iran: the Il
  Khanid period* 702
Ardalan, N. 691
Area handbook for Iran 16
'Aref 624
Arent Madelung, A. M. 670
Aresvik, O. 530
Armenia: cradle of civilisation 235
Armenian architecture 694, 698
Armenian studies
  Western journal articles 784
Armenians 235
Armenians: a people in exile 235
Arms and armed forces 368-369, 431,
  444, 446, 455, 462, 480, 489-493
  arms transfers 369, 444, 455, 493
  Pahlavi period 489-491
  statistics 565
*Arms trade registers, the arms trade
  with the Third World* 565
Arnold, A. 52
Arnold, Matthew 613
Art
  bronzes 683
  calligraphy 683, 689, 716, 746, 750,
    754

folk art 713-728
history 683, 685, 688, 750
jewellery 689
manuscript illumination 689,
  747-749, 756-757
miniatures 4, 68, 686-687, 741, 743-
  744, 747-749, 751-752, 755, 757
modern 681-683
paintings 683-689
paper-cutting 689
pottery 683, 688-689, 728
Qashqa'i 745
Scythian 683
Shiraz school 687
silverware 683
and tradition 681-682
Art collections
  Amery collection 684
  Bodleian Library, Oxford 741
  British Library 743
  German museums 732
  India Office Library 742
Art exhibitions 748
  Islamic 734
  New York (1940) 739
  Qashqa'i tribal (1976) 745
  Sasanian 733
Art galleries
  Asia House 733
*Artisans and guild life in the later
  Safavid period: contributions to the
  social-economic history of Persia*
  160
Artists 681, 684, 716
Arts 2, 6, 13, 20-22, 108, 280, 525, 575,
  681-728
  11th-14th centuries 685
  14th century 686
  16th century 687
  19th century 690
  Achaemenian 108, 112-113, 683
  Armenian 235
  decorative 689
  Median period 108
  mediaeval Islamic period 137
  modern Islamic period 159
  Mongol period 750, 755
  patronage 752
  Persian Gulf 7
  pre-Islamic period 108, 112-113, 115
  Qajar 684
  Safavid period 154, 163, 168, 751,
    755

258

Sasanian period 733, 755
support from Pahlavi government
    683
visual 681-690
see also Architecture, Art, Music,
    Folk art, Theatre, Film
Arts of Islam 734
Aryanpur-Kashani, A. 264-266
Aryanpur-Kashani, M. 264-265
Asaria, I. 388
Asayesh, K. 223
Asfar 275
Ashmolean Museum, Oxford 735, 738
Ashraf, A. 332
Asia House Gallery
    Sasanian art exhibition 733
Asia Society 733
Asmussen, J. P. 286
Aspen Institute for Humanistic Studies
    11
Assersohn, R. 410
Astronomy 280
    Isma'ili 143
    Safavid period 170
    Timurid period 129
Atesh-kadeh 662
Atkin, M. 146
*Atlas of geographical maps and
    historical documents on the
    Persian Gulf* 47
*Atlas of Iran: White Revolution
    proceeds and progresses* 48
Atomic energy 517
Attar, Farid ud-Din 640-641
Authority 316, 394, 480
    judicial 475
    modernist 348
    Pahlavi period 480, 489
    regional 485
    traditional 345
Autobiography
    Gholam Hosein Sa'edi 608
Avery, P. W. 147
Avesta
    Gathas 609
Avesta 110, 292, 295, 780
Avestan hymn to Mithra 292
Āyandegān 26
Ayoob, M. 441
Azad 668
Azar, L. A. B. 662
Azarbaijan
    dialect 259

music 704
Azari, F. 318
Aziz, T. 460

B

Ba'ath Socialist Party 460
Baba, Mirza 684
Babism 270, 344
Babylon 90
Badian, E. 98
Baghdad
    conquered by Il Khan Hulagu 128
    institution of caliphate 140
Bagley, F. R. C. 174, 194, 473, 669
Baha'is
    treatment under Islamic Republic
        408-409
Bahar 624
Bahar, S. 318
Bahrambeygui, H. 569
Bahrein islands 414-415, 471
*Bahrein islands, a legal and diplomatic
    study of the British–Iranian
    controversy* 414
Baillie Fraser, J. 690
Baker, T. D. 232
Bakhash, S. 148-149, 370, 432
Bakhtiar, L. 691
Baldick, J. 622
Baldwin, G. B. 226-227
Ball, W. 67
Ballads 624
Baluch tribes 243-244
Baluchestan 243-244
    geography 26
    political history 26
*Baluchestan: its political economy and
    history* 26
Bam 38
Banani, A. 175, 672, 759
Banisadr, President 370
Bank Markazi 216
Banking 184, 501
    19th-20th centuries 158
    periodical 772
*Banking and empire in Iran: the history
    of the British Bank of the Middle
    East. Volume 1* 184
Banks 505
Barahani, Reza 667
Barthel, G. 371

259

Barthold, W. 27
Bartholomew world travel map: the Middle East 28
Bartsch, W. H. 774
Bashiri, I. 245
Bashiriyeh, H. 372
Batatu, H. 354
Bauer, J. 319
Bausani, A. 116-117
Bayat, A. 557
Bayat, M. 176, 344, 395
Bazaar
  role of *'olama* 315, 339
  Tehran 315
Bazargan, Premier Mehdi 370, 552
Beaumont, P. 29
Beazlay, E. 692
Beblawi, H. 461
Bedil, Abdul Qadir
  biography 583
Behind the veil in Persia and Turkish Arabia: an account of an Englishwoman's eight years' residence amongst the women of the East 56
Behn, W. H. 775
Behnam, J. 217
Behrangi, Samad 668, 768
Behzadnia, A. A. 552
Beihaqi, Abu al-Fazl 142
Belles-lettres 633
Bengston, H. 99
Bergman, H. 531
Berlin 664
Betteridge, A. H. 320
Bharier, J. 218, 497, 774
Bible 288
Bibliographical guide to Iran 777
Bibliographies 115, 773-787
  'Ali Shari'ati 312
  Ayatollah Sayyid Mahmud Taleghani 403, 488
  British holdings Persian serials 786
  culture 773
  economic history 781
  economy 497, 774
  history 773
  L. P. Elwell-Sutton 150, 778
  literature 781
  mass media 760
  opposition groups 775
  Pahlavi period 779

Qajar period 787
Sayyid Jamal al-Din Afghani 201
scholars 782
science 783
Shi'ite law 483
Western journal articles 784
Bibliography of Iran; a catalogue of books and articles on Iranian subjects, mainly in European languages 780
Bibliography on Qajar Persia 785
Biggest deal 410
Bilharzia 335
Bill, J. A. 345
Binyon, L. 757
Bio-bibliographies 782-783
Bio-bibliographies de 134 savants. Acta Iranica 20, répertoires, vol. 1 782
Biographies 8
  Abdul Qadir Bedil 583
  Amir Khosrou 621
  Ayatollah Ruhollah Khomeini 199, 212, 402
  Ayatollah Sayyid Mahmud Taleghani 488
  Bozorg Alavi 664
  Hakim Sana'i 597
  Imam 'Ali 200
  Jalal al-Din Rumi 610
  Malkom Khan 193
  Mary Bird 208
  Mohammad Mossadeq 195
  Mohammad Reza Shah Pahlavi 199, 205
  monarchs 199
  Musa Sadr 192
  Naser al-Din Shah 215
  Nasir-i Khusraw 652
  poets 642, 678
  philosophers 199
  politicians 199
  Prophet Mohammad 194, 209
  Reza Shah Pahlavi 196, 199, 213
  Sadeq Hedayat 607
  Safavid artists 154
  Sayyid Jamal al-Din Afghani 201
  scientists 199
  Shari'ati, 'Ali 191, 312
  Sheikh Mosleh al-Din Sa'di 662
  Zoroaster 199
Bird, Mary
  biography 208

260

Birds 79
Birks, J. S. 553
Birth control 337
  see also Family planning
Bishop, I. 690
Bismarck period (1873-90)
  foreign relations 422
Black, D. 713
Blair, S. 748
Blake, G. H. 29
Blind owl 674
Blind white fish in Persia 63
Blunt, W. 68
Bobek, H. 74
Bodleian Library, Oxford
  manuscript collection 741
Bogdanov, L. 623
Bombaci, A. 588
Bonine, M. E. 30
Book collections
  India Office Library 729
Book of government or rules for kings
  653
Book of Sufi chivalry 282
Book production 752-753
Bookbindings 753
Books 180
  illustration 716, 747, 750-751, 755-
  756
  see also Miniatures
Border disputes
  Shatt al-Arab river 24
  Frontier Treaty (1937) 41
Borujerdi, J. 400
Bosworth, C. E. 3, 7, 27, 50, 118-120,
  141, 147, 149-150, 161, 174, 176,
  186, 215, 244, 247, 273, 280, 285,
  421, 473, 478, 584, 598, 693, 717,
  778
Bound phraseology 253
Bowen, J. C. E. 642-643, 649
Bowen–Jones, H. 532
Boyce, M. 100, 289-291, 589, 693, 714
Boyle, J. A. 4, 116-118, 121-122, 126,
  128, 131, 134-135, 626, 685
Bradley, C. P. 442
Branscomb, L. M. 580
Bresciani, E. 99
Bricault, G. C. 512
Bride of acacias 671-672
Britain
  dispute with USSR 210

Iran–Britain agreement (1919) 185
  military intervention 421
  occupation of Iran (1941-46) 213,
  447, 456
  relations with Iran 144, 152, 184,
  214, 346, 414-415, 421, 423, 449
  role in fall of Mossadeq 357-358, 362
  severance of diplomatic links 454
  withdrawal from Persian Gulf (1971)
  415
  in Persia 144, 238
British ambassador
  in Tehran 206
British Institute of Persian Studies,
  London 87
British interests in the Persian Gulf,
  1747-1780 144
British Library
  manuscript collection 743-744
British Military Intelligence 375
British Museum
  bronze collection 736
British Society for Middle Eastern
  Studies Bulletin (BRISMES) 761
British War Office 55
Bronze collections
  Adam collection 737
  Ashmolean Museum, Oxford 735
  British Museum 736
Bronzes
  Luristan 683
Brooklyn College Conference 428
Browne, E. G. 53, 177, 590, 730
Brunner, C. J. 731
Bryn Mawr College, Pennsylvania 113
Buddhist imagery 591
Budget 770
Buf-e Kur 607, 674
Building crafts 728
Bureaucratic system 386
  creation 175
  emergence of middle class 310, 345
Burn, A. R. 101
Burrell, R. M. 7, 415
Bushehr
  British residents in 238
Business 355
  periodical 762
Busse, H. 155
Bustan of Sa'di 661
Butler, W. J. 474
Buyid dynasty 130

261

Byron, R. 54

C

Cahill, K. 232
Cairo University, School of Law 501
Calder, N. 475
Calendar 250
Calendar of documents on Indo–
  Persian relations (1500-1750) 165
Caliph
  original meaning 285
Caliphate 347
  Umayyad claims 285
Caliphate and kingship in medieval
  Persia 140
Caliphs 97, 285
Calligraphers and painters 754
Calligraphy 683, 689, 750, 754
  designs and motifs 716
  exhibition 746
Calligraphy from Iran 746
Cambridge history of Iran, vol. 1: the
  land of Iran 34-37, 39-40, 45, 49,
  73-74, 78-79, 88, 217, 225, 241,
  525, 532, 538, 541, 548
Cambridge history of Iran, vol. 2: the
  Median and Achaemenian periods
  98, 101-104, 108, 111
Cambridge history of Iran, vol. 3: the
  Seleucid, Parthian and Sasanian
  periods 107, 115, 286-287, 589,
  617, 714
Cambridge history of Iran, vol. 4: the
  period from the Arab invasion to
  the Saljuqs 124
Cambridge history of Iran, vol. 5: the
  Saljuq and Mongol periods 116-
  118, 121-122, 126, 131, 134, 626,
  685
Cambridge history of Iran, vol. 6; the
  Timurid and Safavid periods 129-
  132, 136-139, 156, 159, 166, 169-
  170, 270, 277, 515, 629-630, 632,
  639, 696, 700, 726, 751-752
Campbell, R. 360, 403
Canby, S. L. 431, 490
Capital development 362, 494
Capitalism 314, 351
  and feudalism 314

and Islam 309
Capitalism and revolution in Iran 351
Carbonneau, T. E. 411
Carmelite Order 151
  Isfahan 151
Carpets 2, 4, 688, 713, 718, 722, 726
  see also Kilims, Rugs
Carr, C. D. 431, 443
Carswell, J. 694
Carter, A. 209
Carter, M. L. 591, 733
Carter, President Jimmy 410, 442, 453
Caskel, W. 99
Caspian Sea 234
Catalogue of the ancient Persian
  bronzes in the Ashmolean Museum
  735
Catalogue of the Library of the India
  Office: vol. 2, part 6 729
Catalogue of the Persian manuscripts in
  the library of the University of
  Cambridge 730
Catalogues 157, 729-746, 786
Catholicism 16th-18th centuries 151
Cattle-breeding
  14th-18th centuries 156
Caucasus 55
  Kilims 713, 724
Censorship 620, 759
Censuses
  housing (1956 and 1966) 229
  population (1956 and 1966) 229
Central Asia
  history 120, 125
Central Asia
  literature 583
Central Intelligence Agency (CIA) 413
  role in coup d'état (1953) 357-358,
  362, 522
Centre College of Kentucky 380
Centre for Middle Eastern and Islamic
  Studies, University of Durham 505
Cento (Central Treaty Organization)
  520
Characteristics
  Islamic Revolution 314
  physical 303
  rural population 307
  social 303
  tribal 307
  urban population 307

262

Chatwin, B. 54
Checkmate: fighting tradition in central Asia 55
Chelkowski, P. J. 5-6, 592, 603, 710-711
Chick, H. 151
China
 17th-century 57
Chittick, W. C. 783
Chivalry
 Sufi 282
La chouette aveugle 674
Christianity 286, 288
 history 286, 288
Christians 151, 288
 Muslim relations 311
Christians in Persia: Assyrians, Armenians, Roman Catholics and Protestants 288
Chromite 40
Chronicle of the Carmelites in Persia and the papal mission of the XVIIth and XVIIIth centuries 151
Chronologies 69, 71-72, 98, 111, 212, 214, 457
 Constitution 487
 foreign policy 424
 Iranian Revolution 378, 410, 413
 political events 387
Chubak, B. 669
Chubak, Sadeq 669, 767-768
Chubin, S. 416-417, 433, 444
Church Missionary Society 56
Churches
 architecture 694
CIA (Central Intelligence Agency) 413
 role in coup d'état (1953) 357-358, 362, 522
Cinema 712
Cities 38
 maps 28
 religious institutions 313
 slums 230, 339, 549
 social structure 316
Cities and trade: Consul Abbott on the economy and society of Iran 1847-1866 511
Civil war
 Russian 55
Clagett, B. M. 411
Claims Settlement Agreement 411

Clarification of questions: an unabridged translation of 'Resaleh Towzih al-Masael' 400
Clark, B. D. 32, 219
Clarke, J. I. 31-32
Class structure 230, 386
 characteristics 314
 élite 262, 343, 363, 367, 392
 income distribution 308, 425, 477
 in Islamic Revolution 314
 merchants 339
 middle class 310, 345
 mobility 225
 professionals 345
 upper class 570
 working class 310, 557-560, 563
 see also Social structure
Classical Persian literature 587
Classical Persian music: an introduction 709
Clawson, P. 505, 523
Clays 34
Clergy
 fundamentalist 173, 176-177, 182, 300, 313, 315, 372
 legitimizing power 182
 see also 'olama
Climate 7, 14, 37, 74, 97
 Semnan 33
Clinton, J. W. 593
Coal 40
Cockcroft, J. D. 314
Coins and coinage 111
 Achaemenian 113
 introduction by Cyrus the Great 111
Cole, J. R. I. 317, 373, 392, 419
Coleing, L. 745
Collected Persian poems: the golden pomegranate 642
Collected Persian poems: poems from the Persian 643
Collections
 antiquities 738
 art 684, 732, 741-744
 bookbindings 753
 books 729
 bronzes 735-737
 manuscripts 730, 740-741, 743
 Sasanian seal stones 731
Colombia
 land reform 363

263

Columbia University, Ohio 236
Comment on the Iranian claims concerning the Iraqi-Iranian Frontier Treaty of 1937 and the legal status of the frontier between the two countries in Shatt al-Arab 41
Commerce 501
  19th-20th centuries 158
Commercial companies 512
Committee Against Repression in Iran 558
Committee for the Defence of Political Prisoners in Iran 350
Committee on the International Migration of Talent 227
Communications 548, 569
  role in development 758
  statistics 770
Communism 364
  and land reform 363
Communist movement in Iran 364
Companies 512
Comprehensive Persian–English dictionary 268
Concise Persian–English dictionary 265
Conference of birds 641
Conflict and intervention in the Third World 441
Conflict in the Persian Gulf 463
Connel, J. 33
Conscription 489
Conservation 77
Constitution
  1906 190, 482, 487
  amendments 482, 487
  Islamic Republic 472, 476, 481
Constitution of the countries of the world: Iran 487
Constitution of the Islamic Republic of Iran 472
Constitutional Fundamental Laws 177
Constitutional government 171
Constitutional movement 149, 171-190, 504
  impact of the West 171
  in Tabriz 181
Constitutional revolution (1906) 171-172, 176-177, 376
  photographs 177
  resistance from clergy 176-177
Constitutionalism

in literature 601
Construction industry 568
Consumer protection 526
Contemporary Iran 18
Contributions to the anthropology of Iran 303
Cook, J. M. 102
Cooper, R. 546
Co-operatives 533-534, 537
Copper 40, 80
Cordesman, A. H. 462
Cosmography 783
Cosmology 783
Costa, A. 69
Costello, D. P. 674
Cottam, R. W. 178, 392
Cottrell, A. J. 7, 445, 491
Council for Ten Days Dawn Celebration 476
Countercoup: the struggle for the control of Iran 357
Country Profile: Iran 762
Country Report: Iran 762
Coups d'état
  Reza Khan (1921) 185, 196, 213
  CIA (1953) 357-358, 362, 386, 522
Court poetry 593
Courts
  religious 478
  secular 478
Cover, W. W. 16
Craft design 715-716, 723
  see also Handicrafts
Criminal law 474
Cronin, C. 570
Crop production 542
Cry from the heart: the Baha'is in Iran 409
Cuisine 15
Cults
  Mandaeans 233
  pagan 100
Cultural geography 29
Culture 1-4, 6, 9-10, 13, 20-21, 23, 85, 92, 106, 108, 120, 208, 299, 306, 586, 637
  19th century 150
  Achaemenian period 108, 113
  Baluch tribes 244
  bibliography 773
  conflicting values 301
  dissemination into Asia Minor and

264

the Fertile Crescent 96
Elam (Khuzestan) 103
Fars province 307
impact of constitutional revolution
   176
importance of craft design 715-716,
   723
influences of iconography 113
Iranian – Arab–Islamic assimilation
   96
Mandaean 233
mediaeval Islamic period 121, 124,
   137
Median period 104, 108
migrant–non-migrant contrast 231
and modernism 176, 188
periodicals 764-765
Persian Gulf 7
pre-Islamic period 103-104, 106, 108,
   113
prehistoric 90
Qajar period 150
role of education 575-577
Western 509
women in 321
Currency 250
Curtis, J. 81
Curtis, M. 393
Curzon, G. 152, 690
Cyrus the Great 100, 102, 111
   establishment of Achaemenian
      empire 102
   foreign policy 111
   march to Persia 114
   military campaigns 111, 114
   religious beliefs 100, 111

D

Dabashi, H. 594
Dabestan 272
Dam construction 544, 546
   Khuzestan 545
Dam construction in Iran 544
Dams
   maps 46
Daneshvar, Simin 620
Daniel, E. L. 123
*Daramad of chahargah: a study in the
   performance practice of Persian
   music* 706

Darbandi, A. 641
D'Arcy Oil Concession (1901) 519
Dari 786
Darius I 99
Darius III 100
Darius, R. G. 374, 383
Dash Akol 712
Dasht-e Kawir
   water supply 543
Dashti, A. 194, 595
Daudpota, U. M. 596
Davidian, Z. N. 179
Davis, D. 641
Dawn and twilight of Zoroastrianism
   297
Death penalty 406
Débâcle: the American failure in Iran
   453
De Bruijn, J. T. P. 597
Defence 431, 489-493
   statistics 770
de Filippis, L. 383, 446
Dehkhoda, A. A. 265
de Menasce, J. P. 617
De Misonne, X. 78
Democracy 347
Demography 7, 9, 35, 222, 425, 573
   Fars province 307
   households 308
   migrant–non-migrant contrast 231
   rural 221
   statistics 551
   Tehran 569, 571
   see also Population
Demotte 748
Denman, D. R. 533
Denny, N. 552
Department of Classical and Near
      Eastern Archaeology, Bryn Mowr
      College, Pennsylvania 113
Department of the Environment 76
Department of Geography, University
      College, London 33
de Planhol, X. 241
*Descriptive catalogue of the Persian
   paintings in the Bodleian Library*
   741
Deserts 5
   architecture 692
   life and customs 56
Developing countries
   19th century 310

Developing countries *contd.*
  patterns of migration 227-228, 231
  see also Third World
Development 19, 21, 179, 302
  impact on upper class 570
  Pahlavi period 564
  role of Islam 395
  role of mass media 758
  women's role 332
  see also Modernization
Development, agricultural 528-531
Development, capital 362, 494
Development, economic 327, 329, 368,
    464, 494-497, 502-503, 505-506,
    509
Development, educational 226-227
Development, industrial 505, 523-524,
    526-527
Development, political 387, 464
Development, rural 528
Development, social 230, 304, 310, 387
Development, socio-economic 229
Development, socio-political 190, 343,
    395
*Development of the Iranian oil
    industry: international and
    domestic aspect* 516
*Development of large-scale farming in
    Iran: the case of the province of
    Gorgan* 539
Development programmes 570, 573
Dewan, M. L. 34
Dez Irrigation Project 545
Dhamija, J. 715
Dhofar rebellion 418
Diakonoff, I. M. 103-104
Dialects 259
  Larestani 248
  Masal 252
  Tati 259
  Tehrani 255
Diaries 27, 58-60, 66, 75
  foreign ambassadors' 206, 211
  London 1976-1979 207
  Naser al-Din Shah 203
  Tehran, 1974-1979 206
*Diary of HM the Shah of Persia,
    during his tour through Europe in
    AD 1873* 203
Diba, F. 195
Dictatorship 380, 387
Dictionaries 264-269

  scientific 267
  technical terms 269
Dictionary of scientific terms 267
Dietrich, A. 601
Diplomacy 426
Discourses of Rumi 655
Diseases, Endemic 335
Dissent
  19th-century Shi'ite 344
Dissidents 421
Divan 593, 610, 652, 658, 660, 756
*Divan of Manuchehri Damghani: a
    critical study* 593
Divorce 473
Doctors 334
  migration to USA 232
Domestic policy
  Mohammad Reza Shah Pahlavi 358
  on Kurdish nationalism 237
Donohue, J. J. 271
Doroudian, R. 534
Dowlatshahi, A. 716
Drake, H. 653
Drake, S. 745
Drama 5, 592, 627, 669, 676
  passion plays 710-711
Dreyfuss, R. 375
Drower, E. S. 233
Dual sovereignty 185
Dualistic economy 495
Duchesne-Guillemin, J. 105, 782
'Dunsterforce' 55
Dunsterville, Major General 55
Dwyer, C. Brown 407
Dynastic struggles 136, 138-139
Dynastic territories 44
Dyson-Hudson, N. 243

                        E

Earthquakes 25
East India Company
  trade with Persian Gulf 144
East Iranian quadrangle 39
Eastern Caucasus
  Russian expansionist policies 146
Eastwick, E. B. 662
Echo of Iran 8-9
Ecology 29, 78, 234
  and population distribution 241
Economic characteristics

migrant–non-migrant contrast 231
Economic conditions
  Sistan-Baluchestan 26
Economic development 494-497, 502-
  503, 505-506
  effect on women 327, 329
  impact of foreign institutions 505
  Middle East 464
  revolutionary period 368, 509
*Economic development in Iran: 1900-
  1970* 497
Economic geography 29, 35
Economic history 497, 503-504, 515
  14th-18th centuries 159
  19th-20th centuries 55, 158, 505
  1930s 523
  Achaemenian period 102
  Afghan occupation 163
  bibliography 781
  reforms, 19th century 188
  rural, 14th-18th centuries 156
  Safavid period 156, 168, 515
  Timurid period 156, 515
  under Karim Khan Zand 164
  urban, 14th-18th centuries 156
Economic history of Iran, 1800-1914
  158
*Economic origins of the Iranian
  Revolution* 384
Economic planning 510
Economic policy
  Islamic government 387, 390
  Pahlavi government 496, 500
Economic recession 461
Economic sectors 495-497
Economic structure
  Islamic Republic 377, 384, 403
Economics 304, 387, 426
  bibliographies 497, 774
  and Islam 194, 488
  Persian Gulf 7
Economy 9, 16, 20, 35, 55, 179, 184,
  280, 369, 386-387, 396, 438, 494-
  510
  and agriculture 156, 503, 532, 537-
  539
  cause of Iranian Revolution 384, 386
  cause of migration 230
  development programmes 327, 573
  dualistic 495
  effect of Gulf War 461, 468
  fall in oil revenues 461

forecasts and projections 384, 506,
  510, 567
fourth plan (1968-72) 494
growth and distribution 308
international 505, 507, 514
and Islam 318
Islamic Republic 384, 509
Pahlavi era 187, 495, 503-504, 510
periodicals 762, 765, 769-772
Persian Gulf 459, 469, 505
revolutionary period 368, 370, 380,
  384, 386, 509-510
role of industrialized nations 499,
  505
role of oil 495, 499-500, 503, 508,
  518-519, 527, 567
role of OPEC 507
statistics 425, 500, 564, 567, 770
third plan (1962-68) 494
traditional and modern 33
USA involvement 362, 448, 452
village 242
Western 509
*Economy of Iran, 1940-1970: a
  bibliography* 774
Education 1, 20, 307, 574-578
  administration 575
  development 226-227, 574-576
  higher 575, 578
  history 574, 576-577
  impact on migration 227
  laws 574
  Pahlavi period 575
  primary 575
  reforms 310, 574-575
  religious 576-577
  role in modernization 574-575
  secondary 575
  statistics 551, 564, 566, 770
  technical colleges 180
  US aid 452
  women's role 332, 574
*Education and social awakening in
  Iran: 1850-1968* 574
Educational institutions 573
Egypt 316
  economy 498
  housebuilding 568
  land reform 363
  stability 436
Egyptians
  political ideas 347

Ehlers, E. 776
Eilers, W. 575
EIU Regional Reviews 762
Elahi, C. 341, 343, 449
Elam (Khuzestan)
   history 103
Electoral Laws (1906 and 1909) 177
Electricity 525, 581
Elementary Persian grammar 246
Elgood, C. 93, 153
Eliash, J. 300
Elites
   letters 262
   political 343, 363, 367, 392, 396
Ellis, H. S. 498
Elwell-Sutton, L. P. 150, 196, 246,
   346, 376, 431, 595, 598, 777-778
   bibliographies 150, 778
Emami, K. 681
Emery, J. J. 513
Emigration *see* Migration
*Employee-supervisor attitudes in banks:
   a comparative study between the
   Netherlands and Iran* 555
Employment 503, 549-556
   banks 555
   policies 554
   statistics 551
*Employment and income policies for
   Iran* 554
Enayat, H. 347, 394
Encyclopaedia Iranica 22
Encyclopaedias 22
   science 783
Endemic diseases 335
Energy
   crisis 499
   periodical 772
   policy 431, 517, 581
*Energy policy in Iran: domestic choices
   and international implications* 581
*English amongst the Persians during
   the Qajar period* 238
English–Persian collegiate dictionary
   264
Entertainment 1
Environment 29
   and population distribution 241
*Epic images and contemporary history:
   the illustrations of the great
   Mongol Shahnama* 748
Epic literature 623, 644

*Epic of the kings: shāh-nāma, the
   national epic of Persia by Ferdowsi*
   644
Erdmann, H. 732
Erdmann, Professor Dr. Kurt 732
Eshqi 624
Eskandar Beg Monshi 154
Eslami 767
Esposito, J. L. 271, 395
E'tesami, Parvin 624, 670
Ethnic relations 311
Ethnicity
   Makran area 50
Ethnoarchaeology
   Ain Ali 89
   Aliabad 83
   Hasanabad 89
   Shirdasht 89
Ethnography 22-23
Ettela'at 263
Ettinghausen, R. 6, 682-683
Études Mithraiques 92
Etymology 247
Eura, K. 785
Eurasian steppes
   Scythian art 683
Excavations 575
Executions 404-406
Exhibitions
   Asia House Gallery (1978) 733
   calligraphy 746
   Islamic art (1976) 734
   London (1931) 748
   New York (1940) 739
   Qashqa'i tribal art 745
   Sasanian art 733
*Expenditure of oil revenue: an optimal
   control approach with application
   to the Iranian economy* 508
Exports 514, 567
   oil 518

F

Faces in a mirror: memoirs from exile
   204
*Faces of Persian youth: a sociological
   study* 298
Factories 524
Fada'iyan 340, 351, 366
   and women's rights 359

268

Falk, S. J. 684
Fall of the peacock throne: the story of Iran 10
Fall of the Safavi dynasty and the Afghan occupation of Persia 163
Fall of the Shah 197
Fallah, R. 499
False dawn: Persian poems by Nāder Nāderpour 680
Family laws 486
Family laws of Iran 486
Family life 316, 321, 326
  impact of development programmes 570
  Yomut Turkmen 234
Family planning 220, 223, 337
  legal aspects 484
  Pahlavi era 484
Family protection law (1967) 473
Famine 55
Famouri, J. 34
Fani, Sheikh Mohammad Mohsen 272
Fard-Saidi, M. 416
Fardi, M. A. 514
Farhat, H. 301
Farid, A. M. 434
Farmanfarmaian, K. 229, 302, 334, 529, 540, 570, 582, 758
Farmayan, H. F. 180, 348
Farmers
  response to modernization 528
Farr, C. F. A. 704
Farrokhzad, Forugh 671-672, 768
Fars
  history 155
Fars province
  Qashqa'i nomads 240
  social change 307
Farsnameh-ye Naseri 155
Farzad, M. 599, 767
Fasā'i, H. 155
Fassih, E. 673
Fātemeh Fātemeh ast 324
Fatemi, F. S. 447
Fatemi, K. 448
Fathi, A. 181-182, 321
Fauna 7, 35, 73, 76, 78-79, 97
  amphibians 73
  birds 79
  domestic animals 78
  mammals 76, 78
  reptiles 73

Fazel, G. R. 239
Fazlollah, Sayyid 270
Fehrest-e maqālāt-e Farsi: 1339-1345 (1960-1966) 773
Fekrat, M. A. 495
Felt-making 719
Feminism 318-333
Fendereski, Mir 277
Ferdousi 613, 623, 644, 756-757
Ferdows, A. H. 322
Ferdows, A. K. 322
Fernea, E. W. 326, 619
Ferrier, R. 515
Fertile Crescent 316
Fertility 217, 221-222, 224, 337
Fesharaki, F. 431, 500, 516-518
Festivals
  pre-Islamic 714
Feudalism 134, 538
  Islamic teachings 309
Field, H. 303
Field Museum of Natural History 303
Fifty poems of Hafiz 646
Filippani-Ronconi, P. 94
Film 712, 760
Finance 503, 505
  14th-18th centuries 156
  19th-20th centuries 158
  and industrialization 523, 526
  periodical 772
Firouzi, F. 477, 571
Firouz, E. 76
First cities 90
First four caliphs 97
Fiscal policy 179
Fisher, M. M. J. 576
Fisher, W. B. 34-37, 39-40, 45, 49, 73-74, 78-79, 88, 217, 225, 241, 525, 532, 538, 541, 548
Fisheries 489
Fishing
  14th-18th centuries 156
FitzGerald, E. 649-650
Floor, W. M. 396, 478, 505, 523-524, 559
Flora 7, 35, 74-75, 77, 97
  conservation 77
Flower, J. 541
Folan, J. B. 16
Folk art 713-728
Folk-literature 598, 603, 605
Folk tales of ancient Persia 605

269

Folklore 22
  Alamut 42
  Mandaean 233
Foltin, Jr., B. 706
Food processing industry 525
Food-treating crafts 728
Forbes-Leith, F. A. C. 55
Forbis, W. H. 10
Forces of modernization in nineteenth century Iran: an historical survey 180
Ford, I. D. 568
Foreign aid
  USA 452, 579-580
Foreign capital
  statistics 449
Foreign collections 729-746
Foreign exchange 500, 505
  and foreign development 523
Foreign investment 526
  and railway construction 547
Foreign policy 179, 426-427
  18th century 146
  chronology 424
  Cyrus the Great 111
  Iranian Revolution 373, 383
  Iraq 418
  Islamic Republic 377, 419, 428
  and modernization 425
  Mohammad Reza Shah Pahlavi, 358, 418
  Pahlavi era 418
  Qajar period 424
  regional 418, 420
Foreign policy of Iran: a developing nation in world affairs 1500-1941 424
Foreign relations 9, 85, 210, 387, 414-488, 520, 770
  16th-18th centuries 165
  Britain–USSR rivalry 210, 238
  impact of Arab-Israeli conflict 416
  mediaeval Islamic period 132
  Qajar period 214, 238
  regional 417, 420, 429-439, 449
  Sasanian period 107
  strategic significance 417, 428, 431
  under Afghan occupation 163
  with Bahrein 414-415, 471
  with Britain 144, 152, 184, 214, 238, 414-415, 421, 423, 449
  with Germany 422, 456

  with the Gulf States 429-439
  with Iraq 237, 418, 432
  with Saudi Arabia 431, 435, 442
  with USA 420, 427, 431, 440-446, 448-450, 452-453, 455, 457-458
  with USSR 420, 427, 441, 444, 447, 449, 451, 454, 456, 520
  World War I 422-423
Foreign relations of Iran: a developing state in a zone of great power conflict 417
Foreign schools 575
Forughi, M. 'A. 661
Foruzanfar, Badi' al-Zaman 655
Four eminent poetesses of Iran: with a brief survey of Iranian and Indian poetesses of neo-Persian 611
Fragner, B. G. 95, 156
Fraser, J. 157
Friedl, E. 323
From the Levant 52
Frontier Treaty (1937) 41, 438
Frye, R. N. 96, 106-107, 124-125, 717
Fullerton, A. 75
Fundamentalism 171, 173, 176, 182
  'olama 173, 176-177, 182, 300, 313, 315, 372, 394, 396
  and women 318

G

Galdieri, E. 695
Galerkina, O. 747
Ganji, M. 564
Ganji, M. H. 37
Gans-Ruedin, E. 718
Gas 179, 517
Gathas 609
Gāthās of Zarathustra 609
Gaube, H. 38
Geldner, K. F. 292
Genealogy
  Safavid dynasty 163
Genghis Khan 135
Geographical distribution guide to endemic diseases of Iran 335
Geographical texts 27
Geography 9, 14, 22-24, 26-33, 35-36, 38, 41-44, 46-48, 74, 97
  agricultural 532
  Baluchestan 26

cultural 29
economic 29, 35
historical 27, 38, 44, 47
human 216-217, 225, 241, 335
Khorram-rud valley 542
Makran 50
Middle East 29
physical 33-36
political 29
regional 36
and water supply 546
Geology 25, 34, 39-40, 45, 49-51, 65
Makran mountain range 39
Zagros mountain range 45
Geomorphology 49
*German–Persian diplomatic relations:
1873-1912* 422
Germany
Bismarck era (1873-90) 422
foreign relations 422, 456
military intervention 421
Gershevitch, I. 98, 101-104, 108, 111,
247, 292
Gerson-Kiwi, E. 705
Gervers, M. 719
Gervers, V. 719
Ghani, A. 583
Ghanoonparvar, M. R. 600
Gharbzadegi 666
ghazal 584, 606, 640
Ghazan reforms 134
Ghazni
royal palace 588
Ghirshman, R. 109
Ghoreyshi, A. 449
Ghotbi, A. 560
Gilan republic (1920) 185
Gitisetan, D. 779
*Glory of the Shia world: the tale of a
pilgrimage* 59
Gluck, J. 720
Gluck, S. H. 720
Gnoli, G. 95, 110
GNP (Gross National Product) 503
statistics 564
God's shadow: prison poems 667
Goethe, Johann Wolfgang von 625
Golchin 767
Gold 40, 80
*Golden age of Persia: the Arabs in the
East* 96
Golestan 662

Golestan, Ebrahim 768
Good, B. J. 334
Gordon, H. 377
Gordon, M. 463
Gorgan
history 82
large-scale farming 539
Gorgani, F. al-Din 645
Government
19th century 152
absolute 177
constitutional 171
dissident 421
Iraqi 460
Jewish autonomous 287
local 485
provisional 370
Qajar period 148-149
Safavid period 629
Government, Islamic 368, 376, 385,
390, 394, 399
administration 485
agricultural policy 549
attitudes to Westernization 323
economic policy 387, 390
economic problems 510
energy policy 431, 517
militant ideology 385
oil policy 432
and oppression 481
policies for women 329
role in Persian Gulf 432
see also Islamic Republic
Government, Pahlavi 480
and Anglo–Iranian Oil Company 346
attitude towards minorities 239
bibliography 779
consolidation of power 397
economic policy 496, 500
employment policies 554
income policies 554
land reform policy 386
modernization policy 11, 19
reform programme 16
structure 372, 379
support for arts 683
trade policy 526
see also Pahlavi era; Pahlavi,
Mohammad Reza; Pahlavi, Reza
Grabar, O. 685, 748
Graf, K. H. 661
Graham, N. A. 513

Grammar of southern Tati dialects 259
Grammars 246, 249-251, 255, 258-259
Gray, B. 749-752
Grayson, B. L. 450
Greek expansion 99, 101, 108
Greek language 254
*Greeks and Persians from the sixth to
    the fourth centuries* 99
Green, J. D. 378
Grenbäck, E. 565
Griffith, W. 418
Grimwood-Jones, D. 777
Gross National Product (GNP) 503
    statistics 564
Grube, E. J. 686
Grunebaum, G. E. von 17
Guerrilla movement 340, 351, 359
Guest, G. D. 687
Guide to the contents of the Qur'an 281
Guide to the mammals of Iran 76
Guidebook
    archaeology 71
    see also Travel guides
Guilds
    bazaar craftsmens' and tradesmens'
        160
*Gulf and the search for strategic
    stability: Saudi Arabia, the military
    balance in the Gulf, and trends in
    the Arab–Israeli military balance*
    462
*Gulf in the early 20th century: foreign
    institutions and local responses*
    505, 523, 547
Gulf in the 1980s 439
Gulf War 377, 387, 389, 434, 459-470,
    489, 506, 509, 520, 673
    causes and background 460, 466,
        468, 470
    economic effects 461, 468, 470
    impact on oil companies 467, 470
    impact on society 468, 470
    problems for West 463, 470
Gurney, J. 786
Gynaecology
    Safavid period 153

H

Haass, R. 431, 435
Haddad, G. M. 349

hadith 322
Haeri, S. 479
Hafez 587, 606, 625, 632, 640, 646, 756
Haft Ourang 756
Haft paikar: the seven beauties 654
Haidari, A. A. 260
Hairi, A.-H. 601
Hajjar, S. G. 464
Hakim Maryam (*see* Bird, Mary)
Haldane, D. 753
Halliday, F. 419, 434, 451
Hamoud, S. H. 501
Hamun-e Moshkel 243
Hanaway, W. L. 5, 602-603
*Handbook of classical and modern
    Mandaic* 233
Handbooks 14, 16, 18, 70, 72
    Persian Gulf 7
Handicrafts 525, 713-728
    19th-20th centuries 158
    building 728
    carpets 2, 4, 688, 713, 718, 722, 726
    designs and motifs 715-716, 723
    felt-making 719
    food-treating 728
    Kilims 713, 724
    leatherwork 728
    lustre ware 727
    metalwork 688-689, 728
    modern Islamic period 159
    pottery 683, 688-689, 728
    rugs 719, 721, 723, 725
    Safavid period 160
    textiles 688-689, 716, 728
    woodwork 728
Harper, P. O. 733
Harrington, Jr., F. A. 76
Harrison, J. V. 39-40
Harrow, L. 697
Hartman, S. S. 17, 293
Harverson, M. 692
Hasan, Muhammad 684
Hasht Behesht
    architecture 699
Hayes, B. 604
Hayes, G. S. 221
Health 56, 334-338
    doctor–patient relationship 334
    in rural areas 221
    primary health care 336
    statistics 770
Health, Public

reforms 310
Heart's witness: the Sufi quatrains of Awhaduddin Kirmani 651
Hedayat, Sadeq 198, 615, 674-675, 712, 767-768
  biography 607
Hedāyat's The blind owl forty years after 607
Hedges, R. E. M. 80
Heikal, M. 379
Hejazi, Mohammad 767
Hekmat, F. 605
Hekmat, M. 335
Helms, C. M. 465
Hemmasi, M. 228-229
Hendershot, C. 452
Herat 38
Heritage of Persia 106
Hermansen, M. K. 324
Herring, R. 767
Hertz, M. F. 411
Heston, W. L. 198
Hickman, W. F. 492
High level manpower in Iran: from hidden conflict to crisis 561
Higher education 575, 578
Highlights of Persian art 683
Hillenbrand, C. 149-150, 174, 176, 215, 244, 273, 421, 478, 778
Hillenbrand, R. 696
Hillman, M. C. 380, 606-608, 665, 676, 680
Historical atlas of Iran 44
Historical atlases 44, 166
  Persian Gulf 47
Historical gazetteer of Iran: Mashad and northeastern Iran 23
Historical gazetteer of Iran: Tehran and northwestern Iran 23
Historical geography 27, 38, 44, 47
Historical geography of Iran 27
Historical sources 115, 676, 702
Historiography 95, 142
History 1-4, 9-10, 13-14, 22-23, 65, 69, 92-190, 208, 279-280, 351–352, 369, 379, 381, 470, 576
  Abbasid rule 119, 123
  Achaemenian period 98, 101-104, 108, 111-113
  Afghan occupation 162-163
  Afghanistan 120
  agriculture 530

Algair's Agreement (1975) 237
anti-British riots 342
Arab conquest 123-125
architecture 701
armed forces 491
Armenians 235
arts 154, 683, 685, 688, 750
Baluchestan 26
bibliography 773
Buyid dynasty 130
Central Asia 120, 125
Christianity 286, 288
constitutional movement 149, 171-190
constitutional revolution 171-172, 176-177
coup d'état (1921) 185, 196, 213
coup d'état (1953) 357-358, 362, 386
dam construction 544
D'Arcy Oil Concession (1901) 519
Dhofar rebellion 418
dual sovereignty 185
dynastic territories 44
eastern Caucasus 146
economy 497, 503-504, 515
education 574, 576-577
Elam (Khuzestan) 103
establishment of Iranian state 5
Fars 155
Feudal system 134
foreign policy 424, 427
foreign relations 133, 152
Frontier Treaty (1937) 41
Ghazan reforms 134
Gilan republic (1920) 185
Greek expansion 99, 101, 108
guilds 160
Gulf War 466
Gorgan 82
iconography 113
Imperial Bank of Persia 184
Iran–Britain agreement (1919) 185
Iranian Constitution (1906) 97
Iranian Revolution 368, 374, 376, 380-381, 384, 391-392
Isfahan 68
Islam 3, 97, 279, 353
Islamic conquest 106, 109, 119
Islamic Revolution (1979) 172
Isma'ilis 126
Khurasan 123, 125
Khuzestan 103

273

History contd.
kingship 94, 113, 480
Kurds 130
land reform 533, 535
language 125, 246, 260
mass media 759
Media 104
mediaeval Islamic period 116-143
Median period 81, 98, 101-104, 108, 111-113
medicine 93, 153, 170
military campaigns 98, 101, 104, 111, 114, 162
modern Islamic period 144-170
modernist movement 171-190
Moghul Empire 157, 165
Mongol period 116-118, 121-122, 125-126, 128, 131, 134
music 709
mut'a marriages 479
nationalism 177-178, 185
occupation of Iran (1917) 55
oil industry 522
Ottoman Empire 154
Parthian period 81, 107, 115
periodicals 764-765
Persian empire 99-101, 114
politics 348
post-constitutional period 97
Persian Gulf 7
pre-Islamic 98-106, 306
Qajar period 5, 145-150, 155, 174, 190, 215
rural markets 540
Safavid period 5, 68, 119, 129, 132, 136-139, 145, 151, 153-154, 156, 159-160, 166-170
Saljuq period 116-118, 121-122, 124, 126, 131, 134
Sasanian period 96, 107, 115
sciences 129, 154, 170
secularist movement 171-190
Seleucid period 107, 115
Semnan 33
Shatt al-Arab border dispute 24
Shi'ism 145, 283
Sistan 119, 141
socio-political 190, 343
Tehran riots (1963) 197
Timurid period 129, 132, 136-139, 156, 166, 169
trade 144, 515

Treaty of Friendship and Commerce (1856) 440
Treaty of Golestan 147
tribalism 242
Turkish 3
Turkmanchai treaty (1828) 146
Turkmen dynasties 139
Turks 135
Twelfth Imam 127
White Revolution (1963) 179
women 189, 321, 329
women's movement 318
working class 563
World War I 62, 97
World War II 62
Zoroastrianism 100, 110, 297
History of modern Iran, an interpretation 190
History of Nadir Shah, formerly called Thamas Kuli Khan, the present emperor of Persia 157
History of Persia 97
History of Persia under Qajar rule 155
History of Persian earthquakes 25
History of Persian literature 612
History of Persian literature from the beginning of the Islamic period to the present day 622, 633
History of Shah 'Abbas the Great 154
History of the Shah Isma'il Safawi 167
History of the world-conqueror 128
History of Zoroastrianism 100
Hodgson, M. G. S. 126
Hooglund, E. 535, 668
Hooglund, M. E. 325, 354, 397, 668
Hormoz
vegetation 77
Horufis 270
Hosein, Saddam 237
Hostage crisis
USA 199, 389, 410-413, 428, 440, 450
Hostage to Khomeini 375
House building market in the Middle East 568
Housego, J. 721
Households
socio-economic and demographic characteristics 308
Housing 433
censuses (1956 and 1966) 229
housebuilding market 568

Hoveyda, A. 'A. 197
Hoveyda, F. 197
Howard, I. K. A. 200
Hoyt, E. P. 183
Human geography 216-217, 225, 241
  endemic disease distribution 335
Human rights 350, 369, 404-409, 474
*Human rights and the legal system in
  Iran* 474
Humanity 360
  in Islam 194
Humboldt University, Berlin 371
Hume-Griffith, M. E. 56
Hunting
  14th-18th centuries 156
Hurewitz, J. C. 420
Hussain, J. M. 127
Hutt, A. 67, 697
Hydropower 581

I

Ibn Mohammad Ibrahim 57
Ibn Yamin 647
Ibn Yamin 647
Ice-houses 692
Iconography
  Achaemenian period 113
  Hasht Behesht 699
Identity
  and social change 298, 301, 306
Ideology
  Gulf War 466
  Islamic 314, 390-403, 464
  political parties 482
  religious 390-403
  revolutionary 372, 385, 428
  and sexuality 317
'Ideoloji-ye nehzat-e mashrutiyat-e Iran
  174
Idris Shah 272, 659, 662
Il-Khan Hulagu 128
Il-Khans 122, 134-136
  architecture 700, 702
  fall of the empire 136, 138, 159
  socio-economic conditions 134
Illiteracy
  campaign against 575
Illustrations 65, 69, 184
  Alamut mountain rocks 42
  Baha'is 408-409

carpets 718, 722
craft designs 715
dam construction 544, 546
folk-literature 605
Isfahan 68
landscape 208
Mandean peoples 233
Masjed-e Jom'eh mosque 695
rugs 725
Safavid period 168
Shahnameh 748, 756-757
tribal weaving 721
Imagery
  Mithra 591
Imam 'Ali
  biography 200
*Imam 'Ali: source of light, wisdom and
  might* 200
Imam Reza
  tomb in Mashhad 59
Imami Shi'ite jurisprudence 475
Imami Shi'ite movement 127
Imams
  teachings on women 322
*Immortal rose: an anthology of Persian
  lyrics* 640
*Impact of the oil technology on Iran:
  1901-1951* 519
*Impacts of large-scale farms on
  development in Iran: a case study
  of certain aspects of the Iranian
  agrarian reform* 531
Imperial Bank of Persia 547
  history 184
Imperialism 380
Imports
  statistics 449
In search of Omar Khayyam 595
*In the service of the peacock throne: the
  diaries of the Shah's last
  ambassador to London* 207
*In the shadow of Islam: the women's
  movement in Iran* 333
Income
  policies 554
Income distribution 308, 425, 477, 567
  statistics 308, 566
Index Iranicus 773
Index of articles in Western journals
  784
Index on Censorship 350
India 54

India contd.
  Baluchestan 244
  invasion by Nadir Shah 162
  land reform 363
India Office Library
  book collection 729
  paintings 742
Indian language 254
Indian Ocean
  role in international politics 430
  security 416
Indo–European languages 254
*Indo–Persian relations: a study of the
    political and diplomatic relations
    between the Moghul empire and
    Iran* 165
Industrial companies 512
Industrial development 505, 523-524,
    526-527
  see also Modernization
Industrial relations 557
Industrialization in Iran, 1900-1941 524
Industrialized nations
  disruption of oil supplies 517
  role in economy 499
  technology trade 513
Industry 179, 355, 386, 503, 523-527,
    558, 770
  14th-18th centuries 156
  19th-20th centuries 158
  appliance 527
  construction 568
  food processing 525
  manufacturing 202
  mining 525
  oil 179, 195, 346, 357, 454, 457-458,
    495, 503, 516-522, 525
  reforms 310
  statistics 564, 566, 770
Inflation 380, 567
*Influence of Arabic poetry on the
    development of Persian poetry* 596
Inlow, E. B. 480
Inside the Iranian Revolution 389
Insler, S. 609
Institute for Rural Sociology,
    University of Giessen 531
Institutions 18
  educational 573
  foreign 505, 547
  political 380, 482
  religious 313, 315

Intelligentsia 345, 594, 615
  contrast with traditionalism 171
  and modernism 381
  Muslim 309
International Commission of Jurists
    474
International Congress of Art and
    Archaeology 85
International Covenant on Civil and
    Political Rights 404
International Human Rights Law 404
*International Journal of Middle East
    Studies (IJMES)* 763
International Labour Office 554
International law 369
*International and legal problems of the
    Gulf* 459
*International migration of high-level
    manpower: its impact on the
    development process* 227
Internationalism 419
Introduction to Persian 255
*Introduction to Shi'i law: a
    bibliographical study* 483
Investment 309, 500
  foreign 526
  in oil 518
Investors
  statistics 449
Ionians
  architecture 112
*Ionians in Pasargadae: studies in old
    Persian architecture* 112
Iqbal, A. 610
Iraj 624, 767
Iran almanac and book of facts 9
*Iran at the end of the century: a
    Hegelian forecast* 384, 506
Iran between two revolutions 172
Iran: a bibliographic research survey
    776
Iran: briefing 405
Iran–Britain agreement (1919) 185
Iran Carpet Company 722
Iran – the continuing struggle for power
    377
Iran: continuity and variety 5, 603
*Iran: diplomacy in a regional and
    global context* 445
*Iran: economic development under
    dualistic conditions* 495
Iran: an economic profile 496

Iran: essays on a revolution in the making 380

Iran faces the seventies 20, 226, 313, 315, 348, 420, 494, 502, 537, 573, 578, 638, 681-682, 708, 759

Iran: from the earliest times to the Islamic conquest 109

Iran: from monarchy to republic 371

Iran: from religious dispute to revolution 576

Iran: highway map 43

Iran: the impact of United States interests and policies 1941-1954 458

Iran in the service of world peace 179

Iran–Iraq agreement (1975) 445

Iran–Iraq Boundary Treaty (1937) 41, 438

Iran–Iraq conflict: questions and discussions 460

Iran–Iraq war *see* Gulf War

Iran and Islam 50, 141, 147, 161, 186, 247, 285, 473, 584, 598, 693, 717

Iran and Islam: in memory of the late Vladimir Minorsky 3

Iran: Journal of the British Institute of Persian Studies 764

Iran media index 760

Iran: monarchy, bureacracy and reform under the Qajars: 1848-1896 148

Iran: the new imperialism in action 355

Iran: official standard names approved by the US Board on Geographic Names 51

Iran: past and present 19

Iran: past, present and future 11, 21, 301, 306, 308, 332, 341, 343, 426, 449, 485, 499-500, 507, 514, 526, 528, 534, 551, 564, 566-567

Iran: precapitalism, capitalism and revolution 314

Iran: religion, politics and society 12

Iran: a revolution in turmoil 239, 339-340, 368, 390, 401, 489, 509, 518, 549-550

Iran since the Revolution: internal dynamics, regional conflicts, and the superpowers 428

Iran under the Pahlavis 94, 187, 196, 310, 418, 482, 491, 503, 522, 533, 572, 575, 592

Iran under the Safavids 168

Iran–United States Claims Tribunal 411

Iran–United States Claims Tribunal; 1981-1983 411

Iran: the untold story 379

Iran, violations of human rights: documents sent by Amnesty International to the Government of the Islamic Republic of Iran 406

Iran who's who 8

Iranian bulletins: the news bulletins of the Committee for the Defence of Political Prisoners in Iran 350

Iranian carpets: art, craft and history 718

Iranian cities 38

Iranian city of Shiraz 31

Iranian Constitution with amendments 487

Iranian crisis of 1941 – the actors: Britain, Germany and the Soviet Union 456

Iranian Culture Foundation 780

Iranian experiment in primary health care, the West Azerbaijan project 336

Iranian national epic 623

Iranian Oil Refining Company 305

Iranian opposition to the Shah 775

Iranian Plateau 316

   architecture 692

Iranian Revolution (1979) 172, 205, 212, 314, 368-414, 428, 431, 433-435, 457, 462-465, 506, 576, 673, 770

   causes and background 372, 374-376, 378, 380-381, 384, 386-387, 391-392

   chronology 378, 410, 413

   consequences for USA 440, 444, 448, 450, 453, 455, 457

   economic issues 370, 510

   effect on agriculture 535

   foreign policy 373, 383

   historical context 368, 384

   hostage crisis 410-413

   human rights 404-409

   ideology 314, 390-403, 428

   impact on minorities 374

   impact on oil companies 467

   implications for Middle East 374, 383, 417, 428, 431-436, 439

   international reactions 384, 436

   'olama 372

Iranian Revolution *contd.*
  and OPEC 374, 517
  and PLO 374
  political issues 370
  role of migration 230
  role of oil-workers 563
  society 314, 370
  support from pastoral tribes 239
  women's role and status 189, 319-
    320, 325, 329, 333, 373, 380
  see also Revolutionary period,
    Ayatollah Khomeini, Islamic
    Republic
*Iranian Studies: Bulletin of the Society
  for Iranian Cultural and Social
  Studies* 765
*Iranian Studies: Journal of the Society
  for Iranian Studies* 765
Iranian Women's Solidarity Group 318
*Iranian working class: a survey of
  conditions, repression and
  struggles* 558
Iranians: how they live and work 1
Iranica: twenty articles 13
Iranische Kunst in Deutschen Museen
  732
*Iran's foreign policy 1941-1973: a study
  of foreign policy in modernizing
  nations* 425
Iran's men of destiny 199
*Iran's politics and government under
  the Pahlavis, an annotated
  bibliography* 779
*Iran's secret pogrom: the conspiracy to
  wipe out the Baha'is* 408
Iraq
  agreement with Iran (1975) 445
  economy 498
  effect of Gulf War 465, 470
  Frontier Treaty (1937) 41
  government 460
  housebuilding 568
  military strategy 465
  Ministry of Foreign Affairs 41
  relations with Iran 237, 418, 432
  Shatt al-Arab border 24
  Shi'ite movement 354
  stability 436
  war with Iran 377, 387, 389, 434,
    459-470, 489, 491, 506, 509, 520
Iraq: eastern flank of the Arab world
  465

Iraq and Iran: roots of conflict 466
Iraqi School 639
Iron 40, 80
Irons, W. 234, 243
Irrigation 534, 541-546
  Mashhad 541
  Zagros mountains 542
*Irrigation in the Zagros mountains:
  Iran* 542
Isfahan 38, 85
  Afghan defeat 162-163
  architecture 68, 694, 698
  Carmelite Order 151
  family planning practices 337
  Hasht Behesht 699
  history 68
  migration from (1960s) 232
  travel guide 68
*Isfahan is half the world: memories of a
  Persian boyhood* 198
Iṣfahān: Masǧid-i ǧum'a 695
*Iṣfahān, New Julfa: the houses of the
  Armenians* 698
Isfahan, pearl of Persia 68
Ishaque, M. 611
Islam 195, 270-285, 393
  19th-century movements 271
  attitudes to family planning 220
  and capitalism 309
  comparison with Judaism 393
  concept of women 194, 322, 326,
    330
  and economics 194, 318, 488
  history 3, 97, 279, 353
  humanity 194
  Kingship 94
  militant role 385, 388, 391, 398
  and modernization 271, 274
  mysticism 278, 280
  and nationalism 271
  and ownership 488
  Pahlavi period 395
  philosophy 271, 274, 276-277
  as a political force 145, 279, 312, 354
  re-emergence 271, 389, 393
  in revolutionary period 395
  role in development 395
  and secularism 271
  and sexuality 317
  Shi'ite beliefs 283
  and socialism 271
  tradition of dissent 344

and women 194, 322, 326, 329-330, 333
and work 552
see also individual religions
Islam and capitalism 309
Islam and development: religion and sociopolitical change 395
Islam and its cultural divergence 17, 635
Islam and ownership 488
Islam and the plight of modern man 274
Islam and Revolution: writings and declarations of Imam Khomeini 399
Islam in the political process 394
Islam in transition: Muslim perspectives 271
Islam in the world 279
Islamic architecture: Iran 1 697
Islamic art and design 689
Islamic banking: the adaptation of banking practice to conform with Islamic law 501
Islamic bookbindings: in the Victoria and Albert Museum 753
Islamic city of Gurgan 82
Islamic conquest 106, 109, 119, 123-125, 167
Islamic Consultative Assembly 476
Islamic Consultative Assembly of the Islamic Republic of Iran 476
Islamic ideology 390-403
Islamic Iran and Central Asia (7th-12th centuries) 125
Islamic life and thought 276
Islamic movement 361, 388, 391, 398
Islamic movement: a system's approach 361
Islamic nationalism 271, 372
Islamic painting: a survey 755
Islamic period 3, 85, 95, 97, 170
   mediaeval Islamic era 116-143
   modern Islamic period 144-170
   pre-Islamic era 98-115
   see also Government, Islamic
Islamic Republic 197, 212, 368-413, 448
   anti-Baha'i protest 408
   economic problems 509
   economic structure 377, 384, 403
   foreign policy 377, 419, 428

fundamentalist clergy 372
human rights 404-409
minorities 387
political structure 377
social problems 509
social structure 382, 403
status of women 318, 320-322, 326-329, 333, 373
see also Government, Islamic
Islamic Revolution *see* Iranian Revolution
Islamic Revolution: achievements, obstacles and goals 388
Islamic Revolution in Iran 391
Islamic values and world view: Khomeyni on man, the state and international politics 402
Ismael, T. Y. 466
Isma'ilis
   astronomy 143
   challenge of Saljuq state 126
   defeat by Mongols 126
   philosophy 143
Isma'ilism 116, 126, 284, 652
Issawi, C. 158, 502-503, 781
Italian Archaeological Mission 588
Ivanow, W. 42, 284

J

Jabbari, A. 380, 488
Jacobs, N. 304
Jackson, P. 129-132, 136-139, 156, 159, 166, 169-170, 270, 277, 515, 629-630, 632, 639, 696, 700, 726, 751-752
Jacqz, J. W. 11, 21, 301, 306, 308, 332, 341, 343, 426, 449, 485, 499-500, 507, 514, 526, 528, 534, 551, 564, 566-567
Ja'far al-Sadeq 127
Jaffery, Y. 612
Jahan, Shah 583
Jalayirids 136
Jamalzadeh, Mohammad'Ali 198, 677, 768
Jami, Hakim Nuruddin Abdurrahman 587, 622, 648, 756
Jangali movement 185
Jansen, G. H. 398

279

Japan
  17th-century 57
Javadi, H. 613, 660, 671
Jawan, H. B. 767
Jazani, B. 351
Jazayery, M. A. 614
Jewellery 689
  prehistoric 81
Jews 236
  settlement 287
jinn 283
John, L. B. 411
Johnson, G. C. 561
Jones, D. 734
Jones, D. Lloyd 411
Jones, G. 184
Jordan
  housebuilding 568
Judaism
  comparison with Islam 393
  Sasanian period 287
Judicial system 474
  Pahlavi 480
  punishments 406
  Qajar period 478
  reforms, 19th century 188
  status of *'olama* 300
Julfa
  religious orders 151
Jurisprudence 483
  Imami Shi'ite 475
Juvaini, 'Ala-ad-Din 'Ata-Malek 128

K

Kachmir 272
Kaczmarczyk, A. 80
Kadkani, M. R. S. 622
Kamioka, K. 248
Kamshad, H. 261, 615
Kangavar 83
Karanjia, R. K. 352
Karapetian, K. 698
*Karim Khan Zand: a history of Iran,
  1747-1779* 164
Karim Khan Zand (1747-79) 164
Karimi-Hakkak, A. 616, 678
Karl Marx University, Leipzig 371
Kashani, J. 199
Kasra, P. 650
Kassicieh, S. 467

Katouzian, H. 185, 504
Kattani, S. 200
Kazemi, F. 230
Keddie, N. R. 12, 186, 201, 317, 373,
  381, 392, 419
Kellens, J. 782
Kennedy, E. S. 129
Kennedy, H. 130
Kent, R. G. 249
Ker Porter, Sir Robert 690
Kerbela 97
Kerman
  life and customs 56
  travellers' accounts 56, 63
Kermanshah 32
  dissident government 421
Kermanshah: an Iranian provincial city
  32
Kessler, J. 672
Ketab al-Futuwat 282
Keyhan 263, 360
Keyvani, M. 160
Khademadam, N. 531
Khalili, A.-U. J. 200
Khalizadeh Rezai, G. 758
Khamseh 756
Khamsin 766
Khan, H. A. H. 59
Khan, N. 59
Khan, Reza
  coup d'état (1921) 185, 196, 213
  see also Pahlavi, Reza Shah
Khan, Thamas Kuli *see* Nadir Shah
Khanlari 767
Khanom Maryam *see* Bird, Mary
Khayyam, Omar 595, 599, 649-650
Khomeini, Ayatollah Ruhollah 199,
  271, 273, 368-413, 399, 400, 453
  biographies 199, 212, 402
  exile 197, 379
  philosophy 400, 402
  speeches 399
  theological interpretations of
    religious authority 273
Khorram-rud valley
  geography 542
Khosrou, Amir
  biography 621
Khurasan
  history 123, 125
  under Abbasid rule 123
Khuzestan 103

dam construction 545
Khuzestan province
  mechanized agriculture 362
Kiani, M. Y. 82
Kilims 713, 724
  see also Rugs, Carpets
*Kilims: the art of tapestry weaving in
  Anatolia, the Caucasus and Persia*
  724
*King and kingship in Achaemenid art:
  essays on the creation of an
  iconography of empire* 113
King, M. 336
Kingship 94, 480, 482
  in Achaemenid art 113
  mediaeval Islamic period 140
Kinship terms 254
Kirk, D. 220
Kirmani, Awhaduddin 651
Know the Middle East 70
Koelz, W. N. 58
Koran see Qur'an
Koury, E. M. 374, 382-383, 385, 427,
  436, 446
Kramer, C. 83
Kröger, J. 733
*Kūfic inscription in Persian verses in
  the court of the royal palace of
  Mas'ūd III at Ghazni* 588
Kunkel, G. 77
Kurdish revolt, 1961-1970 237
Kurdish revolt (1961-70) 237
Kurds 130, 237
Kuwait
  housebuilding 568

L

Labour laws 558-560
Labour movement 557-563
Labour unions and autocracy in Iran
  562
*Labour unions, law and conditions in
  Iran (1900-1941)* 559
Ladjevardi, H. 562
Laffin, J. 70
Lāhuti 624
Lake, C. M. 481
Lambton, A. K. S. 131, 161, 250, 536-
  537
Land 35

Land and revolution in Iran, 1960-1980
  535
Land reform 20, 351, 397, 433, 528-
  530, 533-540
  history 533, 535
  Khuzestan 362
  policy 386
  and politics 363
Land Reform Law (1962) 363, 536
  implementation regulations (1964)
  363
*Land reform and politics: a
  comparative analysis* 363
Land tenure 535, 537
Land utilization 532, 534, 569
Landlords 534, 537-538
Landownership
  statistics 564
Landscape
  photographs 67
Lang, D. M. 235
Language 2, 4, 17, 22, 125, 245-269,
  306, 311, 780
  Abjad alphabet 250
  Arabic 246, 250-251, 629
  dialects 248, 252, 255, 259
  dictionaries 264-269
  grammars 246, 249-251, 255, 258-259
  history 125, 246, 260
  in the Persian Gulf 7
  Indo-European 254
  Kinship terms in 254
  Mandaic 233
  mediaeval 245
  Old Persian 247, 249
  Parthian 589
  periodical 765
  prehistoric 90
  pre-Islamic period 115
  readers 260-263
  see also Linguistics
Larestani dialect 248
*Lārestāni studies 1 – Lari basic
  vocabulary* 248
Large-scale farming 531, 534, 539, 545
  Gorgan 539
Latin 254
Law, H. D. G. 262
*Law and human rights in the Islamic
  Republic of Iran* 404
Lawless, R. I. 505, 523, 547
Laws 299

281

Laws *contd.*
  criminal 474
  education 574
  family 473, 486
  family planning 484
  Gulf War 459, 466
  human rights 404
  international 369
  labour 558-560
  Persian Gulf 459
  Shar'iah 486
  Shatt al-Arab dispute 24
  Shi'ite 483
  taxation 477
  women 321, 331
  Zoroastrianism 294
  see also Legislation
Lead 40
League of Iranian Communists 366
Leatherwork 728
Lebanon
  economy 498
Lecoq, P. 782
Ledeen, M. 453
Left in contemporary Iran 366
Legacy of Islam 280
Legacy of Persia 2
Legal status of the Arabian Gulf states 471
Legal system 471, 473-375, 477-481, 483-486, 488
Legal theory
  power of the Shah 480
Legends
  influence on literature 598
  Mandaean 233
Legislation
  Family Laws 486
  Family Protection Law (1967) 473
  nationalization of oil industry 519
  Security Organization Act (1957) 474
  taxation 477
Lenczowski, G. 94, 187, 196, 310, 418, 421, 454, 482, 491, 503, 522, 533, 572, 575, 592
Lescot, R. 674
Letter of Tansar 289
Levasseur, G. 474
Levy, R. 644
Lewis, W. 453
Libraries 575

Bodleian Library 741
British holdings Persian serials 786
British Library 743-744
India Office 729, 742
University of Cambridge 730
Liddel, R. 197
Lieberman, S. S. 337
Life and customs 1-22, 53-56, 208, 714
  19th century 152, 679
  Mandaeans 233
  pre-Islamic era 115
  prehistoric 90
  urban 307
Life and Letters, vol. 63, no. 148 767
Life and works of Abdul Qadir Bedil 583
Life and works of Amir Khusrau 621
Life and works of Jalal-ud-din Rumi 610
Lillich, R. B. 411
Linguistics 22, 234, 245, 247-248, 252-254, 256-257, 263, 630
  19th century 615
  bound phraseology 253
  dialects 248, 252, 255, 259
  Indo–European 254
  morphology 252, 259
  Old Persian 247, 249
  phonology 252, 256, 259
  syntax 245, 249, 253
List of the historical sites and ancient monuments of Iran 84
Lister, H. 542
Literacy
  statistics 564, 566
Literary criticism 585-586, 588, 590, 592-594, 599-604, 606-609, 615, 618-620, 624-625, 631, 633, 635-638
Literary history 583-584, 586-589, 591-593, 595-598, 601, 603, 605-606, 609-614, 617, 621-623, 625-626, 628-634, 639
Literary Review 768
Literature 2-6, 13, 17, 20-22, 53, 245, 255, 280, 380, 583-680, 780
  9th-15th century 587, 622
  12th-14th century 626
  16th-18th century 584
  Armenian 235
  ballads 624
  belles-lettres 633

bibliography 787
censorship 620
classical 587, 592-593, 605, 621-622,
    625, 633-634, 637-638, 640-663
and constitutionalism 601
drama 5, 592, 627, 669, 676, 710-711
epic 623, 644
fiction 615, 635, 712
folk-literature 598, 603, 605
imagery 591
impact of European literature 624
influence of Zoroastrianism 296, 609
Kufic inscription 588
mediaeval Islamic period 137
modern Islamic period 159
modernist 381, 592, 594, 600, 603,
    614-615, 622, 624, 633, 635-636,
    638, 664-680
and mysticism 625
and nationalism 637
novels 592, 607, 665, 673-674, 676-
    677
oral 605
Pahlavi era 600
Parthian 589
periodicals 765, 767-768
Persian Gulf 7
poetry 4, 583-587, 590, 592-597, 599,
    604, 606, 610-611, 618-619, 621-
    622, 624, 626, 628-629, 631-632,
    634, 639-640, 645-647, 652, 657-
    658, 660, 667, 670-672, 676, 678,
    680, 767-768
pre-Islamic period 115, 612
prose 615, 626
and religion 597
religious 353, 617
romances 602, 645, 648
Safavid 141, 163, 629
Sasanian 591, 617
short stories 592, 665, 668-669, 675-
    676, 768
Sufi 622, 631, 641, 648, 651, 659
Timurid period 630
Turkmen period 630
Little black fish and other modern
    Persian stories by Samad Behrangi
    668
Living tradition of Iran's crafts 715
Living with the desert: working
    buildings of the Iranian plateau
    692

Lloyd Jones, D. 411
Local government 485
Lockhart, L. 69, 132, 136-139, 156,
    159, 162-163, 166, 169-170, 270,
    277, 515, 629-630, 632, 639, 696,
    700, 726, 751-752
Loeb, L. D. 236
Loghatnameh 265
Logic 783
London Mercury 767
Looney, R. E. 384, 506
Loveless, C. 713
Lowenfeld, A. F. 411
Luft, P. 505, 547
Luristan bronzes 683, 736-737
Luschey-Schmeisser, I. 699
Luso–Brazilian Council 758
Lustre ware 727

M

M. A. Jamālzāda: Once upon a time
    677
MacDonald, C. G. 374, 382-383, 385,
    427, 436, 446
Mace, J. 251
MacEoin, D. M. 273, 353
McLachlan, K. 7, 538
Macuch, Rudolph 233
Magic
    Mandaean 233
Mahdavi, M. 543
Mahdavi, S. 326
Mahdi, A.-A. 386
Mahsatī of Ganja 611
Majles 476, 482
Major companies of the Arab World
    and Iran 512
Major companies of Iran 512
Major voices in contemporary Persian
    literature 676
Makran
    anthropology 50
    ethnicity 50
    geography 50
    society 50
Makran mountain range
    geology 39
Malaria 335
Malayer 38

283

Malkom Khan, M.
  bibliography 193
Mallowan, M. E. L. 109, 111
Mammals 76, 78
*Man, Islam and Western schools of
  thought* 360
Man and society in Iran 299
Mandaeans 233
*Mandaeans of Iraq and Iran: their
  cults, customs, magic legends, and
  folklore* 233
Mandaic language 233
Manganese 40
Mani 780
Manichaeism 780
Manpower 219, 222, 503, 549-556, 558
  cause of Iranian Revolution 561
  effect of oil industry 556
  in agriculture 550
  migration to cities 549-550
  migration to Tehran 229
  migration to West 226-227
  Persian Gulf 553, 556
  policy 554
  statistics 566
Manson Bier, C. 733
Manteq al-teir 641
Mantle of the prophet 577
Manual of classical Persian prosody 634
Manuchehri Damghani 593
Manufacturing industry 202
Manuscript illumination 689, 747-749,
  756-757
  see also Miniatures
Manuscripts 157
  Bodleian Library, Oxford 741
  British Library 743-744
  medical 740
  University of Cambridge 730
  UCLA 740
Map of Iran: river basins 46
Maps and atlases 28, 35
  dams 46
  disease distribution 335
  historical 44, 47, 166
  north-east 23
  north-west 23
  population density 335
  roads 43
  river basins 46
  Tehran 23
  White Revolution 48

Marble 40
Markets 540
Marlik (Cherāgh-Ali tape) 86
Marriage 217
  ethnic communities 217
  mut'a 479
  in rural areas 221
  Shi'ite 283
Martin, B. G. 422
Marxism 360
  and economy 506
*Marxism and other Western fallacies:
  an Islamic critique* 360
Mary Bird in Persia 208
Masal dialect 252
Mashayekhi, M. B. 221
Mashhad
  irrigation 541
  migration from (1960s) 232
  tomb of Imam Reza 59
  Vakil Abad prison 60
Mashed and northeastern Iran 23
Masjed-e Jom'eh mosque 695
Masjid-i 'Atiq mosque 703
Masjid-i 'Atiq of Shiraz 703
Masnavi 610, 656, 659
*Masnavi i ma'navi: the spiritual
  couplets of Maulana Jalālu-'d-Din
  Muhammad i Rumi* 659
Masonry
  Ionian 112
Mass media 9, 20, 307, 758-760
  bibliography 760
  bulletins on human rights 350
  campaign for family planning 337
  and development 758
  history 759
  role in US relations 457
Masterpieces of Persian art 739
Masterpieces of Persian carpet 722
Mas'ud III 588
Mathematics
  Timurid period 129
Matheson, S. A. 71
Mawarannahr book painting 747
Mazandaran
  rural markets 540
Mazdeism 110
Mazzaoui, M. M. 5, 263
Mead, P. A. 221
Mechanics
  Safavid period 170

Mechanization 362, 539
Media 104
Mediaeval Islamic period 116-143
Median period 81, 98, 101-104, 108,
    111-113
  arts 108
  culture 104
  fall of the empire 104
  military campaigns 104
  religion 104
  society 104
*Medical history of Persian and the
    eastern Caliphate: from the earliest
    times until the year AD 1932* 93
Medicine
  doctor–patient relationship 334
  history 93, 153, 170
  Western influence 93
*Medieval history of Iran, Afghanistan
    and Central Asia* 120
MEED (Middle East Economic Digest)
    769
Mehner, H. 572
Mehr Yasht 292
Mehran, H. A. 507
Meissenburg, M. L. 16
Melamid, A. 525, 548
Melville, C. P. 25
Memoirs 197-198
*Memorial volume of the Vth
    International Congress of Iranian
    Art and Archaeology* 85
Menasce, J. P. de 617
Merchants 339
  19th century 161
Mercury 80
MERI Report: Iran 770
MERIP Reports 771
Merleau, M. 99
*Mersad al-ebad men al-mabda ela'l-
    ma'ad* 278
Meshkati, N. 84
Mesopotamia
  Catholicism 151
Metal technology
  prehistoric 80
Metalwork 688-689, 728
  Timurid period 752
Metropolitan Museum of Art
  seal stone collection 731
Mexico 363
Middle class

  bureaucratic 310
Middle East 393, 441, 464
  balance of power 428-429
  construction industry 568
  geography 29
  handbooks 70
  impact of Iranian Revolution 374,
    383, 417, 428, 431-436, 439, 455
  manpower 553
  mediaeval Islamic period 130
  periodicals 761, 763
  revolutionary movements 349
  rugs 723
  sociology 316
  technology trade 513
  university studies 761
  women and the family 326
  see also Persian Gulf
*Middle East from transition to
    development* 464
Middle East: a geographical study 29
Middle East Newsletter 772
*Middle East Newsletters: Gulf States,
    Iraq, Iran, Kuwait, Bahrain,
    Qatar, United Arab Emirates,
    Oman* 772
Middle East and North Africa 762
*Middle East Research and Informative
    Project* 354
Middle East Research Project,
    American Enterprise Institute 498
Migrants 433, 478
  British in Persian Gulf 144
  contrast with non-migrants 231
  educational characteristics 226, 231
  role in Islamic Revolution 230
  role in politics 230
Migration 219, 222, 226-232, 433
  determining factors 229-230
  doctors to USA 232
  impact of modern education 226-
    227, 231
  internal 228-231
  manpower to Tehran 229
  manpower to West 226-227
  prehistoric 88
  rural-urban 228-231, 549-550
  to Gulf States 553, 556
  to Shiraz 231
  urban-urban 231
*Migration in Iran: a quantitative
    approach* 228

Milani, A. 564
Milani, F. 618-620, 672
Militancy 353, 366, 385, 398
    Islamic 398
Militant Islam 398
Military 425-426, 431, 462, 489-493
    19th century 511
    Iraqi 465
    reforms, 19th century 188
    in revolution 368
    statistics 425
    see also Arms and armed forces
Military campaigns 101
    Alexander the Great 98
    Cyrus the Great 111, 114
    Median 104
    Mongol 122
    Nadir Shah 162
    Reza Shah Pahlavi 196
    Shah Isma'il Safavi 167
Military intervention
    World War I 421
Military rule 349
Miller, M. K. 305
Millspaugh, A. C. 202
Millward, W. G. 263
Mind of a monarch 352
Mineral resources 7, 40, 65, 97
    periodical 772
Miniatures 4, 68, 686-687, 741, 743-
    744, 747, 749, 755, 757
    Safavid period 749, 751
    Shahnameh 748, 757
    Timurid period 726, 749, 752
    see also Manuscript illumination;
    books
Mining
    14th-18th centuries 156
Mining industry 525
Ministry of Culture and Arts 85
Ministry of Roads 43
Minorities 233-244, 316, 393, 433
    Armenians 235
    attitudes of Pahlavi government 239
    Baha'is 408-409
    Christian 151
    English, Qajar period 238
    impact of Iranian Revolution 374
    in Islamic Republic 387
    Jews 236
    Kurds 237
    Mandaeans 233

marriage 217
and nationalism 178
relations 311
women in 321
Yomut Turkmen 234
Minorsky, V. 3, 13, 754
Mins, L. 355
Mir Damad 277
Mirani, S. K. 327
Mirza, M. W. 621
*Mirza Malkum Khān: a study in the
    history of Iranian modernism* 193
Mirza, Sayid 684
Mission to Iran 211
Missionaries 151
    American 450
    Church Missionary Society 56
    Rezaiyeh 311
Mitchell, G. 734
Mithra 292
    imagery 591
Mithraism 92
Moayyad, H. 670, 677
Mobility 219
*Modal system of Arab and Persian
    music – AD 1250-1300* 707
Modal systems 705-707, 709
Modaressi Tabātabā'i, H. 483
Modern Islamic period 144-170
*Modern Islamic political thought: the
    response of the Shi'i and Sunni
    Muslims to the twentieth century*
    347
Modern Persian 251, 258
Modern Persian prose literature 261,
    615
Modern Persian prose reader 261
Modern Persian reader 260
Modernist movement 171-190
Modernization 175, 180, 190, 271, 306,
    381, 433, 464, 482
    of agriculture 528-531, 533-539
    effect on population distribution 222
    and foreign policy 425
    impact on society 307
    impact on traditional political
        thought 340, 343-345, 347, 364,
        393, 527
    impact on upper class 570
    and industry 527
    and Islam 271, 274
    legitimization 182

and literature 381, 592, 603, 614, 622, 624, 633, 636, 638
Pahlavi era 11, 19, 171-173, 175, 178-179, 183, 187, 196, 213, 509
political system 345
Qajar period 174, 176, 180-182, 188
resistance from traditionalists 176-177, 527
role of education 574
role of religious leaders 173, 176-177, 182
shift of public opinion (1979) 197, 509
see also Development; Reform programme
Modernization of Iran: 1921-1941 175
Modernization policy 11, 19, 55
Moghari, M. 519
Moghul Empire 157, 165
decorative arts 689
poetry 642
Mohammad Mossadegh: a political biography 195
Mohammad Naim, C. 17
Mohammad, Prophet 97, 130, 209, 285
Mohammad, Shah 583
Mohammed 209
Moherijo-Daro 90
Mojahedin 340, 366
and women's rights 359
Molla Sadra 275
Momeni, J. 216, 218-224, 231-232, 305, 337, 571
Monarchs 480
biographies 199
Mongol period 118, 121-122, 125-126, 128, 131, 134-135
arts 750, 755
Islamic mysticism 278
military campaigns 122
poetry 583
politics 122
religion 116-117
socio-economics 134
Montague, J. 223
Monuments 84
Achaemenian 113
Moore, R. 223
Moorey, P. R. S. 735-738
Morals pointed and tales adorned: The bustān of Sa'di 661
Morier, J. 59, 679, 690

Morphology
Masal dialect 252
Tati dialects 259
Morrison, G. 622, 633, 645
Mortality 222
Mortimer, E. 350
Mosha'sha' movement 270
Moshir al-Douleh 180
Mosques
architecture 685, 695, 703
Mossadegh era: roots of the Iranian Revolution 365
Mossadeq, Premier Mohammad 379
biography 195
domestic policy 365
fall of government (1953) 357-358, 362
oil nationalization 346
Mossavar-Rahmani, B. 581
Mossavar-Rahmani, Y. L. 484
Mostafavi, R. 767
Mostofi, A. 44
Motahhari, Ayatollah Mortaza 271
speeches 368, 401
Motamen, H. 508
Mottahedeh, R. P. 133, 577
Mozaffaroddin Shah (1896-1907) 66
Muhsin, J. 468
Murdoch Smith, R. 690
Museums 575
Ashmolean, Oxford 735, 738
British Museum 736
German 732
Metropolitan Museum of Art 731
Victoria and Albert 753
Music 280, 301, 575, 704-709
Azarbaijan 704
classical 704, 708-709
contemporary 708
modal systems 705-707, 709
sitar 621
Music of professional musicians of northwest Iran (Azerbaijan) 704
Musical instruments 709
Muslim Institute, London 391
Muslims 270-285, 316, 361
Christian relations 311
intellectuals 309
Islamic identity 274
natality 220
political ideas 347
see also Shi'ites

Mut'a marriages 479
Muzaffarids 136
Mystical poems of Rumi: first selection, poems 1-200 657
Mystical poems of Rumi: second selection, poems 201-400 660
Mysticism
  and dissent 344
  Islamic 278, 280, 360
  in literature 625
Mysticism and dissent: socioreligious thought in Qajar Iran 344
Mythology
  influence on literature 598

N

Naderpour, Nader 680, 768
Nadir Shah (1736-47) 157
  military campaigns 162
Nadir Shah: a critical study based mainly upon contemporary sources 162
Nafici, H. 712, 760
Na'ini, Sheikh Hosein 271
Najafbagy, R. 555
Najmabadi, F. 526
Namazi, M. B. 485
Names, Place 51
Nanes, A. 440
Naqavi, S. A. R. 486
Naraghi, E. 306
Naser al-Din Shah Qajar (1848-96) 203
  administrative reforms 148
  biography 215
  diary 203
  modernization attempts 180, 215
Nash, G. 408
Nashat, G. 188-189, 319-320, 322-325, 327-330, 359, 407, 479, 484, 618
Nasir-i Khusraw
  biography 652
Nasir-i Khusraw: forty poems from the Divan 652
Nasirean ethics 663
Nasr, S. H. 44, 274-277, 283, 652, 783
Nassar, J. R. 467
Natality
  Muslim 220
National identity 298, 301, 306
  evidence in literature 637

Nationalism 306, 347, 380, 393, 419, 447
  1950s 418, 425
  effect of allied occupation 447
  in literature 637
  Islamic 271, 372
  Kurdish 237
  and minorities 178
Nationalism in Iran 178
Nationalist movement 177-178, 185
  periodical 766
  oil 195, 346, 357, 454, 457-458, 503, 519, 522
Natural gas 581
Natural resources 29
Nava'i, Mir 'Ali-Shir 756
Naval Intelligence Division, Admiralty War Staff 14
Nawata, T. 252
Near East
  Armenians 235
Near Eastern Centre, University of California at Los Angeles 17
Negahban, E. O. 86
Nersessian, V. 784
Nettl, B. 706
Netzer, A. 17
Neuman, S. G. 431, 493
Neusner, J. 287
New Julfa
  architecture 694, 698
New Julfa: the Armenian churches and other buildings 694
New selection from The rubaiyat of Omar Khayyām 649
New unabridged English–Persian dictionary 266
New York
  Asia House Gallery 733
  Exhibition of Persian Art 739
  Metropolitan Museum of Art 731
New York University
  Annual Round Table Series 5
News programmes 760
Newspapers 590, 759, 786
  19th century 180
Newton, J. K. 665
Nezam al-Mulk 653
Nezam al-Saltareh 421
Nezami 756
Nezāmi Ganjavi 654
Nicholson, R. A. 610, 658

288

Nightingale's lament: selections from the poems and fables of Parvin E'tesami (1907-41) 670
Nima, R. 387
Nineveh 90
Nirumand, B. 355
Nishapur 282
Nöldeke, T. 623
Nomads 58, 219, 225, 239-244
  and ecological conditions 241
  Qashqa'i 240
  Shi'ite 239
  Sunni 239
  see also Pastoral tribes
Nore, P. 563
North Africa 316
Novels 592, 607, 665, 673, 676-677
Nuclear power 581
Nuclear weapons 462
Numismatics
  pre-Islamic period 115
Nuptiality 222
Nuri, Sheikh Fazlollah 271
Nylander, C. 112

O

O'Ballance, E. 237
Oberlander, M. 45
Oberling, P. 240
Occultation of the Twelfth Imam: a historical background 127
Occupations 307, 341, 559
  statistics 551
Oceanography 7
Odell, P. R. 520
Of piety and poetry: the interaction of religion and literature in the life and works of Hakim Sanā'i of Ghazna 597
Oil 179, 355, 358, 425-426, 455, 464, 516-522
  concessions (1901-51) 516, 519
  disruption of supplies 437, 517
  exports 518
  fall in revenues 461, 500
  Persian Gulf 342
  potential resources 518
  price 499
  price increase 418, 500, 503, 517

  production 518
  and regional security 431, 433-434, 437-438, 455, 516
  role in economy 495, 499-500, 503, 508, 518-519, 527, 567
Oil and class struggle 563
Oil companies 505
  effect of war and revolution 467
Oil Company 516
Oil industry 516-522, 525, 581
  class composition 563
  development 516
  effect on labour market 556
  energy policy 517
  history 522
  implications of fall of Shah 518
  international 520
  nationalization 195, 346, 357, 454, 457-458, 503, 519, 522
  Pahlavi period 495, 518
Oil policy 432
Oil-producing nations 429, 446, 508
Oil and security in the Arabian Gulf 434
Oil supply in the 1980s 437
Oil-workers
  role in Iranian Revolution 563
Oil and world power 520
O'Kane, J. 57
Okazaki, S. 539, 785
'olamā 173, 176-177, 182, 300, 313, 315, 326, 372, 394, 396
Old Persian 247, 249, 780
  grammar 249
Old Persian: grammar, texts, lexicon 249
Old routes of western Iran 64
Olson, R. 380
Olson, W. J. 423
Oman
  military intervention 491
Omar, Caliph 97
On the sociology of Islam 312
Once upon a time 677
OPEC (Organization of Petroleum Exporting Countries) 507
  impact of Iranian Revolution 374, 517
Oppenheimer, M. F. 513
Opposition groups 368, 377, 381, 387-389, 509
  bibliography 775

289

Organization of Iranian People's
  Fada'iyan Guerrillas *see* Fada'iyan
Organization of Petroleum Exporting
  Countries (OPEC) 507
  impact of Iranian Revolution 374,
  517
*Orientalia Romana, 6: The first
  European colloquium of Iranology
  (Rome, June 18th-20th, 1983)* 95
*Origins of modern reform in Iran,
  1870-80* 188
Ornaments 716
Orthography 17
Osman, Caliph 97
Ottoman Empire 154
  decorative arts 689
Ouseley, Sir William 690
Outcast: Jewish life in southern Iran
  236
Ownership
  and Islam 488

P

Paganism 100
Pahlavi, Ashraf 204
Pahlavi era 19, 97, 179, 205-206
  agricultural policy 549-550
  attitude towards minorities 239
  clergy-state relations 173
  development 564
  economy 187, 495, 503-504, 510
  education 575
  family planning 484
  Islam 395
  literature 600
  manpower migration 549
  modernization 171-173, 175,
    178-179, 183, 187, 196, 213, 509
  oil industry 495, 518
  politics 187, 482
  relations with USA 413
  revival of Kingship 94
  secularization 173
  social development 310
  society 187, 378
  see also Government, Pahlavi;
    Pahlavi, Reza Shah; Pahlavi,
    Mohammad Reza Shah
Pahlavi, Farah 11
  art collection 684

Pahlavi Foundation of Iran
  symposium, September 1975 11
Pahlavi, Mohammad Reza Shah (1941-
  1979) 172, 183, 204-205, 352, 504,
  521
  arms transactions 369
  and the army 489
  biographies 199, 205
  collapse of régime (1979) 369-370,
    387, 389, 447-448, 462
  consolidation of power 387, 397, 480
  coronation (1967) 179, 455
  domestic policy 358
  economy 510
  exile 457
  foreign policy 358, 418
  industrial development 526
  modernization policies 509
  and oil industry 518
  and political élites 367
  reinstatement (1953) 357, 386
  relations with USA 355, 358, 362,
    443, 448, 455, 457-458
  social change 204, 338, 378
  support for arts 683
  see also Government, Pahlavi;
    Pahlavi era
Pahlavi, Reza Shah (1925-1941) 55, 97,
  190, 204, 213, 592
  abdication (1941) 456
  biographies 196, 199, 213
  economy 503-504
  exile 213
  foreign policy 424
  military campaigns 196
  role in social development 196, 310
  see also Government, Pahlavi;
    Pahlavi era
Pahlavi University, Shiraz 227
Paintings 683, 688-689
  14th century 685-686
  16th century 687
  India Office Library 742
  miniatures 4, 68, 686-687, 741, 743-
    744, 747-749, 755, 757
  Qajar 684
  Safavid 750
  Shiraz school 687
Pakistan
  land reform 363
  military rule 349
Pakravan, K. 437

Palaces
  Hasht Behesht 699
Paper-cutting 689
Paquin, G. A. 723
Parliament *see* Majles
Parsik 780
Parsis 780
Parsism 293
Parsism: the religion of Zoroaster 293
Parsons, A. 206
Parthian language 589
Parthian period 81, 107, 115, 780
  language and literature 589
Parvin-i I'tiṣāmī 611
Pasargade 87
Pasargade 87
  Ionian architecture 112
Passion plays 710-711
Pastoral tribes 104, 219, 224-225, 239-244
  art 745
  characteristics 307
  density and movement 335
  Gamshadzai 243
  isolation from politics 239
  religious institutions 313
  Shi'ite 239
  Sunnite 239
  weaving 721, 725
  Yarahmadzai 243
  see also Nomads
Pastoralism 225, 242
Path of God's bondsmen from origin to return 278
Patronage
  arts 752
Paved with good intentions: the American experience and Iran 457
Paydarfar, A. A. 224, 231, 307
Pearce, B. 309
Peasantry 58
  effects of land reform 534-535, 537, 545
  and marketing system 540
  migration to cities 549-550
  support for Iranian Revolution 375
Pendlebury, D. 648
Penton, C. J. 720
Periodicals 759, 761-772, 786
  archaeology 764
  banking 772
  business 762

culture 764-765
economy 762, 765, 769-772
energy 772
finance 772
history 764-765
language 765
literature 765, 767-768
Middle East 761, 763
minerals 772
nationalist movement 766
politics 765, 769-772
security 772
society 765, 770
Perry, J. R. 164
Persepolis 11, 91, 302
Persepolis: the archaeology of Parsa, seat of the Persian Kings 91
Persia 14, 69
Persia: an archaeological guide 71
Persia: history and heritage 4
Persia and the Persian question 152
Persian architecture 701
Persian cooking: a table of exotic delights 15
Persian designs and motifs for artists and craftsmen 716
Persian diary 1939-1941 58
Persian doctrine of dastga-composition: a phenomenological study in the musical mode 705
Persian empire 99-101, 114
  collapse 109
Persian expedition 114
Persian grammar 250
Persian Gulf 415
Persian Gulf 463
  arts 7
  balance of power 428-429, 462
  British in 144, 238, 414
  British withdrawal (1971) 415
  culture 7
  economy 7, 459, 469, 505
  Gulf War 377, 387, 389, 434, 459-470, 491
  handbook 7
  historical atlas 47
  history 7
  impact of foreign institutions 505
  labour migration 553, 556
  language 7
  legal problems 459

Persian Gulf *contd.*
  literature 7
  politics 342, 385, 459, 466, 468-469
  religion 7
  role in international politics 430, 444
  role of USSR 463
  security 374, 383, 417, 428, 432-434,
    436-439, 444, 446, 462
  society 7
  trade with East India Company 144
  urbanization 7
  US policy 442, 446
  US security 383, 446, 455, 462-463
Persian Gulf and Indian Ocean in
    international politics 430
Persian Gulf: Iran's role 438
Persian Gulf oil in Middle East and
    international conflicts 429
Persian Gulf states, a general survey 7
Persian land reform: 1962-1966 536
Persian landscape: a photographic
    essay 67
Persian letters: a manual for students of
    Persian 262
Persian lustre ware 727
Persian medical manuscripts at the
    University of California, Los
    Angeles: a descriptive catalogue
    740
Persian metal technology 700-1300 AD
    80
Persian miniature painting and its
    influence on the art of Turkey and
    India: the British Library
    collections 744
Persian miniatures: from ancient
    manuscripts 749
Persian oil: a study in power politics
    346
Persian painting 750
Persian painting in the fourteenth
    century, a research report 686
Persian paintings in the India Office
    Library: a descriptive catalogue
    742
Persian poetic metres 599
Persian poets of Sind 628
Persian Railway Syndicate 505, 547
Persian revolution of 1905-1909 177
Persian stronghold of Zoroastrianism
    290
Persians amongst the English: episodes

  in Anglo–Persian history 214
Perspectives on nomadism 243
Pesaran, M. H. 308, 509
Pessyan, H. A. S. 84
Petrochemicals 581
Petrodollars 500
Petrushevsky, I. P. 134
Petsopoulos, Y. 724
Philippines
  17th-century 57
  land reform 363
Philology 285
Philosophers 275, 284
  biographies 199
Philosophy 22, 53, 299
  Ayatollah Ruhollah Khomeini 402
  Islamic 271, 274, 276-277
  Isma'ili 143
  Safavid period 168
  Shi'ite 381
  on women's role 324
Phonology 256
  Masal dialect 252
  Tati dialects 259
Photographs 303
  Armenians 235
  Bozorg Alavi 664
  constitutional revolution 177
  early 20th century 177
  historical 62
  Islamic architecture 697
  Jews 236
  landscape 67
  New Julfa 694
  poets 678
  working class 558
Physical characteristics 303
Physical geography 33-36
Pictorial tile cycle of Hašt Behešt in
    Işfahān and its iconographic
    tradition 699
Pigeon towers 692
Pilgrimage 59
Pinder-Wilson, R. 700
Piscatori, J. P. 394
Place names 51
Plague by the West (Gharbzadegi) 666
Plaksin, D. 747
Plan and Budget Organization 327
Plan Organization 544
Planhol, X. de 241
Planning 568-573

PLO (Palestine Liberation
    Organization)
  impact of Iranian Revolution 374
Poetry 4, 585-587, 592, 597, 599, 604,
    610-611, 618-619, 624, 628, 631-
    632, 634, 645-647, 652, 657-658,
    660, 667, 670-672, 676, 678, 680,
    767-768
  10th-15th century 643
  12th-14th century 626
  court 593
  ghazal 584, 606, 640
  influence of Arabic poetry 596
  Iraqi school 639
  Mogul Empire 642
  Mongol period 583
  and music 709
  political 590, 594, 671-672
  ruba'is 595, 649-650
  sabk-e Hendi 584, 621, 633, 639
  Safavid period 629, 639
  Sufi 622, 641, 648, 651, 659
  Timurid period 639
Prose 615, 626
  Sufi literature 622
Point IV programme 579
Police state 355
Political development 387
  Middle East 464
  and trade unions 562
*Political economy of modern Iran:
    despotism and pseudo-modernism,
    1926-1979* 504
Political élite 262, 343, 363, 367, 392,
    396
Political elite of Iran 367
*Political environment of economic
    planning in Iran, 1971-1983: from
    monarchy to Islamic Republic* 510
Political events
  chronology 387
Political geography 29
Political history 348, 355
  Abbasid 123
  Afghan occupation 163
  Baluchestan 26
  mediaeval Islamic period 118, 121,
    124, 136-139
  Mongol period 122
  pre-Islamic period 115
  Qajar period 150, 152
  reforms, 19th century 188

  Safavid period 166, 168
  Shi'ite dissent, 19th century 344
Political institutions 380, 482
Political leadership 343
Political movements 353
  Islamic 388, 391, 398
  Shi'ite 373
Political parties 482
  Ba'ath Socialist Party 460
  ideology 482
  Rastakhiz Party 341
  Tudeh Party 364, 366
Political poetry 590, 594, 671-672
Political poetry of modern Persia 590
Political prisoners 404-407, 664, 667
  women 407
*Political and social history of Khurasan
    under Abbasid rule, 747-820* 123
Political stability 363
Political structure 770
  Islamic Republic 377
  Yomut Turkmen 234
Political system 341, 343, 345, 396
  modernized 345
Political theory
  power of the Shah 480
Political unrest 368, 370, 372
Political writings
  19th century 180
Politicians
  biographies 199
Politics 9, 12, 16, 20, 54, 184, 211, 280,
    304, 314, 339-367, 369, 383, 393,
    438, 451, 463, 576, 666
  1960s 340, 343, 345, 348-349, 363
  1970s 340-343, 345, 350, 359
  anti-British riots 342
  bazaar-clergy alliance 339
  cause of Iranian Revolution 386
  communist influences 364
  and constitutionalism 172, 187
  effect of land reform 528
  guerrilla movement 340, 351, 359
  and human rights 350
  impact of oil industry 519
  Indian Ocean 430
  international 402
  involvement of USA 357-358, 362
  Islamic Republic 377
  isolation of pastoral tribes 239
  and Judaism 393
  and land reform 351, 362-363

Politics *contd.*
  modernization period 340, 343-345, 347, 364
  and nationalism 178, 185
  and oil 342, 346, 355, 357
  Pahlavi era 187, 482
  periodicals 765, 769-772
  Persian Gulf 342, 385, 459, 466, 468-469
  and railway construction 547
  and religion 480
  revolutionary period 370, 384-386
  role of Armenians 235
  role of Islam 145, 279, 312, 354
  role of migrants 230
  role of Persian Gulf 430, 444
  role of Qashqa'i 240
  and Shi'ite *'olamā* 173, 176-177, 182, 300, 313, 315
  social bases 172
  under the Shah 341, 348, 351-352, 355-358, 362, 367
  and women 318, 329, 332
Politics in the Gulf 342
Politics of Iran: groups, classes and modernization 345
Politics of oil and revolution in Iran 432
Politics, polemics and pedagogs: a study of United States technical assistance in education to Iran . . . 452
Pollution control 459
Polygamy 473
Polygyny 305
Poor
  role in politics 339
  support for Iranian Revolution 375
  women 319
Pope, A. U. 688, 701, 739
Population 14, 35, 69, 216-225, 433
  19th century 511
  censuses 229
  characteristics 219
  distribution 216-217, 219, 223, 225
  family planning 220, 223, 336
  fertility 217, 221-222, 224
  forecasts 222
  growth 216-219, 223
  in Islamic Republic 382
  marriage 217, 221
  Median 104

  and modernization 222
  mortality 222
  natality 220
  nomadic 58, 219, 225
  nuptiality 222
  prehistoric 90
  redistribution 228-231
  rural 217-218, 224-225
  statistics 564, 566
  tribal 104, 219, 224-225, 239-244
  urban 217-219, 222, 224-225
Population distribution 532
  ecological determiners 241
  maps 335
Population of Iran 216, 218-224, 231-232, 305, 337, 571
Post-constitutional period 97
Post-revolution Persian verse 624
Pottery 4, 683, 688-689, 728
  Amlash 683
  designs and motifs 716
  Timurid period 752
Poverty 380
Poverty and revolution in Iran: the migrant poor, urban marginality and politics 230
Prehistory 80-91
  jewellery 81
  metal technology 80
  Zoroastrianism 100
Pre-Islamic era 98-106, 306
  literature 612
  women's status 189
Pregnancy 221
Preliminary report on Marlik excavation 86
Press and poetry of modern Persia 590
Price control 526
Price increase
  oil (1973) 418, 500, 503
  19th century 511
Pride and the fall: Iran 1974-1979 206
Prigmore, C. S. 338
Primary education 575
Primary health care 336
Principles of Persian bound phraseology 253
Prison papers of Bozorg Alavi 664
Prison system 474
Profane practices 475
Prisoners
  political 404-407

Prisons
Evin 407
Vakil Abad 60
Private enterprise 498, 526
*Private enterprise and socialism in the
Middle East* 498
Production 511
Islamic teachings 309
Programmes
public affairs 760
*Prophet and the age of Caliphates: the
Islamic Near East from the sixth to
the eleventh century* 130
Prophet Mohammad 97, 130, 209, 285
biography 194
teachings on women 322
*Prophets of doom: literature as a socio-
political phenomenon in modern
Iran* 600
Public affairs 316
television programmes 760
Public health
reforms 310, 573
Publications 575

Q

*Qajar Iran: political, social and cultural
change, 1800-1925* 149-150, 174,
176, 215, 244, 273, 421, 478, 778
*Qajar paintings: Persian oil paintings of
the 18th & 19th centuries* 684
Qajar period 145-150, 155, 174, 190,
215
administration 148-149, 215
ambassadors 214
Anglo–Persian relations 214
Baluch tribes 244
bibliography 785
culture 150
fall of dynasty 196
government 148-149
intellectual writings 180
Isfahan 68
judicial system 478
modernization 174, 176, 180-182,
188
oil-paintings 684
political history 150, 273
Shi'ism 5, 145, 273
Shi'ite political dissent 344

social change 150, 273
women's status 189
qanats 63, 541, 543
Qara Quyunlu 139
Qashqa'i nomads 240
art exhibition 745
Qashqa'i nomads of Fars 240
*Qashqa'i of Iran: World of Islam
Festival 1976* 745
Qazi Ahmad 754
Qazvin
dialect 259
Qeshm
vegetation 77
Qom 576-577
Quarterly Economic Review 762
Quietism 353
Qur'an 281, 285
cantillation 707
teachings on women 330
Qurratu'l-'Ayn 611

R

Rābi'ah of Quzdar 611
Ra'di 767
Radio 759
Radji, P. C. 207
Raffat, D. 664
Rahman, F. 330
Rahman, M. 624
Rahnoma, Hamid 767
Railways 505, 547
Rainfall 37
Rajaee, F. 402, 488
Ramazani, N. 15
Ramazani, R. K. 383, 424-427, 438,
455
Rashid al-Din Fazl Allāh 135
Rashidun caliphs 130
Rassekh, S. 573
*Ravaged and reborn: the Iranian army,
1982* 492
*Rawdatu't-taslim: commonly called
tasawwurat* 284
Razavi, H. 510
Razi, G. H. 380
Rāzi, Najm al-Din 278
Read, S. J. 79
Readers 260-263
Reagan, President Ronald 442

295

Recent trends in Middle East politics and Iran's foreign policy options 416
Recent United States policy in the Persian Gulf (1971-82) 442
Redhouse, J. W. 203
Redwell, E. H. 647
Reform programme 16, 349
  see also Modernization
Regional authorities 485
Reid, J. J. H. 242
Reign of the ayatollahs: Iran and the Islamic Revolution 370
Religion 2, 12, 17, 20-22, 108, 115, 299, 369, 381
  Achaemenian period 108
  akhbari-osuli debates 277
  Babism 270
  Catholicism 151
  Christianity 286, 288
  fundamentalism 171, 173, 176-177, 182
  Horufis 270
  Imami-Shi'ite movement 127
  Islam 195, 270-285
  Isma'ilism 116, 126, 284
  and literature 597, 635
  Mandaeans 233
  Mazdeism 110
  mediaeval Islamic period 121, 124, 136-137
  Median period 104, 108
  Mithraism 92
  modern Islamic period 159
  Mongol period 116-117
  Mosha'sha' movement 270
  'olamā 173, 176-177, 182, 300, 313, 315
  Parsism 293
  Persian Gulf 7
  and politics 145, 393, 480
  pre-Islamic period 100, 104-105, 108, 110-111, 115
  Qajar period 5, 145, 273
  religious orders 151
  Roman Catholicism 288
  Safavid period 270, 277
  Saljuq period 116
  Shi'ism 5, 116-117, 145, 166, 173, 176-177, 182, 270, 273, 277, 283
  and social change 145, 273, 314-315
  Sufism 272, 277, 282

Timurid period 270, 277
  under Cyrus the Great 111
  and women 194, 322, 326, 329-330, 333
  Zoroastrianism 100, 105, 110, 289-297
Religion and politics in contemporary Iran: clergy-state relations in the Pahlavi period 173
Religion and politics in the Middle East 393
Religion of the Sufis 272
Religious education 576-577
Religious ideology 390-403
Religious institutions 313, 315
Religious literature 353
Religious protest
  anti-Baha'i 408
Religious riots 386
Religious rituals 397
Repression
  working class 558, 560, 563
Reptiles 73
Resaleh Towzih al-Masael 400
Research Centre of International Agrarian Development, Heidelberg 531
Resources
  mineral 7, 40
  natural 29
Retail trade 548
Return of the Ayatollah: the Iranian Revolution from Mossadeq to Khomeini 379
Revolution 349
  and capitalism 351
  constitutional (1906) 171-172, 176-177, 376
  Iranian (1979) 172, 205, 212, 273, 368-414
  Russian (1917) 421
  White (1963) 48, 179, 205, 376, 386, 503-504, 530, 538
Revolution in Iran: the politics of countermobilization 378
Revolution in Iran: a reappraisal 374, 382-383, 385, 427, 436, 446
Revolutionary ideology 372, 385, 390-403
Revolutionary period 389
  economic development 509-510
  economy 368, 370, 380, 386

ideology 392
Islam 395
politics 370, 384-386
society 370-371, 378, 386, 392
US–Iranian relations 413
villages 397
Revolutionary tribunals 404
Revolutions and military rule in the Middle East 349
Rezaiyeh
ethnic relations 311
missionaries 311
Rezun, M. 356, 456
Riazul Islam 165
Rice, C. C. 208
Rice, D. T. 755
Richard, Y. 381
Richter–Bernburg, L. 740
Ricks, T. 380, 668, 768
Rim of prosperity. The Gulf: a survey 469
Riots
religious (1963) 386
Tehran (1963) 197
Rise and fall of the Shah 358
Ritual practices 283
Rituals
religious 397
Rivāyat-i hēmīt-i asawahistān: a study in Zoroastrian law 294
River basins
maps 46
Rivers 541
Riza Shah Pahlavi: the resurrection and reconstruction of Iran, 1878-1944 213
Road to Oxiana 54
Roads 548
maps 43
Roaf, S. 692
Robinson, B. W. 741-742
Rodinson, M. 209, 309
Roemer, H. R. 136-139, 166
Rogers, J. M. 689
Roman Catholicism 288
Roman Empire
influence of Kingship 94
Romances 602, 645, 648
Ronaghy, H. A. 232
Roosevelt, K. 357
Root, M. C. 113
Roots of Revolution: an interpretative
history of modern Iran 381
Rose, E. 625
Rose-garden of Sheikh Moslihu'd-din Sadi of Shiraz 662
Rosen, B. N. 428
Ross, D. 53
Royal hunter: art of the Sasanian empire 733
Royal Persian manuscripts 756
ruba'is 595, 599, 649-650
Rubā'iyāt of 'Umar Khayyām 650
Rubin, B. 457
Rudbar 86
Rugs 719, 721, 723, 725
see also Carpets, Kilims
Rumi, Jalal al-Din 586-587, 631, 640, 655-660
biography 610
Rumi the Persian, the Sufi 586
Rundle, C. 470
Rural development 528, 549
Rural economy 534-536
14th-18th centuries 156
Rural life 5, 58, 536
Khuzestan 545
Rural population 217-218, 224-225
characteristics 307
demography 221
migration to cities 228-231
Russia and the West in Iran, 1918-1948: a study in big-power rivalry 454
Russia and Iran, 1780-1828 146
Russian Revolution (1917) 421
Russo–Persian wars 146-147
Ruthven, M. 279
Rypka, J. 626

S

sabk-e Hendi 584, 621, 633, 639
Sabri-Tabrizi, G. R. 627
Sadarangani, H. I. 628
Saddam's Iraq: revolution or reaction? 468
Sadeq Chubak: an anthology 669
Sādeq Hedāyat: an anthology 675
Sadeqi, Bahram 768
Sa'di, Sheikh Mosleh al-Din 587, 640, 661-662
biography 662
Sadiq, Muhammad 684

Sadr al-Din Shirazi and his transcendent theosophy: background, life and works 275
Sadr, Musa
    biography 192
Sadroddin Shirazi *see* Molla Sadra
Sa'edi, Gholam Hosein 608, 627, 668
Safa, Z. 629-630
Safa-Isfahani, N. 294
Safavi, Shah Isma'il 166-167
Safavid medical practice . . . 153
Safavid period 5, 68, 119, 129, 132, 136-139, 151, 153-154, 156, 159-160, 166-170
    administration 169
    architecture 696
    arts 154, 163, 168, 751, 755
    astronomy 170
    collapse of dynasty 132, 159, 162-163
    decorative arts 689
    economy 156, 158, 515
    genealogy 163
    guilds 160
    handicrafts 160
    Isfahan 68, 162
    literature 141, 163, 629
    mechanics 170
    medicine 153, 170
    miniatures 749, 751
    paintings 750
    philosophy 168
    poetry 629, 639
    politics 166, 168
    religion 270, 277
    science 154, 170
    Shi'ism 5, 145, 166, 270, 277, 629
    society 166, 168-169
    technology 170
    travellers' accounts 170
Saffarzadeh 618
Safineh-ye Suleimani 57
Saghafi-Nejad, T. 582
Sahāb, 'A. 46-48
Saikal, A. 358
Saleh, A. P. 487
Saleh, J. S. 266
Salinger, P. 412
Saljuq period 116-118, 121-122, 124, 126, 131, 134
    administration 131
    religion 116
    socio-economics 134

Sallee, S. 671
Salmanzadeh, C. 545
Salzman, P. C. 243
Sana'i, Hakim 640
    biography 597
Sanasarian, E. 331, 359
Sanitation 573
Sarbadars 136
Sarhad plateau 243
Sar-o tah-e yek karbas 198
Sarwar, G. 167
Sasanian period 96, 107, 115
    administration 107
    arts 733, 755
    Christian Church 286
    fall of the empire 115
    foreign relations 107
    Judaism 287
    literature 591
    seal stones 731
    silverware 683, 717
    taxation reforms 107
    Zoroastrianism 296
Sasanian stamp seals in the Metropolitan Museum of Art 731
Saudi Arabia
    housebuilding 568
    relations with Iran 431, 435, 442
    stability 436, 462
    United States policy 442, 444
Savin, R. 60
Savory, R. M. 7, 154, 168-169, 310
Sayyid Jamal ad-Din 'al-Afghani': a political biography 201
Scarce, J. 690
Schacht, J. 280
Scharlan, K. 49
Schimmel, A. 631-632, 732
Schlamminger, K. 725
Scholars
    bibliography 782
School of Law, Cairo University 501
School of Law, University of Virginia 411
School of Oriental and African Studies, London 3
School principal 665
Schools 575
Schwartz, R. M. 311
Science 22, 299, 579-582
    bibliography 783
    and the Islamic tradition 276, 280

298

modern Islamic period 159
Safavid period 154, 170
Timurid period 129
Scientific dictionary 267
Scientists
  biographies 199
Scythian art 683
Sea transport 548
Seal stone collection
  Metropolitan Museum of Art 731
Seals
  Achaemenian 113
Sears, W. 409
Seccombe, I. 556
Second International Congress on
  Mithraism 92
Secondary education 575
Secularism
  and Islam 271
Secularist movement 171-190
Secularization
  Shi'ite political dissent 344
Security
  impact of Iranian Revolution 374,
    383, 417, 428, 431-436, 439
  Indian Ocean 416
  periodical 772
  Persian Gulf 431, 433-434, 437-438,
    455
*Security in the Persian Gulf 1: domestic
  political factors* 433
*Security in the Persian Gulf 4: the role
  of outside powers* 444
Security of the Persian Gulf 376, 431,
  435, 443, 490, 493, 517
Security Organization Act (1957) 474
Sedehi, A. 487
Sedghi, H. 332
*Selected poems from the Divāni Shamsi
  Tabrīz* 658
Seleucid period 107, 115
  manual for rulers 653
Semnan 33
Semnan: Persian city and region 33
*Sense of unity: the Sufi tradition in
  Persian architecture* 691
Settlements 30, 109
  Jews 287
Seventh Sokol Colloquium on Private
  International Law 411
Sexuality
  and Islam 317

and Shi'ite social protest 317
and women's oppression 318
*Shadow of God and the hidden Imam:
  religion, political order and
  societal change in Shi'ite Iran from
  the beginning to 1890* 145
Shafi'i Kadkani, M. R. 633
*Shah: the glittering story of Iran and its
  people* 183
*Shah Mozaffar Al-Din's European
  tour, AD 1900* 66
*Shahanshah of Iran on oil: Tehran
  agreement – background and
  perspectives* 521
*Shahanshah: a study of the monarchy
  of Iran* 480
*Shāh-nāmah of Firdausi: the book of
  the Persian Kings* 757
Shahnameh 623, 644, 757
  illustrations 748, 756-757
Shahryari, P. 267
Shah's story 205
Shaki, M. 253
Shamlu, Ahmad 585, 768
Shams-e Tabriz 610, 658
Shari'ah law
  banking 501
Shari'ati, 'Ali 271, 312, 324, 354, 360,
  380, 391
  bibliography 312
  biography 191, 312
Shatt al-Arab border dispute 24
  Frontier Treaty (1937) 41
*Shatt al-Arab river dispute in terms of
  law* 24
Shea, D. 272
Sheehan, M. K. 458
Sheikhism 344
Sherif, F. 281
Sherley, Sir Antony 61
Sherman, L. B. 411
Shi'ism 5, 116-117, 283, 306, 391, 576
  history 145
  Imami jurisprudence 475
  militancy and quietism 353
  modern Islamic period 145
  'olamā 173, 176-177, 182, 300, 313,
    315, 372, 394, 396
  philosophy 381
  Qajar period 5, 145, 273
  Safavid period 5, 145, 166, 270, 277,
    629

299

Shi'ism *contd.*
  and sexuality 317
  and social protest 317, 373, 392, 419
  and sovereignty 393
  Timurid period 277
  treatise 400
  see also Babism
Shi'ism and social protest 317, 373,
  392, 419
Shi'ite community 192, 340
  conflict with Sunnites 347
  revolutionary traits 192
Shi'ite Islam 283
Shi'ite law 475, 483
Shi'ite leaders 239
Shi'ite *'olama* 173, 176-177, 182, 300,
  313, 315
Shi'ite scholars 277
Shi'ite tribes 239
Ship of Sulaiman 57
Shiraz 31, 85, 320, 325, 397
  archaeological discoveries 88
  folk-tales 605
  Iranian Jews in 236
  Masjid-i 'Atiq 703
  migration from (1960s) 232
  migration to 231
  power struggles 397
Shiraz Art Festival 710
Shiraz painting in the sixteenth century
  687
Shirazi, Sadr al-Din 275
Shiraz school 687
'Shirin painter' 684
Short stories 592, 665, 668-669, 675-
  676, 768
Shorter Oxford Dictionary 266
Shuster, W. M. 210
Shu'ubis
  conflict with Arabs 133
*Shu'ubiyah controversy and the social
  history of early Islamic Iran* 133
Siam
  Iranians in 57
  travellers' account 57
Sick, G. 413
Siddiqi, A. H. 140
Siddiqui, K. 361, 388, 391
Silsby, S. P. 362
Silver 80-81
  Sasanian period 683, 717
Sims–Williams, U. 786

Sinclair, C. A. 553
Sind
  poets 628
Sindhi Adabi Board 628
Sistan
  history 119, 141
Sistan–Baluchestan
  economic conditions 26
*Sīstān under the Arabs, from the
  Islamic conquest to the rise of the
  Saffāvids (30-250/651-864)* 119
Sitar 621
Siyasat-nameh ya Siyar al-Moluk 653
Skrine, C. 62
Slums 230, 339, 549
Small finds 81
Smith, A. 63
Smith, H. H. 16
Smith, M. 99
Social change 298-317, 338
  cause of migration 230
  conflicting values 301
  development programmes 570, 573
  education 574, 578
  effects of modernization 307
  Fars province 307
  impact of West 306
  and loss of national identity 298,
    301, 306
  Pahlavi era 204, 338, 378
  political system 345
  Qajar period 150
  and religion 315
  revolutionary period 314
  women 318-327
  and youth 298
*Social change in a southern province of
  Iran* 307
Social characteristics 9
  Islamic Revolution 314
  migrant–non-migrant contrast 231
Social conditions 304
  13th century 610
  16th-18th centuries 151
  19th-20th centuries 208
  women 330, 332
  working class 558-560, 563
Social conflict 18, 298
*Social and cultural selections from
  contemporary Persian* 263
Social development 230, 387
  19th century 310

Middle East 464
Pahlavi era 310
Social history
  mediaeval Islamic period 133, 136
  under Abbasid rule 123
Social life 386
Social mobility 225
Social problems 20, 666
  disease 335
  family planning 220, 223, 337
  Islamic Republic 509
  rural–urban migration 228-231
Social sciences and problems of
  development 229, 302, 334, 529,
  540, 570, 582, 758
Social services 179, 334-338
  family planning 337
  welfare 334-338, 573
Social status 305, 380
  women 189, 320-322, 326-327, 329-
  331, 373
Social structure 14, 216-219, 298-317,
  386, 396
  and authority 316
  Baluchistan 244
  cities 316
  classification by income 477
  early 20th-century 55
  Islamic Republic 382, 403
  migrants 230
  Qashqa'i nomads 240
  Semnan 33
  Shiraz 31
  statistics 425
  villages 316
  Yomut Turkmen 234
Social welfare 334-338, 573
Social work 338
Social work in Iran since the White
  Revolution 338
Social writings
  19th century 180
Socialism 347, 498
  and Islam 271
Society 1, 10, 12, 16, 18, 211, 299, 314,
  369, 381, 396, 509
  19th-century 65
  Achaemenian 102, 114
  and agriculture 532, 537-538
  cause of Iranian Revolution 386
  consequences of Gulf War 468
  early 20th century 190

felt-making 719
forecasts and projections 506
impact of oil industry 519
impact of US policy 455
Makran area 50
marriage 217, 221
Median 104
Pahlavi era 187, 378
periodicals 765, 770
Persian Gulf 7
pre-Islamic era 102, 104, 115
and religion 145, 314
revolutionary period 370-371, 378,
  386
role of Armenians 235
role of *'olama* 313
role of women 189
rural 5
Safavid period 166, 168-169
and sexuality 317
traditional 299
tribal 316
under Afghan occupation 163
under Karim Khan Zand 164
under Mohammad Reza Shah
  Pahlavi 378
women 56, 311, 318-333
Society and economics in Islam:
  writings and declarations of
  Ayatullah Sayyid Mahmud
  Taleghani 403
Socio-economic development 12
  effects of migration 229
  household characteristics 308
  mediaeval Islamic period 121, 124,
  134, 137
  see also Social development;
  Economic development
Socio-economics 496
  effect of land reform 528, 535, 537-
  538
  and large-scale farming 531
Socio-political development 190, 343,
  395
  19th century 273
Socioreligious thought
  Qajar Iran 344
Sociology 145, 309, 312
  development 304
  élites 367
  Islam 198
  Middle East 316

301

Sociology *contd.*
  religious rituals 397
*Sociology of development: Iran as an
  Asian case study* 304
*Sociology of the Middle East: a
  stocktaking and interpretation* 316
Sohrab and Rustum 613
Soils 34
Soleiman, Shah 699
Solid fuel 581
Sorraya in a coma 673
Soucek, S. 27
South Persian Rifles 423
Special schools 575
*Spirit of Allah: Khomeini and the
  Islamic Revolution* 212
Spiritual movements 277
Spooner, B. 3, 50, 244, 313
Sports 575
*Sports and pastimes: scenes from
  Turkish, Persian and Mughal
  paintings* 743
Sprachman, P. 666, 677
Springborg, R. 441
Spuhler, F. 726
State and revolution in Iran, 1962-1982
  372
State University of Groningen,
  Netherlands 24
Statistics 23, 564-567
  agriculture 564, 566, 770
  arms trade 565
  communication 770
  defence 770
  demography 551
  economic 425, 500, 564, 567, 770
  education 551, 564, 566, 770
  employment 551
  foreign capital 449
  GNP 564
  health 770
  importation 449
  income distribution 308, 566
  industry 564, 566, 770
  investors 449
  landownership 564
  literacy 564, 566
  manpower 566
  military 425
  occupation 551
  population 564, 566
  social structure 425

trade 514, 564, 566, 770
  urbanization 566
  welfare 770
Stauth, G. 314
Steel 80
Stein, Sir Aurel 64
Steingass, F. 268
Stempel, J. D. 389
Stern, S. M. 141
Stewart, D. P. 411
Stobaugh, R. B. 522
Stonework
  Ionian 112
Straits of Hormuz
  rights of passage 459
Strangling of Persia . . . 210
Strategic significance 417, 428, 431-
  432, 451, 462
Streams 541
Strikes 560
Stronach, D. 81, 87
*Structure of Christian–Muslim relations
  in contemporary Iran* 311
*Studies in art and literature of the Near
  East* 6
*Studies in the phonetics and phonology
  of modern Persian: intonation and
  related features* 256
Successors of Genghis Khan 135
Sufi literature 622, 631, 641, 648, 651,
  659
Sufism 116, 272, 277
  chivalry 282
Sullivan, W. H. 211
Sunderland, E. 88, 225
Sunnism 116
Sunnite jurisprudence
  contrast with Shi'ite 475
Supplementary Fundamental Laws 177
Surgery
  Safavid period 153
*Survey of Persian art, from prehistoric
  times to the present* 688
Survey of Persian handicraft 720
Suvashun 620
Swaan, W. 68
Sykes, P. M. 59, 65, 97
Syntax 245, 249
Syria
  housebuilding 568
Szemerenyi, O. 254
Szentadorjany, J. 16

302

T

Tabari, A. 333
Tabas wedge 39
Tabataba'i, 'A. S. M. H. 283
Tabatabai, S. E. 380
Tabriz
    migration from (1960s) 232
    role in constitutional movement 181
Taheri, A. 212
Tahmasb Mirza, Prince 162
Tai, H.–C. 363
Taiwan
    land reform 363
Tajik 786
Taleghani, Ayatollah Sayyid Mahmud
    403, 488
    bibliography 403
Tales from the Masnavi 656
Taleshi
    Masal dialect 252
Tamerlane *see* Timur
Tangsir 669
Tansar 289
Tape Nush-i Jan 81
taqiyah 283
Tarbiyat 590
Tarikh-e Beihaqi 142
Tarikh-e Sistan 119
Tati dialects 259
Tavallali 767
Tavallodi digar 671
Tavana, J. 269
Tavassoli, G. A. 312
Taxation 526
    14th-18th centuries 156
    Sasanian period 107
Taxation laws 477
Ta'zieh 710-711
Ta'ziyeh: ritual and drama in Iran 711
*Teachings of the Magi: a compendium
    of Zoroastrian beliefs* 296
*Technical assistance in theory and
    practice: the case of Iran* 579
Technical colleges 180
*Technical cooperation with Iran: a case
    study of opportunities and policy
    implications for the United States*
    580
Technical dictionary 269
*Technical dictionary of oil industry
    terms* 269

Technology 513, 579-582
    and manpower 549
    oil 519
    Safavid period 170
    US aid 579-580
Technology trade with the Middle East
    513
Tehran 23, 38
    bazaar 315
    British ambassador in 206
    demography 569, 571
    Evin prison 407
    labour migration to 229
    migration from (1960s) 232
    riots (1963) 197
    seizure of American Embassy (1979)
    440
    urbanization 569-571
Tehran Oil Agreement (1971) 521
Tehran School of Social Work 338
Tehran: an urban analysis 569
Tehrani dialect 255
Tehranisa, H. 258
Teleki, S. 16
Television 759
    programmes 760
*Tell the American people: perspectives
    on the Iranian Revolution* 369
*Ten thousand miles in Persia or eight
    years in Iran* 65
Territory 69
Textiles 688-689, 716, 728
    14th-18th centuries 726
    designs and motifs 716
*Textual sources for the study of
    Zoroastrianism* 291
Teymourtash, Abdol Hosein Khan 356
Thackston, Jr., W. M. 255
Thaiss, G. 315
Thamas Kuli Khan 157
Theatre 575, 710-711
Theocracy 390
Theology 277
Theosophy 275
Third World 309
    dependence on arms transfers 493,
    565
    economic problems 499
    relationship with Superpowers 441
    see also Developing countries
XXXV International PEN Congress
    598

Thisen, F. 634
Thompson, C. T. 540
Threat from the East: Soviet policy from Aghanistan and Iran to the Horn of Africa 451
Through Persia by caravan 52
Tikku, G. L. 17, 635
Times 350
Timur 136-138
Timurid period 129, 132, 136-139, 156, 166, 169
   architecture 700
   economy 156, 515
   literature 630
   metalwork 752
   miniatures 726, 749, 752
   poetry 639
   pottery 752
   religion 270, 277
   sciences 129
Titley, N. M. 743-744
'To be' as the original of syntax: a Persian framework 245
To Persia for flowers 75
Tofigh, F. 566
Topography 74
Toponymy 50
Torture 405-406, 667
Touring Iran 72
Tourism 67-72
Toward a theory of historical narrative: a case study in Perso–Islamicate historiography 142
Towhidi, J. 256
Towns 23, 65
   maps 28
Trachoma 335
Trade 309, 425-426, 511-515
   18th century 144
   19th century 152, 511
   19th-20th centuries 158
   arms 565
   foreign 514
   history 515
   policy 526
   retail 548
   statistics 514, 564, 566, 770
   technology 513
   with USA 448
Trade unions 557-563
Trading companies 505
Traditional crafts of Persia: their development, technology, and influence on Eastern and Western civilizations 728
Traditionalism
   impact of modernization 340, 343-345, 347, 364, 393, 527
Traditions 18, 298, 301
   Mandaean 233
   pre-Islamic period 115
Transport 71, 202, 503, 547-548, 567
   19th-20th centuries 158
   railways 505, 547
Travel guides 67-72
Travellers' accounts 52-66
   17th-century 57, 61
   19th-century 52-53, 65, 180, 690
   20th-century 54-56, 58, 60, 62-64, 66
   archaeological 64
   Kerman 56, 63
   mediaeval Islamic period 132
   Safavid period 170
Travelogues 27, 198
Travels to Persia 61
Treaty of Friendship and Commerce (1856) 440
Treaty of Golestan 147
Tribal rugs: an introduction to the weaving of the tribes of Iran 721
Tribalism and society in Islamic Iran, 1500-1629 242
Tribes *see* Pastoral tribes
Tristan and Isolde 645
Triumphal sun: a study of the works of Jalāladdin Rumi 631
Troyer, A. 272
Truman, President 579
Tudeh party 364, 366
Tup-e lastiki 669
Turkey 316
   economy 498
   felt-making 719
   history 3
   military intervention 421
   military rule 349
Turkish dynasties 96
Turkistan
   invasion by Nadir Shah 162
Turkmanchai treaty (1828) 146
Turkmen
   Yomut 234
Turkmen dynasties 139
   Aq Quyunlu 139

Turkmen period
  literature 630
Turks 135
Turner, B. S. 314
Turner, T. 563
Tusi, Nasir ad-Dīn 284, 663
Twelfth Imam 127
*Twenty-three years: a study of the
  prophetic career of Mohammad*
  194

U

Umayyads 119, 130
Undiscovered Kilim 713
*Union catalogue of Persian serials and
  newspapers in British libraries* 786
United Nations
  mission to Bahrein 415
  sources for migration trends 228
  sources for Muslim natality 220
United Nations Declaration on Human
  Rights 405
*United States and Iran: a documentary
  history* 440
*United States and Iran: the patterns of
  influence* 455
United States–Iranian relations 450
Unity in the ghazals of Hafez 606
Universal Declaration of Human
  Rights 404
Universities
  Middle East studies 761
University College, London 33
University of California at Los
  Angeles, Near Eastern Centre 17
University of Cambridge
  manuscript collection 730
University of Durham, Centre for
  Middle Eastern and Islamic
  Studies 505
University of Giessen, Institute for
  Rural Sociology 531
University of Texas at Austin 30
University of Virginia, School of Law
  411
Upper class
  impact of development programmes
  570
Upton, J. M. 190
Ur 90

Urban agriculture 33
Urban economy
  14th-18th centuries 156
Urban population 217-219, 222, 224-
  225, 307
  characteristics 307
  impact of development programmes
  570
  and rural migrants 228-231
Urbanization 219, 222, 568-573
  Persian Gulf 7
  statistics 566
  Tehran 569-571
US Board on Geographic Names 51
US Department of Agriculture 58
USA
  administration 355, 442, 453
  ambassador 211
  arms transfer 444, 455
  consequences of Iranian Revolution
  440, 444, 448, 450, 453, 455, 457
  economic aid 452
  financial experts 210
  hostage crisis 199, 389, 410-413, 428,
  440, 450
  migration to 232
  Point IV programme 579
  policy towards Persian Gulf 442, 446
  policy towards Saudi Arabia 442,
  444
  relations with Iran 420, 427, 431,
  440-446, 448-450, 452-453, 455,
  457-458, 491
  role in fall of Mossadeq 357-358, 362
  security in Persian Gulf 383, 446,
  455, 462-463
  seizure of American Embassy,
  Tehran (1979) 440
  support for the Shah 355, 358, 362,
  443, 448, 455, 457-458
  technical assistance 579-580
USSR
  allied occupation of Iran (1941-46)
  213, 447, 456
  'Arc of Crisis' 451
  arms transfer 444
  civil war 55
  dispute with Britain 210
  expansionist policies, eastern
  Caucasus 146
  foreign policy, 19th century 152
  military intervention 421

305

USSR *contd.*
  policy towards Iraq 444
  relations with Iran 420, 427, 441,
    444, 447, 449, 451, 454, 456, 491
  role in Persian Gulf 463
  Yomut Turkmen 234
  USSR in Iran: the background history
    of Russian and Anglo–American
    conflict in Iran . . . 447

V

Vaghefi, M. R. 527
Vahidi, M. 546
Vakil Abad, Iran: a survivor's story 60
Vakil Abad prison, Mashhad 60
Vakil, F. 510, 567
Vali, A. 314
Van Nieuwenhuijze, C. A. O. 316
Vanished Imam: Musā al-Sadr and the
  Shia of Lebanon 192
Varaq-pareh-ha-ye zendan 664
Vegetation 74, 77
  Semnan 33
  Zagros mountains 542
Vegetation of Hormoz, Qeshm and
  neighbouring islands (southern
  Persian Gulf area) 77
Veil wearing 320
Venice 54
Victoria and Albert Museum 753
Village economy 242
Village ethnoarchaeology: rural Iran in
  archaeological perspective 83
Villages 23, 65, 230
  politics 354
  power struggles 397
  religious institutions 313
  social structure 316
Violence 355
Vis and Ramin 645
Visual arts 681-690
von Grunebaum, G. E. 17

W

Wagstaff, J. M. 29
Waldman, M. R. 142
Walker, P. E. 143
Ward, P. 72

Warner, R. 114
Water and irrigation in Iran 546
Water supply 532, 534
  Dasht-e Kawir 543
  geographical problems 546
  Mashhad 541
  and population density 225
Water use 33, 541
Waterfield, R. E. 288
Watermills 692
Watson, O. 727
Watson, P. J. 89
Watt, W. M. 285
Waugh, T. 205
Wealth
  Yomut Turkmen 234
Weaver of tales: Persian picture rugs
  725
Weaving 721, 724-725
Weber, Max 145
Webster's International Dictionary 266
Weights and measures 250
Weischer, B. M. 651
Welch, S. C. 756
Welfare 334-338, 573
  statistics 770
Wells 541
Wells, R. 636
West Azarbaijan 311
  primary health care project 336
Western response to Zoroaster 105
Westernization
  effect 509, 519
West-östlicher divan 625
Whinfield, E. H. 659
White House 413
White Revolution (1963) 48, 179, 205,
  376, 386, 503-504, 530, 538, 573
Whitehouse, R. 90
Whitworth Art Gallery 745
Wickens, G. M. 66, 637, 661, 663
Wilber, D. N. 18-19, 91, 213, 702-703,
  787
Wilkinson, J. V. S. 757
Williams, A. N. 380
Wills, Dr. C. 690
Wilson, C. E. 654
Wilson, P. L. 651-652, 725
Windfuhr, G. 257-258
Windle, C. 305
Windmills 692
Winter, H. J. H. 170

Women 56, 311, 318-333
    emancipation 333
    and fundamentalism 318
    history 189, 321, 329
    identity 324
    in Iranian Revolution 189, 319-320,
        325, 329, 333, 373, 380
    in Islamic Republic 318, 320, 322,
        326-329, 333, 373, 380
    and Islamic teaching 194, 322, 326,
        329-330, 333, 380
    legal rights 321, 331, 473
    oppression 318
    poets 611, 618-619
    political prisoners 407
    and politics 318, 329, 332
    in religious minorities 321
    roles 321, 324, 332, 574
    social conditions 330, 332
    social status 189, 320-322, 326-327,
        329-331
    veil wearing 320
    views on Westernization 323
Women and the family in Iran 321
*Women and the family in the Middle
    East: new voices of change* 326,
    619
*Women of Iran: the conflict with
    fundamentalist Islam* 318
Women and revolution in Iran 189,
    319-320, 322-325, 327-330, 359,
    407, 479, 484, 618
Women's movement 331, 333
    history 318
*Women's rights movement in Iran:
    mutiny, appeasement, and
    repression from 1900 to Khomeini*
    331
Woodwork 728
Work 1
    and Islam 552
Work and Islam 552
*Workers and Revolution in Iran: a
    Third World experience of
    workers' control* 557
*Workers say no to the Shah: labour law
    and strikes in Iran* 560
Working class
    industrial 310
    role in Iranian Revolution 557, 563
    social conditions 558-560, 563
World Bank 573

World of Islam Festival (1976) 745
World War I 62, 97, 422-423, 504
    military intervention 421
World War II 62, 417
World War in Iran 62
*Wrath of Allah: Islamic Revolution and
    reaction in Iran* 387
Wright, D. 214, 238
Wright, O. 707
Writers' Association of Iran 616
Wulff, H. E. 728

X

Xenophon 114

Y

Yamada, M. 248
Ya'qub b. Laith 119
Yar-Shater 5, 20-22, 107, 115, 215,
    226, 259, 286-287, 313, 315, 348,
    420, 494, 502, 537, 573, 578, 589,
    617, 638-639, 675, 681-683, 708,
    714, 759
Yasefi, M. 552
Yazd 30
    architecture 693
    life and customs 56
    Zoroastrian community 290
*Yazd and its hinterland: a central place
    system of dominance in the central
    Iranian plateau* 30
Year amongst the Persians . . . 53
Yeganeh, N. 317, 333
Yomut Turkmen 234
*Yomut Turkmen: a study of social
    organization among a Central
    Asian Turkic-speaking population*
    234
Yorke, V. 439
Youth
    in guerrilla movements 340
    in social change 298
    support for Iranian Revolution 375
Youth organizations 575
Yushij, Nima 768
*Yusuf and Zulaikha: an allegorical
    romance* 648

Z

Zabih, S. 364-366, 417
Zaehner, R. C. 295-297
Zagros mountains
    geology 45
    irrigation 542
Za'imi, K. 746
Zan-e Mosalmān 324
Zarathustra *see* Zoroaster
Zaryab, A. 44
Zia, General 398
Zinc 40
Zonis, E. 708-709
Zonis, M. 367, 578
Zoroaster 100, 110
    biography 199
Zoroaster's time and homeland: a study
*on the origins of Mazdeism and
related problems* 110
Zoroastrian architecture 693
Zoroastrian Pahlavi writings 617
Zoroastrianism 100, 105, 110, 289-297,
    301, 780
    history 100, 110, 297
    impact on Greece 105
    impact on Israel 105
    influence on literature 296, 609, 618
    laws 294
    Sasanian period 296
    see also Mithraism, Parsism and
        Babism
Zoroastrians 291
    Yazd 290
Zurvan 295
Zurvan: a Zoroastrian dilemma 295

Map of Iran

This map shows the more important towns and other features.

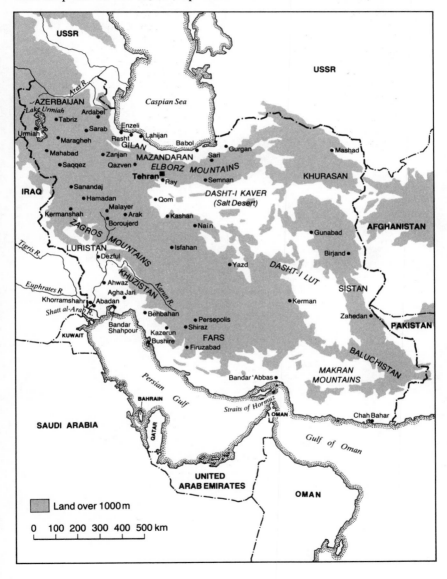